Understanding Mass Communication

Understanding Mass Communication

Melvin L. DeFleur
University of Miami

Everette E. Dennis
University of Minnesota

Houghton Mifflin Company   Boston
Dallas   Geneva, Ill.   Hopewell, N.J.   Palo Alto   London

Printed in the U.S.A.

Library of Congress Catalog Card Number: 80-82762

ISBN: 0-395-29722-2

Contents

Preface

No one would deny that the lives of most Americans are influenced in great measure by the activities of the mass media in our culture — we receive a considerable amount of our entertainment, our awareness of national and international events, and our assessment of consumer products from television, movies, radio, newspapers, magazines, and advertising of all kinds. Of course, the effects of each medium on its audience have existed from that medium's inception, as history shows us. Nevertheless, it has been only comparatively recently that observers have systematically analyzed the media in terms of their effects on individuals and society as well as in terms of their specific functions. Today, the media are an acknowledged arena for research efforts that have often resulted in the development of new concepts, explanations, and bodies of knowledge. In turn, those research findings have often brought about modifications in media practices — one celebrated example being the impact that the Surgeon General's report on televised violence had on certain of the networks' programming policies.

This book is based on our strong conviction that students can best understand mass communication by studying it in its totality — by devoting equal attention to the daily activities of the individual media and to the concerns and discoveries of the researchers who study the effects of mass communication. The organization of the text reflects this conviction. In Part I, the first three chapters set the stage, looking closely at the basic process of human communication and the special features of mass communication, the origins and technical nature of each of the media, and the conflicts that are created as the media function within a web of other social institutions in modern society. Chapters 4 through 7 in Part II present a detailed introduction to each of the major media as industries. These chapters discuss the scope, distribution, organization, and day-to-day activities of the American print, film, and broadcasting media. In Part III, Chapters 8 through 11 assess the influences of the media from several viewpoints. The focus is on direct and indirect effects on individuals, on society as a whole, and on culture. In these chapters the student can learn much about the nature of research and its problems. Chapters 12 and 13 in Part IV examine three major practical activities and services that depend extensively on mass communication: formulating and presenting the news, advertising our nation's products and services, and providing public relations influences. Finally, Chapter 14 offers insights and advice to students who are interested in careers in mass communication.

Understanding Mass Communication does more than summarize the work of others. It presents innovative analyses and full explanations of such difficult concepts as *meaning, free press, popular culture, taste, media, mass, mass media*, and *direct and indirect effects*. It also sets forth several new theoretical frameworks — among them an explanation of human communication as a biosocial process, and (its corollary) the "meaning theory" of mass communication effects — that have been developed especially for this text and do not appear elsewhere.

We have designed the text to challenge students and to spark discussion, not merely to present information. The flow of topics, both within and between chapters, presents a logical sequence and accumulative learning experience. The discussions of contemporary communication research and industry operations are thorough, critically acute, and written in a style to engage the interest of the typical student. Our intent throughout has been to balance thoroughness with thoughtfulness and liveliness.

The authors wish to acknowledge the significant contributions to this text made by Dr. Timothy G. Plax of the Rockwell International Corporation. Dr. Plax, a noted specialist in the field of speech communication, brought important ideas and principles from his discipline to bear upon those from journalism and sociology that constitute the basis of this text. With Melvin DeFleur, Dr. Plax wrote the original drafts of Chapter 1, "The Process of Mass Communication," and Chapter 10, "Indirect Effects of the Media." His contributions to other chapters in the book also helped to enrich their substance.

Finally, we would like to thank the following individuals who read the manuscript and offered significant suggestions for improvement: James Buckalew, San Diego State University; Douglas N. Freeman and John P. Garrison, Auburn University; Kathleen Matichek, Normandale Community College; Roger Wimmer, University of Georgia; and Churchill Roberts, University of West Florida.

M.D.
E.D.

Understanding Mass Communication

The Nature of Mass Communication

1 The Process of Mass Communication

> "When I use a word," Humpty Dumpty said, in a rather scornful tone, "it means what I choose it to mean — neither more nor less."
>
> LEWIS CARROLL, *Through the Looking Glass*

Social observers often praise or blame mass communication for all sorts of things: for bringing Americans closer together; for driving them apart; for educating the country's children; for making them more violent. Yet a television soap opera, *Jaws*, the *New York Times*, the *Golf Digest*, the morning disc jockey's program, and this book are all examples of mass communication. What do they have in common? To understand and assess mass communication and its effects, we need first to define what we're talking about. By describing five steps in the process of mass communication, we will develop a definition that points to the similar features of all mass media.

The heart of all communication is the sharing of meanings by a communicator and the receiver of the communication. But meanings cannot be seen or touched; how can they be shared? The ability to share meanings is what makes us uniquely human. This chapter therefore examines meanings, how we learn them

*Shared meanings are central to an under-
standing of the basic processes of communication. Animals communicate without language; human beings use symbols for more
complex interactions. Mass communication is
an even more elaborate process, but it is
founded on the basic communication act.*

and how we share them, in both face-to-face and mass communication.

Try to imagine what our society would be like if all the mass
media were to disappear suddenly. We would have no television,
movies, newspapers, radio, magazines, or books. It is difficult to
conceive of life without such media. They provide us with an incredible flow of information and entertainment: beautiful music,
exciting sports events, the latest news, soap operas, silly games,
serious drama, advertising puffery, and political bombast — the
list is almost endless. The media sometimes bore us or even
make us mad, but on the whole most Americans are happy to have
them as a familiar part of everyday life.

Actually, life without the mass media would not only be pretty
dull but it might even be impossible as we know it. We are all
very *dependent* on mass communication.[1] This dependency is

both social and personal. For example, the mass media are critical to almost every industry that must sell goods. In this sense they are an indispensable link in the economic and industrial activities that provide jobs for millions of workers. The media are also large industries in their own right and provide employment and investment opportunities for many Americans. Mass communication has also become a central part of American politics. No one who has followed a recent presidential election would deny that television is an important medium by which candidates gain exposure for their ideas and themselves.

At a more personal level, mass communication is woven deeply into our day-to-day existence. We listen to the radio in the car and use it as a background for many kinds of work and recreation. We look to the newspaper for all kinds of consumer information, from the best buys at the supermarket to job openings. During the day millions of people avidly follow the latest adventures on their favorite soap opera. At night they watch the news or their favorite comedy. Magazines and books bring us specialized information needed for school, for hobbies, or for understanding public affairs in depth. Going to the movies has long been part of our lives. In other words, we use the mass media in dozens of ways every day to gratify our needs for entertainment and enlightenment, or for simple and practical purposes.

But there is another, darker side to this dependency. Critics of the media tell us that mass communication can do things to us that we really do not want. Some say it weakens our characters, shapes the way we think, modifies the opinions we hold, erodes our morals, and influences many of the decisions we make. Others are more positive. They say the media enrich our lives. They provide us with satisfying forms of entertainment and make us more aware of public issues and problems. We suspect that all of this is probably true and that mass communication is influencing not only us, but our neighbors, our friends, and beyond them the nation or even the world.

In spite of all the controversy, we *like* our television set, our newspaper, and our other media and would not want to part with them. Still, their effects are worrisome. Are they really good or bad? Are they powerful or trivial? Should we resist them or ignore them? How do we decide?

In this book we try to develop an understanding of these issues and more. We deal not only with mass communication as a process but also with the purposes, products, and effects of the media. We begin by looking at what mass communication is and how it is both similar to and different from other types of communication.

Defining Mass Communication

Mass communication cannot be defined in a quick and simple way because it includes many technologies, groups, kinds of content, types of audiences, and different effects. All these aspects must be taken into account in developing a good definition. Therefore, we need to proceed one step at a time, describing each major feature of mass communication before pulling them together into an overall summary definition.

An appropriate beginning is to note that mass communication must be considered as a process. Any *process* consists of a series of stages or steps by which something is transformed during a set of distinctive operations. A good example is human digestion: in this process food is operated on at various stages by specific parts of the body to be transformed into the energy that we all need to survive. Another illustration is the process of refining gasoline from crude oil, a series of mechanical and chemical operations that eventually yield the product we buy at the gas station. Although mass communication has little to do with digestion or gasoline, it too is a process with several stages.

Mass Communication as Process

We can distinguish five distinct stages that make up the process of mass communication. Summarized briefly, these stages are

1. *Professional communicators* formulate various kinds of content for eventual presentation to different segments of the public for a variety of purposes.
2. These messages are disseminated (that is, sent out) in a relatively rapid and continuous way through the use of *mechanical media* (for example, print, film, or broadcasting).
3. The message reaches relatively *large and diverse* (that is, mass) audiences who attend to the media in selective ways.
4. Individual members of the audience interpret the messages they select in such a way that they experience *meanings* that are more or less parallel to those intended by the professional communicators.
5. As a result of experiencing such meanings, members of the audience are *influenced* in some way. That is, the communication has some effect.

Professional Communicators. The first stage in the mass communication process occurs when some type of message is shaped into a form suitable for transmission by one of the mass media. Usually this shaping is done by specialists who make their living working for some part of the communications industry. These are the professional communicators; they originate, edit, and disseminate news, entertainment, dramas, and comedy, that is, the content of the print, film, and broadcasting media. They are the producers, editors, reporters, and so on.

Professional communicators depend on a host of groups to help formulate and disseminate their messages. Creative people — artists, composers, authors, directors, and actors — shape messages into specific forms for eventual transmission. Technicians operate the mechanical and electronic aspects of the media. Sponsors trying to sell their products supply the funds to finance the communicators. Other auxiliary groups supporting the professional communicators include agencies that prepare commercial advertising, wire services that provide new reports, and polling groups that tell communicators how many people they are reaching.

The purposes and goals of all these people vary. Some may be motivated by their salaries, others by the chance to enhance their reputations, a love of their work, a desire for excellence, a belief in the message they're communicating, or, most likely, a combination of these motives. In the United States, however, this variety of individual goals is overshadowed by one fact. Most of these people work for organizations with one overriding goal: to make money. With few exceptions, the organizations that control American mass communications are private businesses devoted to making money for their owners. The organization's demand for profits shapes the work of the individual communicators and through them the messages that are communicated.

Rapid and Continuous Dissemination. The second stage in the process of mass communication is moving the message across distance and time. A clear feature of our modern media is that they transmit information relatively rapidly. Whereas centuries ago it took months or even years of painstaking work by hand to reproduce a single manuscript, today high-speed presses run off thousands of copies of a book that can be distributed around the country in a matter of days. Once a film is produced, thousands of copies can be sent to theaters all over the country to millions of viewers within days. Obviously, radio and television are the most rapid types of mass communication. The audience receives the message at virtually the same time it is transmitted.

Besides being rapid, modern mass communication is usually continuous rather than sporadic. That is, the messages are sent on the basis of a schedule, not on the basis of someone's whim. Newspapers appear every day; magazines appear weekly or monthly. Television and radio broadcasts follow a fairly rigid time schedule, with programs planned for each week. Books and films are released less regularly as publishers and movie producers provide a continuous flow of their products to the public.

Use of Mechanical Media. Dissemination in mass communication has another characteristic: it involves the use of mechanical media. Long before the age of television and radio, people used various media to extend their ability to communicate. A *medium* is any object or arrangement of objects that is used to communicate a message; it is any device used for moving information over distance or preserving it through time. (*Media* is the plural of *medium.*) In the past people used cave drawings, flags, smoke signals, drums, and handwritten manuscripts as media. Today the media of mass communication are mechanical and electronic devices that depend on elaborate technology, such as computerized typesetting equipment for the print media and satellites for the broadcasting media.

Each medium has advantages and limitations that influence how it is used for disseminating messages. Print, for example, depends on the learned habits of reading and writing. Both the communicator and the receiver must follow certain rules of language if the printed word is to communicate anything. Print is thus useless if you're communicating with a child who doesn't know how to read or with a person who doesn't speak your language. Furthermore, only certain kinds of messages can be transmitted by print, and the communicator can directly transmit only visual stimuli. It would be silly to try to transmit an opera via the newspaper.

It would be equally silly to use television to transmit want ads or to transmit a college text on anatomy by radio. Television, radio, and movies are much better than print at transmitting some things, such as moving images and sounds. They can give us a sense of being on the scene and seeing things for ourselves. But they too have limitations. They give us transitory messages; once received, the message is gone. Usually the audience cannot review the message. Print, on the other hand, is ideal for transmitting messages that must be interpreted at the reader's own pace and referred to over and over again — messages such as those in a book of poetry or a technical manual.

Large and Diverse (Mass) Audiences. The term *mass* in mass communication needs explanation. It came to be a part of the name of the process many years ago. It refers to the social nature of audiences rather than just to their size. The meaning of the word *mass* grew out of a set of beliefs popular among intellectuals early in this century concerning the nature of modern society.

They believed at the time that urban-industrial societies were increasingly made up of individuals whose social ties to others were slipping away. Such observers saw that the large extended family of rural life, which included grandparents, aunts, and uncles, was breaking down as people flocked to the cities. They saw immigration mixing people with different origins and cultural backgrounds. Bringing such diverse people together in cities, they assumed, would result in a society in which social bonds between people would be weak rather than strong.

Essentially, then, this is what was meant by a *mass society:* a society in which people act as individuals rather than as members of families or other kinds of groups. Thus, modern society was thought to be a kind of "lonely crowd" made up of people who did not know each other well and were not bound to each other by strong friendships, loyalties, or family ties. In fact, their many differences in origin and culture, the analysts felt, would thrust people apart rather than bring them together.

It was this kind of society that early students of mass communication saw as the audience of the media that were developing at the beginning of this century. In other words, the audiences were thought to be not only large but socially diverse. More important, they were thought to be made up of individuals who responded to media content in ways that were not influenced by social relationships with others. The importance of the "mass" idea is that individuals in such diverse audiences were thought to be particularly easy to influence by propaganda and other forms of mass communication. Because (in theory) each person was isolated, the influences of mass media messages were not softened by social influences from other sources, such as the family and other groups.

Today, we no longer assume that the audiences for the mass media are like a lonely crowd. We understand that people in an urban and industrial society still maintain strong relationships with their families and other groups. They are not at the mercy of every form of propaganda that comes along. But the idea that the audience for mass communications is large and diverse is still sound. The older ideas implied in the word *mass* may not describe these audiences, but clearly large numbers of people from all walks of life can be involved and we still use the term.[2]

Similarities of Meaning. The essence of human communication, whether it is face-to-face communication or a television message sent to millions, is the achievement of parallel sets of meanings between those sending and receiving the message. By *meanings* we refer to a person's inner responses to a message — the internal experiences it evokes. If the internal responses of images, interpretations, and feelings of the receiver do not match more or less those intended by the communicator, then parallel sets of meaning have not been achieved and communication has not occurred. When communication does occur, then communicator and receiver are linked by their experience of parallel sets of meanings; they "share" the meaning of the message.

Influencing People. The last stage in the process of mass communication is the outcome of the preceding stages. As a result of sharing meanings with the communicator, people in the audience are *changed* in some way. Such changes are the basis of media influences, and they range from the trivial to the deeply significant. For example, at a simple level a person may learn new facts from hearing a weather report on the radio. Thus, providing a person with new information is a form of change brought about by the medium. Or, again at a rather trivial level, a person may be entertained by reading the comics in the Sunday paper. Thus, causing a person to feel better is a form of media influence.

At a more complex level, mass communications can change our shared understandings by introducing new symbols and meanings. For example, prior to the events in Iran of 1979 and 1980, few Americans knew what was meant by the term *ayatollah*. But with their intensive news coverage of the hostage crisis and the Ayatollah Khomeini, the media established a new word and new meanings for millions of Americans. Thus, mass communications can change our language and our understanding of the world.

Mass communications can also alter our feelings about social issues. By giving widespread and one-sided publicity to an issue, the media can alter people's opinions and attitudes toward that issue. For example, the Soviet invasion of Afghanistan in 1979 was almost uniformly denounced by the American news media. Earlier, it had appeared that the two superpowers were becoming more friendly as they moved toward adopting a treaty limiting nuclear arms. But the shift toward more negative attitudes toward the Soviet Union in the wake of the invasion of Afghanistan made it possible for President Carter to gain support for a boycott of the Olympic Games in Moscow during the summer of 1980. Thus, attitude formation and change are important forms of influence that can result from exposure to mass communications.

Exposure to mass communications may also change overt behavior. After hearing or seeing an advertisement, a member of the audience may buy a new brand of breakfast food. Or, more significantly, as a result of a media campaign a citizen may decide to take the time to vote and may be convinced to support a specific candidate. Other possible influences on overt behavior are more debatable. Some people believe that some modern music encourages youngsters to use drugs or to engage in sexual behavior. Others charge that media portrayals of violent behavior stimulate children to defy authority and act more aggressively.

It is such forms of change that deeply concern social observers of the mass media. Not many of us are troubled when someone learns a few facts from a weather report or feels better after reading the comics. But many people are deeply concerned by the possibility that the mass media may be controlling our politics or stimulating our children to engage in harmful behavior. In other words, *influence on people* is not only the final stage in the mass communication process but also the "bottom line" of concern to the public. It is for this reason that communication researchers have spent so much time trying to understand the effects of mass communication, and it is for this reason that in later chapters we will look closely at what fifty years of research has revealed about such media influences.

Each of the stages we have described must be part of an adequate definition of mass communication. With these stages in mind, we can now define mass communication as follows:

> *Mass communication* is a process in which professional communicators use mechanical media to disseminate messages widely, rapidly, and continuously to arouse intended meanings in large and diverse audiences in attempts to influence them in a variety of ways.

Mass Media and Other Media

Using this simplified definition, we can now see which forms of communication should or should not be considered as mass communication and which mechanical devices should be considered as mass media. For example, is the telephone a mass medium? What about a large museum? Should a rock concert, the theater, the church be included in our study of mass communication?

According to our definition, talking on the telephone is not a form of mass communication because there is usually only one person at each end of the line. Furthermore, these persons usually are not professional communicators, and there is no large, diverse audience. A museum is not a form of mass communication because it does not involve rapid dissemination with mechanical media. The rock concert does not qualify either, because it is a form of direct communication and does not involve messages disseminated over distance by mechanical media. Similarly, any situation in which live performers and an audience can see each other — as in a theater or church, at a sports event, or at a parade — is not an example of mediated communication. Thus by our definition they are not forms of mass communication. Large-scale advertising by direct mail might qualify, except that it is not continuous.

The record industry is more difficult to classify. In may ways it resembles the book industry, and it comes very close to fitting our definition of mass communication. But listening to music generally does not result in the same kind of shared parallel meanings as does reading a magazine or watching television. In fact, the meanings of the communicating musicians and the listener may differ greatly. Thus, although records often provide an important part of the content of mass communications, we will classify the record industry as an auxiliary service and not as a major mass medium in its own right.

The major mass media, therefore, are print (books, magazines, and newspapers), film (principally commercial motion pictures), and the broadcast media (radio and television). Many other forms of mediated communication are worth studying; but print, film, and broadcasting fit our definition most closely, and it is on them that we focus attention. We will look at their history, how they fit into modern society, how they work, and how they affect their audiences.

Before examining these specifics, however, we need to have more than a definition of mass communication; we need a deeper analysis of human communication generally. We have said that in mass communication more or less parallel sets of meanings are achieved between the communicator and the audience. In fact, experiencing parallel sets of meanings is the heart of all human communication. How does it happen? And does the existence of mechanical media make mass communication totally different from face-to-face communication? If an audience is large and diverse, is communication fundamentally different from communication between two people? Just what are the essential elements of all human communication?

Elements of Human Communication

Take a simple example of human communication. One person says hello to another, who nods in reply. The exchange takes just a few seconds, but it involves the ability to perform a variety of activities: (1) activities of the brain, because both parties must remember what the word *hello* means; (2) psychological activities, both because the listener must perceive the word and because if the two persons know what the word means they must have learned its meaning at some time; (3) cultural activities, because they are using language, which is an important part of their culture; and (4) sociological activities, because the exchange is an example of social interaction.

We cannot explore each of these aspects of communication in great detail, but we can provide a basic explanation of how they contribute to human communication. Our approach will be something like that of a high-speed camera tracking a speeding bullet: by slowing down a process that in reality occurs almost instantaneously, we will try to capture a glimpse of each step in the process of human communication.

Symbols, Memory, and Meaning

The basic act of communication begins when one person decides that he or she wants to use a given language *symbol* (such as a word or some object for which there is a standard interpretation) to arouse a specific set of meanings in another. By *meanings* we refer to inner subjective responses of images, interpretations, and feelings of understanding such as those aroused by each word that we know. The act of communication is completed when the internal responses of meaning of the *receiver* (the person to whom the message has been sent) are more or less parallel to those intended by the communicator. Thus, the act of communication results in a correspondence of inner meanings between communicator and receiver.

Memory and meaning. A person would not be able to initiate an act of communication using standardized language symbols unless he or she had an adequately functioning memory from which to draw meanings. The same is true of the individual who receives and interprets the message. In addition, as we have already noted, the two parties could not experience parallel meanings unless they learned the same cultural rules that link the symbols and what they are supposed to represent. But the big question is, *how do people remember meanings* so that they can engage in such activities?

Memory functions are based in the central nervous system (brain) of the human being. They depend upon biochemical and electrical processes that take place within the molecular structure of nerve tissue. Without becoming too technical, we need to grasp how this works because it has profound implications for the study of the effects of mass communication! These implications will become clear in later chapters. Thus, the ideas we present here on the workings of memory as an essential part of human communication are needed as a foundation for further analyses of the relationship between memory functions and media effects.

The most important concept that has emerged from studies of the physiology of memory is the trace.[3] The term *trace* refers to experiences stored in the brain in such a way that they are capable of being recalled. Scientists have concluded that every experience of which the individual has ever been aware or unaware is *indelibly registered* within the nerve cells of the brain. This process of registering traces of experience is called *imprinting*. Imprinting appears to involve some of the most basic biochemical processes of living organisms. The precise mechanics of how traces of experience are imprinted into neural tissue are as yet a subject of much debate: "One theory is that memory stems from . . . changes in neurons, brought about by experience; it has also been suggested that memory involves the formation of new neural circuits developed in the learning situation. Moreover, there is some evidence that there is more than one kind of memory, and that each may involve different processes."[4] But whatever the exact nature of imprinting, one thing appears to be clear: *every experience of which we are ever aware imprints a permanent record of that experience.*

The brain contains billions of cells. Each cell may have a capacity for storage of many "bits" of retrievable experience. Thus, the total trace capacity of human memory would appear to be astounding. Not every record, however, is immediately available for conscious recall. Psychological theories, such as those of Freud, indicate that it can be difficult for a person to recall some kinds of experiences. Emotions, fears, or other factors may interfere. The fact that we all forget most of what we experience leads to the conclusion that the brain might "overload" if we could remember everything at once!

In spite of these limitations on recall, research studies seem to support the idea that our traces provide for the storage of all our experiences, whether we can readily recover them or not. In fact, medical studies of people have shown that an incredible amount of detail is available for potential recall. For example, one neurologist has been able to show that delicate electrical stimulation of various areas of the brain by tiny electrodes — needlelike devices that carry minute electric currents — can set into motion a mental "replay," in rather vivid detail, of earlier personal experiences that had long been forgotten. In these experiments subjects who underwent electrode stimulation of specific areas of the brain were able to reexperience activities undergone many years earlier.

This "reliving" was complete in every detail and occurred at the same speed as the original experience. For example, in one experiment a subject "saw" a play that she had seen as a child. Another repeated an experience of visiting friends and relatives that had taken place many years earlier.

Hypnosis has also been used to remove blocks to memory. One of the most dramatic accounts shows the degree to which imprinted traces of earlier experience can retain even the most insignificant details. Under hypnosis an elderly bricklayer "described in detail the bumps on bricks in a wall he had built when he was in his twenties. When the wall was checked, it was found that the bumps were there, just as he had said."[5] It remains a mystery why some individuals can recall experience more readily from their traces than others. People with "photographic memories" appear to have almost total recall even without electrode stimulation or hypnosis. Most of us, however, have only partial conscious access to our stored experiences.

In summary, then, we may assume that a trace depends on a permanent biochemical change in nerve cell structure. We may also assume that it provides a psychological record of subjective experience. Although the exact nature of the biochemistry is not yet understood, it appears that the imprinted trace is the basis of human memory. Thus, the trace has two aspects: it is a modification of nerve cell structures, and it has an associated capacity to store details of prior experiences for potential recall.

Meaning and Language Symbols. The importance of the trace explanation of human memory for understanding the basic act of communication is that it enables us to understand how a communicator can formulate a meaning experience for a given symbol. As a result of learning the language of our culture, and other imprinting of experience, we have billions of traces stored in our memories. These traces can be selectively recalled or retrieved in various patterns or configurations and linked to words or other symbols according to the language rules we have learned. *The meaning for a given language symbol, then, is a specific trace configuration that we have learned to recover for that symbol.*

What we have seen thus far is that in initiating an act of communication a person must identify an appropriate configuration of traces and then determine if a given symbol (likely to be known to others) is a suitable means for expressing the desired meaning. To accomplish this, the individual must *search* his or her total array of stored traces for appropriate meanings. This search can be assumed to involve a *comparison* process, much like a computer searching through a vast data bank. When potentially suitable imprinted experiences have been *identified*, they can be brought together into a configuration that seems to represent the desired meaning.

Assigning a particular language symbol to a set of intended meanings is called *labeling*. Selecting a suitable label to express what the communicator has in mind is a critical part of communicating. It is this step that changes the intended message from internal meanings located in the traces of the communicator to a form that can be responded to by the other party. However, before that can happen there is still the matter of overcoming the distance between the two parties. The message must be sent or transmitted in some way across the space between them.

How is the language symbol converted into a form that can be transmitted and received by the other person? To do this the person initiating the communication uses parts of the anatomy that are involved in speaking, gesturing, writing, or typing. These behaviors are forms of voluntary action and need not be discussed in detail here. For our purposes we need simply note that through such actions the communicator *transmutes* (changes in form) what began as trace configurations into what we will call *information* — events in the physical world that can be apprehended by the receiver.[6] *Information* can be defined as physical events that conquer time or distance. Simple examples are the vibrations of air molecules that make up sound waves, or the patterning of light that forms visual stimuli. Such physical events can be detected by the receiving person who is within auditory or visual range of the communicator.

It is important to stress that we are describing in great detail all the stages in the complex process of interpersonal communication. We are looking closely at activities that are virtually instantaneous. The activities of the communicator in remembering, identifying a trace configuration to express meaning, labeling that meaning, and transmuting the label into a physical form actually take place in an instant.

Perceiving and Understanding the Message. The person toward whom a message is directed engages in activities that are, in many ways, reverse forms of those of the communicator. First, we can assume that the receiver is paying attention to the communicator. This implies a state of readiness to perceive the patterns of physical events (the information) that has been transmitted. *Perception* is the mental activity by which sensory input from our eyes and ears is classified into recognizable categories and meaning. For example, when a receiver perceives a word, he or she must first *identify* the incoming pattern of physical events as a known language symbol rather than some other type of event. This implies that that the receiver understands that the communicator expects some specific pattern of internal meaning response. Once the symbol has been perceived, the receiver begins the process of assigning meaning (interpreting).

The assignment of meaning to a language symbol by the receiver is *reverse labeling.* In labeling, it will be recalled, a communicator assigns a symbol to intended meaning (a specific configuration of traces). In reverse labeling, a receiver assigns a pattern of meaning to a perceived symbol. To assign such meaning, the individual searches and compares candidate trace configurations. Once the receiver has decided which pattern of internal experiences corresponds best to the perceived symbol, the receiver has *interpreted* the message. That is, the symbol has activated a pattern of subjective experiences — images, understandings, and feelings — that have been stored in the memory functions of the receiver, a pattern that was imprinted as a result of earlier learning. Thus, if both parties have followed the cultural rules of the language being used, the internal meaning experiences of the receiving person are more or less *parallel* to those the communicator intended and built into the message. At this point, the basic act of communication has taken place.

Complexity and Accuracy

Thus far, we have explained the act of human communication at a very simple level with the message going only one way and consisting of only a single word. But common sense tells us that interpersonal communication is more complex an activity. People use elaborate patterns in their messages. Furthermore, things often go wrong. People may fail to understand what the other person is saying, or they may misread a written message. In other words, there are various sources of inaccuracy in communication. Finally, communication is a back-and-forth process as people respond to the content of each other's meanings, ask for clarification, indicate agreement, and so on.

Patterns in Messages. We seldom communicate with only a single word. We normally put words together into patterns according to rules, as in sentences, paragraphs, and various kinds of grammatical constructions. These patterns themselves introduce meanings into the messages that go beyond the meanings associated with each of the words used. For example, the pattern "The boy hit the car" implies a meaning totally different from the pattern "The car

*Posture, facial expressions, and mode of dress
are all factors in nonverbal communication.
The photographs on these two pages capture
a range of emotions and attitudes — pride,
anticipation, happiness, worry, expectancy.*

hit the boy," even though the words are identical. Patterns themselves have their own meanings.

These patterns pose no serious problem in understanding the nature of communication. People learn the patterns and their associated meanings as part of their language, just as they learn the meanings of each word. Thus, the use of patterns by communicators and receivers follows the same general principles as we have described in the one-word case. Such patterns correspond to configurations of traces that are aroused in both communicator and receiver in a parallel manner.

Accuracy in Communication. The second issue we noted above is accuracy in communication. We know from everyday experience that the meanings intended by communicators and those aroused in receivers are not always perfectly parallel. In fact, complete accuracy — a perfect match between the meanings of both parties — is unlikely except in the case of very trivial messages. Collectively, the disrupting factors that reduce similarity of meanings between communicator and receiver are called *impedance,* which can be defined as any reduction in correspondence between the trace configurations of the communicator and those the receiver uses in interpreting the message.

Impedance can take a variety of forms, depending on its causes. One kind results from such factors as poor acoustics, dim light, disruptive sounds, or any similar physical condition that interferes with the transferring of information. Impedance can also be caused by psychological, social, or cultural conditions that reduce similarities between the meanings of sender and receiver. Conditions of this kind include memory failure, faulty perception, or unfamiliarity with the language. Obviously, the greater the amount of any type of impedance, the less accurate the communication will be.

Feedback and Role Taking. Finally, our analysis of the basic act of communication described it as essentially a one-way process in which a message is originated by one person, goes through the various stages described, and is completed by the receiving individual. In reality, human communication goes back and forth between the two parties. For one thing, the communicator in the face-to-face situation is ever alert to various kinds of verbal or nonverbal cues coming from the receiver. These provide feedback.

Feedback is essentially a reverse communication initiated by the receiver and directed back toward the communicator. The communicator takes feedback cues into account to try to minimize impedance. Feedback is usually provided on an ongoing basis so that it can have a substantial influence on the communicator's selection of words and meanings. Thus, when two people are in face-to-face communication, meanings are interpreted back and forth as the messages of the one stimulate feedback from the other.

When the communicator interprets feedback cues correctly and adjusts message content so that impedance is minimized, he or she is engaged in *role taking*. Role taking can be defined as the use of feedback by the communicator to judge which symbols will best arouse the intended meanings in the receiver. We can conclude from our simple theory of communication, therefore, that *the greater the amount of feedback provided, the more effective role taking will be. It follows that the more effective the role taking, the less impedance there will be in the communication.*

Interpersonal and Mass Communication Compared

Having looked closely at the nature of human communication, we can now ask how mass communication differs from face-to-face communication. Recall that mass communication depends on the use of mechanical media and is addressed to a large, diverse audience. Do these factors alter communication in some fundamental way? Or is mass communication just a specific form of human communication?

Consequences of Using Media

In communication between two people, the introduction of a medium clearly has consequences. Talking on the telephone, for example, does not permit the same rich feedback as face-to-face communication does. Face to face, the communicator can easily detect a puzzled look, raised eyebrows, a smile, or a frown. All these cues help the communicator know how the message is being received — indeed, whether it is being received at all. On the telephone, however, the communicator receives feedback only if the other person decides to say something, or at least to make a sound. (Sometimes, of course, silence itself says something.) The limitation on feedback reduces the ability of the communicator to engage in effective role taking. The result may be a reduction in accuracy. Mechanical problems — for example, static or crossed lines — may also produce impedance.

Still, talking on the telephone is clearly human communication. It relies on imprinted traces, learned patterns of meaning, labeling with language symbols, transmission of information over distance, perception by the receiver, reverse labeling, and the experience of parallel meanings by the receiver and communicator. In short, communication through the medium of the telephone follows the same stages as face-to-face communication, although the possibility of impedance is greater when a medium is used.

Using a mass medium is obviously somewhat different from using the telephone. Feedback is reduced even further. You cannot interrupt the television reporter who is using an unfamiliar word, confusing you, or making you angry. When a newspaper, radio, or television is the medium, the communicator has no immediate contact with any member of the audience. Thus mass communication is, in many respects, a one-way activity; and direct feedback is almost nonexistent.

True, the communicator may get responses from a portion of the audience at some later time, but this feedback cannot serve as the basis for role taking while the message is being disseminated. Thus, the communicator is left with little more than indirect, delayed feedback such as letters to the editor, the results of polls and rating services, movie reviews, and box office receipts. These sources may provide useful information for shaping future communication, but they provide no basis for role taking while the message is being disseminated.

What all this means, of course, is that accuracy in mass communication is difficult to predict. To the problems posed by the lack of immediate feedback are added the possibilities of mechanical impedance — typographic errors or bad printing, static or electrical failure, and so on. Generally, then, because the sources of potential impedance are many and because effective feedback is very limited, communication through the mass media is likely to be less accurate than face-to-face communication. But communication through mass media, like communication through the telephone, is still human communication.

Clearly, the use of any medium brings limitations. One may write a letter, make a tape-recorded message for a friend, shoot a home movie, or broadcast a message to tens of millions of people. Such mediated communication is not the same as that between people who are face to face; but there is no doubt that all such forms follow all the basic steps of face-to-face communication.

Consequences of Large, Diverse Audiences

Our analysis has shown that mass communication differs from face-to-face communication not only in its use of mechanical media but also in its dissemination to large, diverse audiences. The basic activities of a professional communicator and the members of the audience, however, are the same if there is one receiver or a million: imprinted traces in the memories of the communicating parties, patterns of meaning, labeling, reverse labeling, and so on. Without these activities, similarities of meaning could not be achieved. The fact that there may be millions of individuals at the receiving end does not change the underlying biological, psychological, and sociological aspects of communication. Thus, we can conclude that mass communication is a special form of interpersonal communication; it is not a completely unique process.

The existence of a large and diverse audience, however, can have important effects on the choice of the form and content of communication. What kind of message, after all, is likely to appeal to a large and diverse audience? How does one share meanings with millions of strangers? If the communicators try to take the role of their receivers, how do they define that role when their audience is large and diverse, especially when feedback is so limited? The safest course is to assume that the audience has limited intellectual capacity, likes to be entertained, and has little interest in delving deeply into any one subject. Then the communicator is more assured that a large part of the audience will get at least most of the message. The existence of a large and diverse audience, therefore, encourages messages that are low in their intellectual demands and high in their entertainment content.

Social and Cultural Influences

For simplicity we have said little about the influence of society and culture on communication. Of course, language itself is a central part of culture. In addition, when a person mails a letter, talks on the telephone, or uses a citizens' band radio, that activity is deeply embedded in the society's economy, regulations and laws, day-to-day customs, and established traditions. Even in a communication between two people, a truly complete understanding of the exchange would require an explanation of all social and cultural influences.

The influences of society and culture are even more significant when one looks at mass communications. For example, each medium has its own history. One aspect of each medium's history is the series of mechanical advances that led to the current technology. Another aspect is the effect of economic and political institutions and cultural values on the development of the medium. In the next chapter we review the history of each medium, examining both the technological background and the influence of the social setting on the medium's development.

Summary

Mass communication is a process that begins when professional communicators formulate a message. They disseminate their message rapidly and continuously through the use of mechanical media to large and diverse audiences. When members of the audience perceive the message, similarities are achieved between the intended meanings of the communicator and the meanings aroused in members of the audience. This experience changes the audience in some way — often trivially, but sometimes in ways that have profound implications for their personal lives and for society. According to the definition of mass communication developed from this analysis, the major mass media are print (including newspapers, magazines, and books), film (that is, commercial motion pictures), and broadcasting (radio and television).

Mass communication is not a unique process but rather one form of human communication. Thus the essence of mass communication, like all human communication, is the arousal in the audience of sets of meanings more or less parallel to those intended by the communicator; that is, meanings are shared by the communicators and the receivers.

This sharing, and the meanings themselves, depend on configurations of traces. A *trace* is a record of experience imprinted in the brain through a change in the nerve cells and available for recall. Every experience of which we have ever been aware is registered in this manner. Each language symbol we have learned has associated with it a pattern of such traces. That pattern is the meaning we experience for that language symbol.

In the process of communicating, the communicator first identifies an appropriate pattern of traces that constitutes the meaning to be conveyed, labels that meaning with a symbol, changes the symbol into a form that the receiver can detect, and finally transmits it. The receiver perceives the symbol, associates it with his or her learned version of its meaning from stored traces, and interprets the message. Usually, the communicator transmits not isolated words but patterns of words. Such patterns are interpreted by the receiver in the same manner as a single word.

Impedance, whether from physical conditions, cultural differences, or other sources, often reduces this sharing of meaning; that is, it leads to inaccuracies in communication. Feedback and role taking can increase the accuracy of communication. When a medium is used, however, feedback and role taking become more difficult and accuracy is likely to decline.

Notes and References

1. For a detailed discussion of the nature and consequences of such dependency, see Melvin L. DeFleur and Sandra Ball Rokeach, *Theories of Mass Communication*, 3rd ed. (New York: McKay, 1975), pp. 261–275.
2. The largest audience is that for television, which currently reaches

more than 76 million households in the United States. *TV Guide*, February 16, 1980, p. A–83.

3. Alexander R. Luria, *The Neuropsychology of Memory* (Washington, D.C.: V. H. Winston & Sons, 1976) pp. 1–16.
4. Robert A. Wallace, *Biology: The World of Life*, 2nd ed. (Santa Monica, Ca.: Goodyear Publishing Co., 1978) p. 310.
5. Ibid, pp. 309–310.
6. Claude E. Shannon and Warren Weaver have a particularly interesting treatment of this process. See *The Mathematical Theory of Communication* (Urbana: The University of Illinois Press, 1949).

2 The Development of the Mass Media

Blessed are they who never read a newspaper, for they shall see Nature, and through her, God.

HENRY DAVID THOREAU, *Essays and Other Writings*

For centuries people have sought ways to communicate over distances and preserve their communications over time. The long history of these attempts has helped shape today's media. This chapter reviews a number of milestones in the history of efforts to extend human speech through media. At every point in this history the media were influenced not only by the available technology but also by social institutions and culture. To examine this history we will look at the development of each medium separately. We begin with the story of the development of early media and the emergence of the first mass medium, print.

The First Media

The long effort to develop media for communication did not begin when newspapers first appeared on the streets, when the earliest movies were shown, or when radio signals were first transmitted. A *medium*, we have said, can be any object or arrangement of objects used as a device to transmit to human meanings. The first media appeared in prehistory, even before people could write. Through century after century, in all parts of the globe, people slowly developed ingenious ways to expand their ability to communicate beyond the spoken word, across both time and distance. It took thousands of years for the first modern medium — print — to be developed.

Media in Preliterate Societies

Some anthropologists believe that our ancestors used complex language more than 300,000 years ago. In any event, it was a very long time ago. By 27,000 B.C. prehistoric people were representing ideas through pictures or drawings. The results of their work can still be seen in caves in northern France and Spain. They left beautiful representations of bison, reindeer, wild horses, and extinct animals on the walls of these caverns.[1] The messages contained in the drawings are not easy to understand today because we know relatively little about their meanings to the people who produced them.

These wall drawings were only one of the media used by prehistoric peoples. Little is known about what techniques were tried first or about their effects on the people. But at various points in prehistory some inventive individual must have come up

Members of preliterate societies often communicated with each other by means of paintings and drawings — centuries later, these cave paintings seem more permanent than some of our ephemeral modern communication.

with each of the new techniques. People marked trails by notching trees and indicated directions or boundaries with piles of stones. In pottery, weaving, sculpture, and humble articles of everyday use, many preliterate people incorporated decorative motifs that seemed to convey meanings of deep significance. For example, they invented standardized designs, like swastikas, crosses, serpents, birds, and animals. They embellished their products with symbols that were meaningful in their culture. In dances, ceremonies, and rituals they represented myths and legends that expressed their group's central values. They used special clothing, hair styles, and body markings to signify ranks, honors, and special privileges. Bodily adornments, tattoos, and scars often signified a person's status in society, such as the position of warrior, priest, or chieftain, or their condition as married or unmarried.

Even with these media, the ability of preliterate people to extend their communication beyond face-to-face speech was very limited. Without writing or paper, they had little that could overcome time but pictorial representations on wood, bark, skin, or stone. Their ability to communicate over distances (*telecommunications*) was limited by the sharpness of their eyesight or hearing and even by weather conditions. Smoke signals, for example, can be seen at a distance only in daylight and under favorable conditions. Something more was needed. That something was writing — the most significant human accomplishment of all time.

| **The Invention and Spread of Writing** | The first step toward true writing was taken thousands of years ago when people arranged pictures or drawings in a sequence to tell a story. Such *pictographic writing* was a slow, laborious way to communicate. Eventually it was replaced by *ideographic writing*, in which simplified or stylized pictures stand for specific things. For instance, a drawing of the sun might stand for a day, a whip for subjugation, and a bundle of grain for a good harvest. Obviously, for such symbols to be useful there had to be widespread agreement about what stood for what. |

The ancient Egyptians used ideographic writing extensively, developing highly stylized symbols known as *glyphs*. Often they carved glyphs into stone to decorate tombs or public buildings. But the glyphs were more than mere decorations. For those who could read them, they transmitted complex messages. By about 4000 B.C. the Egyptians were using these symbols to record accounts of wars, religious ideas, and the deeds of important leaders.

However, writing with glyphs was laborious and complicated. Thousands of symbols were required to refer to the many words and

Paper making was an early and essential step in the development of mass communication through the printed word.

concepts in a language. The symbols had to be carved into stone, and stone was difficult to move over distance. Under such conditions, ordinary people did not learn to read or write. Only small numbers of scribes, who were usually controlled by political and religious leaders, used the written language.

A major step forward was taken when people found materials to replace stone as a writing surface. The Mayan tribes of Central America, for example, used thin white bark as a writing surface. In several parts of the world, and at various times, scribes began to imprint symbols on small clay tablets, or paint them on materials such as papyrus, parchment, and bark with brush and ink. With these media, writing was quicker and the written messages would be transported fairly easily.

The ideographic symbols were increasingly simplified and standardized. Eventually, over a period of centuries, scripts were developed in which characteristic shapes and forms (such as the letters of the various alphabets) came to stand for the sounds of the language.[2] Such *phonetic writing* greatly simplified the recording of speech. Fewer symbols are needed to represent all the words of a language in phonetic writing than in ideographic writing. The development of phonetic scripts made it possible to write many of the world's principal languages.

Once simplified written languages as well as portable media such as papyrus were available, easily understood messages could be preserved through time and moved over distance with relative ease. Long before the birth of Christ, books, historical records, commercial documents, legal codes, scientific treatises, and scriptures began to be part of many cultures. By the time of the Greek and Roman civilizations, however, only a small part of the population could read and write. Widespread literacy was still centuries away.

Predecessors of Modern Books

Although lengthy written documents are almost as old as writing itself, books as we are familiar with them — with leaves bound together between covers — did not appear until about the fourth century A.D. Earlier, when papyrus and parchment came into use, sheets were joined together in long rolls to form *volumen*. These scrolls were hard to use and difficult to store. It was Roman jurists who decided to fold sheets together, collect many sheets at their folds, and bind those sheets between covers, forming a *codex*.[3] We can consider these codices the first books. The Maya also produced codices before they were conquered by the Spanish. They produced long folded sheets (like an accordion) bound between two wooden end pieces. Their written accounts used glyphs rather than phonetic script. The Maya had libraries of codices, but their Spanish conquerors burned the libraries, and only three codices survive.

All these books were, of course, handwritten. In Europe monks laboriously produced books by copying each letter by hand on parchment.[4] Among the most beautiful of these *manu scripti* were those produced in Irish monasteries in the sixth to eighth centuries. Most were religious works, although, as time passed, interest in other topics would grow.

Even before Europeans began using parchment, which is made from the skin of goats or sheep, the Chinese were using a cheaper and more abundant material — paper. Since the fifth century A.D. paper had been used widely in China. Its manufacture and use spread westward slowly.[5] In A.D. 751 Islamic soldiers captured a group of Chinese paper makers in Turkestan. The prisoners taught their captors how to make paper, and its use spread to the

Moslem world. By 950 paper had completely replaced papyrus in Egypt. It was being used in Morocco by the 1100s, and a few years later the Moors took it to Spain. By the 1300s paper was being used in virtually all parts of Europe, although it was not produced in England until the late 1400s or on the American continent until the late 1600s. This early paper was made from linen rags, not wood pulp. Meanwhile, the Chinese preceded the West in another invention — printing.

The Printing Press

As early as the second century A.D., the Chinese were reproducing documents by taking rubbings of texts that had been carved in stone. During the sixth century, they introduced another method: reverse images of letters or illustrations were cut into blocks of wood and then the blocks were inked. When paper was pressed against the blocks, the letters appeared in white against the inked background. During the ninth century the Chinese tried yet another printing method — *movable type* — although they did not develop the idea fully.

The use of movable type was the key to developing a method of reproduction that was simple and cheap compared with copying by hand. Individual pieces of type were made for each letter of the alphabet. The pieces were put together to form a page, but they could then be reused to form other pages. In 868 the teachings of the Buddha were printed by movable type in China in a book known as the Diamond Sutra. In 1456 Johann Gutenberg printed his 42-line Bible in Germany, which many have called the first book printed by movable type in the Western world.

Others were involved in preparing the first printed books in the West, but Gutenberg stands out. He put together a sturdy, workable printing press from the parts of a winepress and cast his type in metal. Gutenberg's Bible was a work of great precision and beauty. Moreover, in a world accustomed to the hand-copied manuscript, the existence of 200 absolutely identical copies of a book was astonishing. But Gutenberg did not enjoy fame; he died a pauper shortly after his press was taken over to pay for his debts.

By the end of the 1400s, printers had established their craft in every major capital in Europe. The first press to operate in England was that of William Caxton, who printed the first book in English, *Recuyell of the Hystoryes of Troye*, in 1476. (It was a translation from the French version that had first been printed in Belgium in 1475.) Caxton turned out dozens of titles, including many literary classics and translations. Other printers quickly followed his example. By about the time when Columbus first

*Johann Gutenberg's invention of movable
type in the fifteenth century revolutionized
communication and altered the course of
Western history.*

sighted land in the New World, presses were operating all over
Europe, and books had been published on almost every topic then
known.

Print in the New World began very early. In 1539 Juan Pablo
set up a press in Mexico City and printed the first book in the
Americas. It was a religious work entitled *Breve y mass compen-
diosa doctrina cristiana*. This book, like the many others that
followed, was printed under the authority of the Spanish arch-
bishop of Mexico. Thus printing had begun in the Americas approximately a century before the Pilgrims arrived at Plymouth
Rock.

**The Print
Revolution**

Gutenberg's invention touched off a veritable revolution in the
Western world. Prior to the invention of the press, book knowledge was concentrated in the hands of a few. As use of the printing press spread, more and more books appeared in the ordinary
languages of the people. Earlier, most books had been prepared
in Latin — the language of religious authorities. Thus, when
printing spread, developments in science, philosophy, and re-

ligion slowly became available to almost anyone who was literate and could afford to purchase a book. Even though literacy was scarcely widespread and books were expensive, there were probably more than 20 million books printed in the West before Columbus made his historic voyage. (The average press run was only about 500 copies per book, so this number represents a very large number of titles.) As presses and the technology of printing were improved during the 1600s and 1700s, and as paper became more available, the number of books printed each year continued to mount.

The development of education contributed greatly to this growth in book publishing. The great European universities had started as early as the twelfth century. More were established every year until, by the sixteenth century, universities were common in all Western European countries. Changes in religions brought a considerable demand for Bibles and other religious works. In addition, the growth of science, philosophy, and literature all added to the demand for more and more books.

At first, books were not seen as a political force. But as soon as those in authority realized that printing could be used to circulate ideas contrary to the wishes of those in power, it came under strong regulation. In England, for example, Henry VIII established a list of prohibited books and a system of licensing in 1529. In spite of these measures, numerous documents were circulated expressing political opinions. When the Tudors controlled the Crown in the mid-1500s, they were very effective at censoring England's presses.[6] This suppression was to last more than a century.

Book Publishing in America

The first printing press in North America was set up at Harvard College in Cambridge, Massachusetts, where the first book was published in 1640, the *Whole Book of Psalmes* (often known as the *Bay Psalm Book*). The college controlled the press until 1662, when the Massachusetts legislature took it over.

Book publishing was slow to develop in the North American colonies, in part because of restrictions by local government, but political dissent around the time of the Revolution stimulated it. In the decades following the Revolution, New York, Boston, and Philadelphia were established as centers of publishing.

By the 1840s a large reading audience existed in America. Cheap paperback reprints of popular books appeared, and then sensational fiction. The cheap paperback was thus established, at this early date, as an important part of American publishing. By 1855 the United States far surpassed England in the number of books sold. That year saw the first publication of *Leaves of Grass,* *Hiawatha,* and Bartlett's *Familiar Quotations.* Probably no other book in American history had as much impact on its time as one published during this period: the antislavery novel *Uncle Tom's Cabin.* Thus, even before the Civil War, book publishing in the United States was well established as a business, as a shaper of American culture, and as a mass medium.[7] During the remainder of the nineteenth century, books continued to develop into a major form of mass communication.

Although advances in technology have altered the methods of producing books, the industry has changed surprisingly little since the nineteenth century. The industry is more commercialized and larger today, and about 40,000 titles are published each year. Of these, fiction makes up only about 10 percent. College textbooks account for a large portion of the books published; nearly 80 million copies are sold each year. In recent years many publishing companies have merged, and others have been acquired by large corporations.

Books today are the most respected medium. They allow the slow, thorough development of ideas that serious and complex subjects demand. But they are also a diverse medium. Everything from Einstein's theory of relativity to hard-core pornography is available in books. The future of books might thus seem secure, but so did the future of radio and the movies in the 1940s. New media appear all the time, and it is not impossible that books might some day be obsolete. Changes in reading ability have already influenced college textbooks: they must be easier to read now than they were a decade ago. Such changes could have larger effects on the publishing industry in years to come. At present, however, the book remains the only form of communication that allows a topic to be set forth in great detail and great depth. For this reason, its death in the near future is unlikely.

Newspapers in America

In a sense the history of newspapers is as long as the history of books. About the time of Christ, the Romans posted daily news sheets in public places. In the mid-1500s leaders of Venice made news of the war in Dalmatia regularly available to the public. To receive a copy, Venetians had to pay a small coin, a *gazetta.* Another forerunner of newspapers was apparently printed in Germany in 1609, but little is known about it. Better known is the *coranto,* which was first sold to the London public in 1621. Published somewhat sporadically as single sheets, the corantos dealt only with foreign news.

Today's newspapers, however, have several characteristics not found in these earlier publications. Edwin Emery, a distinguished historian of journalism, has defined a true newspaper as a paper that (1) is published at least weekly, (2) is produced by a mechanical printing process, (3) is available to people of all walks of life (for a price), (4) prints news of general interest rather than items on specialized topics such as religion or business, (5) is readable by persons of ordinary literacy, (6) is timely, and (7) is stable over time.[8] By this definition the first true newspaper was the *Oxford Gazette*, later called the *London Gazette*. First published in 1665 under authority of the Crown, the *Gazette* appeared twice weekly. Its publication continued into the twentieth century.

The first daily newspaper in English, the *Daily Courant*, began publication in London on March 11, 1702. A newspaper of high quality and considerable integrity, the *Courant* had a high literary level and appealed primarily to an educated elite. Like almost all newspapers, it recovered its costs mainly from advertising.[9]

The English newspapers, like other publications, were legally subject to censorship by the Crown, although after the late 1600s censorship was rarely enforced. In the American colonies censorship came mostly from the governors representing the Crown. These governments soon had a lively, independent press on their hands.

The Eighteenth-Century American Press

The growth of newspapers in the American colonies was of course closely related to cultural, economic, and political circumstances. Both population and commerce grew steadily in the colonies, creating a market for news of shipping and trading as well as advertising. Political tensions also grew, and the colonists often published their criticisms of the Crown's government of the colonies. One of the more significant criticisms appeared in Boston on September 25, 1690. It was a four-page paper titled *Publick Occurrences. Both Foreign and Domestick*. The paper was the work of Benjamin Harris, a printer who had fled to Boston from London, where the authorities had first jailed him and later seized one of his publications. This was the paper's first and last issue. In it, Harris managed to insult both the Indians, who were allies of the British, and the French king. The governor of Massachusetts banned Harris's paper on the grounds that it had been published without authority and contained material disapproved by the government.

Because of its short life, *Publick Occurrences* is not credited with being the first American newspaper. That honor goes instead to a rather dull publication called the *Boston News-Letter*, which first appeared in April 1704. John Campbell, the publisher, was also the postmaster of Boston, a position that allowed him to mail the paper without postal charges. (For early colonial papers, a connection with a post office was almost indispensable.) In its first issue the *News-Letter* solicited advertising. The small one-page paper also noted, immediately under its banner, that it was "published by authority." The result, according to Edwin Emery, was a paper that was "libel-proof, censor-proof, and well-nigh reader-proof." [10] Because of a lack of public interest, the paper was never a financial success.

Somewhat better was the *Boston Gazette,* which William Brooker began in 1719. It was much like the *Boston News-Letter,* but both its printing and its news information were somewhat improved. The *Gazette's* first printer was James Franklin, who was the older brother of Benjamin Franklin. At the age of thirteen, Ben Franklin was apprenticed to his brother and began to gain firsthand experience with printing.

In 1721 James Franklin started his own paper, the *New England Courant.* The *Courant* was not "published by authority" and had no connection with a post office. It included shipping reports and information from nearby towns, but it appealed most to those who liked literary essays and controversial opinions. It was the first newspaper in the colonies to undertake a crusade on a public issue: in the midst of an outbreak of smallpox in Boston, it argued strongly against smallpox inoculations.

The *Courant* was quite successful, and it became increasingly bumptious. It criticized this person, poked fun at another, and finally attacked the governor himself. Eventually, James Franklin was thrown in jail for a month. He was ultimately forbidden to publish the *Courant* or any paper "of like nature" — a restriction he got around by making his brother Ben publisher.

Young Ben Franklin had set type for the paper and done all the other chores of a printer's apprentice. He had tried his hand at writing essays, signing his first works as "Silence Dogood" and slipping them under the door of the print shop at night. They were printed and provoked many replies by other essayists. When his brother was in jail, Ben operated the print shop and paper. In 1723 he ran away from Boston and six years later took over the *Pennsylvania Gazette* in Philadelphia. Franklin not only made the paper a success but also established a small chain of newspapers.

The colonial papers were small, both in their dimensions (they were usually about ten by fifteen inches) and in their number of pages (usually about four). By 1750 most Americans who could read had access to a newspaper. In 1783 the first daily newspaper was founded, the *Pennsylvania Evening Post and Advertiser.*

Although many papers were started in the colonies, most published only a few issues and died. The papers were severely limited by technology, by the fact that literacy was not widespread, and by their system of financing. The hand press used in 1790 was little different from that used by Gutenberg in the mid-1400s. Paper was still made from rags, not wood, and was both expensive and always in short supply. The papers' news was scarcely up to date. Furthermore, the newspapers limited their own audience. Many were *partisan papers;* that is, they consistently argued for one point of view. When political parties developed at the end of the eighteenth century, each party had some papers under its control. Some papers were even subsidized by one of the political parties. After the Revolution, *commercial newspapers* also grew; they concentrated on shipping and foreign news, which was of interest to merchants and businessmen but to few others. All the papers, commercial and partisan, were aimed at a comparatively well-educated segment of society and were expensive. Around the time of the Revolution a newspaper might cost six to ten dollars a year, about as much as a worker's salary for one or two weeks.

In spite of these limitations, the colonial press established a tradition of journalism that was an important part of the emerging society. Many papers defied local authorities. They showed that the press could be a political weapon. Writers such as Thomas Paine and Samuel Adams helped build public support for independence. After the war the most famous arguments for the Constitution (the *Federalist Papers*) were first presented in newspapers. From its beginnings the American press thus established itself as an important political force separate from the government.

The Penny Press

By the early part of the nineteenth century, the technological problems of newspapers were beginning to be solved. It was a time when new machines were being driven by animal, water, and even steam power to accomplish tasks with astonishing rapidity and uniformity. The old screwtype press had been extremely slow. A well-trained team of two printers working full speed could put out only 200 sheets per hour at most. Then in 1827 the first power press in the United States was put into operation in Boston. It was driven by a horse going around a track about thirty feet in diameter.[11] This press could turn out between 500 and 600 impressions an hour, presumably depending on the strength and speed of the horse. By the early 1830s, steam-powered rotary presses could produce 4,000 sheets per hour printed on both sides.

These technological improvements meant that newspapers could greatly increase their circulation if the audience and money could be found. Both the population and percentage of people who could read had increased, but existing newspapers were still very expensive. They sold for six cents a copy, and for a working man who made only four or five dollars a week they were a luxury. If a daily newspaper was going to increase its circulation greatly, it would have to reduce its price and hope to recover the costs and make a profit through the sale of advertising space.

On September 3, 1833, a strange little newspaper that took just this approach appeared on the streets of New York. It was published by Benjamin Day and was called the *New York Sun*, with the slogan "It Shines for All." Its content was clearly designed to appeal to the less-sophisticated reader. Day hired a "reporter" who wrote interesting stories about local happenings, with an emphasis on crime, human interest, accidents, and humorous anecdotes. The *Sun* was sold on the streets by newsboys for only a penny. This system of distribution worked well. The newsboys purchased the papers in lots of a hundred for 67¢. If they sold the whole hundred they could earn 33¢. Day made his profit on advertising, although the profit on a single copy was very small.

The paper was an instant hit. It was soon selling over 8,000 copies a day. From there its sales doubled. Three years later it was selling 30,000 copies per day.

Within a few months the *Sun* had competitors, and the mass press had become a reality. Together these newspapers are known as the *penny press*. Particularly noteworthy was the *New York Herald*, founded in 1837 by the colorful James Gordon Bennet. Bennet imitated Day, but he also added many features that became part of modern journalism — for example, a financial page, editorial comment, and more serious local, foreign, and national news.

The penny papers were vulgar, sensational, and trivial in many respects. But publishers like Bennet had begun to carry basic economic and political news as well as editorial points of view regarding public matters. They were bringing some significant firsthand information and ideas to people who had not been readers of earlier newspapers.

The Great Expansion

The two decades preceding the Civil War saw an enormous expansion of American society. Vast numbers of people moved west, and the industrial and mechanical arts flourished. The general technological growth of the society was reflected in the

THE SUN.

NUMBER 1.]   NEW YORK, TUESDAY, SEPTEMBER 3, 1833.   [PRICE ONE PENNY.

PUBLISHED DAILY,

AT 222 WILLIAM ST............BENJ. H. DAY, PRINTER.

The object of this paper is to lay before the public, at a price within the means of every one, ALL THE NEWS OF THE DAY, and at the same time afford an advantageous medium for advertising. The sheet will be enlarged as soon as the increase of advertisements requires it—the price remaining the same.

Yearly advertisers, (without the paper,) Thirty Dollars per annum.—Casual advertising, at the usual prices charged by the city papers.

Subscriptions will be received, if paid in advance, at the rate of three dollars per annum.

FOR ALBANY—PASSAGE ONLY $1.

The large and commodious steamboat COMMERCE, Capt. R. H. Fitch, will leave the foot of Courtlandt street on Friday, at five o'clock, P. M. for Albany, stopping at the usual landing places to land and receive passengers. Passage $1. For particulars apply to the captain on board.

REGULAR DAYS.

From New York, Mondays, Wednesdays, Fridays.
From Albany, Tuesdays, Thursdays, Saturdays.   a29

FOR NEWPORT AND PROVIDENCE.

The splendid steamboat BENJAMIN FRANKLIN, Capt. E. S. Bunker, and the PRESIDENT, Capt. R. S. Bunker, will leave New York at 5 o'clock, P. M. every Monday, Wednesday and Friday. For further information apply to the Captain on board, foot of Courtlandt-st. or at the office, 14 Broad st.   a2

FOR HARTFORD—PASSAGE 1 DOLLAR.

THROUGH BY DAYLIGHT.

The splendid low-pressure steamboat WATER WITCH, Capt. Vanderbilt, leaves the foot of Catherine street every Tuesday, Thursday, and Saturday mornings, at 6 o'clock, and arrives in Hartford at 7 o'clock the same evening. Passage One Dollar—meals extra.

The above boat leaves Hartford on Mondays, Wednesdays, and Fridays, at the same hours.   a2 tf

FOR LONDON—To sail 10th of Sept.—The

new packet ship Montreal, Champlin, Master, will sail on the 10th inst. For freight or passage, having elegant accommodations, apply to the Captain, on board, Pine-st. wharf, or to

JOHN GRISWOLD, Agent, 68 South st.   a2

FOR LIVERPOOL—The fast-sailing ship

Tallahasse, S. Glover, Master, will be ready to receive cargo in a few days, and have despatch. She has excellent accommodations for both cabin and steerage passengers. For freight or passage, apply to

WOOD & TRIMBLE, 107 Maiden-lane.

FOR HAVRE—The Packet ship Formosa,

Orne, master, will sail on the 8th Sept. For freight or passage apply to the captain on board,

WM. WHITLOCK, Jr. 46 South st.   a2

FOR LIVERPOOL—Packet of the 8 Sept.—

The packet ship Roscoe, J. C. Delano, master, is now in readiness to receive cargo. For freight or passage apply to the captain on board, foot of Maiden lane, or to

FISH, GRINNELL & CO. 134 Front st.   a2 a10

FOR KINGSTON, JAM.—Packet 10th Sept.

The elegant coppered ship Orbit will sail as above. For freight or passage, having splendid accommodations, if state rooms, apply to

B. AYMAR & CO. 34 South st.   a2

FOR NEW ORLEANS.—Packet of the 8th

September, the very fast sailing coppered ship, Nashville, Capt. Rathbone, will sail as above.— For freight or passage, having handsome accommodations, apply to

E. K. COLLINS, 68 South st.

N. B. A lighter is in readiness to receive cargo at Pine street wharf.   a2

FOR NEW ORLEANS—Packet of Sept. 15.

The ship Tennessee, Capt. Sears, will sail as above. For freight or passage, having handsome accommodations, apply to

SILAS HOLMES & CO. 62 South st.

N. B. A lighter is in readiness to receive cargo.

AN IRISH CAPTAIN.

"These are as sweet a pair of pistols as any in the three kingdoms;" said an officer, showing a pair to a young student of his acquaintance, "and have done execution before now; at the slightest touch, off they go, as sweet as honey, without either recoiling or dipping. I never travel without them."

"I never heard of highwaymen in this part of the country."

"Nor I." replied the officer, "and if I had I should not trouble myself to carry the pistols on their account—Highwaymen are a species of sharks who are not fond of attacking us lobsters; they know we are a little too hard to crack. No, my dear sir, highwaymen know that soldiers have not much money, and what they have they fight for."

"Since that is the case, how come you to travel always with pistols?"

"Because," answered the officer, "I find them very useful in accommodating any little difference I may accidentally have with a friend, or which one friend may chance to have with another."

"Do you often settle differences in that way?"

"Why, I was twice out before I arrived at your age.— The first time was with a relation of my own, who said he would see my courage tried before he would contribute with the others towards the purchase of my first commission; so I sent him word that I would be happy to give him one proof the very next morning, and when we met, I touched him so smartly in the leg, that he has halted ever since. But all his doubts being now removed, he cheerfully contributed his quota with the rest of my relations, and we have been very good friends ever since."

"Pray what gave you occasion for the second?" said the young student.

"How it began originally is more than I can tell," answered the captain; all I know is, that a large company of us dined together; we sat long, and drank deep, and I went to bed rather in a state of forgetfulness, and was awaked in the morning from a profound sleep, by a gentleman who began a long story, how I had said something that required explanation; and also, that I had accidentally given him a blow, but he supposed I had no intention to affront him, and so he continued talking in a roundabout kind of way, without coming to any point. So I was under the necessity of interrupting him, "upon my conscience, Sir, (said I,) I am unable to declare, with certainty, whether I had any intention of affronting you or not, because my head is still a little confused, and I have no clear recollection of what passed, nor do I fully comprehend your drift at present, but I conjecture that, you wish to have satisfaction; if so, I must beg you will be kind enough to say so at once, and I shall be at your service." Finding himself thus cut short, he named the place and the hour. I met him precisely at the time. His first pistol missed fire, but I hit him in the shoulder. At his second shot, the bullet passed pretty near me, but mine lodged in his hip, and then he declared he was quite satisfied. So as I had given a blow the preceding night, and two wounds that morning, upon declaring himself satisfied, I said I was contented."

"You would have been thought very hard to please, if you had made any difficulty."

"I thought so myself," rejoined the captain, "and so the affair ended, he being carried home in a coach, and I marching from the field of battle on foot."

"Pray, may I ask if you ever was in a battle?"

"No," replied the captain with a sigh, "I never was; I never had that good fortune, though I would give all the money I have in the world, and all the money I am owing, which is at least treble the sum, to be in one to-morrow."

"Provided you had a good cause;" replied the young student.

"I should not be squeamish respecting the cause, provided I had a good battle: that, my dear, is what is the most essential to a conscientious officer, who wishes to improve himself in his profession. I have much reason, therefore, to wish for a war; and at the present juncture it would be much to the advantage of the nation in general, as it is dwindling into a country of shopkeepers, manufacturers, and merchants. And you must know, too, that I am pretty fortunate, having already stood thirteen duels, and I never was hit but once."

"Thirteen! what, have you fought thirteen duels?"

"No, no!" replied the captain, "the last shot fired at me completed only my sixth duel."

Wonders of Littleness.—Pliny and Elian relate that Myrmecides wrought out of ivory a chariot with four wheels and four horses, and a ship with all her tackling, both in so small a compass, that a bee could hide either with its wings. Nor should we doubt this, when we find it recorded in English history, on less questionable authority, that in the twentieth year of Queen Elizabeth's reign a blacksmith of London, of the name of Mark Scaliot, made a lock of iron, steel, and brass, of eleven pieces, and a pipe key, all of which only weighed one grain. Scaliot also made a chain of gold, of forty-three links, which he fastened to the lock, and key, and put it round the neck of a flea, which drew the whole with perfect ease. The chain, key, lock, and flea, altogether weighed but one grain and a half!

Hadrianus Junis saw at Mechlin in Brabant, a cherry-stone cut into the form of a basket; in it were fourteen pair of dice distinct, the spots and numbers of which were easily to be discerned with a good eye.

But still more extraordinary than this basket of dice, or any thing we have yet mentioned, must have been a set of turnery shown at Rome, in the time of Pope Paul the Fifth, by one Shad of Mitelbrach, who had purchased it from the artist Oswaldus Norhingerus. It consisted of sixteen hundred dishes, which were all perfect and complete in every part, yet so small and slender that the whole could be easily enclosed in a case fabricated in a peppercorn of the ordinary size! The Pope is said to have himself counted them, but with the help of a pair of spectacles, for they were so very small as to be almost invisible to the naked eye. Although his holiness thus satisfied his own eyes of the fact, he did not, we are assured, require of these about him to subscribe to it on the credit of his infallibility; for he gave every one an opportunity of examining and judging for himself, and among the persons thus highly favored, particular reference is made to Gaspar Schioppius, Johannes Faber, a physician of Rome.

Turrianus, of whose skill so many wonderful things are related, is said to have fabricated iron mills, which moved of themselves, so minute in size, that a monk could carry one in his sleeve; and yet it was powerful enough to grind in a single day, grain enough for the consumption of eight men.

A Whistler.—A boy in Vermont, accustomed to working alone, was so prone to whistling, that, as soon as he was by himself, he unconsciously commenced. When asleep, the muscles of his mouth, chest, and lungs were so completely concatenated in the association, he whistled with astonishing shrillness. A pale countenance, loss of appetite, and almost total prostration of strength, convinced his mother it would end in death, if not speedily overcome; which was accomplished by placing him in the society of another boy, who had orders to give him a blow as soon as he began to whistle.

Newspapers were an elite and expensive form of communication until the advent of the Penny Press, which was cheap and readily available and which made the mass press a reality. The New York Sun was an early and important leader of the Penny Press.

improvement of news gathering, printing, and newspaper distribution. Increasingly sophisticated steam-powered rotary presses were capable of printing, cutting, and folding thousands of finished newspapers per hour. The telegraph linked major cities, leading to the rapid transmission of news stories to the editor's desk. On the very day that Samuel F. B. Morse sent the historic first message by telegraph from Washington to Baltimore (May 25, 1844), he also sent over the wire the news of a vote in Congress. Newspapers in all parts of the country began to use the "magnetic telegraph."

The new railroads and steamboats also promoted the growth of newspapers. They could deliver daily newspapers across substantial distances so that communities beyond the larger cities could receive the news in a timely manner. The ancient dream of conquering both time and distance with an effective medium of communication was slowly becoming a reality.

The 1840s also saw the birth of the first wire service. In 1848 several papers agreed to share the cost of telegraphing foreign news from Boston. This was the beginning of the Associated Press. Other newspapers purchased national and foreign news reports prepared by the AP. The service was a boon to smaller newspapers that could not afford to keep their own reporters in Washington, much less overseas.

The Civil War stimulated newspapers enormously. People on both sides of the conflict were desperate for reports of victories and losses. There were hundreds of reporters in the field, and they often devised ingenious methods for getting their reports out ahead of their competitors.

Of special significance was the development of pictorial journalism. One of the country's leading photographers, Mathew Brady, persuaded President Lincoln to let him make a photographic record of the war. Brady was given unrestricted access to military operations and the protection of the Secret Service. During the war, he and his team prepared some 3,500 photographs, one of the most remarkable photographic achievements of all time.[12] It would be a decade, however, before technological improvements would enable newspapers to print photographs.

The Rise of Yellow Journalism

From the end of the Civil War to the turn of the century, the American nation went through a series of important social and cultural changes. Millions of immigrants arrived from Europe, some to take up farms and others to swell the populations of the cities. Industrialization increased at an ever faster pace. New machines were invented to make farming, transportation, mining, manufacturing, and even home life less burdensome.

Mathew Brady, a prototype of the modern photojournalist, photographed the Civil War in such dramatic detail that he brought a new realism to nineteenth-century periodicals.

Newspapers took part in these changes. Vigorous new editors revitalized and reshaped older papers while others established newspapers in the growing cities of the West. Newspaper "barons" developed chains, and the mechanics of printing became one of the wonders of the time. Cheap paper was being made from wood as early as 1867. By the end of the century, the newspaper publisher had at his disposal a rapid news-gathering system, cheap paper, linotypes, color printing, cartoons, electric presses, and, above all, a corps of skillful journalists. The newspaper had settled into a more or less standard format much like what we have today. Its features included not only domestic and foreign news but also a financial page, letters to the editor, sports news, society reports, women's pages, classified sections, and advice to the lovelorn. Newspapers were complex, very competitive, and extremely popular.

It was their competitiveness that led to one of the most colorful periods in the history of American newspapers. The key to financial success in a newspaper — then as now — was to attract as many readers as possible. By showing advertisers that their messages would be seen by more people than in a competing paper, a publisher could attract more ads at higher prices and enjoy greater revenues. During the last decade of the century, the competition for readers led to a trend toward sensational journalism.

The first steps were taken when the penny papers began increasing their emphasis on crime, human interest, and humor. Another step occurred when Joseph Pulitzer succeeded in building the circulation of the Sunday *World* in New York to over 300,000 in the early 1890s. To do this, he combined good reporting with crusades, an emphasis on disasters, melodramatics, sensational photographs, and comic strips in color — all to increase reader interest. Pulitzer crusaded against corrupt officials and for civil service reform and taxes on luxuries, large incomes, and inheritances. He pioneered the use of colored comics in newspapers, which did much to spur the circulation of his Sunday editions. One cartoon in particular made history. It featured a bald-headed, toothless, grinning kid, clad in a yellow sacklike garment. The "Yellow Kid," as the character came to be called, appeared in settings that depicted life in the slums of New York and was extremely popular.

It was William Randolph Hearst who mastered the art of attracting readers through appeals to sympathy and anger, the bizarre, and the picturesque. Hearst purchased the *New York Journal* in 1895, determined to build its flagging circulation to surpass that of Pulitzer's paper. Seeing the popularity of the Yellow Kid, Hearst

EDITION FOR GREATER NEW YORK

NEW YORK JOURNAL

AND ADVERTISER.

NO. 5,572. Copyright, 1898, by W. R. Hearst.—NEW YORK, THURSDAY, FEBRUARY 17, 1898.—16 PAGES. PRICE ONE CENT

DESTRUCTION OF THE WAR SHIP MAINE WAS THE WORK OF AN ENEMY.

$50,000!

$50,000 REWARD!
For the Detection of the
Perpetrator of
the Maine Outrage!

Assistant Secretary Roosevelt Convinced the Explosion of the War Ship Was Not an Accident.

The Journal Offers $50,000 Reward for the Conviction of the Criminals Who Sent 258 American Sailors to Their Death. Naval Officers Unanimous That the Ship Was Destroyed on Purpose.

$50,000!

$50,000 REWARD!
For the Detection of the
Perpetrator of
the Maine Outrage!

NAVAL OFFICERS THINK THE MAINE WAS DESTROYED BY A SPANISH MINE.

George Eugene Bryson, the Journal's special correspondent at Havana, cables that it is the secret opinion of many Spaniards in the Cuban capital that the Maine was destroyed and 258 of her men killed by means of a submarine mine, or fixed torpedo. This is the opinion of several American naval authorities. The Spaniards, it is believed, arranged to have the Maine anchored over one of the harbor mines. Wires connected the mine with a powder magazine, and it is thought the explosion was caused by sending an electric current through the wire. If this can be proven, the brutal nature of the Spaniards will be shown by the fact that they waited to spring the mine until after all the men had retired for the night. The Maltese cross in the picture shows where the mine may have been fired.

Hidden Mine or a Sunken Torpedo Believed to Have Been the Weapon Used Against the American Man-of-War---Officers and Men Tell Thrilling Stories of Being Blown Into the Air Amid a Mass of Shattered Steel and Exploding Shells---Survivors Brought to Key West Scout the Idea of Accident---Spanish Officials Protest Too Much---Our Cabinet Orders a Searching Inquiry---Journal Sends Divers to Havana to Report Upon the Condition of the Wreck. Was the Vessel Anchored Over a Mine?

BY CAPTAIN E. L. ZALINSKI, U. S. A.

(Captain Zalinski is the inventor of the famous dynamite gun, which would be the principal factor in our coast defence in case of war.)

Assistant Secretary of the Navy Theodore Roosevelt says he is convinced that the destruction of the Maine in Havana Harbor was not an accident. The Journal offers a reward of $50,000 for exclusive evidence that will convict the person, persons or Government criminally responsible for the destruction of the American battle ship and the death of 258 of its crew.

The suspicion that the Maine was deliberately blown up grows stronger every hour. Not a single fact to the contrary has been produced.

Captain Sigsbee, of the Maine, and Consul-General Lee both urge that public opinion be suspended until they have completed their investigation. They are taking the course of tactful men who are convinced that there has been treachery.

Washington reports very late that Captain Sigsbee had feared some such event as a hidden mine. The English cipher code was used all day yesterday b the naval officers in cabling instead of the usual American code.

If the Penny Press expanded the audience for the American newspaper, the practitioners of "Yellow Journalism," the sensational press of the 1890s, dramatically accelerated newspaper circulation from tens of thousands of readers to millions. Rival papers competed vigorously for the attention of readers.

simply bought the cartoonist from his rival with a large salary. He added other writing and editorial talent. Then he published more comics, more sensational reports, and more human interest material — which led to increased circulation.

As Hearst's publication began to rival Pulitzer's circulation, the two newspaper barons led their papers into practices that came to be called *yellow journalism*. In part the label was used because the Yellow Kid symbolized the newspapers' mindless intellectual level. Their papers were preoccupied increasingly with crime, sex, sob stories, exposés of sin and corruption in high places (many of which were gross exaggerations), sports, sensational photographs, misrepresentations of science, indeed anything that would attract and hold additional readers. It was said that each issue of Hearst's *San Francisco Examiner* was designed to provoke one reaction: when the readers opened their papers and saw the headlines, Hearst wanted them to say, "Gee whiz!" The idea that newspapers had any responsibility to the public seemed abandoned.

As the century came to a close, the period of yellow journalism seemed to be ending with it. Newspapers became somewhat more responsible. Then, during the 1920s, another form of yellow journalism emerged. This new *jazz journalism* retained much of the sensationalism of the nineteenth century's yellow journalism and added two new elements. One was the tabloid format, copied from London papers; that is, their dimensions were smaller, making them easier to read. The other new element was the bold and more dramatic use of photographs. For example, on January 14, 1928, the entire front page of the *New York Daily News* consisted of a brief headline and photograph of a woman at the moment of execution in the electric chair. An enterprising photographer had smuggled a camera into the death chamber and snapped the picture just as the electricity surged through the woman's body. The gruesome details of the woman's reactions and a graphic description of the apparatus were given below the picture.

Gradually, the excesses of jazz journalism moderated, just as those of the penny press of the early 1800s had. Almost everyone read a newspaper every day, and the battles for circulation moderated. Newspapers were the major mass medium; they left no large segment of the population untouched. By the beginning of the new century, the newspaper was in its golden age.

Yellow journalism and its offshoot, jazz journalism, are more than historical curiosities. They represent an approach to newspaper publishing that seeks circulation and profit at the expense of integrity and objectivity in reporting. It is an approach that represents an abandonment of responsibility toward the public and thus betrays the confidence that the U.S. Constitution puts in the press. Under the First Amendment to the Constitution, the government is forbidden to regulate the press. Instead, the nation is to trust that under a free press there will be a flow of objective information that will allow citizens to make intelligent political decisions.

The public did not deserve the excesses of yellow journalism. This is as true today as it was decades ago. Yet elements of yellow journalism can still be found in publications that "expose" and "reveal" the secret lives of famous people, that distort scientific issues, that play on people's hopes and fears concerning medicine and health, and so on. The *National Enquirer* is probably the best-known example of this kind of journalism today; unfortunately, it is not the only one.

Twentieth-Century Trends

By the beginning of the twentieth century, the newspaper had virtually the same kind of content and format as we see today. Even though newspapers use modern technology, such as computers, their appearance and production and distribution techniques have much in common with those of 1910. But there have been significant changes in other areas — specifically, in circulation, ownership, competition, and styles of reporting.

Circulation. The American newspaper reached its peak of popularity at about the time of World War I. During those years more newspapers were sold per household in America than at any time before or after. Since that time, increases in newspaper circulation have not kept pace with the growth in population, as Table 2.1 shows.

The newspaper enjoyed its golden age in the early twentieth century for several reasons. First, broadcasting and the movies were in their infancy; they were not serious contenders for either the attention of the public or the advertising dollars of business and industry. Furthermore, newspapers had matured. Their problems of news gathering and reporting, distribution, and printing had largely been resolved by the turn of the century.

Ownership and Competition. While newspapers were undergoing a relative decline in circulation, a closely related change was taking place in their patterns of ownership. Because of the rising costs of production, limitations on new markets, and the inroads of competing media, many papers ceased to be competitive. They either stopped publication altogether or were purchased by their rivals in order to consolidate production and other facilities. In 1914

Table 2.1 The Growth of Daily Newspapers in the United States, 1850–1977

Year	Total circulation of daily newspapers (thousands)	Circulation per household
1850	758	0.21
1860	1,478	0.28
1870	2,602	0.34
1880	3,566	0.36
1890	8,387	0.66
1900	15,102	0.94
1910	24,212	1.36
1920	27,791	1.34
1930	39,589	1.32
1940	41,132	1.18
1950	53,829	1.24
1955	56,147	1.17
1960	58,882	1.12
1965	60,358	1.05
1966	61,379	1.06
1967	61,561	1.05
1968	62,535	1.03
1969	62,060	1.00
1970	62,108	0.99
1971	62,231	0.97
1972	62,510	0.94
1973	63,147	0.93
1974	61,901	0.89
1975	60,655	0.85
1976	60,976	0.84
1977	61,495	0.83

Sources: U.S. Bureau of Census, *Historical Statistics of the United States, Colonial Times to 1957* (Washington, D.C., 1960), Series R 176, p. 500; Series R 169, p. 500; Series 255, p. 16; Series A 242–44.

U.S. Bureau of Census, *Historical Statistics of the United States, Continuation to 1962 and Revisions* (Washington, D.C., 1965), Series R 170, p. 69.

U.S. Bureau of Census, *Statistical Abstract of the United States* (Washington, D.C., 1973), pp. 53, 503.

U.S. Bureau of Census, *Current Population Reports: Population Characteristics,* Seies P 20, no. 166 (August 4, 1967), p. 4 (and forthcoming reports). *Editor and Publisher, International Yearbook* (New York: Editor and Publisher Co.), an annual.

Note: Figures after 1960 include Alaska and Hawaii.

some 2,250 daily newspapers were being printed in the United States. By 1950 the number had dropped to 1,772. Since that time, the number of American daily papers has remained relatively constant at approximately 1,750. This number is likely to remain stable for the foreseeable future.[13] The number of owners and independent newspapers, however, has dropped and is likely to continue to drop even further as more newspapers are taken over by chains and conglomerates.

Styles of Reporting. During the history of journalism, styles of reporting have ranged from a concentration on human interest and sensational topics to a vigorous pursuit of factual information about critical public issues. In the eighteenth-century colonial press, essays that argued for one side of a controversy were popular. During the nineteenth century, when the wire services were born, *objective reporting* gained prominence; impersonal reports that stated the facts but avoided opinions were favored.

Later, yellow journalism and sensationalism were the predominant styles. In this century still other styles have emerged. One can contrast the 1928 pictorial report of the woman in the electric chair with the *investigative reporting* that led to the public exposure of the Watergate scandal and, ultimately, the resignation of President Nixon. Rather than arguing a point or simply reporting the circumstances of an event, investigative journalists play the role of detective.

Serious investigative reporting is a style that has increasingly characterized good newspapers as the medium has matured. An extension of investigative reporting is *precision journalism*. This form of reporting uses the tools of social science (for example, polls, questionnaires, and statistical analyses) as aids in assembling objective information. Both investigative reporting and precision journalism indicate increasing professionalism in the modern newspaper.

American Magazines

Magazines have a much briefer history than newspapers, but they depend on the same technological developments and social trends that gave rise to the print media in general. Ben Franklin published a magazine in 1741, but it lasted for only six issues. For all practical purposes, American magazines began during the middle of the nineteenth century. However, it was the social trends of the last half of that century that allowed magazines to survive as a mass medium.

The cities grew rapidly during the late 1800s and continued to grow in the twentieth century. Literacy increased steadily, as did the affluence of the middle class. Modern transportation, a reliable mail service, and demands for specialized information all played a part in the emergence of the modern mass-circulation magazine. In the years after the great depression of 1893, a time that magazine historian Frank Luther Mott has called the "more of everything era," "every interest had its own journal or journals — all the ideologies and movements, all the arts, all the schools of philosophy and education, all the sciences, all the trades and industries, all the professions and callings, all organizations of importance, all hobbies and recreations."[14] In other words, while newspapers were providing their readers with varied content, magazines zeroed in on special interests. They were largely directed toward audiences who shared an interest in a particular subject.

Toward the end of the century there was a massive increase in both the number of magazines and their circulations. Several began to appeal to a national audience and national advertisers; they achieved circulations of over 1 million subscribers. In 1900 somewhat over 5,500 periodicals were appearing regularly in the United States. By 1905 there were more than 6,000. New titles appeared, died out, and reappeared. Magazine publishing was thus a dynamic field, as it is today.

Some magazines were extensions of publishing firms; for example, *Scribner's*, *Harper's*, and *The World's Work* (published by Doubleday). These journals previewed and displayed the publishers' new books, teasing readers and catching their interest with sample chapters of forthcoming books. Other popular magazines began by appealing to particular interests among some segment of the population (for example, *True Confessions*, *Field and Stream*, and *Silver Screen*). Some magazines became important instruments of social change. They called for reforms in politics, industry, health care, and child labor. For example, at the turn of the century, *McClure's* attacked the powerful Standard Oil Company, political bosses in major cities, and other instances of corruption and the abuse of power. President Theodore Roosevelt gave these magazines the name *muckrakers*.

By World War I, the muckraking magazines were declining. Even today, however, magazines are often the first medium to publish calls for needed social change. Ralph Nader began his first crusade for consumer protection in the pages of the *New Republic* long before he was nationally famous.

As the muckraking magazines declined, those publishing light fiction and feature articles grew. The early 1920s saw the birth of a new breed of magazines with the founding of *Time,* a weekly interpretation of the news. It would be imitated by *Newsweek* and *U.S. News & World Report.* As television grew in the 1950s, magazines aimed at a mass general audience with no specialized interests began to fail. But magazines aimed at particular groups of people or people with specialized interests — such as women or hunters or gardeners — have fared well.

In 1950 there were 6,960 periodicals published in the United States; by 1978 the number had risen to 9,732.[15] Magazines today are a significant form of mass communication. By combining many of the features of the more timely newspapers with the greater flexibility and in-depth discussion of books, they have retained an important role as a mass medium.

Motion Pictures

The history of the motion picture as a mass medium is short, spanning less than a century. But the events that led to motion pictures go back many centuries. The first step in this story was the solution of a series of complex technical problems. A motion picture, after all, is a series of still pictures projected rapidly on a screen in such a way that smooth motion is perceived. Before this illusion of motion could be achieved, problems in optics, chemistry, and even human physiology had to be solved. Lenses, projectors, cameras, and roll film had to be invented. Only then were the movies born.

Magic Shadows on the Wall

The first problem to be solved was how to focus and project an image. Convex quartz lenses for magnifying and concentrating the rays of the sun were used as early as 600 B.C. Centuries later, Archimedes earned fame by frightening the Romans with a lens during the defense of Syracuse. He is said to have mounted a large "burning glass" on the city's wall that could set fire to the Roman ships. The story may or may not be true, but it indicates that the ancients had begun to solve one of the main problems associated with cameras and projectors — how to use lenses to focus light.

A major advance was made in the mid-1600s. The concept of projecting a visual image by passing light through a transparency was the subject of experiments by a German priest, Athanasius Kirscher. Kirscher was able to put on a "magic lantern show" for his fellow scholars at the Collegio Romano in 1645. He had painted his slides himself. His projected images of religious figures could barely be seen, but his show was a sensation. No one had ever seen anything like it. In fact, there were dark rumors that he was in league with the devil and was conjuring up spirits through the practice of the "black arts."[16]

The public became increasingly aware of the idea of the projected image in the eighteenth century. Showmen produced shadow plays and projected images of ghostlike figures for the entertainment of their audiences. By the mid-1800s, relatively reliable light sources were available in the form of improved lanterns with reflecting mirrors and condensing lenses. The simple oil-burning lantern was eventually replaced by a powerful light produced by burning hydrogen gas and oxygen through a cylinder of hard lime. Ultimately, of course, electric lights provided the necessary source of illumination.

Photography Develops

The science of lenses and projection had advanced more rapidly than that of photography. Until the nineteenth century, people could project images but no one had been able to capture images to form a still picture. With advances in the science of chemistry in the late 1700s and early 1800s, however, the stage was set for the development of photography. An artist, Louis Daguerre, and a chemist, Joseph Nièpce, along with others, worked for several years on the problem. Nièpce died shortly before success was achieved, but his partner Daguerre was able to carry on.

In 1839 Daguerre announced the process, the *daguerreotype*, and showed examples of his work to the public. The photographs were sharp and clear. The daguerreotype used a polished copper plate coated with gleaming silver. The plate was exposed to iodide fumes to form a thin coating of light-sensitive silver iodide. After the plate was exposed briefly to a scene, the image registered on the plate. Chemical baths then "fixed" the image on the plate. Because Daguerre's pictures were much clearer and sharper than those of others (who tried to use paper), his process was adopted all over the world.[17]

Photography was received enthusiastically in the United States. Soon there were daguerreotype studios in every city, and itinerant photographers traveled the back country in wagons to take portraits. As chemistry and technology improved, such pioneers as George Eastman transformed photography from an art practiced by trained technicians to a popular hobby. More than anything else, it was Eastman's development and marketing of flexible celluloid roll film that made popular photography a success.[18] The availability of flexible film also made motion pictures technically feasible, making it possible to bring together the technology of photography with progress in the study of visual processes and the perception of motion.

The Illusion of Motion

Motion pictures, of course, do not "move." They consist of a series of still pictures in which the object in motion is captured in progressively different positions. When the stills are run through a projector at the correct speed, an illusion of smooth motion is achieved.

At the heart of this illusion is a process called *visual lag* or *visual persistence:* "The brain will persist in seeing an object when it is no longer before the eye itself."[19] We "see" an image for a fraction of a second after the thing itself has changed or disappeared. If we are presented with one image after the other, the *visual persistence* of the first image fills in the time lag between the two images so they seem to be continuous.

The discovery of visual persistence by Dr. Peter Mark Roget in 1824 and its study by eminent scientists of the time led to widespread interest in the phenomenon. Toys and gadgets were produced that were based on visual lag. For example, a simple card with a string attached on each end can be twirled with the fingers. If a figure, say a dog, is drawn on one side of the card and a doghouse on the other, and the card is twirled, the dog seems to be jumping in and out of the doghouse.

Few of these gadgets were of historical importance, but one does stand out as a step in the development of the motion picture: the *Zoetrope*, later known as the "wheel of life," a cylinder mounted on a vertical spindle. Cards showing figures in successive movement — such as a man running or a horse jumping a fence — were mounted inside. A viewer could peer into the cylinder through slits and see one card at a time as the cylinder revolved. The result was the illusion of smooth motion.

The illusion of motion came under intense study by such scientists as Joseph Plateau, who studied timing, color intensity, and other matters related to the perception of movement. By the middle of the century, the wheel of life (or *phénakistiscope* as it became called) was highly developed. When elaborated and combined with the photography of things in motion, its principles provided the basis for movies.

Capturing and Projecting Motion on Film

During the closing decades of the nineteenth century, various attempts were made to photograph motion. A major advance was the result of a bet. Governor Leland Stanford of California and some of his friends made a large wager as to whether a running horse ever had all its feet off the ground at once. To settle the bet, they hired an obscure photographer named Eadweard Muybridge. Muybridge photographed moving horses by setting up a bank of twenty-four still cameras, each of which was tripped by a thread as the horse galloped by. His photographs showed that a horse did indeed have all four feet off the ground at once.

The photographs created such interest that Muybridge took many more, refining his techniques for photographing moving things. He eventually traveled to Europe to display his work and found that others had been making similar studies. Interest in the photography of motion became intense, but in 1890 no one had yet taken motion pictures as we do today. Further advances in both cameras and projectors were needed.

During the late 1880s and early 1890s, various crude motion picture cameras were under development, and a number of showmen were providing audiences with moving pictures based on serially projected drawings. Then during the 1890s, a virtual explosion of applications of film and viewing procedures occurred. By 1895 French audiences were seeing brief motion pictures projected on a screen by August and Luis Lumière. The audiences were greatly impressed. Other applications of the new technology soon followed, and a number of individuals clamored for the title of inventor of the motion picture. But it was William Dickson, assistant to Thomas Alva Edison, who perfected the motion picture camera.

Meanwhile Edison and Thomas Armat developed a practical and reliable projection system. Edison and his partner obtained U.S. patents and began to manufacture their projector, the Vitascope. Edison also set up a studio to produce short films — mostly of vaudeville acts — for use with the projector. Although it had many shortcomings, the Vitascope worked reliably. Its major flaw was that it projected at a wasteful forty-eight frames per second, whereas sixteen frames easily provide the illusion of smooth motion.

Because Edison, ever the penny pincher, declined to spend $150 to obtain foreign patents, his machines were quickly duplicated and patented in Europe. In fact, numerous improvements were incorporated that soon made Edison's original machines obsolete. Furious patent fights in the courts later threatened to kill the new medium.

Then Edison decided to exhibit his moving pictures in a peep show device called the Kinetoscope. For a nickel, one could turn a crank, look inside the machine, and see a brief film on a small screen. This one-viewer-at-a-time approach, Edison thought, would bring a larger return on investment than projecting to many people at once. Needless to say, Edison's approach did not catch on; instead, the industry developed on the theater model. Such pioneers as the Lumière brothers and others in Europe had seen this clearly. By 1896, however, Edison was projecting motion pictures to the public in New York for the first time in America. In general, by 1900 all the scientific and technological problems of the motion picture had been resolved. It had taken centuries to achieve some of the solutions, but the medium was now ready for mass use. Millions of people would be eager to pay to be entertained by its magic shadows.

The Expanding Movie Industry

The first couple of years of the new century were marked by experimentation. Many of the early films ran for only a minute or so. Just the sight of something moving on the screen could thrill an audience. Then the makers of motion pictures began to seek longer films and more interesting content. One-reel films were produced on every conceivable topic, from prize fights to religious plays. They were exhibited at vaudeville halls, saloons, amusement parks, and even opera houses.

By 1903 both American and European producers were making films that were up to twenty-five minutes or more in length and that told a story. Some, such as *Life of an American Fireman* (1903), *The Great Train Robbery* (1903), and *A Trip to the Moon* (1902), have become classics. Production and distribution of films expanded at an extraordinary pace.

The Nickelodeons. When films became available on a rental basis, it made the local motion picture theater possible as a small business venture. The investment needed was modest, and the profits could be high. One could rent a vacant store, add some cheap decorations, install folding chairs, buy a projector, piano, and screen, rent films, and open the door for business. Harry P. Davis and John P. Harris of Pittsburgh did exactly that in 1905. They charged five cents for admission and called their theater "The Nickelodeon." In a week they made $1,000 playing to near-capacity houses.

The success of the first nickelodeon greatly impressed the entertainment world, and there was a stampede to set up others in cities all across the nation. Within a year there were 1,000 in operation, and by 1910, 10,000 were exhibiting films. National gross receipts for that year have been estimated at $91 million.[20]

The early theaters were concentrated in the industrial cities of the Northeast. Movies were made to order for that time and place. America was a nation of immigrants, most of whom were newly arrived and many of whom lived in Northeastern cities. Since these

The first movie houses, called nickelodeons, gave their patrons larger-than-life visuals on the silver screen. In that age of silent movies, sound effects and music were provided by the theater pianist or organist.

early movies were silent, language posed no barrier for the audience. Going to the movies was cheap so they provided entertainment for people at the bottom of society. Even the illiterate could understand their stereotyped plots, overdramatized acting, and slapstick humor. The nickelodeons have therefore been called "democracy's theaters."

The early movies proved to be popular beyond the wildest dreams of their pioneers. In New York City alone, more than a million patrons a week were attending the nickelodeons in the early 1900s. Although the nickelodeons were associated with the slums and ghettos, movies had become big business. Corporations had been formed to produce, distribute, and exhibit the films.

Movies for the Middle Class. While the nickelodeons brought the motion picture to the urban poor, the industry was anxious to lure the huge mass of middle-class families into the theaters. But movies were associated with low taste and the least prestigious elements of society. To shake this image and bring middle-class patrons to the box office, longer, more sophisticated films were produced. Attractive theaters were built in better neighborhoods, and movie palaces opened in the central business districts. The star system came: particular actors and actresses played prominent roles in the films and became widely known as personalities — even idols and love goddesses. The star system provided a tremendous boost to the popularity of motion pictures.

By 1914 an estimated 40 million patrons attended movies every week. An increasing number were women and children. The movies had been accepted by the middle class, and the era of the nickelodeon was over. Meanwhile, as Europe entered World War I, Hollywood had been established as the center of American movie making. The closing of industries in Europe because of the war opened the world market to American film makers. They took advantage of the opportunity, and a huge growth in film attendance occurred all over the globe. American films have tended to be popular in the world market ever since.

The Talkies. Since the 1890s, inventors had tried to combine the phonograph and the motion picture to produce movies with synchronized sound. Few of their contraptions worked well. The sound was either weak and scratchy or poorly coordinated with the action in the film. The public soon tired of such experiments; movie makers thought that talking pictures posed insurmountable technical problems.

But the technical difficulties were overcome by the mid-1920s. American Telephone and Telegraph used its enormous capital resources to produce a reliable sound system. Then Warner Brothers signed an agreement with AT&T, and the transition to sound was ready to begin. Warner produced a new feature including sound for the 1927–1928 season. It starred Al Jolson and was called *The Jazz Singer.* Actually, it included only a few songs and a few minutes of dialogue; the rest of the film was silent. But it was an enormous success, and other talkies followed quickly.

Almost overnight, the silent movie was obsolete; the motion picture with a full sound track became the norm. With improvements in technical quality, theaters, acting, and other aspects of the medium, motion pictures entered their maturity.

The Golden Age. The period from 1930 to the late 1940s in many ways represents the peak years of the movies (see Table 2.2).

Table 2.2 The Growth of Motion Picture Attendance in the United States, 1922–1977

Year	Average weekly movie attendance (thousands)	Weekly attendance per household
1922	40,000	1.56
1924	46,000	1.71
1926	50,000	1.78
1928	65,000	2.23
1930	90,000	3.00
1932	60,000	1.97
1934	70,000	2.24
1936	88,000	2.71
1938	85,000	2.52
1940	80,000	2.29
1942	85,000	2.33
1944	85,000	2.29
1946	90,000	2.37
1948	90,000	2.22
1950	60,000	1.38
1954	49,000	1.04
1958	40,000	0.79
1960	28,000	0.53
1965	21,000	0.37
1974	17,904	0.26
1975	19,808	0.28
1976	19,992	0.27
1977	20,385	0.27

Sources: U.S. Bureau of Census, *Historical Statistics of the United States, Colonial Times to 1957* (Washington, D.C., 1960), Series H 522, p. 225; Series A 242–44, p. 15.

U.S. Bureau of Census, *Historical Statistics of the United States, Continuation to 1962 and Revisions* (Washington, D.C., 1965), Series H 522, p. 35.

U.S. Bureau of Census, *Statistical Abstract of the United States* (Washington, D.C., 1968), tables 11, 302, pp. 12, 208 (1973); tables 53, 347, 349, pp. 41, 211, 212.

U.S. Bureau of Census, *Current Population Reports: Population Characteristics*, Series P-20, No. 166 (August 24, 1967), pp. 1, 4.

Note: Figures do not include Alaska or Hawaii.

During these two decades, movies were the dominant form of mass entertainment in America, and a few major studios dominated the movies. Companies such as MGM, 20th Century Fox, Paramount, RKO, and Republic controlled the movies from their conception to their showing in local movie theaters.

The 1920s brought changes in moral codes in the United States. In its struggle for increased profits, the movie industry began to introduce subject matter that was sexually frank by the standards of the times. Their attempts are reminiscent of the episodes of yellow journalism during the struggle for circulation by the newspapers. But when major religious groups actively opposed such movies, the industry took steps to police itself. In 1930 the Motion Picture Producers and Distributors Association adopted its first code for censoring films prior to exhibition. The standards in the code changed from time to time and became increasingly puritanical. By the mid-1930s, for example, the code banned words such as *broad, hot* (woman), *fairy, pansy, tart,* and *whore.* Bedroom scenes always showed twin beds and fully clad actors. The code was rigidly enforced, and by the beginning of World War II (1941) the movies had become a wholesome, if bland, form of family entertainment.

The Decline. Receipts at the box office held steady until the late 1940s. By then, some 90 million tickets were being sold weekly. With the rise of television, though, the movies underwent an increasingly sharp decline. By 1970 only 15 million tickets were being sold during an average week.

To draw patrons back to the theaters and away from their television sets, movie makers turned to gimmicks such as three-dimensional films and, once again, to themes and topics that could not be found on television. The major studios made movies that were often increasingly violent and sexually explicit. In addition, a large, if somewhat underground, pornographic film industry came into existence.

Today an occasional motion picture may draw record crowds because of a unique monster or other special effects (*Jaws, Star Wars*), violence (*The Godfather*), a sensational theme (*The Exorcist*), or an explicit portrayal of sex (*Deep Throat*). Movie attendance has increased somewhat. The current audience for films is mainly younger people rather than the entire family. New types of theaters (with multiple rooms and screens) have helped revive the industry somewhat. But the golden age of the movies has passed. Most neighborhood movie theaters closed long ago, and television has replaced film as America's most popular form of entertainment. Generally, the movie industry is surviving by adapting to its smaller audience, with films for a more youthful audience, and by the revenues that television pays the industry for both making and broadcasting films.

Broadcasting

Devices that could conquer both distance and time were a dream for centuries. Giovanni della Porta had written in the sixteenth century of the "sympathetic telegraph" for which learned men were searching.[21] It was to use a magnetic lodestone that would sensitize two needles so they would act in unison. The needles were to be mounted on separate dials, something like compasses, in such a way that if one needle were moved to a given position on its dial, the other would move to a parallel position immediately — even though the devices were far from each other. With the alphabet arranged around each dial, messages would be sent and received over distances.

The special lodestone was never found, but the slow accumulation of science and technology, and its more rapid acceleration in the twentieth century, eventually yielded communication devices that would have astounded Giovanni della Porta. The telegraph was first, followed by the telephone. The wireless telegraph was followed quickly by the radiophone. These eventually led to home radio and then, at mid-century, to home television. These applications of scientific principles were spurred in the late nineteenth century by an ever-increasing need for rapid communications as nations developed powerful military forces and commercial interests that literally spanned the globe.

The Growth of Technology

The Greeks marvelled at static electricity but did not understand its nature. By the 1700s European scientists were generating gigantic static charges, but they still didn't understand its nature. Slowly, experiment followed by experiment succeeded in revealing how electricity worked, how it could be stored in batteries, and how it could be used in the telegraph, the light bulb, and the electric motor. It was the discoveries of scientists such as Volta, Ampère, Faraday, and Maxwell that laid the foundations for our radio and television. Their scientific principles were then applied by such people as Samuel Morse, Guglielmo Marconi, and Philo T. Farnsworth.

Communicating Via Wires. The era of instantaneous telecommunication began on May 24, 1844. On that day Samuel F. B. Morse sent the dramatic words "What hath God wrought?" in code by electricity across about twenty miles of copper wires strung on poles between Washington, D. C., and Baltimore, Maryland. Within a few years, such wires connected all the major cities of the United States. The telegraph began to play a key role as a communications medium for business, the military, and newspapers. Underseas cables soon followed, and the United States was linked with Europe by 1866. Yet the telegraph obviously was not a medium for the general public. It would be more than half a century before the public at large would have a device in their homes for instantaneous mass communication without wires.

The telegraph set the stage for the structure of ownership that would eventually characterize the electronic media in the United States. Even though the federal government had paid for Morse's original line to Baltimore, it declined to exercise control over the telegraph. The medium became the property of a private corporation to be operated for profit. This pattern was followed for the telephone, radio, and television as they developed.

A Telegraph Without Wires. Meanwhile, a German scientist, Heinrich Hertz, had been experimenting with some curious electromagnetic waves that he had produced in the laboratory. By 1888 he had demonstrated the existence of such effects, which we know today as radio waves. A few years later, a twenty-year-old Italian youth, Guglielmo Marconi, had read everything he could find about these waves. He built his own devices to produce and detect them on his father's estate. His idea was that by systematically generating radio waves, messages in Morse code could be sent and received without wires. By 1895 he had succeeded in sending messages over a considerable distance. With the aid of family and friends, he went to England and patented his device. With considerable financial backing, Marconi then built powerful versions that were able to span the Atlantic.

Radio in this dot-and-dash form had enormous practical advantages over the telegraph, which depended on wires. Ships at sea could communicate with land. Various stations could all hear the broadcast of a home station simultaneously. For England, as well as for other nations with numerous colonies, a large navy, a huge merchant marine, and far-flung commercial enterprises, the wireless telegraph was a godsend.

The Radiotelephone. It was 1906 when voices, instead of the Morse code, were first heard over the air waves. Reginald A. Fessenden in the United States had built a system for using existing transmitters and receivers to send music and the human voice over the air. Then a simple radio receiver — the crystal detector — was invented. It stimulated a horde of radio fans to build their own home receivers.

It was Lee De Forest who brought the radio into its own by inventing the vacuum tube, which allowed vastly more sophisticated circuits and applications. The vacuum tube — and its later replacement, the transistor — made small reliable receivers possible. As a result, portable radio transmitters and receivers about the size of a breadbox played important roles in World War I. By this time, radio communication had advanced sufficiently for a pilot to receive and transmit from an airplane to people on the ground.

Another advance occurred in 1935. Working alone for ten years, Edwin H. Armstrong developed static-free radio broadcasting: frequency modulation (FM). His approach stunned the scientific world and opened a whole new field of transmission and reception to supplement amplitude modulation (AM).

Home Radio

The idea of manufacturing small and simple radio receivers for use in the home seems obvious and practical in retrospect. But during the early days of the medium David Sarnoff, who would soon head RCA, was one of the very few who deemed it worthwhile. Radio was thought to be suitable only for commercial and military purposes, not for family use. No stations were broadcasting to interest ordinary people.

Then events took a rather curious turn. Several people began to play Victrola music on the air over small transmitters. Dr. Frank Conrad, an engineer for Westinghouse in Pittsburgh, was one. He had a small transmitter in a room over his garage so that he could continue his experiments at home after work. To see how far his signal would reach, he played records and asked people to write in with requests. He was swamped! Amateur radio enthusiasts were eagerly tuning in on his broadcasts. Dr. Conrad and his family became the world's first disc jockeys.

Westinghouse, the first manufacturer of home receivers, had Dr. Conrad build a more powerful transmitter (200 watts) on the roof of the Westinghouse plant in Pittsburgh. A metal shack was constructed as a studio, and radio station KDKA was in business on November 2, 1920. The first broadcast was the election returns in which Warren G. Harding defeated James M. Cox for the U.S. presidency. The audience was probably between 500 and 1,000 listeners. Thereafter, home radio sets sold like the proverbial hotcakes in the Pittsburgh area.

Financing the Medium. KDKA was followed very quickly by similar stations in other cities. Suddenly the sale of home receivers was big business. For example, RCA sold $11 million worth of receivers in 1922, but by 1925 sales had jumped to $50 million.[22]

At first, people played with their home receivers like toys. They marvelled at their ability to pick up signals from hundreds of miles away. During the mid-1920s there were no regular programs. Those who operated transmitters broadcast whenever they felt like it and sent out over the air whatever struck their fancy. Still, receivers were selling by the millions.

Before long people tired of just trying to receive a signal from far away. They wanted to be entertained. The major barrier to regular programming was, of course, financial. No one had figured out how private enterprise could make a profit from broadcasting entertainment. Various proposals were debated. Some felt that licensing each receiver (as in Great Britain) would yield enough income so that a public trust could operate transmitters. AT&T wanted the medium to operate like a public telephone booth. That is, they would own and operate the transmitters; anyone who wished to broadcast could pay for the use of the facilities.

Early radio brought messages and entertainment to an enraptured audience at home or, as in this photograph, in such public places as hotel lobbies.

When they tried to implement this plan in the early 1920s it was a dismal failure. The customers they anticipated did not appear. Others suggested that wealthy individuals should endow stations as they endowed libraries and museums. The last thing leaders in the industry wanted was either government control of the medium or its use as a means of huckstering over the air.

The turning point came in 1922 when a few stations sold time to advertisers. First a company bought ten minutes to read a message about real estate lots for sale on Long Island; then a cosmetics firm sponsored a program. Within months, the medium turned to commercial sponsors for financing.

Advertising revenues stabilized the new medium. By the middle of the 1920s regular broadcasts had been established, and people could tune in weekly to their favorite programs. The programs included comedy, concerts, sports, drama, lectures, and news commentary. The networks were established by using long-distance telephone lines so that local stations could broadcast programs that originated elsewhere. First NBC was set up in 1926; CBS followed in 1927. ABC owes its origins to a court decision in 1943 that forced NBC to give up some of its stations, which became the nucleus of ABC.

Frequency Allocation. The popularity of radio had at least one undesirable side effect: near chaos over the air waves. The problem arose from the simple but important fact that the number of frequencies is limited. Without regulation, stations frequently interfered with each other's broadcasts. Some stations increased the power of their transmission or changed the time of their broadcasts; some changed from frequency to frequency, trying to find one free from interference. For a while Secretary of Commerce Herbert Hoover assigned frequencies to stations on an informal basis, but the courts ruled that his actions were illegal. Finally, the industry convinced a reluctant Congress to design legislation to control broadcasting hours, power, and frequencies so that stations would not interfere with one another. The result was the Radio Act of 1927, which provided a temporary solution while the problem was studied.

The Federal Communications Act of 1934 finally placed the government in the position of allocating frequencies and licensing transmitters of all types in order to control their use in the public interest. The act also established the Federal Communications Commission (FCC) and gave it strong regulatory powers. Although its powers have changed from time to time, the FCC continues to have jurisdiction over the use of all radio frequencies by transmitters in the United States — including those used by aircraft, the police, marine operators, citizens' band radios, AM and FM radio stations, and television.

Radio's Heyday. No one could have foreseen the massive growth of radio that took place during the 1930s and 1940s. Radio became a major entertainment medium with its own star system. It broadcast music and made big bands and individual musicians famous. It presented plays, comics, opera, sports broadcasts, and hundreds of other types of programs. In particular, it brought rapid and dramatic news coverage by distinctive commentators and announcers with their own special styles. Radio not only expanded the consciousness of its listeners concerning events in the world but also placed before them personalities that were larger than life — such as Franklin D. Roosevelt, patent medicine man Dr. Brinkley, and the political priest Father Charles E. Coughlin. It was through their radio broadcasts that these men gained a following and a place in history.

Even the Great Depression of the 1930s did not slow the growth of radio. If anything, the hard times helped the industry. Advertisers were looking for ways to stimulate sales, and they turned to radio because the listening audience was continuing to grow. People who were unemployed or hard-pressed economically hung on to their radios despite their troubles. Radio was free, and it brought music, comedy, plays, and other forms of amusement into their homes to provide a bright spot in the face of hardship. The furniture could be repossessed and the car remain unrepaired, but the radio would be kept.

Radio Meets Television. As the television industry grew after World War II, radio's profits dropped, but radio survived by adapting. It gave new emphasis to information and music and less to dramas and comedies. Network and national programming declined, and radio became more and more a local medium — with independent stations and local programs, local news, and local sports. Radio today is economically healthy and growing. In particular, FM broadcasting has become popular.

Television

The histories of radio and television are closely intertwined. The three major television networks were radio networks first, and the same companies that developed home radio and pioneered commercial broadcasting developed television.

Early in the 1920s such corporations as General Electric and RCA allocated small budgets for experiments with television.

The idea seemed farfetched and futuristic to many in the industry, but work in the laboratory was authorized in the hope that it would somehow pay off. General Electric employed an inventor, Ernst Alexanderson, to do what he could, and by 1927 he had developed a workable system.

Even though the country had entered the age of corporate research and development, the lone inventor continued to play a role. Gutenberg had put together a workable printing system; Morse had made the telegraph a reality; Edison and Armat had perfected the motion picture; Marconi had developed a practical wireless; and Armstrong had developed FM broadcasting (over which television signals are broadcast). Incredibly, television, too, was invented independently by a genius working in isolation on a shoestring budget. A boy with the unlikely name of Philo T. Farnsworth was in high school in the remote community of Rigby, Idaho. Farnsworth astounded his science teacher when he brought him drawings of a workable television system. The year was 1922, and Farnsworth had single-handedly solved the problems in sending and receiving television signals. By 1930 Farnsworth had patented his device. RCA had been working on the same system but had not patented it. At age twenty-four, Philo Farnsworth forced the corporate giant to meet his terms in order to obtain the rights to manufacture the system.

The Early Broadcasts. The earliest experimental television sets used tiny screens that were about three by four inches. Cameras were crude and required intense lighting. People who appeared on the screen had to wear bizarre purple and green makeup to provide contrast for the picture. In fact, the lights were so intense they almost fried the actors. Nevertheless, in 1927 Herbert Hoover, then secretary of commerce, appeared on an experimental broadcast.

By 1932 an experimental television station, complete with studio and transmitting facilities, had been built in the Empire State Building. RCA set aside a million dollars to develop and demonstrate television. In 1936 it began testing the system, broadcasting two programs a week.

But the new industry was about to be nipped in the bud. The Japanese attacked Pearl Harbor in December 1941, and survival monopolized the country's attention. All the electronics manufacturers turned to producing for the armed forces. Not until 1945 did these companies return to making products for the civilian market. In the immediate postwar years, however, television stations were quickly established in many major cities, and the pub-

Entertainers like Dave Garroway, an early host of "The Today Show" (seen here typically perched on a stool), found television the ideal medium for conveying their personalities.

lic began to buy sets as fast as they could be manufactured. TV had become a mass medium for home use.

The Television Generation. From 1948 through 1952, the federal government slowed the spread of television by refusing to assign licenses to transmitters. The purpose was to study the broadcasting situation thoroughly and allocate appropriate frequencies to TV, FM radio, and other forms of broadcasting. As a result, many American cities could not receive television until after the freeze was lifted.

During the freeze, the FCC developed a master plan that governs TV broadcasting today. The system prevents one television station from interfering with the broadcasts of another. Thus the chaos that characterized early radio broadcasting was avoided. When the freeze was lifted in 1952, television spread quickly throughout the United States. Today, only a few remote corners of the country cannot receive signals.

In the decades that followed, television was so successful that social commentators often spoke of the "television generation." Most Americans born after World War II had never known a world without television, and the medium was presumed to have shaped their lives in significant ways. Today television is the most popular medium of all. Many families own several sets, and audiences for some programs run into the tens of millions. Color has all but replaced black and white. Cable television is fast becoming commonplace and challenging dominance of the medium by the three major networks. Satellites in space can relay programs coming from all parts of the world, as well as from space itself.

We have seen in the present chapter that each of the mass media has had a long and fascinating history. It is difficult today to imagine a world in which the only media for communications were carvings on stone and the beating of a drum. The communications world we live in has changed so radically from those early times — or even from the time of our grandparents — that it is not surprising that we have not yet determined all the implications of these changes. In later chapters we examine these media in more detail — their financial bases, social organization, and day-to-day functioning. Then we will be able to turn to the task of assessing their impact on individuals and society.

Summary

Media, whether primitive or modern, are extensions of speech that permit communication beyond the range of the unaided human voice. The most significant event in the centuries-long development of communications was the invention and spread of writing. When paper and printing were also developed, the book as we know it today became a reality. From the time of Gutenberg's printing press in the fifteenth century, the publication of books grew rapidly. Today books are our most important medium for the expression of complex ideas. In this sense they are the most significant form of mass communication for society and culture. Even so, the future of books is not a certainty. As new devices develop and reading ability changes, books might be replaced by other media.

The history of newspapers and magazines overlaps that of books because they share the same basic technology. However, newspapers as they are defined today did not appear until the seventeenth century. By the early 1700s a daily newspaper was being published in England.

Newspaper publishing in America began in the 1600s and developed during the 1700s. These papers were small and expensive, intended mainly for the more educated segments of society. By the early 1830s, however, rapidly developing technology made it possible to publish a newspaper for the ordinary citizen. From these beginnings the American newspaper industry expanded swiftly. In the late nineteenth century it passed through a period of sensationalism known as yellow journalism. Today the industry has consolidated ownership through chains, developed new styles of reporting, and retained its vigor as a financially strong industry.

Magazines are a related medium, serving a role that includes elements of both the book and the newspaper. Magazines have been important as an entertainment medium, a source of news reports, and a stimulus to social change.

Motion pictures have a technological history that extends back into several centuries of scientific development. That history includes inventions in optics, photography, and electrical technology, and discoveries in the psychology of perception. By 1896 silent motion pictures were being shown in America; by the end of the 1920s talkies were common. The movie industry changed from a mere novelty into a huge entertainment medium in about four decades. When television appeared, the audience for movies declined, making numerous adjustments in the industry necessary.

Broadcasting in all its forms also has a long technological history. Its major developments occurred during the present century when the wireless telegraph and telephone came into use. As a household medium, radio broadcasting began in the 1920s. Two decades later, radio was in its golden age. Television, whose growth soared during the 1950s and 1960s, has not displaced radio, but it has caused the medium to find a new role.

Notes and References

1. Douglas McMurtrie, *The Book: The History of Printing and Bookmaking* (New York: Oxford University Press, 1943) p. 1.
2. Hendrik D. L. Vervliet, ed., *Through Five Thousand Years* (London: Phaidon Press, 1972) p. 18.
3. McMurtrie, *The Book*, pp. 76–77.
4. Falconer Madan, *Books in Manuscript: A Short Introduction to Their Study and Use*, 2nd ed. (London: 1920).

5. Robert Hamilton Clapper, *Paper: An Historical Account of Its Making by Hand from the Earliest Times Down to the Present Day* (Oxford: 1934).

6. Frederick Seibert, *Freedom of the Press in England, 1476–1622* (Urbana: University of Illinois Press, 1952) chs. 1–3.

7. John Tebbel, *The Media in America* (New York: Thomas Y. Crowell, 1974).

8. Edwin Emery, *The Press in America*, 3rd ed. (Englewood Cliffs, N.J.: Prentice-Hall, 1972) p. 3.

9. Marvin Rosenberg, "The Rise of England's First Daily Newspaper," *Journalism Quarterly*, 30 (Winter 1953), 3–14.

10. Emery, *The Press in America*, p. 31.

11. John W. Moore, *Historical Notes on Printers and Printing, 1420 to 1886* (New York: Burt Franklin, 1968) pp. 36–37, originally published in 1886.

12. An excellent selection of Brady's photographs can be seen in Phillip B. Kunhart, Jr., *Mathew Brady and His World* (New York: Time-Life Books, 1977).

13. For a review of such trends, see Raymond B. Nixon, "Trends in U.S. Newspaper Ownership: Concentration with Competition," *Gazette XIV*, No. 3 (1969).

14. Frank Luther Mott, *A History of American Magazines, Vol. IV, 1855–1905* (Cambridge: Harvard University Press, 1957) p. 10.

15. *Ayer Directory of Publications* (Philadelphia: Ayer Press), 1978. See also U.S. Bureau of the Census, *Historical Statistics of the United States, Colonial Times to 1970*, Series R 232–243.

16. Martin Quigley, Jr., *Magic Shadows: The Story of the Origin of Motion Pictures* (Washington, D.C.: Georgetown University Press, 1948) pp. 9–10.

17. Josef M. Eder, *History of Photography* (New York: Columbia University Press, 1945) pp. 209–245, 263–264, 316–321.

18. There were several claimants to the invention of celluloid roll film in the late 1880s. Eventually, the courts awarded a legal case on the matter to the Rev. Hannibal Goodwin. However, Eastman produced it in his factory and marketed it to the public. Frederick A. Talbot, *Moving Pictures: How They Are Made and Worked* (London: William Heinemann, 1923).

19. Talbot, *Moving Pictures*, p. 2.

20. Tino Balio, ed., *The American Film Industry* (Madison: University of Wisconsin Press, 1976) p. 63.

21. John Baptista Porta (or Giovanni Battista della Porta), *Natural Magick*, ed. Derek J. Price (New York: Smithsonian Institute for Basic Books, 1957). This is a modern reprint of the work first published in the late 1500s.

22. Erik Barnouw, *Tube of Plenty: The Evolution of American Television* (New York: Oxford University Press, 1975) p. 36.

3 The Media in an Economic and Political Environment

A newspaper is a private enterprise, owing nothing to the public.

Wall Street Journal, January 20, 1929

Most Americans today accept without a second thought the fact that their mass media are privately owned. They also accept the credo that it is essential in a democracy to have something called a "free press." Many even believe that we have such an arrangement, and that the mass media are free of governmental interference. Few citizens worry that economic considerations limit the content of the media. Similarly, the majority are unconcerned or even unaware of continuing controversies that erode any literal meaning of a "free press."

We do not suggest that the United States should shift to some other set of arrangements for the mass media, or that what we have now is bad. But we do try here to show some of the costs that Americans share because we have chosen our present system. The focus is on economic and political institutions. We try to show how the content of media is sharply influenced by private ownership and how the media are limited in various ways from presenting a completely free flow of the news. To do so we examine the following questions: Why did the American media develop as private, profit-making enterprises; how do they operate as businesses today; and what are the influences of economics on them? What is the basis for the freedoms from government control that the American media enjoy; what are the limitations on these freedoms; and how are those limitations imposed?

American Economic Values

The American media for the most part are privately owned businesses that are operated for a profit. In this sense they are very different from their counterparts in, say, the Soviet Union, Great Britain, or China. In fact, in most countries the government either operates the media directly or supervises and controls them extensively. In the United States the media are profit-oriented in part because American society is committed to a set of values that defines profit, private ownership, and freedom from government control as very desirable.

It was almost inevitable that the media in America would develop as private enterprises. From the beginning American society has approved the profit motive and individual initiative. The New Englanders were traders and entrepreneurs who roamed the world to trade in fish, furs, lumber, slaves, and rum. Their fellow colonists to the south developed the land to derive a profit from cotton, tobacco, and other agricultural products. It was an industrious nation that was constantly in search of ways to turn an honest (or maybe not so honest) dollar.

The foundation for a strong commitment to competitive private enterprise began with the underlying beliefs of the *Protestant ethic,* which has been described by German sociologist Max Weber.[1] The Pilgrims subscribed strongly to this set of beliefs. They were Protestants who valued hard work, frugality, and self-denial. Through hard work they thought that they could aid God in fulfilling His plan for the universe. By frugality they believed they could become prosperous — and prosperity, they believed, was a sure sign that they were being guided by the hand of Providence. By self-denial they avoided temptations, reducing the risk of squandering their capital. In more modern dress these values still pervade the work ethic dear to the American middle class. However, as the nation developed, other beliefs helped influence American economic values. The pioneer life of the frontier stressed self-reliance and rugged individualism. This was later compounded with *social Darwinism* — a philosophy that valued "natural selection" and "survival of the fittest" in business competition.

It was out of these orientations that Americans shaped their economic institutions. Competition, private ownership, and profit making seemed natural to generations of earlier Americans. For the majority of Americans today, they still do.

As the early media appeared, they became part of the economic system based on these values. Even the earliest colonial newspapers were private enterprises. If they did not produce sufficient revenue to defray the costs of their production and distribution, they simply went out of business. The newer media of the twentieth century found no government subsidy waiting to support them; they too developed as private, profit-making, competitive businesses. Movies had to make it on their own as a form of popular entertainment. In spite of early resistance, radio as a household medium had little choice but to derive its support from advertising. Television followed and spread quickly because the system of economic support — local and national advertising — had already been developed in radio broadcasting.

Many intellectuals deplore the economic basis of the American media on the grounds that it produces much content of low quality. Defenders of the system point out that by and large, when Americans turn to print, film, and broadcasting, they have more to choose from than anyone else in the world. In many respects, however, the critics have a valid point. Private ownership of the media and the search for profits, as we shall see, have led to an emphasis on popular culture. The tastes of the majority of consumers dominate media content. It is abundantly clear that such content often lacks artistic, intellectual, or educational merit.

The Media as Businesses

Because they are profit-making enterprises, the American media share two important characteristics. First, they are ruled by the *law of large numbers.* That is, whatever content will attract the largest number of consumers and produce the most advertising dollars will be the content provided. Content that can attract large numbers of consumers will tend to crowd out content that cannot. It is no secret that the people with low artistic and intellectual tastes far outnumber the people with highly developed tastes. Although there are exceptions to this crude law of large numbers, it generally accounts rather well for the low intellectual and artistic level that prevails in American mass communications. Newspapers, magazines, television, and radio depend on advertising revenue. Advertisers are looking for programs that will reach the largest possible number of purchasers of beer, soup, and soap. Movies and books do not depend on advertisers for revenue, but here too the law of large numbers plays a key role in determining which films and books are produced.

A second characteristic of America's modern media is increasingly concentrated ownership; fewer and fewer people own more and more of the media. As the costs of the media have risen, large corporations are more and more frequently their owners. A given newspaper, magazine, television network, or motion picture studio is likely to be, not independently owned, but part of a huge corporation or conglomerate.[2]

Behind these similarities are significant economic differences among the media. In developing as businesses, each medium had to adapt to its own continually changing economic circumstances. Competition from other media and the rising costs of services, labor, talent, and materials influenced their success and their content. In Part 2 we look at each medium in more detail, but here we can get an overview of the constraints that economic considerations place on the media.

The Print Media

Newspapers. The early colonial papers paid their costs through both advertising and subscriptions. Then, beginning with the penny press of the nineteenth century, newspapers began to depend on advertising as their main source of revenue, opening new economic frontiers. When it became clear that with increased circulation advertising could support a newspaper sufficiently to reduce its price, the elite press gave way to the popular press. The papers now emphasized human interest, crime, humor, and so on. From time to time they resorted to sensationalism as well. Over the years they became more and more dependent on advertising. In 1880 the average newspaper devoted 25 percent of its space to advertising. By World War I advertising accounted for about 50 percent; and today, for 60–70 percent.[3] Until about 1880, subsidies from political interests also paid part of the costs of many newspapers. From the time of Thomas Jefferson, political parties arranged to have newspapers serve as their pipelines to the public.

By the beginning of the twentieth century, most newspapers had severed their ties to political parties and lost their subsidies. Consequently, they became more general in their point of view and more comprehensive in their coverage of the news.

The dependence on advertising discourages newspapers from dealing harshly with the business community that supports them. But what would newspapers be like without support from advertisers? A single copy of a daily newspaper would cost nearly a dollar at the newsstand. Delivered to one's door, an annual subscription would cost about $300. At the same time the content might be noticeably altered as a result of freeing the paper from dependency on advertising. For example, one might see more headlines along the lines of "Local Supermarket Chain Sued for Insects and Rat Hair in Hamburger," "Local Automobile Dealers Regularly Cheat Customers," "City's Movie Theaters Declared Fire Traps." Newspapers might be more eager to print stories that were damaging to local businesses — businesses that today help pay the costs of publishing the paper.[4] Under today's arrangements publishers who lose the good will of the business community risk losing advertising money as well.

The end of advertising revenue would probably have other effects as well. Sports, news, and the financial section of the paper all require complex logistics. Without advertising revenue, the papers might not be able to continue many of these features. In fact, without advertising revenue, newspapers might become much as they were before the penny press arose in the nineteenth century, if they could survive at all.

Clearly, advertising support for newspapers is a mixed blessing. Dependency on it may bias publishers in favor of the values and interests of merchants and businesses. But the approximately $9 billion spent annually for newspaper advertising brings content and services that only such astronomical sums can produce.

The constraints introduced by dependence on advertising are by no means the only ones felt by the press. Faced with continually rising costs for materials, labor, and services, newspapers have had to increase their income to meet costs or go out of business. Several hundred newspapers have folded for one reason or another since the peak of their popularity at about the time of World War I. In fact, the reduction of the number of newspapers in America has been one of the most significant trends in newspaper publishing in this century.

The prospects of starting a new daily newspaper in a major city are very limited. It would require as much as $50 million to start a newspaper in a city like San Francisco or Chicago. Furthermore, a new paper's chances of getting a share of the available advertising revenues would be very low. Thus, anyone wanting a newspaper in a city would be well advised to purchase an existing paper. And, of course, this is precisely what has happened over the years. Existing papers have been bought by large corporations that already own papers elsewhere. The papers can then consolidate some activities and management for substantial savings.[5]

The result of these trends has been reduced competition among

With imaginative art work and bright messages, nineteenth-century advertisers used newspapers to hawk their wares. This ham and bacon parade ad uses a prestige appeal to attract an audience interested in quality.

Contemporary newspaper grocery ads like this one serve a quite utilitarian purpose, providing consumers with product prices that can be used in comparative shopping.

newspapers. While the number of daily papers in the United States has more or less stabilized at around 1,750, competition among papers has declined sharply. Most surviving papers are quite profitable, but few cities have competing papers that are independently owned.

Books and Magazines. Book publishing is not a large industry when compared with such giants as General Motors, IBM, or General Foods. In 1980 all American book publishers together produced about $4 billion in retail sales both here and abroad. Many publishers are small, and some 80 percent of the total sales are produced by only about 20 percent of the companies. Although the book publishing industry has grown over the last quarter century, it is still one in which rather small firms produce and sell very specialized products.

Advertising plays virtually no role as a source of revenue for book companies. Instead, they depend on the outright sale of their products to consumers. Thus the wholesale price of a book must be enough both to cover its costs and to yield a profit. That price has been going up steadily. In 1970 a hardback college text or a well-manufactured technical book could be purchased for about $10. By 1980 its price had nearly doubled.

Their high price might be one factor keeping the sale of books down. On the average, Americans do not read a lot of books. Current estimates put the figure at about five to ten books per year. Probably, the number of book readers has declined as television has grown in popularity, but it is difficult to make such comparisons over time because the proportion of American society that is illiterate has declined and the percentage with advanced education has increased.

Although advertising does not play the role in book publishing that it plays in many other media, and although books have a smaller audience than many other mass media, the law of large numbers does operate in the book industry, but in modified form. Like any business, book publishers want to maximize their profit margins and produce dividends for their stockholders. They must therefore keep their costs of production down and maximize their sales. This basic economic principle plays a key role in every decision that is made from the time a publisher expresses interest in a manuscript or idea to the time the finished product is delivered to a retail outlet. It has the effect of screening out some books that could be of great interest to a very specialized audience and placing an emphasis on acquiring and publishing manuscripts that will attract wide interest. In the textbook field, for example, it is far easier to interest a publisher in a basic book that will be used by students in large introductory courses than in an advanced technical book that will interest only a small number of specialists. For the same economic reasons, it may be difficult to find a publisher for poetry, short stories, *avant garde* fiction, or other works that are unlikely to attract a large number of purchasers.

Unlike books, magazines depend on advertising revenues to cover much of the cost of production. By the turn of the century the magazine for a general audience was well developed because such magazines provided excellent vehicles for advertising. By 1929 the nation's leading 365 magazines had an average readership of about 95,000 each. By 1950, 567 major magazines were reaching, on the average, over 223,000 readers each.[6] But as more and more Americans watched television, the general-interest magazines failed. The main reason is that it costs about half as much to reach a thousand people with a television ad as with a magazine ad.[7] The general-interest magazines tried to buck this trend, but they eventually failed in the face of the competition of television.

The near death of *Harper's* in 1980 dramatically illustrated the economics of magazines today. *Harper's* was a monthly magazine aimed at a fairly educated, prosperous, and influential audience, but it had survived for 130 years. In 1979 it had a circulation of about 325,000 — but relatively little advertising and losses of more than $1.5 million. By mid-1980, it was announced that the magazine would cease publication later in the year. Its fall reported to be not television — whose coming it had survived — but competition from more specialized magazines. Increasingly, reported the *Washington Post,* "advertisers found the Harper's audience too difficult to define. They couldn't predict whether the Harper's reader was interested in whiskey, cars, power tools, sports clothes or any combination of the above."[8] However, a private foundation came to the rescue and *Harper's* was saved, but in the process it became a nonprofit organization.

In contrast, an advertiser knows that a magazine like *Gourmet* is a great one in which to advertise expensive food processors and high-quality cooking pans. It would make little sense to advertise such products in a shot-gun approach on television. The same is true of fishing tackle, boating goods, model railroad parts, and special diet products. Such advertising of specialized products in specialized magazines for specialized readers pays off, and in 1978 alone, advertisers spent over $2 billion on magazines. Specialized magazines make money because they can reach their readers with advertisements that are closely related to their focused interests.

Thus the trend in magazine publishing has been toward increasing specialization. Among the vast American population there are enough people with particular specialized interests that a magazine devoted to those interests can be a success. There are thousands of magazines that appeal to specialized target audiences, such as *Organic Gardening, Model Railroader, Firehouse, Identity* and *Nuestro* (for Italian Americans and Hispanics, respectively). To these we can add *Weight Watchers' Magazine* for those yearning to be thin, and *F. I. B.* for those who claim that fat is beautiful, and thousands more.

The situation of magazines in the 1980s can be summed up in a tongue-in-cheek comment made by Marc Connelly, a writer for *Holiday* magazine, at a reception in Portugal several years ago. When each journalist was asked to stand and identify his or her magazine, Connelly claimed that he was a writer for *Popular Wading*, which he said was devoted to enthusiasts of shallow water sports. He maintained that his magazine specialized in such topics as the ravages of "immersion foot" and other dangers of the sport. The hosts of the party smiled politely, but to the other writers Connelly's description was hilarious because it seemed to sum up what has happened to American magazines in the last two decades as specialization came to rule the industry.

The Movies

Anyone who doubts that the movies are big business can consider the fact that even a Hollywood potboiler costs from $15,000 to $18,000 *a minute* to shoot. Large additional costs are involved in distributing the final version to a worldwide market and exhibiting it in theaters. An enormous investment is required to produce and market even the most mediocre film.

It is therefore not surprising that many of the movies we see are made and owned by the same film companies that have dominated the industry for decades — companies such as Columbia, Paramount, Twentieth Century Fox, United Artists, Universal, and Warner Brothers. Since the 1960s, however, independent companies have made more and more films. The studios therefore have less control over the medium, while independent producers have more. But because a movie requires such a large financial investment, most of the independent companies rely on the major companies for financial backing. Thus the major companies still get the largest share of box office receipts and thereby retain some influence on what movies are made.

Economic influences on the film industry are very similar to those on the other media in one very important respect: the law of large numbers prevails. Movie producers seek above all to maximize the size of their audiences. In the 1930s and 1940s they did so by being the dominant form of family entertainment. Their content had to conform to the prevailing mores of the time. When television developed in the 1950s, it presented entertainment for the same general audience, reflecting basically the same tastes, themes, and content as the movies, but it did so at far less cost and inconvenience to the consumer. As television thus stole the movies' audiences, the movies had to change to survive.

At first the movies tried to regain their audience through technical gimmicks. There were experiments with huge screens, three-dimensional films, and special sound effects. Most of these devices failed to boost ticket sales significantly. As the struggle continued, movie makers turned to showing more violence and more explicit sex — content that audiences generally could not find on television. But even that did not slow the stampede to television.

The movie industry has had to adapt to the fact that the size and composition of its audience has changed. Whereas in the 1930s and 1940s the whole family would go to the movies, today people under thirty account for over three-fourths of the annual audience. Today movies try to appeal to a new generation of moviegoers, and it is their tastes that govern content. Movie makers still seek films with universal appeal, such as romance and adventure, but they make many movies with very specific groups in mind. The violent movie filled with fistfights, spectacular auto chases, and blazing crashes is made for a young audience with limited education and undeveloped aesthetic tastes. Movies are made specifically for such groups as children, lovers of animals in the wilderness, World War II buffs, aviation enthusiasts, and rebellious teenagers. Pornographic movies are made with yet other groups in mind.

Despite the problems the movie industry has faced, audiences pay nearly $1.5 billion a year at the box office. Another billion comes to the industry from foreign sources, and about half a billion comes from the sale of films to television. Movie making is a high-risk industry, but one with the potential for very high profits. *The Godfather*, for example, was produced several years ago and is still bringing in dollars. By the time it completes its runs and reruns here and abroad, including its television showings, it will probably gross about $150 million for its producers and distributors. Of course, for every film that succeeds as *The Godfather* did, a dozen or more are dismal failures at the box office. But the

The box office draw of the film The Godfather
*(1971), starring Marlon Brando and Robert
DeNiro, was so strong that the movie's producers made a sequel,* Godfather II *(1974),
starring Al Pacino.*

movie industry today is in good shape financially and has adapted
well to the challenges of competing media.

The very medium that caused the movie industry most of its
problems is now one of its major sources of revenue — television.
Television has an almost insatiable appetite for films. They cost
less per minute of air time than live broadcasts and can attract
more viewers than many other kinds of content. Subscription

television and tape cassettes have increased the market for films. Although these trends may lead to a decline in sales at movie theaters, they will clearly add to the revenues of the film industry.

Broadcasting

The economic situation of the broadcasting industry differs strikingly from that of other media. For example, there is no clear trend toward concentration of ownership of radio or television stations; FCC rules limit the number of stations one person or company can own. Additional differences arise from the importance of local programming in radio and from the growth of cable television.

According to FCC regulations, a given individual or organization can own no more than seven television stations. Only five of those can be VHF stations (that is, those channels numbered from 2 to 13). Individuals or groups can own no more than seven AM radio stations and seven FM stations. Also, owners of broadcast television stations cannot own a cable system in the same community as their television station.

The networks, however, represent a different kind of concentration: the concentration of control over programming. Their influence goes far beyond the stations they actually own. The networks produce or purchase programs and then pay local stations to carry the programs. Networks now provide about 65 percent of all broadcasting hours by their affiliates. Since more than 40 percent of the commercial VHF stations in America are affiliated with one of the three major networks, it is clear that the networks have substantial control over what we see and hear on television. CBS and ABC are independent corporations, but NBC is a subsidiary of RCA, the giant that has survived since the earliest days of broadcasting.

Many critics deplore the virtual monopoly that these three networks enjoy over the content that is broadcast nationally. Their only competition for viewers at present is the ETV (Educational Television) network, which is part tax-supported through the Corporation for Public Broadcasting (CBP). But ETV has a very limited budget and provides almost no competition to the commercial networks in terms of its share of the national audience. At present only 5 percent of the money that pays for television broadcasting in this country goes into noncommercial television.[9] Even when stations supported by schools, communities, or other noncommercial sources are included, the viewing audience for "public" television in the United States is still minor.

The networks are less influential in radio broadcasting. When television appeared, the revenues of the radio networks declined drastically. In 1979 the networks received only thirty cents for each five dollars in advertising that went to local radio stations.

Among the broadcast media, radio appears to have the fewest economic problems. AM radio seems to be losing much of its audience and revenue to FM radio, but radio as a whole is prospering. It has a unique place in the media system as a provider of music, weather reports, information on local events, and summaries of the news. The Public Broadcasting Service of CPB supports some educational broadcasts. Radio reaches people when a color spectacular on television would be out of place, or when reading a newspaper or going to a movie is not an alternative. Furthermore, it is unlikely that this role will be taken over by another medium.

Radio is healthy, but economically it is dwarfed by television. Currently television receives about 20 percent of all dollars spent for advertising in the United States; newspapers receive about 30 percent. But television's share of these dollars is increasing. In fact, since there are far fewer television stations, they receive a larger *per station* share of advertising revenue and higher net profits than the more numerous individual newspapers. According to Professor Arnold H. Ismach, "On the basis of return per dollar of investment, television stations are more profitable than newspapers. They are more profitable than any other enterprise, short of Arizona land sales and the illicit drug trade." [10]

The principal reason for this profitability is the eagerness of sponsors to advertise on television. Their eagerness is based solidly on the operation of the law of large numbers. With some 76 million households owning at least one television set in 1979, and with each set turned on for an average of more than six hours daily, the audiences for an advertisement can be awesome. For example, the average daily audience for most of the daytime serials (soap operas) is in the tens of millions. For special events, such as superbowl football or programs such as *Roots,* audiences can be five or six times as large. It is little wonder, then, that manufacturers of household products or other consumer goods eagerly stand in line with cash in hand to get their messages on commercial television.

Competition for advertising time has driven the cost of advertising on commercial television as high as $250,000 per minute for major sports events broadcast to gigantic audiences nationwide by CBS in 1979. Table 3.1 lists the costs of advertising on several network programs. Local advertising is much cheaper; for example, a minute during a popular program presented in the evening in Albuquerque, New Mexico, cost from $500 to $1,000 in

Table 3.1 1980 Prices for Prime-Time Network TV Commercials

Program	Cost per 30-second unit
M*A*S*H	$150,000
60 Minutes	145,000
Laverne and Shirley	130,000
Happy Days	130,000
Little House on the Prairie	110,000
CHiPs	100,000

Sources: *Advertising Age*, September 10, 1979, p. 98, and *Broadcasting*, January 8, 1979, p. 23.

1979. Still, the costs are going up. In recent years, the cost of advertising on television has risen as much as 20 to 30 percent per year, and the end is nowhere in sight.

The high price of television advertising, and television's resulting profitability, is based mainly on the absence of strong competitors. A limited number of licenses are available in each city because of FCC regulations. Owning a television station licensed to transmit in a good market area is equivalent to having a partial monopoly on an important product that is in great demand — audience attention to advertising messages. The three large commercial networks have an even more profitable partial monopoly because they command national audiences and receive the largest share of the broadcasting advertising dollar. For every $5 received by local stations for advertising, the networks receive $8.30. Thus ABC, CBS, and NBC are red hot money makers.

But the rosy picture of profitability that prevails in television may end in the relatively near future. Changes are going on that may do to ordinary broadcast television what that medium did to the movies in past decades. Cable television is the most important of these changes.

It all started innocently enough in rural and mountainous areas that did not receive clear television signals. People in those remote areas received programs through wires from a central facility that picked up the signals either through a large community antenna or by wire from other locations. This was fine with the broadcasters because it expanded the number of people who could view their programs and thus the number who could see advertisements.

Now, however, cable television poses a threat to broadcasters.

Cable companies began operating in cities, not just in remote regions. Very soon about one in three U.S. households will receive cable television. The cables can now reach about half the television sets in use in the United States. Recent federal rules have made it easier for cable television to grow, and all signs indicate that during the early 1980s this new kind of television will develop even more rapidly.

Cable television presents problems for the over-the-air broadcasters because it spreads the audience over more channels. Advertisers may be reluctant to spend their dollars on a station's services, or even a network's efforts, if they cannot be assured of a large audience of potential customers. Needless to say, cable television has been vigorously opposed by the commercial broadcasters.

For its users, cable television has the advantage of providing up to thirty-six channels, rather than the usual four or five that are broadcast in a typical city. Some channels may pick up commercial-free broadcasts from satellites; sports events from a city like Atlanta might be shown to viewers in a city like Los Angeles via cable. Of course, cable has the disadvantage to users that they must pay for it.

Standard television broadcasting has also been challenged by the appearance of devices for taping programs off the air or for playing back programs that have been prerecorded. This trend toward using video cassettes may change the viewing habits of Americans, but it is not likely to change the economic structure of the industry or the content of its programs. In fact, although cable television and cassette recorders both appeal to large numbers of people, even those who can afford to use them will undoubtedly continue to view standard broadcasts.

Political Protections: The Constitutional Framework

Politics as well as economic considerations place limitations on the media in a society. In Great Britain newspapers are privately owned, yet it is a crime to publish anything from public documents unless authorization is obtained. Reporters are allowed to report only what is said at a trial, nothing more. Pretrial publicity is not permitted. In the United States many Americans take special pride in having freedom of speech and a "free press." Yet in 1972 the courts ruled that the government could censor a book by Victor Marchetti and John D. Marks, *The CIA and the Cult of Intelligence.* When the book was published, it had 168 blank spaces as a result of the censor's cuts.

The media certainly have more freedom in the United States

than in most nations, but here, too, they must operate within a system of constraints imposed by the government. The political environment of the American media has two fundamental elements. First, a belief in the freedom of the press was embodied in the U.S. Constitution. Second, as freedom of the press has come in conflict with other rights and freedoms and as American society has changed, legal limitations on freedom of the press have been established. We begin an examination of these limitations by looking at the constitutional guarantee of a free press that arose from America's colonial experience.

The Historical Legacy

The Colonial Heritage. Colonial America was, of course, ruled by England. Governors representing the Crown were appointed for each colony to ensure that English laws and English policies prevailed. With English law came a specific set of legal relationships between the press and the government. The principle embedded in those laws was *prior restraint;* that is, the government could not only punish those responsible for illegal publications but also *prevent* the publication of material it did not like. The government, in other words, could censor publication.

In England the Crown had not enforced its prior restraint laws for many decades before the Revolution, although it had jailed or fined some whose publications it did not like. English pamphleteers and newspapers in the eighteenth century often criticized the government without reprisal. The situation in the colonies, however, was another matter. Rebellions were an ever-present possibility in overseas possessions. In the colonies the governors representing the Crown could and sometimes did require that any material commenting on the government's activities be reviewed and approved by the governor's office before publication.

As the eighteenth century wore on, colonial newspapers and pamphleteers began to follow the English example; criticism of the Crown's representatives increased. Occasionally, colonial governors would decide to crack down. As we saw in Chapter 2, Ben Franklin's brother James was among those who suffered the consequences; he went to jail for the criticisms he published.

One of the most celebrated cases involving freedom to publish occurred in New York with the encouragement of a group of anti-establishment merchants. John Peter Zenger, publisher of the *New York Weekly Journal,* had repeatedly published criticisms of the governor of the colony. The governor finally took action and had Zenger arrested on November 17, 1734.

Zenger was charged with *libel* (that is, publishing material that tends to damage a person's reputation). Actually, Zenger's case involved what has been called criminal libel — defaming the state, in this case the crown and its governor. The case dragged on for months while the governor, trying to ensure Zenger's conviction, manipulated the courts and Zenger remained in custody. Meanwhile, Zenger's wife continued to publish the paper, including strong criticisms of the governor and his administration. The public looked on with fascination.

The high point of the trial was the defense of Zenger by a prominent lawyer, Andrew Hamilton. According to British law (and American law, too, until the nineteenth century), the truth of what was published was no defense against the charge of libel. But Hamilton, over the objections of the judge in the case, appealed to the jury to find Zenger not guilty because what Zenger had published was true. He urged them to assert the right of citizens to speak out against the government. Hamilton's appeal was successful, and Zenger became a popular hero.

The Zenger case did not change the laws regarding libel, but it did put public opinion firmly behind the idea that newspapers should be allowed to print the truth even if it was contrary to the wishes of the government. The principle of prior restraint, too, remained a part of the legal system for many years, but it was seldom enforced.

Following the Zenger trial, colonial newspapers became increasingly bold, and the governors of the colonies did little to suppress them. During the time just before the Revolution, various writers published essays and editorials that urged independence from England. Pieces by Thomas Paine, Samuel Adams, Isaiah Thomas, and John Dickensen were widely read and helped gain the public support needed in the fight against England.

The First Amendment. Curiously enough, in spite of the key role played by newspapers, pamphlets, and broadsides in mobilizing support for the Revolution, the framers of the U.S. Constitution did not mention freedom of the press in the original document. For one thing, they could not agree on what the concept meant in practical terms or how such a provision could be enforced. In addition, some of the framers argued that there was no need to guarantee such freedoms in the Constitution.

Shortly after the Constitution was ratified, however, the states passed amendments that guaranteed the freedoms we have come to know as the Bill of Rights. Prominent among these is the First Amendment, which states, "Congress shall make no law . . .

abridging the freedom of speech, or of the press." These words are known as the *free speech* or *free press clause* of the First Amendment. (The amendment also includes guarantees of freedom of religion and freedom of assembly.) At first glance, the clause seems clear and unambiguous. Yet through the years the press and the government have become enmeshed in a tangle of issues that have confused the public, perplexed the most able jurists, and placed a variety of constraints on those who operate the mass media.

How could such confusion occur? At the outset we should recognize that even in the first days of the Republic, many of the founders had mixed feelings on the merits of a "free press" and on the extent to which it should be free. Some had qualms because it seemed obvious that newspapers were instruments of political power. For example, newspaper enthusiasts today are fond of quoting Thomas Jefferson, who said: "Were it left to me to decide whether we should have a government without newspapers, or newspapers without government, I should not hesitate a moment to prefer the latter." Less frequently quoted is the qualifying sentence that followed: "But I should mean that *every* man should receive those papers and be capable of reading them" (italics added). And almost never quoted are the disillusioned remarks of Jefferson the politician, after being opposed frequently by the press. He bitterly noted: "The man who never looks into a newspaper is better informed than he who reads them, inasmuch as he who knows nothing is nearer to the truth than he whose mind is filled with falsehoods and errors."

Almost all Americans will nod vigorously in agreement if asked if they believe in freedom of the press. It ranks with motherhood and the flag in national esteem. But when pressed on some specific case, such as pornography, criticism of their favorite public figure, or unfavorable stories about themselves, their assent to a free press is likely to vanish. Belief in freedom of the press is often based not on the idea that the government simply has no right to control it but on the belief that a free press is the best method for ensuring a well-informed public and a stable democracy. When the press seems to be doing a poor job of informing the public, support for its freedom is likely to diminish.

The debate over freedom of the press became more complicated when film and the broadcast media appeared. Are they forms of speech and press and therefore protected by the First Amendment? In 1915 the Supreme Court ruled that cinema was a "business, pure and simple, originated and conducted for profit" (*Mutual Film Corporation v. Ohio*). Therefore, the Court went on to say, it was not protected by constitutional guarantees of free speech and a free press. Then in 1952 the Supreme Court reversed this decision. The State of New York had said that an Italian film (*The Miracle*) could not be exhibited in the state because it was "sacrilegious." When the case was appealed to the Supreme Court, the Court ruled that the state had no power to censor films on religious grounds.[12] The effect was that films gained the protection of the First Amendment.

Radio and television present a more complicated situation. Whereas the number of "channels" available to the print and film media is, theoretically at least, unlimited, the number of frequencies that can be used for broadcasting is severely restricted. On the basis of this difference between broadcasting and the print media, a host of government regulations regarding broadcasting have grown up. As we shall see later in this chapter, the regulations are generally compromises between the principle that "the public owns the airwaves" and the Constitution's guarantee of freedom of speech.

Perhaps the greatest source of conflict over the right to a free press, however, comes from the fact that it is not the only right or freedom in town. The right to a free press sometimes seems in conflict with society's right to maintain order and security. For example, the press's exercise of its freedom may conflict with the ability of the police and courts to do their jobs or with the government's ability to maintain secrets it deems necessary for national security. Freedom of the press can also conflict with the rights of individuals, such as the right to privacy and the right to a fair trial. As a result of these conflicts, the courts have frequently ruled against the right of the press to publish anything it pleases. The most important limitations on the press imposed by the courts concern libel, coverage of trials, obscene material, and government secrets.

Protection from Libel

Injunctions against saying untrue, defamatory things about others have ancient origins. Among the Ten Commandments is the injunction, "Thou shalt not bear false witness against thy neighbor." In ancient Norman laws it was written, "A man who falsely called another a thief or manslayer must pay damages, and holding his nose with his fingers, must publically confess himself a liar."[13] The idea that a person whose reputation has been damaged because of untrue public statements by another is entitled to compensation was passed on to the American colonies through English law. It remains an important part of American law. Not only the reputations of individuals are protected but also those of corporations and businesses. With the development of media with huge audiences, it became possible to "bear false witness" and damage reputations on a very large scale. Serious economic consequences can follow.

Large numbers of libel cases are brought against newspapers, magazines, book publishers, and broadcast stations each year. In such cases the courts are faced with conflicting rights. They must weigh the right of the press to publish freely versus the right of people to preserve their privacy, reputation, and peace of mind. The situation is complicated by the fact that there are no federal statutes concerning libel. It is a matter of state law, and each state has its own laws.

State laws usually give news reporters and the news media some protection against libel suits. They usually allow publication of public records and "fair comments and criticism" of public officials. But it is not entirely clear who qualifies as a reporter under the laws of the states.

In recent years reporters and the media have also received constitutional protection from libel suits. In 1964 the Supreme Court considered for the first time whether state laws regarding libel might be overturned on the grounds that they violate the First Amendment to the Constitution. The case was *The New York Times* v. *Sullivan*. During the height of the conflict over the civil rights of blacks in the South, the *Times* had published an advertisement that indirectly attacked the Birmingham, Alabama, police chief. An Alabama jury ruled that the *Times* had to pay $500,000 in damages because the advertisement included some misstatements of fact. But the Supreme Court overruled the Alabama jury, holding that its decision violated the freedom of the press. Essentially, the Supreme Court held that a full and robust discussion of public issues, including criticism of public officials, was too important to allow the states to restrain the press through their libel laws.

After 1964 it became very difficult for public officials to claim libel damages. Only when the official could show that there had been "malice," "reckless disregard of the truth," or "knowing falsehood" by the press, the Court said, could public officials sue for libel. More recent cases have extended this doctrine to include public figures as well as public officials. However, the laws and practices associated with libel continue to change and standards continue to develop. In a 1979 case, *Herbert* v. *Lando*, the Supreme Court ruled that courts could inquire into the state of mind of a reporter in determining whether there was malice present as a story was written. The media saw this decision as a setback for press freedom.

Members of Congress are totally protected against suits for libel, as long as what they say can be interpreted as being related to their responsibilities as public officials. They therefore can, and often do, make public statements about issues and people with the knowledge that they will not wind up in the courts. The late Senator Joseph McCarthy provides a classic example of the abuse of this protection.

In the 1950s McCarthy gained national and even worldwide attention by claiming that the United States was in the grip of powerful but hidden Communist infiltration. He used the media to whip up public fear of a vast Communist conspiracy. It sometimes seemed that he charged everyone in sight with being "subversive," or a "fellow traveler," or "a card-carrying member of the Communist party." He accused high military leaders, the film industry, the U.S. State Department, educators, artists, business

Television's ability to bring messages to a national audience was exploited successfully by Senator Joseph McCarthy during his controversial hearings in the early 1950s. McCarthy's unscrupulous tactics were later revealed by one of the most influential figures in the history of the media, Edward R. Murrow.

The Media in an Economic and Political Environment   89

leaders, and even the clergy. The media gave his outrageous claims nationwide coverage.

McCarthy's accusations helped create a climate of fear that wrecked reputations and ruined careers all over the nation. Finally, however, the media that had helped McCarthy's rise assisted in his downfall. As a result of his accusations, Congress held formal hearings on Communist influence in the Army. The hearings were televised daily to a national audience. McCarthy's tactics were so outrageous that, after seeing him in action, the public concluded that he was an irresponsible demagogue. He lost credibility, and his bid for power came to an end.

Trial by the Media

The Constitution guarantees freedom of the press, but it also guarantees a fair trial to defendants. Sometimes publicity about a crime and the suspected criminal seems to make a fair trial impossible. The classic example of how the press can turn a trial into a Roman circus and thereby deny the defendant's right to a fair trial occurred in the case of Sam Sheppard.

Dr. Sam Sheppard was a well-to-do osteopathic surgeon in an Ohio city. One night his wife was brutally beaten and stabbed to death under mysterious circumstances in their expensive suburban home. The police were baffled because there were no witnesses and few clues. Nevertheless, after a short time they arrested Dr. Sheppard and charged him with murdering his wife.

Long before the police investigation had been completed, the local newspapers decided that Sheppard was guilty. One headline read, "Quit Stalling — Bring Him In." Another said, "Why Isn't Sam Sheppard in Jail?" Numerous editorials and cartoons proclaimed him guilty. The trial itself was overrun with reporters and photographers, and the jury was not adequately shielded from negative news reports about Sheppard. One newspaper even printed a photograph of Mrs. Sheppard's bloodstained pillow. The photograph had been "retouched" so as to "show more clearly" an alleged imprint of a "surgical instrument."

The prosecutor found no witnesses to the murder, and the only evidence he presented was circumstantial (for example, the fact that Sheppard had been having an affair with another woman). But Sheppard was convicted and spent many years in jail. Finally the Supreme Court reviewed his case. It declared his trial invalid, largely because of the publicity and improper legal procedures. Ohio tried Sheppard again, and he was acquitted. By this time, of course, his life was shattered. He died in 1970, still a relatively young man.

More recently, the Supreme Court in the case of *Gannett* v. *De*

Pasqualle (1979) seemed to say that the press could be barred from certain portions of trials. An uproar followed in which many said the decision was a threat to the coverage of supposedly public trials. This was clarified somewhat in a 1980 Supreme Court decision, *Richmond Newspapers, Inc.* v. *Virginia*, which gave specific constitutional protection for the media to cover public trials.

Moral Values: Obscenity and Pornography

Do parents have the right to protect their children from seeing advertisements for pornographic movies on the street or from seeing pornographic magazines displayed at the corner drugstore? Many Americans would answer yes; the Supreme Court's answers have been ambiguous. The most emotional issue at present is child pornography: magazines and films showing young children engaged in explicit sexual acts with adults and with each other. Public pressure prompted Congress to hold hearings on the issue.

Two very different conceptions of the role of government underlie debates about government regulation of obscene material. Liberals generally deplore censorship of such material. In fact, they often argue that government should not attempt in any way to regulate the moral behavior of its citizens as long as the people involved are consenting adults. Many conservatives are inclined to

Sex in the media, a hotly debated topic for years, is often a multimedia presentation today, as shown in this view of a porno-adult entertainment district of an American city.

see censorship of obscenity as a proper duty of local or even national government. They tend to feel that a safe society can be maintained only through government regulation of such matters as sexual behavior and the use of liquor and drugs. The media become involved in many of these arguments in strange and convoluted ways.

The Supreme Court seemed to side with the conservatives in 1957. That year it announced, "Obscenity is not within the area of constitutionally protected speech or press" (*Roth* v. *United States*). But it has not been easy to determine what is or is not "obscene." In the 1960s material could not be declared obscene if it had "any redeeming social value" whatsoever. Then in 1973 the Court made it easier to ban materials by relaxing this standard. Moreover, it dumped the issue back into the laps of local communities by saying that the material should be judged in terms of the standards that "prevail in a given community" (*Miller* v. *California*). What is obscene in one community may not be obscene in another. But since this decision the Court has overturned some efforts by communities to ban materials. What can and cannot be censored on the grounds that it is obscene is far from clear.

In the face of public pressure, however, the media have censored themselves to some extent. Various industry associations have drawn up codes limiting the treatment of material related to sex. The classic example is the self-regulation of the movie industry in the 1930s. The self-imposed Motion Picture Producers and Distributors Code by the mid-1930s had become so puritanical at one point that not even butterflies could be shown mating. In the 1950s the comic book industry voluntarily (if grumpily) curtailed production of weird and horror comics in response to a public outcry. (Congressional hearings were held to determine whether such comic books were harmful to children.) Even as late as 1965 the American Newspaper Advertising Code prohibited such words as *girlie, homosexual, lesbian, lust, naked*, and *seduce*. It also ruled out horizontal embraces and comments on bust measurements.[14] The National Association of Broadcasters forbids the use of dirty words and explicit sexual content. The relative purity of broadcasting, however, is also a result of the Federal Communication Commission's strict rules against obscenity.

The Government's Secrets During National Crises

In times of national crises such as wars, reporting some kinds of information can give the enemy a clear advantage. The incident of the scholarly spy illustrates the danger. In 1940, before the United States and Germany were actually at war, a German undercover agent was smuggled into the United States and given a suitable cover. His mission was to assess America's future capacity to produce air armaments. Such knowledge would play a vital part in Germany's preparations for air defense.

The spy did not need to sneak around airplane factories or Army and Navy airfields. Instead, he simply spent all his days reading in public libraries. He carefully scrutinized the *New York Times Index* and the *Reader's Guide to Periodical Literature* for published accounts that mentioned aircraft facilities, plans for factories, or existing air armaments. After making copious notes, he was smuggled back to Germany, where he prepared a report to the high command. This report was later acquired by American espionage agents in Germany. It turned out that the scholarly spy had put together an extremely accurate prediction of U.S. production of military aircraft for the years 1941 through 1943. In fact, his assessment was more accurate than that made by the U.S. War Production Board for the same years. Yet all the spy's data had come from newspapers, magazines, and books readily available to the public.[15]

Recognizing the dangers facing their nation, Americans have generally accepted some sort of censorship during wars. Even many fervent civil libertarians agree that the government deserves and requires protection during wartime. But such censorship obviously contradicts the guarantee of a free press and limits the public's right to know. In peace and war, government secrecy has led to many controversies.

Direct Censorship in Wartime. In past wars the government has been able to use several and indirect methods to protect its secrets. One indirect way to control information is to deny access to telegraph, cable, or similar facilities. Reporters then must either let military censors screen their copy or try to transmit it in some other way. For example, when the battleship *Maine* blew up in the harbor of Havana, Cuba, in 1898, the U.S. government immediately closed the Havana cable to reporters. Similarly, when World War I broke out, the British immediately severed the cables between Germany and the United States. American reporters had to use the English-controlled cables between Europe and the United States and submit their copy to rigid British censorship.

The government has also imposed censorship through codes, regulations, and guidelines. During World War I, for example, U.S. censorship was extensive. The Espionage Act of 1917 was a broad set of regulations providing fines and prison terms for anyone interfering with the war effort in any way. Newspapers were outraged by its provisions, and legal battles over the issue went all the way to the Supreme Court. Eventually such censorship was declared unconstitutional, but Congress then passed even stricter laws to control information. For example, the Sedition Act of 1918 made it a crime to publish anything that abused, scorned, or showed contempt for the government of the United States, its flag, or even the uniforms of its armed forces. To enforce the law, such publications could be banned from using the mails.

On December 19, 1941, only a few days after Japanese forces struck Pearl Harbor, President Roosevelt created the U.S. Office of Censorship and charged it with reviewing all communications entering or leaving the United States for the duration of the war. At the peak of its activity, the office employed more than 10,000 persons. Their main objective was to review mail, cables, and radiograms. The press was handled differently. A Code of Wartime Practices for the American Press was issued, and voluntary cooperation was requested from the nation's editors and publishers. The purpose was to deny the Axis powers any information concerning military matters, production, supplies, armaments, weather, and so on. For the most part, those responsible for the content of the print media cooperated very well, often exceeding the guidelines that the government set. A related code was issued for broadcasters, and their cooperation was also excellent.

The system of codes, regulations, and guidelines in World War II worked because the press did cooperate voluntarily. The country was trying to find a way to deny vital information to the enemy without using official censors, and by and large it succeeded. (The case of the scholarly spy occurred before the guidelines were in effect.)

Even when the nation has not been at war and formal guidelines have not been in effect, the press has often censored itself to protect the national interest. In 1960, for example, the Soviet Union shot down an American U-2 spy plane. The incident temporarily ended attempts to improve Soviet-American relations. For a year before the plane was shot down, however, James Reston of the *New York Times* had known that spy planes were flying over the Soviet Union, but "the New York Times did not publish this fact until one of the planes was shot down in 1960." [16]

Challenges to Government Secrecy. Beside these examples of voluntary censorship by the press, we could place a score of examples in which the press and the government have been locked in conflict, disputing the government's right to censor the press. A shared belief in the need for freedom of the press became a tradition very early in the life of the nation, and any effort by the government to limit that freedom has always met with some hostility.

During the Civil War, for example, the fifty-seventh Article of War provided for a court martial, with a possible death sentence, for anyone giving military information to the enemy. During wartime these rules applied to civilians as well as to the military. Newspapers were an indirect source of military information. The leaders of the Confederacy went to great lengths to obtain copies of major Northern newspapers because they often revealed the presence of military units and naval vessels. As a result, the U.S. War Department tried to forbid newspapers to publish any news from which movements of troops or ships could be inferred. The newspapers generally ignored these orders. Even after the war General Sherman refused to shake hands with Horace Greeley, publisher of the *New York Tribune*, maintaining that Greeley's paper had caused a heavy loss of life by revealing troop movements to the enemy.[17]

Thus even in wartime Americans have questioned censorship, asking what kind of controls and imposed by whom? The government has the need to protect itself and the right and a duty to protect the nation. But the press has the right to tell the public what its government is doing, and the public has the right to know. Thus, there is an inherent conflict between the right to a free press and the need to control information that would be damaging to government.[18]

The conflict between government and the press seems to have grown in recent decades as the government itself has grown. Since World War II we have supported a giant defense establishment, a complex web of foreign relationships, and uniquely powerful nuclear weaponry. Government secrecy has grown with all of these. The majority of editors and publishers cooperate with the government when they see that national security is at stake in maintaining secrecy. But as a host of government bureaucrats classify thousands and thousands of documents secret each year, the press — and the public — often wonder how many of these secrets protect national security and how many protect the government from embarrassment. Often it is difficult to determine what is being protected or at what point a secret becomes so damaging to the national interest that the constitutional guarantee of free speech should be overruled. The case of the Pentagon Papers illustrated these questions dramatically.

During the Johnson administration, the Defense Department had put together a forty-seven–volume history of American involvement in Vietnam, including secret cables, memos, and other documents. The history, which came to be known as the Pentagon Papers, was classified as top secret. It documented American political, military, and diplomatic decisions regarding Vietnam from 1945 to 1967. Then in 1971 Daniel Ellsberg, who had worked on the papers but had come to oppose the war, leaked the papers to the *New York Times*. Ellsberg hoped that the release of the history of the war would turn public opinion against it and help bring about its end. Although the documents were both stolen and classified, the *Times* began publishing a series of articles summarizing the papers, including some of the documents in them. A legal uproar followed.

The Nixon administration went to court to stop the *Times* (and later other newspapers) from publishing additional articles on the papers. It argued that publishing the papers would endanger national security. In response, the courts issued a temporary restraining order, stopping the *Times* from continuing its planned series on the papers. In effect, the courts briefly imposed prior restraint.

Eventually, the case went to the Supreme Court, which ruled against the government. The government had failed to convince the Court that publication of the Pentagon Papers constituted a danger severe enough to warrant suspending freedom of the press. Relieved and triumphant, the newspapers resumed their articles on the Pentagon Papers. Ellsberg was later tried for stealing the documents and went to prison. The Court's decision in the Pentagon Papers case, however, is still regarded as controversial, and it settled little. Conflict continues between the press's desire to publish information, the public's right to have information about the operation of its government, and the government's need to protect the secrecy of some activities.

Protection for Reporters' Sources

While the government claims that some secrets are necessary to its survival, the press makes a similar claim. Take the case of Annette Buchanan. In 1966 Buchanan, the editor of the student newspaper at the University of Oregon, published a story about marijuana smoking on the campus. Buchanan was asked by a local court to reveal the names of the people from whom she had obtained much of her information. She refused and was eventually fined $300.

Although this incident involved neither serious crimes nor harsh punishments, it does illustrate all the elements of an important controversy regarding freedom of the press. If Buchanan had given the names of her informants to the police, her credibility with them would certainly have been destroyed. News personnel claim that maintaining the confidentiality of sources is an important part of the machinery of reporting. If reporters are not allowed to keep their sources secret, they will not be able to obtain information that the public should have.

A case with more serious consequences involved Earl Caldwell, a reporter for the *New York Times*. Caldwell had gained the confidence of the Black Panthers in the San Francisco area. At the time, many people considered the Panthers militant and dangerous. Caldwell published several stories about the Panthers, but he did so in a way that did not cost him the group's confidence. A year later, Caldwell was subpoenaed by federal prosecutors. A Black Panther, David Hilliard, had been charged by a grand jury with threatening to kill the president. Caldwell was asked to appear before the grand jury and testify. He refused. In fact, he refused to go anywhere near the grand jury on the grounds that even if he entered the closed session and then refused to testify he would lose the confidence of his informants, who would never be certain what he had said behind closed doors. Because of his refusal Caldwell was held in contempt of court. Later, an appeals court reversed the decision, but later still the U.S. Supreme Court reversed the appeals court decision.

The case caused an uproar among journalists. During the Supreme Court's hearing on the case, the Author's League of America argued:

> Compelling a reporter to identify his sources or divulge confidential information to a grand jury imposes obvious restraints on the freedom of the press to gather information. . . . The threat of such interrogation would induce many reporters to steer clear of controversial issues inducing the "self-censorship" which is repugnant to the First Amendment.[19]

The Caldwell decision appeared to provide a clear basis for legal action against reporters who refuse to divulge such information. Peter Bridges was the first reporter actually jailed as a result of the decision. In 1972 he remained in jail for twenty-one days because he refused to identify the sources for an article he had written on alleged illegal practices involving the Newark Housing Authority. Bridges did answer fifty questions put to him by a grand jury concerning the material in the article, but he steadfastly declined to name his informants.

Some moves have been made to provide legal protection for new media and reporters who do not wish to divulge sources. Many states have passed so-called *shield laws*, which specifically exempt journalists from having to reveal their sources. A good example is New York's 1970 law. Essentially, it protects journalists and newscasters from charges of contempt in any proceeding brought under state law for refusing or failing to disclose the sources of information obtained while gathering news for publication.[20] Some journalists and lawyers argue against such laws, saying that they imply acceptance of the Court's interpretation of the First Amendment. On the other hand, many lawyers oppose shield laws on the grounds that the courts need all the information they can get in order to protect citizens against wrongdoing and to provide fair trials.

The issue of the confidentiality of sources is by no means resolved. In 1978 Myron Farber, a reporter for the *New York Times,* was jailed for contempt by a New Jersey court for refusing to turn over his notes in a murder trial. The defendants' lawyers had claimed that they had a right to see the notes. Not only was Farber punished with civil and criminal convictions, but the newspaper was also forced to pay a fine. All this happened in spite of a New Jersey shield law that supposedly protected reporters' confidential sources. The New Jersey Supreme Court and the U.S. Supreme Court both said that the Sixth Amendment, which guarantees a fair trial, took precedence over the claims of the press.

Political Constraints: The Agents of Control

We have discussed several specific areas in which the freedom of the press guaranteed by the Constitution is limited, not absolute. But in practice the freedom of the press depends not only on this abstract constitutional framework but also on the daily decisions of courts, bureaucrats, and politicians. The constitutional framework itself continues to change; it has evolved and continues to evolve as specific problems and conflicts arise. Moreover, in particular cases the *actual* freedom of the press may differ from its theoretical freedom. We therefore look next at the various agents of political control of the media, including the courts, legislatures, White House, bureaucrats, and even private citizens. These groups may exert both formal controls on the media and informal influence on the flow of information.

The Courts

We have seen that the courts often act as referees in conflicts between the rights of the press, the rights of individuals, and the rights of the government at large. This is nothing new. As early as 1835, the French writer Alexis de Tocqueville observed, "Scarcely any political question arises in the United States, that is not resolved sooner or later into a judicial question." Today conflicts involving the media often lead to lawsuits in local courts. Sometimes these court verdicts are challenged and taken to a state or federal appeals court. Some appeals may be carried further, to the court of last resort, the Supreme Court in Washington.

Often the Supreme Court's interpretations of prevailing law or the Constitution have broken new ground, establishing new policies. In recent years the Court has ruled on many issues affecting the media, including newsroom searches, libel, the confidentiality of journalists' sources, the regulation of advertising, and laws regarding copyright and cable television. These rulings have often been the center of immense controversy. The prevailing view in the press has been that the Supreme Court under Chief Justice Warren E. Burger has been generally, though not always, hostile to the press and its claims. Dan Rather of CBS News went so far as to claim that the Supreme Court has been "repealing the First Amendment" by its decisions. Many legal scholars, however, would disagree.

The Supreme Court is a kind of final staging ground for many media battles. What it and other courts do sometimes mirrors, sometimes second guesses, and sometimes shapes or anticipates what other parts of the government are doing.

The Legislatures

State legislatures write laws that have considerable impact on the mass media. They may amend or rewrite statutes dealing with libel, misrepresentation, business taxation, newspaper advertising, cable television, and many other subjects. Most major lobbying groups for the media, such as state broadcast and newspaper associations, have representatives at their state capitals to watch out for their interests.

The influence of Congress on the media is greater than the influence of state legislatures. Postal rates for books and magazines, for example, loom large on publishers' balance sheets. Like other businesses the media can be hurt or helped by congressional decisions regarding taxes, antitrust policy, affirmative action, and so on. In addition, both houses of Congress have subcommittees that deal specifically with communications issues and policies. Congress has investigated the financial structure of the communications industry, tried to determine whether the television networks were pressuring producers not to release films to pay-cable systems, considered the regulation of television advertising, written a new copyright law, passed laws on campaign spending in the media, and considered a federal shield law. In the late 1960s, Congress authorized the Department of Health, Education and Welfare to study the effects of television, especially the effects of televised violence on children.[21] It allocated a million dollars for the study. Congress was responsible for passing the censorship laws during World War I, as well as for the Freedom of Information Act, which has opened the government to greater scrutiny by the media as well as the general public. Finally, Congress established the agencies that regulate advertising and broadcasting, and it regularly examines, and criticizes, the work of these agencies.

The Executive Branch

The web of government influence gets more tangled when we consider the executive branch, which includes a host of government departments and agencies as well as the White House. Some bureaucrats in federal departments and agencies exercise formal control over information through the government's classification system, but bureaucrats also exercise informal controls over the flow of information to the press and the public. Both federal and state government are composed mainly of large bureaucracies which manage their own public relations. Each group is anxious to create a favorable public image. At the federal level, approximately $150 million is spent each year on domestic public relations by groups such as the FBI, the Department of Agriculture, and the Pentagon. Every division of government has its own information officers and staffs. In spite of the possibility of leaks, reporters must depend heavily on these public relations officers for information about the daily workings of government. Reporters often have no way of assessing the validity of this information. Much of the news that is reported about the government is therefore just what the public relations people hand out to the press. Through press releases, news conferences, and interviews, the bureaucracies thus control most of the news that appears about their agency or group. Obviously this kind of reporting limits the ability of the press to inform the public.

The White House also exercises informal influence on the flow of information. For example, it is a tradition for the president's press secretary to select a limited number of reporters from the pool of those assigned to the White House to cover an important political briefing or social event. The remainder of the press must get the information from those selected. If a member of the pool is seen by the White House as a friend or is in disfavor, that fact can have a significant influence on his or her prospects for firsthand coverage of the news. And it was Nixon's White House that managed for a while to keep the bombing of Cambodia secret not

*Former Vice President Spiro Agnew, a blis-
tering critic of the news media in the 1960s
and early 1970s, added fuel to the adversary
relationship between media and government.*

only from the public and the media but also from the defense bureaucracy.

Spiro T. Agnew demonstrated another way of trying to influence
the press. In 1969, while Agnew was U.S. vice president and the
war in Vietnam was being debated, he made a speech about the
sins of the press. He claimed (in essence) that the news media
were dominated by a liberal Eastern elite and that the views of
more conservative citizens were not adequately represented. He
implied that this constituted a "controlled press" and that perhaps
it was time to "do something about" the situation.

Agnew's speech sent shock waves through the industry, especially through the television industry because television stations
can have their licenses taken away by the government. In fact,
there is some evidence that the networks changed their policies
after Agnew's remarks. For example, in 1971, when some half a
million people flooded Washington, D.C., to protest the war in
Vietnam, the network news media gave the event only minimal
coverage. A short time later they covered Bob Hope's "Honor
America Day" (which took a conservative view) thoroughly.[22]

The White House also has more formal sources of influence on the media. The White House may present legislative proposals to Congress. It may lobby for or against proposals that Congress is considering. Moreover, the president appoints some members of the two regulatory agencies, the FCC and FTC, that have important powers to regulate and guide parts of the media.

The Federal Communications Commission (FCC). Congress created the FCC in 1934, charging it with the task of seeing that the people who run broadcasting stations operate them in the "public interest, convenience and necessity." Just what this means is the subject of considerable debate.

The FCC makes and enforces rules and develops policies that govern all kinds of communications, from the telephone to cable television. For example, the FCC enforces the *equal time rule,* which states: "If a licensee shall permit any person who is a legally qualified candidate for any public office to use a broadcasting station, he shall afford equal opportunities to all other such candidates for that office in the use of such broadcasting station." Building on the equal time rule, which applies only to political candidates, the commission over the years evolved the *fairness doctrine,* which grants equal time to people representing issues and causes. Later the FCC and the courts added a personal attack law, which gives individuals attacked by a broadcast station air time to respond. Other rules govern advertising, ownership of broadcasting stations, and obscenity. The FCC's rulings have the status of law and can be overturned only by the federal courts or by congressional action.

A good deal of the FCC's attention is given to interpreting its own rules as it resolves disputes between broadcasters and various individuals and interests. In some instances these rules are very specific, as is the equal time rule. But in other instances the law is vague, and the commission must wrangle over terms like "the public interest," trying to determine just what the public interest is in a particular circumstance.

The FCC spends much of its time issuing, renewing, and revoking licenses granted to radio and television stations. Much of the wrangling between the commission and the broadcast industry comes at renewal time, when the FCC requests detailed information on programming, looks for evidence of public service, and tries to see whether (and how well) the station serves its community. Although broadcasters often complain of the heavy hand of government, the FCC has been remarkably lenient in renewing licenses. In fact, one critic compared the relationship between the commission and the industry to a wrestling match wherein "the grunts and groans resound through the land, but no permanent injury seems to result."[23]

A case in point is the handling of obscenity. The Federal Communications Act gives the commission the power to revoke the licenses of stations transmitting obscene or indecent material over the airways. There have been numerous instances of stations running pornographic films and comedy routines, but the most the commission has ever done is to levy fines, usually small ones.

Most critics agree that the FCC has not been the most hard-hitting of the federal regulatory agencies, yet its very existence does provide a constraint on broadcasting. Broadcasters regard the FCC as an overly bureaucratic nuisance, but it exists mainly to prevent self-serving station owners from trampling on the public's access to information and expression. This differs markedly from the role of the government in the print media. As Chief Justice Burger stated when he was an appeals court judge:

> A broadcaster seeks and is granted the free and exclusive use of a limited and valued part of the public domain; when he accepts that franchise it is burdened by enforceable public obligations. A newspaper can be operated at the whim or caprice of its owners; a broadcast station cannot.[24]

The Federal Trade Commission (FTC). In December 1978 the Federal Trade Commission began a series of hearings to study the growing concentration of ownership in the media. The FTC wanted to know whether this economic pattern influenced the flow of information. Although the hearings generated no definitive answers, media owners denounced the FTC for its potential interference.

These hearings reflect only a small part of the FTC's interest in mass communications and other industries. Like the FCC, the FTC is an independent regulatory agency of the federal government. It exists for the purpose of preventing unfair competition. In relation to the media, this task generally translates into the regulation of advertising.

Almost from its inception in 1914, the FTC has looked at deceptive advertising as unfair competition. Both it and the FCC have brought suits against manufacturers and the media for false claims or misrepresentations. A classic illustration of such action is provided by the Rapid Shave case. Rapid Shave had a television commercial that opened with actors shaving effortlessly with the product. A voice claimed that shaving was especially easy because the substance had a "deep wetting" ingredient. A demonstration followed in which it was shown that even sandpaper could be shaved clean if Rapid Shave were used. What the audience was not told was that in one version of the commercial the sandpaper had been soaked in water for nearly an hour and a half prior to the demonstration. In another version the shaving demonstration was even easier because it was not done on sandpaper at all: instead, a plexiglass surface over which sand had been sprinkled was used. The case was in the courts for six years, during much of which time the commercial continued to be shown. Finally, the Supreme Court banned such trickery.

Another example of advertising that the FTC found deceptive is provided by Profile bread. The bread's makers claimed that it could help dieters and that each slice had a third less calories. Actually, the manufacturer was simply slicing the bread a third thinner than a standard slice. The advertisement implying that the bread had special ingredients was banned. But the most famous action of all was that taken against the cigarette industry. All advertising of cigarettes was banned from television, and the manufacturers were forced to put a label on each package warning the user of dangers to one's health.

Although the FTC directs its action mainly against individual advertisers, it has a strong indirect effect on the mass media, which are the channels for advertising. When the FTC told Profile to stop implying that its bread had a special ingredient, it clearly influenced the content of advertising.

The FTC issues warnings before moving to formal orders. Some of these orders have the effect of law, and the commission can and has levied fines, some for hundreds of thousands of dollars. Again, these fines have penalized companies, not the media directly.

Decisions by the FTC have defined the scope of deception in advertising, discussed the concept of truth in advertising, and denounced puffery (that is, exaggerated claims in advertising). The FTC also holds conferences on trade practices, issues guides that suggest what advertising and labeling practices should be, hands down advisory opinions in which advertisers ask for advance comments about advertisements, and publishes rules. In recent years the FTC has frequently called on communications researchers to help examine issues such as the effects of television commercials directed toward children.

The Police

In normal times the relationship between the police and the media poses few problems, but in times of tension conflicts often emerge. One can ask how far the police should go in trying to control the media even during outbursts of violence. Perhaps whenever controls on the media are needed during crises, the controls should come from sources other than police. Police methods can be very inappropriate for dealing with the media.

A classic example of such inappropriate police methods is provided by police actions during the August 1968 Democratic National Convention in Chicago. It was the August after President Lyndon Johnson had withdrawn from the presidential race because of opposition to American involvement in the Vietnam War, the August after Robert Kennedy had entered the race and had been assassinated, the August after Martin Luther King had been assassinated. The Democratic convention was a magnet for critics of the war and the government. Many of the critics who came to protest in Chicago dressed and acted in unconventional ways. To many conservative Chicagoans, these visitors seemed not only unconventional but also dangerous and immoral. Mayor Richard

The Democratic National Convention in 1968 was the scene of a brutal confrontation between Chicago police and dissident protestors. Newspaper and broadcast reporters were in the middle of the violence, and a number of them were beaten by the police.

Daley told his police force to keep the protestors under control. The protestors were equally determined to demonstrate their dissatisfaction with the nation.

All this set the stage for a major confrontation between police and thousands of demonstrators. Rioting and violence occurred over several days. The police used a great deal of force against the protestors, who fought back. During the heat of the confrontations, the police were lashing out at everyone in sight, including reporters. A number were injured. Typical of the violence suffered by many people from the news media was the case of Claude Lewis of the *Philadelphia Evening Bulletin*. An officer tried to grab his notes, shouting, "Give me your damn notebook, you dirty bastard!" When Lewis did not comply, he was beaten with a club and had to be treated at a hospital for scalp wounds. Many other people from the media were assaulted or had valuable equipment smashed by police officers.[25]

The Chicago police riot is a dramatic example of how relationships between police and the media can deteriorate. In many cities during recent years, photographers, reporters, and television personnel have been mauled by the police during violent episodes. At the same time, the police have sometimes been justified in charging that the news media often do not act in the public interest. They give publicity to people who stage demonstrations for the very purpose of attracting attention to themselves. Coverage of airplane hijackers, prison rioters, criminals with hostages, and terrorists provides cases in point. In such cases it is not difficult to understand why the police become frustrated by the overwhelming presence of cameras, reporters, and television equipment. Proper conduct of both the police and the press in times of stress remains less than clear.

Pressures from Outside the Government

Reporters and editors share with the rest of us the typical weaknesses of human beings. When approached on a friendly basis by nice people offering free drinks, free meals, or even free trips to exotic resorts, many accept the favors. Such activities are typical of the tactics used by businesses, lobbyists, and press agents who want favorable treatment in the press. Any acceptance by reporters of such "freebies" reduces their objectivity about the behavior of their benefactors.

A Senate investigation of informal influence on the press revealed that many reporters, and even their wives, had accepted all-expenses-paid trips to resorts in various parts of the world.

Their later stories extolled the virtues of being a tourist in the countries that had paid for the trips.

More serious is the case of journalists' trips to South Africa. South Africa maintains strict separation of the races, with severe restrictions on nonwhites. For years some Americans have urged this country to exert pressure on South Africa to end these policies. South Africa, of course, has fought such efforts. In 1965 and 1966 the Republic of South Africa brought more than twenty reporters and editors with known segregationist and right-wing views to visit the country and paid all their expenses. When the story came out, the South African government denied that it was trying to influence American opinion.[26]

Pressure from groups outside the government can influence the media, as the codes against obscenity illustrate. More recently, public opinion has been exerting pressure on the media to reduce the amount of violence they portray, especially on television. Some research studies have seemed to support the conclusion that frequent viewing of violence increases the probability of aggressive behavior by some categories of children. (The findings of these studies will be discussed in more detail in Chapter 8.) As a result, groups such as the Parent-Teachers Association and the American Medical Association undertook a vigorous campaign to convince stations and networks to reduce the amount of violence on television. Many of the liberals who deplore censorship of sexual material enthusiastically joined these efforts.[27] Nothing much happened, however, and the media continue to portray violence in many prime-time programs.

On the whole, Americans have mixed attitudes about censorship and are often more amused than threatened by it. Controls during wartime have usually been accepted, but other kinds of censorship provoke different reactions. Johnny Carson pokes fun at the whole issue with his characterization of Miss Priscilla Goodbody, the fictitious NBC moral censor. But censorship can also be seen in a more ominous light. When dictators take over a country, censorship of the media is one of their first moves. In communities with strict enforcement of public morality, theaters, magazine stores, and newspapers have been shut down if their content contradicted the moral conceptions of those in power.

Overall, our review of freedom of the press has shown that it is often extremely difficult to protect both this freedom and other important rights. As a result, the press and the other media are surrounded by a web of both formal and informal political, as well as economic, constraints.

Summary

In American society today the mass media are privately owned and operated for a profit. Americans generally regard this arrangement as good. Early in our history the Protestant ethic and social Darwinism promoted Americans' belief in private enterprise and competition free from government interference. As each new medium appeared, it was influenced by these basic beliefs and values and developed as a private, profit-making, competitive industry.

Their dependence on profits has had many consequences for American media. First, the law of large numbers prevails; that is, the content of the media is geared for the most part to the tastes of the majority. The media's dependence on profits has also meant that they have had to adapt as economic conditions have changed. Inflationary pressures, for example, have led to a clear trend toward consolidation of newspaper ownership. Rivalry with other media has led to modification in movies, radio, and now television. New media forms, such as cable TV and video tape cassettes, promise more changes to come.

In addition to these economic constraints on the media, there are political constraints as well. Although most Americans approve of and think we have a free press, the mass media in the United States must operate in a complex web of limitations arising from politics and government. The First Amendment forbids Congress to make laws restricting the press, but the freedom of the press often conflicts with other rights, such as the right to privacy and the right to a fair trial. Moreover, obscene material is not clearly under the protection of the First Amendment. During wartime, controls over the press have ranged from outright government censorship via codes and guidelines to voluntary self-regulation by the media.

The courts are frequently referees when the right to a free press and other rights seem in conflict. Legislatures and the executive branch also influence the press, both through formal powers and through their informal influence over the flow of information. Both bureaucrats and politicians can introduce bias in what is reported through their informal influence. The FCC has the power to regulate many aspects of broadcasting. Groups of private citizens as well as public opinion exert yet other pressures on the press.

Thus, although the American media are generally free from direct government control or outright censorship, they are greatly influenced by economic and political conditions. Since economic conditions, legal interpretations, and political pressures constantly change, the media will be modified as well.

Notes and References

1. Max Weber, *The Protestant Ethic and the Spirit of Capitalism*, trans. Talcott Parsons (London: George Allen and Unwin, 1930).

2. Kevin Phillips, "Busting the Media Trusts," *Harper's* (July 23, 1977), pp. 23–24.

3. Don R. Pember, *Mass Media in America*, 2nd ed. (Chicago: SRA, 1977) p. 88.

4. For a fanciful account of such possibilities, see George G. Kirstein, "The Days the Ads Stopped," *The Nation*, June 1, 1967, pp. 555–557.

5. Raymond B. Nixon, "Trends in U.S. Newspaper Ownership: Concentration with Competition," *Gazette*, 14, no. 3, pp. 181–193.

6. T. Peterson, *Magazines in the Twentieth Century* (Urbana, Ill.: The University of Illinois Press, 1964).

7. P. Sandman, D. Rubin, and D. Sachsman, *Media: An Introductory Analysis of American Mass Communication* (Englewood Cliffs, N.J.: Prentice Hall, Inc., 1976).

8. "Finis for Harper's," *Washington Post*, June 18, 1980, p. 1.

9. Tom La Faille, "Corporate Underwriting: The Dragon that Threatens Public Broadcasting," in Robert Atwan, Barry Orton, and William Vestermon, *American Mass Media* (New York: Random House, 1978), pp. 407–414.

10. Arnold H. Ismach, "The Economic Connection: Mass Media Profits, Ownership and Performance," in Everette E. Dennis, Arnold H. Ismach, and Donald M. Gillmor, *Enduring Issues in Mass Communication* (St. Paul: West, 1978).

11. John L. Hulting and Roy P. Nelson, *The Fourth Estate* (New York: Harper & Row, 1971) p. 9.

12. Richard Findlater, *Comic Cuts* (London: Andre Deutsch, 1970) p. 7.

13. William S. Holdsworth, "Defamation in the Sixteenth and Seventeenth Centuries," *Law Quarterly Review*, 40 (1924), 302–304.

14. Findlater, *Comic Cuts*, pp. 21–22.

15. Douglass Cater, *The Fourth Branch of Government* (Boston: Houghton Mifflin, 1959) p. 119.

16. James Reston, *The Artillery of the Press* (New York: Harper & Row, 1966) p. 20.

17. Frank Luther Mott, *American Journalism*, 3rd ed. (New York: Macmillan Co., 1962) pp. 336–337.

18. John L. Hulting and Roy P. Nelson, *The Fourth Estate* (New York: Harper & Row, 1971) p. 9.

19. See "Freedoms to Read and Write and Be Informed," *Publisher's Weekly*, December 13, 1971, p. 29.

20. See *Editor and Publisher*, May 6, 1972, p. 32.

21. *Television and Growing Up: The Impact of Televised Violence* (Washington, D.C.: U.S. Department of Health, Education and Welfare, December 31, 1971).

22. Fred Powledge, *The Engineering of Restraint* (Washington, D.C.: Public Affairs Press, 1971), p. 46.

23. R. H. Coase, "Economics of Broadcasting and Government," *American Economic Review*, Papers and Proceedings, (May 1966), 442.

24. *Office of Communication, United Church of Christ,* v. *F.C.C.* (1966).
25. Hillier Krieghbaum, *Pressures on the Press* (New York: Thomas Y. Crowell, 1972) p. 80.
26. For further examples of such influences, see John Hohenberg, *The New Media: A Journalist's Look at His Profession* (New York: Holt, Rinehart and Winston, 1968).
27. Garry Wills, "Measuring the Impact of Erotica," *Psychology Today,* 11, No. 3 (August 1977), 30–34, 74–76.

The Communication Industries

4 The Print Media

A good newspaper is a nation talking to itself.

ARTHUR MILLER

Newspapers, magazines, and books all package basically the same thing: printed words. Yet all three have been around a long time, and there is no sign that any one of them is about to replace the others. Even in the face of competition from broadcasting, each of the print media continues to reach millions with a sweeping variety of messages.

To understand why they have survived, we introduce three concepts here: form, function, and audience. Then we look at each medium in more detail. Our examination is far from exhaustive, but we will review the diversity within each medium, their similarities and differences, how the various media have influenced each other, how newspapers and book publishers work, and how the print media are financed.

Forms, Functions, and Audiences

Ever since Gutenberg invented his press, words printed on paper have helped shape the history of Western civilization. Almost at once kings, nobles, and clergymen saw the printed word as a weapon in the war for influence on the minds of men and women. Sayings like "The pen is mightier than the sword" became commonplace. Or, in Napoleon Bonaparte's more graphic terms, "Three hostile newspapers are more to be feared than a thousand bayonets."

But writing had been known for centuries. Why did the written word come to have such power only after the fifteenth century? Earlier written works were luxury items for the rich and the powerful. The great potential of the written word was realized only

Los Angeles Times ★ Page 2, Part I

Inside The Times

A tavern in Santa Barbara features videotaped sports events — which draw droves of participants. (Part I, Page 3.)

An analysis of radar measurements of Mars made in 1971 and 1973 has turned up signs of liquid water. (Part I, Page 3.)

Lt. Gov. Mike Curb and nine legislators launched a drive for an initiative to abolish the state inheritance tax. (Part I, Page 3.)

Paul Gann, Republican nominee for the U.S. Senate, formally launched his drive to unseat Sen. Alan Cranston. (Part I, Page 3.)

A purge of Afghanistan's Marxist regime reportedly is under way, aimed at strengthening President Babrak Karmal. (Part I, Page 4.)

A national Ku Klux Klan leader offered to sell his organization to the leader of a rival klan for $35,000. (Part I, Page 5.)

The Senate opened debate on the Alaska wilderness protection bill with the state's senators sharply divided. (Part I, Page 5.)

A gunman assassinated former Syrian Premier Salah Eddin Bitar in a new outburst of Mideast political violence in Paris. (Part I, Page 9.)

Murder charges against two Lompoc prisoners were dropped because they had no counsel in an investigation. (Part II, Page 1.)

Los Angeles school board member Kathleen Brown will move to New York after her marriage to a TV executive. (Part II, Page 1.)

Los Angeles City Atty. Burt Pines, citing a two-term pledge and family considerations, said he would not run again. (Part II, Page 1.)

Douglas A. Fraser is a man who can make the President of the United States dance. (Part II, Editorial Section.)

In Sports

Nadia Comaneci, darling of the 1976 Olympics, had a perfect 10 on the balance beam in Moscow Olympic competiton. (Part III, Page 1.)

Sebastian Coe, world record distance runner, says he will run in the 800- and 1500-meter events, Steve Ovett or no. (Part III, Page 1.)

Dane Iorg hit a three-run homer and Ted Simmons a solo shot to lead St. Louis to a 5-2 victory over the Dodgers. (Part III, Page 1.)

In Business

The International Trade Commission said it will wait until after the presidential election to rule on auto imports. (Part IV, Page 1.)

Pacific Gas & Electric signed a contract to buy electricity from Optimum Energy Development for 70,000 homes. (Part IV, Page 1.)

Eli Lilly & Co. plans to test synthetic insulin on humans and, if tests succeed, begin commercial production (Part IV, Page 1.)

A late rally pushed stock prices to another 3-year high with the Dow Jones industrials gaining 4.69 to 928.67 (Part IV, Page 2.)

In View

Mario Carrera, 17, of Carpinteria High School, the son of a migrant Mexican laborer, heads for Harvard University. (Part V, Page 1.)

Locks, burglar alarms, patrol services, guard dogs —everything but moats—are being offered jittery homeowners. (Part V, Page 1.)

When they're together, Overeaters Anonymous are anything but anonymous about their struggle to kick eating habits. (Part V, Page 1.)

In Calendar

Newcomer Dale Krantz is the female spark of the Rossington Collins Band, comprised of survivors of Lynyrd Skynyrd. (Part VI, Page 1.)

"The Bizarre Imagery of Yoshitoshi" is a sleeper of a show at the County Museum of Art, filled with horrific fantasy. (Part VI, Page 1.)

Richard Crenna stars in the TV movie version of "The Day the Bubble Broke," filming downtown on Spring Street. (Part VI, Page 1.)

Newcomer Sam Neill stars in the movie version of Irwin Shaw's "Nightwork," about to go before the cameras. (Part VI, Page 1.)

News in Brief

TUESDAY, JULY 22, 1980

Compiled from the Los Angeles Times, the Los Angeles Times-Washington Post News Service and major wire and supplementary news agencies.

THE WORLD

German Warship Curbs Lifted

Western European allies lifted the post-World War II curbs on the building of warships by West Germany, allowing it to construct nuclear-powered vessels and more submarines to reinforce defenses of the North Atlantic Treaty Organization. The move followed a recommendation by U.S. Gen. Bernard W. Rogers, supreme commander of NATO, that the Bonn government be allowed to build larger warships in the face of growing Soviet sea power. The allied action came at a London meeting of the West European Union, which oversees German rearmament.

A giant tanker carrying Persian Gulf crude oil blew up and began to sink at Rotterdam, the Netherlands. Its crew apparently escaped unharmed. An explosion ripped through the stern of the 98,000-ton, Liberian-registered Energy Concentration as it began discharging its cargo of about 61 million gallons of oil. The cause of the explosion was not immediately known.

Bolivian soldiers fired into a public square in La Paz to disperse about 200 demonstrators shouting slogans against the new military junta. There was no immediate report of casualties. Labor unions challenged the junta with a general strike, but resistance to the junta appeared to falter. Labor chieftain Juan Lechin, who has been arrested by the junta, called for an end to the strike, and in the nation's important tin-mining region, troops closed in on the last pocket of armed miners fighting the regime.

The United States and Britain called for an international ban on the commercial killing of whales to save the world's largest mammal from extinction as the 24-member International Whaling Commission met in Brighton, England, for its annual week-long conference. Representatives of the whaling industries of Japan, the Soviet Union, Brazil, Iceland, South Korea, Peru and Spain issued a declaration vowing to fight the ban, which was narrowly defeated at the commission's 1979 conference.

An Israeli Cabinet committee decided to transfer two more government departments from Tel Aviv to Jerusalem, virtually completing the program to make Jerusalem the center of government as well as nominal capital. Only the Defense Ministry will remain headquartered in Tel Aviv, the nation's business center. Prime Minister Menachem Begin is preparing to move his own office from West Jerusalem to the mostly Arab eastern sector, captured from Jordan and annexed in 1967.

U.N. Secretary General Kurt Waldheim called the General Assembly to an emergency session today on Palestinian issues. The session was opposed by the United States and Israel, and France expressed reservations about it. Israel's Ambassador Yehuda Z. Blum called the special session illegal. Arab nations have drafted a resolution proposing Nov. 15 as a deadline for Israeli withdrawal from occupied Arab territories.

South Korea's foreign minister, Park Tong Jin, said it would signal "an improvement in their attitude" if the North Koreans want north-south trade, as reported by Rep. Stephen J. Solarz (D-N.Y.) after his five-day visit to North Korea. Park said the south has long been ready for trade with the north. But he was skeptical of other aspects of the north's apparently conciliatory statements to Solarz.

HOT, HUMID DAY—President Carter, in shirt-sleeves, mops his face as he is introduced to crowd in Robards, Ky., by host Dale Sights. The President campaigned in Kentucky and Texas.
STORY IN PART I, PAGE 8
Associated Press photo

THE NATION

Panel to Consider Billy Carter Inquiry

Sen. Edward M. Kennedy (D-Mass.), chairman of the Judiciary Committee, responding to a request from Sen. Robert J. Dole (R-Kan.), will ask the committee to decide whether an investigation is needed into Billy Carter's ties to the Libyan government, a spokesman said. Dole said in a letter to Kennedy that the panel should air "the role of the White House" in a Justice Department decision not to prosecute President Carter's brother. Kennedy, who is challenging the President for the Democratic presidential nomination, will turn the matter over to the full committee at a meeting scheduled for Wednesday, Kennedy's press secretary said. He did not say whether Kennedy himself would make a recommendation.

A federal court in Philadelphia ordered owners of the American tanker Edgar M. Queeny, involved in a collision on the Delaware River five years ago, to pay nearly $16.2 million to the owners of the Marcus Hook oil refinery and an additional $3.07 million to the owners of the tanker Corinthos. The Corinthos was unloading its cargo of crude oil Jan. 31, 1975, when the Queeny, a chemical tanker, began a U-turn from the New Jersey shore and struck the Corinthos. There were 11 known dead and 15 missing from the fire and the explosions that followed.

The Detroit Free Press and 520 striking truck drivers and circulation workers reached tentative agreement on a new contract, but the newspaper is not expected to resume regular publication until Friday. The Teamstears Union, which walked off the job July 12, has scheduled a ratification vote for Wednesday. Details of the new pact were not immediately known, but bargainers said it was basically unchanged from an offer made by the newspaper late last week.

The House voted to create a special commission to investigate the World War II order that uprooted 120,000 Japanese-Americans from their homes and forced them into internment camps for the duration of the war. Although the bill would authorize only an inquiry, it could open the way for Japanese-Americans to file financial claims against the United States. The Senate has passed a similar measure and the bill now goes to a conference committee.

The plight of poor families is becoming "increasingly desperate" as soaring energy costs force them to spend at least 21% of their income on home heating, cooling and other utility bills, according to the Department of Energy's Fuel Oil Marketing Advisory Committee. The panel recommended sharp increases in federal programs to help the poor. It said a minimum $3.5 billion in aid is needed this winter to offset rising prices.

About 200 blacks walked out of a meeting called to air grievances in Miami's racially tense inner city, known as Liberty City. They complained that all they heard was "talk, talk, talk." Tempers flared at the meeting called by Dade County government leaders after Miami Vice Mayor Armando LaCasa said the city would no longer tolerate violence in the black community and Rep. Dante B. Fascell (D-Fla.) said a "truckload of money" would not solve Liberty City's problems. But one black leader, Athalie Range, said such meetings were needed. "If we don't talk, we will blow up—the tops of our heads will come off—death and dying in the streets is imminent," she said.

THE STATE

A Roman Catholic nun, charged with killing her mother during a seven-hour ritual of exorcism, was found innocent by reason of insanity. San Francisco Superior Court Judge Claude Perasso first found Sister Anna Sangiacomo, 45, guilty of involuntary manslaughter and then ruled that she was insane at the time of the slaying. Sister Anna's mother, Mrs. Rose Sangiacomo, 75, died of a heart attack brought on by a Feb. 12 incident at her San Francisco home in which her daughter beat her with a crucifix and a slipper and continued to do so after the elderly woman lost consciousness. Sister Anna, a member of the St. Joseph's of Corondelet order, will be committed to a mental facility.

More than 1,000 residents were evacuated for 2½ hours from part of Truckee after an eastbound Southern Pacific freight train leaked caustic phosphoric acid fumes. Nine persons, including a mother and her two children, railroad workers and Truckee firemen, were hospitalized for treatment of skin burns, lung irritation and nausea. All were in good condition. Phosphoric acid is an industrial chemical used in the production of fertilizer, soft drinks and flavoring syrups.

The five-day-old strike against 36 of San Francisco's biggest hotels continued unabated—but the striking Hotel and Restaurant Employees and Bartenders Union agreed to let one truck cross its picket line at the Hilton. The truck, from St. Anthony's dining room, an organization operated by a religious order that serves meals to the poor in San Francisco's tenderloin, picked up 40 cases of perishable food from the Hilton, where dining facilities have remained closed since the strike began last Thursday. Bargaining talks were set to begin Thursday.

THE SOUTHLAND

In response to a 1979 housing discrimination suit filed in U.S. District Court in Los Angeles, the Justice Department has obtained a consent decree requiring the owners of more than 1,000 metropolitan area apartment units to rent to blacks. The suit charged the owners of 15 apartment complexes in Los Angeles and Orange counties with violating the Fair Housing Act of 1968 by discriminating against blacks. Defendants in the suit were Del Properties and its partners, Robert L. Breece and John Ohanesian.

The California attorney general has asked Los Angeles Superior Court Judge Robert Weil to order Worldwide Church of God Treasurer Stanley Rader to answer more than 150 questions or default on the state's suit demanding financial disclosure from the Pasadena-based sect. Deputy Atty. Gen. Jim Cordi said Rader had appeared for depositions three times but refused to answer almost all questions. The hearing on Cordi's motion is set for Aug. 6.

About 350 firefighters battled winds gusting to 50 m.p.h. to contain a blaze that blackened 2,000 acres of brushland and threatened 60 homes in the Yucca Valley hamlet of Rim Rock. A California Department of Forestry spokesman said the blaze was 50% contained by early evening, and might be full contained this morning—if the winds die. Another fire, 20 miles to the south, burned 200 acres of brush and carved a black trail to within 100 feet of a condominium complex in Palm Springs, but was fully controlled within hours.

A man was shot and critically wounded by sheriff's deputies after he allegedly pointed a pistol at them in a Lawndale bar, the Los Angeles County Sheriff's Department reported. A spokesman said sheriff's Deputies Murry Carter, 42, and John Anthony, 34, entered the bar in response to a disturbance report and were approached by a man later identified as Ricardo Diaz, 27, who ignored orders to halt and then struggled when one deputy attempted to search him. Breaking free, the deputies said, Diaz drew a .22-caliber revolver from his waistband and pointed it at them. Carter and Anthony each fired one shot. Diaz was taken to Hawthorne Community Hospital where he was reported in critical but stable condition with two bullet wounds in his upper body.

The Mexican-American Bar Association of Los Angeles has threatened to renege on its support for the Democratic Party if President Carter does not move to clear Sacramento-based U.S. Atty. Herman Sillas of the bribery charges which threaten his dismissal. The association, fearing that Carter may have already determined Sillas' fate, has asked that a special prosecutor be appointed to the case. Sillas is accused of accepting a $7,500 bribe in May, 1974, from an ex-felon who needed help obtaining an auto dealer license. Sillas, who claims the charges are "uncorroborated," has failed two FBI-administered lie detector tests. He has agreed to take another given by an authority acceptable to him and the government.

ENERGY AND ENVIRONMENT

Firms Challenge New Pesticide Regulations

Thirteen chemical companies and two of their trade associations asked a federal judge in Sacramento to block implementation of the state's new, tighter pesticide regulations. John Conner, a Washington, D.C., attorney representing the plaintiffs, argued before U.S. District Judge Lawrence Karlton that federal law preempts the state's authority to apply stricter pesticide controls in California. The chemical firms and the National Agricultural Chemicals Assn. and the Chemical Specialties Manufacturers Assn. are seeking a temporary restraining order to stop the regulations from going into effect Jan. 1. The judge took the case under consideration and will issue his ruling later.

Animal protection groups asked President Carter to retain a ban on the importation of kangaroo products. The Interior Department, responding to pressure from the Australian government, said kangaroos presently exist in large numbers and proposed that the 1975 ban be eliminated. But eight groups, including the Society for Prevention of Cruelty to Animals, said large-scale importation of kangaroo products could eventually endanger the species.

Farmers who have introduced Chinese geese in Idaho as an alternative to chemical herbicides have learned an important lesson: don't let the gaggle gourmandize. The geese generally stick to weeds and ignore the crops they are meant to protect. "But when they're hungry, you'd better pick them up," said Dennis Sewald, the man who took the birds to Idaho. "If you leave them out there, they'll eat your crop."

Newsmakers- - - -

Boy's Grasp Now Exceeds His Reach

—Most parents are unhappy when their child sucks his thumb. But **Irene and Neal Barnard** of Cleveland are thrilled when 21-month-old **Jacob** does. Their son, the victim of a birth defect, was born without thumbs. Last May, orthopedic surgeon Avrum I. Froimson transformed Jacob's right index finger into a thumb through an operation known as pollicization—from the Latin pollex, meaning thumb. During the two-hour microsurgical procedure, the finger was detached, shortened and moved to the thumb position. In a few months Froimson will make him a left thumb. As Jacob grew, he first used his feet to play with his toys. Later, he picked up things between his second and third fingers. But, as a result of the operation, Jacob can grasp and hold objects firmly for the first time. "He reacted just like it had always been there," said his happy mother.

—Being a musician, "Georgia on My Mind," must have been running through the mind of **Dominic Frontiere,** film score composer, as he and the owner of the Los Angeles Rams, **Georgia Rosenbloom,** were married in Jacksonville, Fla. Hugh Culverhouse, owner of the Tampa Bay Buccaneers, officiated in his capacity as a notary public. Sixty-two guests, including NFL Commissioner Pete Rozelle and owners and administrators of five other football teams, attended. For Georgia Frontiere, 52, it was her seventh marriage. Frontiere, 49, who also has had previous marriages, said he would leave the running of the football team to his wife. "Her knowledge of football is staggering," he said.

—The former press spokesman for the State Department, **Hodding Carter III,** was named anchorman of a planned weekly program on public television, tentatively titled "Inside Story," that will assess news media performance, according to the New York production company, The Press and the Public Project. Carter, 45, stepped down as assistant secretary of state for public affairs three weeks ago.

—**President Carter** has named his wife, **Rosalynn,** to lead the U.S. delegation at the three-day inaugural ceremonies, beginning Sunday, for Peru's newly elected President Fernando Belaunde Terry.

—Author **Lucille Matthews** became the first known woman to swim the five miles from Oakland to San Francisco. Matthews, who would not give her age, was escorted by a kayak and made the swim in 3 hours and 45 minutes.

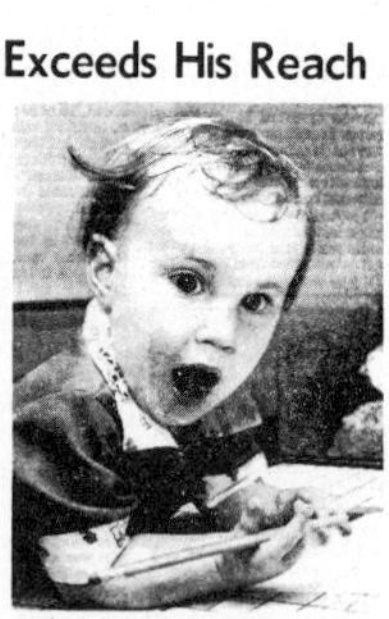

Jacob displays his newly acquired grasp.
Associated Press photo

—**Walter Polovchak,** the 12-year-old Ukrainian boy who does not want to return to the Soviet Union with his family, was granted political asylum, the boy's lawyer announced in Chicago. Attorney Julian E. Kulas said he had learned from Immigration and Naturalization Service officials that "the request I made on Saturday in behalf of my client has been adjudicated and approved." Kulas said the INS decision means Walter may remain in the custody of his parents, Michael and Anna Polovchak, as long as they are in the United States but they cannot force him to leave the country with them. The seventh-grader Saturday told a juvenile court judge, "I would rather never again see my parents than leave Chicago." A final custody hearing is set for July 30.

—**By Jennings Parrott**

This page of the Los Angeles Times *dramatically demonstrates the information function of the press.*

when it became a form of communication used by the common person — and that could happen only after the invention of the printing press made cheap reproduction possible. Once written material could be printed instead of hand-copied, it found new functions and new audiences. These three elements — form, function, and audience — are essential to an analysis of the print media.

The Relationship of Form and Function

By *form* we mean all the physical characteristics of a medium and how it is produced. All the print media share one characteristic: they are composed of words inscribed on some sort of paper by some sort of ink. Their form is strikingly different from those of television and films with their fleeting sounds and images. Even within the print media we find variations in forms. Soon after books were first produced, broadsides (single printed sheets like posters), monographs, and pamphlets were used. These could be produced more quickly and in larger numbers than books. They were followed by newspapers and magazines — forms which are produced quickly and rather cheaply, which deteriorate quickly, and which many people throw away without a second thought.

This diversity of forms suggests a diversity of functions. The earliest printed works were vehicles for authoritative messages. They transmitted religious gospels, the thoughts of the learned, and the commands of government. Modern printed words have far more complex functions. They serve (1) to *inform* (by providing news and information); (2) to *influence* (by providing editorial content and other expressions of opinion); (3) to *entertain* (by providing material that amuses and diverts the individual from weightier concerns); and (4) *as a marketplace* for goods and services (through advertising content).

Yet another, similar way of classifying the functions of the media is

1. *Surveillance* of the environment. Newspapers, for example, "cover" a community, collecting information from a wide variety of sources to give the public a picture of what is happening.
2. *Correlation* of the parts of society. Whereas surveillance is the gathering and distribution of information, correlation provides explanation and interpretation. The press attempts to make sense out of the information it has gathered, telling the public that certain facts are part of a trend or pattern. Whereas news

The Boston Globe

WILLIAM O. TAYLOR, President and Publisher
THOMAS WINSHIP, Editor

JOHN P. GIUGGIO, Executive V.P. & General Manager
RICHARD C. OCKERBLOOM, V.P. Marketing & Sales
DAVID STANGER, V.P. & Business Manager

ROBERT H. PHELPS, Executive Editor
JOHN S. DRISCOLL, Ass't. Executive Editor, Daily
TIMOTHY LELAND, Ass't. Executive Editor, Sunday

ROBERT L. HEALY, Associate Editor   ANNE C. WYMAN, Editor, Editorial Page

Globe Newspaper Company, 135 Morrissey Blvd., Boston, Mass. 02107 — 617-929-2000
A Wholly Owned Subsidiary of AFFILIATED PUBLICATIONS, INC.

DAVIS TAYLOR, Chairman of the Board
WILLIAM O. TAYLOR, President   JOHN I. TAYLOR, Chairman of Executive Committee
JOHN P. GIUGGIO, Executive Vice President and Treasurer

Putting the cards on the table

Aside from budgetary issues, the most important game in the Legislature this year centers on the reform proposals of the special commission on state building contracts. The legislative leadership is now ponderings its next move; it is time for the cards to be played.

Two key bills — one establishing an office of inspector general and the other redrafting state construction contracting procedures — are now in the House Ways and Means Committee. Both arrived there after being altered substantially by the Legislature's Committee on State Administration.

In our view, both should be amended back to their original form and sent to the House floor soon. If they are slipped out in any form moments before prorogation, they will be vulnerable to parliamentary sabotage or to subtle but devastating changes in language and, if enacted, will be open to a pocket veto by the governor.

To be worth its name, the final version of the legislation creating an office of inspector general to monitor state contracting must be considerably stronger than the version approved by the Committee on Administration.

One way or another, the inspector general will be responsible to elected officials; that is the way it should be. But the inspector general should not be responsible to one official, the governor, as the Administration Committee proposed. The special commission's original notion of having the inspector general selected by and accountable to a council consisting of the attorney general, the auditor and the secetary of public safety was a sounder approach.

Second, the charge to the inspector general must include monitoring a wide array of state purchases of goods and services; it should not be limited to building construction and allied services. And third, the inspector general must have the power to do the job and this includes the power to subpoena records and individuals. Those worried about abuses should not forget that the use of subpoenas is always subject to review by the courts.

The contracting procedures bill approved by the Administration Committee also needs reworking. The committee made one major change in the legislation proposed by the special commission, striking proposals to alter the way in which many subcontractors are selected for state projects. The objective of the commission proposal, which eliminates from state law something known as the "filed sub-bid" system, is to allow the general contractor to select subcontractors and thereby to enable the state to hold the contractor responsible for the quality of the work on a state building.

It is a complex matter, but nothing we have seen from opponents of the commission plan suggests how accountability can be built into state building construction without the changes recommended by the special commission and they therefore ought to be restored to the legislation.

From all reports, it appears that the Legislature will soon fold its tent. The early adjournment is designed in part to allow legislators time to campaign for reelection. Surely, those campaigns will be measureably easier if the incumbents can point to their substantive legislative efforts to curb state contracting abuses.

A new try on the T

The MBTA Advisory Board has this week introduced a new proposal for revamping the mass transit system that deserves careful consideration by the Legislature before it prorogues.

Developed in cooperation with public interest groups like the Massachusetts Taxpayers Foundation and the League of Women Voters, the bill correctly concentrates on two major issues: guarantee of reasonable management responsibilities in handling personnel and protection of the cities and towns against the sharply rising costs of the system.

Unlike the ambitious measure filed by the Transportation Committee last week, this bill does nothing to rearrange the present structure of the system. Executive power remains in the hands of the chairman and the 79-member Advisory Board retains budgetary supervision, through its veto power.

The new legislation provides that the state's share of the MBTA deficit should increase by stages to 70 percent over the next three years, covering all forms of service.

The bill also guarantees management the right to train, assign, evaluate and promote personnel irrespective of seniority claims. It permits communities to contract services from other carriers and the MBTA management to make similar arrangements with suppliers. And it allows the hiring of part-time personnel.

These management measures are vital to improving the efficiency of the system. Acting Chairman Barry Locke believes many or all of them are held by management under existing statutes but have been dissipated through tradition or practice. They were all contained in an earlier version of the bill sent to the Legislature by Gov. King. But, because it might take two weeks to check the statutes, and because the Legislature may be gone within that time, Locke should endorse the new proposals as additional security

The Transportation Committee bill, now before the Senate Ways and Means Commitee, deleted the management portion of the original King proposal and is seriously flawed as a result. The Transportation Committee should recall the measure to correct those defects and to reconsider the restructuring of the system in the light of the Advisory Board proposals.

In the event it fails to do so, Sen. Chester Atkins, chairman of Senate Ways and Means, must make every effort to win approval for the amendments in his committee. Gov. King and Mayor White, too, should press for action on these MBTA reforms.

A report to put on the shelf

The marketing of liquor is wrapped in a mystique that defies easy understanding by the outsider. Certainly the sale of alcoholic beverages must be regulated, limited to those of legal age. Certainly its sales must be monitored to ensure the state receives the revenue it is due. Beyond that the buying and selling of liquor ought to be conducted in as open and as competitive an environment as possible.

Recent recommendations by a special commission on the alcoholic beverage industry would constitute excessive meddling. The commission does allow cooperative buying programs with possible reductions in cost for small retailers. And it does propose to increase the number of package store licenses a single firm may hold, from three to seven. Those are steps in the right direction. None of the large chains are approaching a monopoly position; yet they have demonstrated an ability to reduce prices.

Other proposals by the industry-dominated commission are less sound. One calls for the enactment of a so-called "Primary American Source" law. That would prohibit wholesalers from purchasing beer or liquor from out-of-state brand name distributors.

The protection of Massachussets jobs is cited as a principal argument for the primary source rule. That same argument was made in 1978 when a similar proposal was approved by the Legislature. Gov. Dukakis vetoed it, contending the job argument was not compelling. In spite of that veto, distributors have prospered; jobs have not been lost.

Massachusetts consumers, meanwhile, have benefitted from the competition engendered by less expensive liquor bought out of state. And the treasury has profitted as more competitive prices in the commonwealth undercut cross-border traffic in liquor from New Hampshire.

Another commission recommendation would require all retailers to mark up liquor at least 10 percent to eliminate so-called loss leaders. While the state ought to be on guard against predatory marketing practices, it ought not be in the business of mandating specific minimum markups.

The package of special commission recommendations now goes to Gov. King. He may well convert one or all of the recommendations into legislation and ship it to the Legislature for speedy action before adjournment. He would be better advised to do nothing until next session when the legislation can be considered more thoroughly. The special commission's report, on balance, should be put on a shelf to gather dust.

Lady Macbeth of Elmhurst

A few hundred years too late, a New York appeals court has handed down a ruling that would have barred Lady Macbeth's doctor from testifying about statements she makes during the sleepwalking scene. Those lines about the "damned spot" that won't wash away or the "perfumes of Arabia (that) will not sweeten this little hand" would not get past the first objection from Lady Macbeth's defense attorney.

The ruling came in a less poetic case of manslaughter in the Elmhurst section of Queens. There, far from Dunsinane and Birnam Wood, David Knatz was accused of stabbing Charles Flynn to death, apparently because Flynn was making a pass at Knatz' girlfriend, Teresa Lodico. At Knatz' trial, Lodico testified that a day after the killing, he started screaming in his sleep about spurting blood and a bloody knife.

That Knatz was apparently dreaming, "severely detracted from the utterances' reliability," the court said, adding a remark that shows them weaker on their Shakespeare than on their law: "The utterances were ambivalent in content and did not unequivocally relate to the crime." The doctor, you'll recall, knows all too well that "foul whisperings are abroad." Lady Macbeth, he remarks knowingly, "more needs . . . the divine than the physician." The New York judges should have taken a day off to read their Shakespeare.

LETTERS TO THE EDITOR

Carter, the reluctant debater

President Carter's firm reluctance to include John Anderson in a debate against Ronald Reagan, as pointed out by David Broder in "No fair rewriting the news" (June 1), further exposes Carter's ineptitude in defending his past policies and confronting current economic and foreign crises.

The Carter Administration has come up with the half-baked notion that to debate Reagan and Anderson virtually would be to debate two Republicans. It appears more likely that the President fears Anderson's liberal and sometimes radical views might detract voter support, giving Reagan a possible edge. Furthermore, a compelling and impressive speaker like John Anderson could possibly intimidate Carter and his tenuous defense of economic and foreign policies.

Regarding the previous debates with only two parties represented, it is evident that most voters would welcome the overruling of this technicality, since Anderson has captured a sizable portion of public attention, according to recent polls.

Reagan has no objection to including Anderson. The President's decision not to debate Anderson might be interpreted as a badly-placed political ploy, which could have detrimental effects on his re-election.

RICHARD A. VARR
Framingham

'Character' became the campaign code word

Your banner headline in the June 4 Globe, "Carter goes over top in delegate count," was a foregone conclusion and mathematical certainty, news to no one. For the real news of the day, that Kennedy had won five states including California and New Jersey, one had to don his reading glasses and turn to page 10. The import of this news was such that it could have affected, if not the nomination, then certainly the election itself.

This has been the manner of coverage by the press, regrettably including The Globe, of the 1980 presidential campaign. So, again we will be "getting what we deserve"; not that we are so abysmally stupid, but rather because most of us tend to absorb "the news" unquestioningly.

Even Mary McGrory, who had bravely quartered Kennedy, finally succumbed and delivered her own gratuitous (though I hope unintentional) kiss of death. Conjecturing in her column of June 3 as to whether Kennedy's tenacious candidacy was perhaps motivated by a desire to emerge at least as "the conscience of the Democratic Party," she added the crushing qualification that the voters had declared him to be "not a man of conscience." Clearly a non sequitur, for there was no such referendum in the voting, and the verbiage was cruel and crippling. Certainly Chappaquiddick was an issue (overblown or not), but so was the multitude of Kennedy haters; and, mostly, the voting was influenced by the unprincipled cunning of the Carter campaigners — aided, abetted and condoned by the media.

Though "character" became the code word, Sen. Kennedy's performance during the past decade, and the character displayed in the beating he has since uncomplainingly endured, will be hard to equal. True, his opening campaign was a disaster, hampered by his reluctance to say what he easily could have said about the leader of his party. He realized his default too late, and then came out swinging, but still as the gentleman he is.

NATHAN TRABER
Newton

Iran policy legitimizes our bigotry

Tina Bahadori, an 18-year-old, straight A student at Atlantic City High School was deprived of the right to deliver the valedictorian speech. It seems that 57 percent of the faculty signed a petition objecting to honoring her because she is Iranian.

It is clear to me that the most distressing effect of the Carter Administration's handling of the Iranian crisis has been that it has legitimized our hatred and bigotry. In many circles it is no longer considered polite to slander blacks or Jews, and it is even becoming unacceptable to victimize gays and women. Americans seem to have a basic need to hate someone and, thanks to Jimmy Carter, they now feel free to hate Iranians.

I believe deeply in the things my country is supposed to stand for — freedom and equality. When I was younger and learned about the vile way the Germans and Japanese were treated in this country during the World Wars, I felt pleased to be living in a more enlightened age. Perhaps the most profound disappointment of my adult life has been the discovery that nothing has changed.

JAMES WILLIAM MORRIS
Boston

We are still learning

To those who demonstrated at Seabrook:

Why, instead of expending all of your talents to prevent someone from doing something you are against, don't you help him do it better? Yes, I say help him. Help him with all your God-given talent to make the nuclear plant safe. Use your energy to find a way; one day you will find it.

I don't want nuclear power if it is going to deform and kill, and neither does anyone else. Until something better comes along, for God's sake, learn to live with it. The powers that be understand that strict regulations should be in order. Everyone makes mistakes and, unfortunately, this is a learning process. There are tragedies, sickness and death in this process; however, through our mistakes we surge ahead.

PAUL L. MILINAZZO
Waltham

The only drawback

With the latest Seabrook protest behind us, I now have to listen to this seductive male voice (paid for by the electrical companies of America) crooning over the radio that America should use ALL her energy resources, especially her nuclear power. He implies that to do otherwise is wasteful, unwholesome and very un-American.

I say:

If I were in the market for a washing machine and a man offered me a good deal on a wonderful machine with many features that the older, outmoded, more cumbersome models did not have — the only drawback being that if anything went wrong (and of course nothing would) that me, my children and my whole city would die an awful death —

I wouldn't buy it!

JUDY CARR JOHNSON
Cambridge

SEAFARING

What he missed

Too bad Jeremiah Murphy (June 5) didn't talk to the young midshipman from the Guyas who bid us a fond farewell saying, "Boston is a good port and your people are beautiful." Perhaps he missed the look of pride and awe on the faces of visitors who toured the USS John F. Kennedy.

I heartily agree that our politicians are very shortsighted in denying needed appropriations but that is no reason to dismiss the beauty and traditions which surround these fine sailing ships. For shame, Mr. Murphy! Why, next you'll be telling us there are no leprechauns.

BARBARA A. BROWNE
Acton

Matchmaking

We are writing to you about what we think was a very odd side effect of the Tall Ships being in Boston. We are referring to the media's encouragement of single women to go out and "entertain the sailors."

We were happy about the opportunity to have the Tall Ships and their crews here for the 350 celebration. We hope that Boston will always be friendly toward any visitors who may come to our city. Yet, we feel we must draw the line when we women were told to put on our makeup and high heels to ensure that the sailors have a "good time." We must say that we were neither that desperate for men, nor that impressed with the uniforms. It's a sad statement on the status of things, when women are encouraged to act as entertainment commodities for men. Why couldn't we have just been people meeting people?

JEANNE-MARIE BOYER
CYNTHIA KING
and 2 others
Brighton

Nowhere is the opinion function of the press more evident than on editorial and op-ed (opposite the editorials) pages.

POLITICAL CIRCUIT
By ROBERT HEALY

Brooke to run with Anderson?

Political associates of John Anderson have talked with former Sen. Edward Brooke of Massachusetts, now an attorney in Washington, about the number two spot on Anderson's ticket and Brooke has discussed the approach with several of his political people.

Brooke is concerned, however, that if he went with Anderson as a running mate and Anderson failed, he would be burning his bridges forever with the Republican party.

The choice of Brooke, a black, a progressive, and a Republican, would be a bold stroke for Anderson. In the areas Anderson must carry if he is to be a force in the presidential contest — in the large industrial states of the northeast quadrant — it could be a great advantage in moving blacks toward his independent candidacy.

Almost as important as the selection is the timing. Anderson is headed for a minor depression in July and August. Attention will be focused elsewhere.

The Republican National Convention begins its platform hearings after the July 4 weekend and meets in Detroit for the nominating process on July 14. On Aug. 11 in New York, the Democrats come together for their sessions.

At the Democratic convention, Sen. Edward Kennedy could provide a good show. An attempt to dump an incumbent President from the ticket at a convention, whatever the prospects, is sure to produce public interest.

Thus, inside the Anderson camp there is debate about when the choice of the vice presidential candidate should be made. There is an argument for waiting until after the Democratic convention to make certain of the results. But two months of down time in the campaign could present real problems; the public might forget about that third man in the race.

Therefore, Anderson is already deeply involved in the vice presidential selection process. It appears now that because Walter Cronkite has taken himself out of consideration, the field is wide open. Cronkite would have been a spectacular choice and there is some evidence that it was seriously considered. But for Cronkite, who will be phasing out of the anchor position on the TV evening news show, and for the purity of CBS, it was probably a realistic proposition.

Anderson must then look elsewhere. He must analyze the kind of voter he attracts and determine exactly what he needs in a vice presidential candidate to broaden his base.

In his way Brooke would do that.

But the more obvious choice would be a Democrat, one a shade on the progressive side but not so radical as to step all over Anderson's conservative fiscal toes. For balance, since Anderson is from the Midwest and there is no hope for him in the South, which will be cut up between Ronald Reagan and Jimmy Carter, he probably should turn to the East or possibly to California.

In California there is Gov. Jerry Brown and Norman Lear of "All in the Family." One never puts the best fund raiser on the ticket and that would eliminate Lear. Brown has thought about it, as he has about everything political, but late last month in a conversation he suggested that perhaps 1980 was never his year and his "time horizon" may be well into the future. In other words, the country was not ready for Brown and, as he put it, "California."

At the conference of mayors last week in Seattle there was talk of Boston Mayor Kevin White as a possible candidate on the Anderson ticket. White has the same reservations as does Brooke. He would be burning his bridges with the Democrats forever. He would not do that unless he had a real chance of winning. White also would bring something to the ticket. While taking a bath on some local issues in Boston, he is well respected by the national media and outside of Boston he is a symbol of the city of tall ships, a city that is perceived as having made it.

Further, White has been through the vice presidential bit once before with George McGovern in 1972. It was a shattering disappointment to be eliminated after almost making it. He does not want a repeat.

Finally there is Hugh Carey, governor of New York. His major assets are New York and Democratic affiliation. Both Carey and Anderson have a mutual operator in David Garth, the media consultant. This should not be overlooked. Garth could be a force in the selection. He has survived the internal Anderson battles in good shape and has great influence with the governor.

The choice for Anderson may be the most important decision he will make this summer.

Carter: A 'loner' once again

By DAVID S. BRODER

DES MOINES — Like many other Democratic incumbents who will be on the ballot this fall, Sen. John C. Culver has been sweating out the civil war between Ted Kennedy and Jimmy Carter for the presidential nomination.

Personally and politically, Culver is a lot closer to Kennedy, a Harvard friend who first brought him to Capitol Hill as his legislative assistant. But Carter has a loyal following in this state, so Culver was studiously neutral in the Carter-Kennedy battle, knowing he would need support from both sides in his reelection battle with Rep. Charles E. Grassley (R), a formidable challenger.

Neutrality was still the Culver policy last weekend, as he addressed the state Democratic convention.

What got cheers was Culver's declaration that the Democratic Party "has higher missions . . . than to waste time and funds in legal efforts to keep Independent candidate John Anderson off the ballot. The Democratic Party has nothing to fear from the responsible advocacy of candidates of this kind."

As if to demonstrate that Culver had read the mood of the convention correctly, the rules were suspended later in the day to pass a resolution formally criticizing the widely publicized effort by Democratic National Committee lawyers, operating at the direction of the Carter campaign, to challenge Anderson's petitions for ballot access in many states.

Iowa papers made Culver's defense of Anderson's right-to-run the lead on their convention stories — which was probably just what he intended.

There is more at work here than a spirit of fair play. What the Culver incident reveals is a fundamental difference between the tactics that serve Carter's political interests and those that will help many of the other Democrats running for office. It is a difference that will become increasingly obvious and important in comming weeks.

It is hard to exaggerate the threat the Carter strategists see in Anderson's candidacy. The President's game plan is to paint Reagan as such a bogeyman that the divided Democratic constituencies come back home, whatever their misgivings about the record of the past four years.

Anderson spoils that strategy by providing the dissident Democrats another alternative. Carterites fear Anderson could cost them such states as Iowa, Oregon, Massachusetts, Connecticut, New Jersey, Pennsylvania, Michigan — and even New York. Losing any two of the big ones might doom Carter's chances.

But for Democrats like Culver, Anderson could well be a political asset. The maverick Illinois Republican has his strongest support among the well-educated and the young voters. They are so turned off by the Carter-Reagan choice that they might well boycott the election if those were the only alternatives.

If they come out to vote for Anderson, chances are they will also vote for a liberal like Culver over a conservative like Grassley, who is backed by many of the same groups — anti-abortionists, gun-owners, etc. — that Anderson delights in baiting.

Thus, it is no more accidental that Culver defends Anderson's "right" to run than it is whimsical of Carter to put obstacles in Anderson's path.

The situation is developing in a way that almost decrees that Carter will be running even more as a "loner" in 1980 than he was in his 1976 campaign. Then, it was Carter who seemed deliberately to keep his distance from Democratic congressional candidates. This year, it is likely to be those candidates who look the other way when Carter's name is mentioned.

John Culver is not the only Democrat who finds it preferable to link himself in the home-state headlines with the Anderson candidacy than with either Carter or Kennedy.

POLITICS '80

Marionette, no . . .

By ROWLAND EVANS
and ROBERT NOVAK

WASHINGTON — Ronald Reagan's decision to keep William Brock as Republican national chairman corrects two widespread misconceptions, showing that Reagan is a better politician than supposed and that his political operation may be worse than its severest critics imagine.

Shortcomings of his political high command were revealed in unanimous advice that he needlessly outrage party moderates by dumping Brock.

In overriding this advice, Reagan is not the marionette liberals take him for but a politician who covets the presidency.

All Reagan's senior staffers urged him to renege on his month-old promise to retain Brock. Apart from failing to anticipate the firestorm within the Republican Party, their ineptitude is reflected in the simultaneous effort to enlist Bill Timmons as Reagan's national political director. Timmons was invited to California the same week Brock was to be get the coup de grace.

While he staved off disaster in the Brock affair, it enlarged the doubts about the Reagan campaign's readiness for Jimmy Carter.

. . . manageable, yes

By JOSEPH KRAFT

How bad can a man be whose idea of a fun evening is to go home and watch "Little House on the Prairie?"

I have been asking myself that question about Ronald Reagan for some time, and I now have an answer in the form of another question: Can Ronald Reagan control his own right wing?

By himself, Reagan makes a pretty poor excuse for a menace. He comes on warm and friendly and with the decent instincts of the Midwestern small town. Nothing in his record announces that he is — to cite qualities associated with three recent presidents — mean, vicious or megalomaniacal.

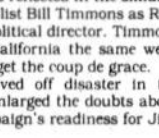

As governor of California he was far less silly than he sounded. His appointments were on the whole good. He did no serious damage to the university. Even though he is often misinformed on details, his errors turn out to be insignificant.

Efforts to paint Reagan as a black villain don't come off. Still, there is the far right wing of the Republican Party. Its members adhere to a wide range of ideas obnoxious to just government and a decent society. They are dead serious in their beliefs, and they line up behind Reagan with an intent to assume mastery of government and shape national policy.

So far the evidence is that Reagan is not going to be particularly good at holding his right wing. He is easy-going and hates bickering. He is given to letting things happen. Those are just the qualities to make a President the prisoner of a determined minority in his entourage.

Only the strong

By JIMMY BRESLIN

NEW YORK — Last November, with the hostages in Iran at Day Six, President Carter asked Ramsey Clark if he could fly to Tehran and use his influence to get everybody freed. Carter placed a White House plane at Clark's disposal. The trip did not work, and Clark flew back home on the White House plane.

Last week, when the hostages were at Day 219 and sitting, Carter was flying around the country to inspect volcanoes. During his flight Carter decided to make comments. He faces Ronald Reagan in the election, and one of the Carter strong points at this time is that Reagan goes around saying a lot of dumb things. Therefore, Carter told the press he felt Ramsey Clark, who this time went to Tehran on his own, should be indicted.

A sensible arrangement of facts shows that if Carter has Clark arrested for going to Tehran, then Carter should have himself arrested as at least an accomplice. Which did not pass through Carter's mind.

Now this week on Monday, on Day 225 for the hostages, Ramsey Clark had a press conference in New York to talk about the hostages and President Carter's threat to have him arrested.

Clark, solemn-faced, was saddened by Carter's position. Rather than go into the facts, the original trip on a White House plane, he just said that the President shouldn't mix politics with prosecution.

Clark went to Tehran at a time when the mightiest nation on earth seems not to have the slightest idea of how to get 53 hostages released. He seems to understand enough about strength to know that it is the heavyweight champion who always says "Excuse me" in a crowded doorway.

At this time, Clark's country is confused by the way fine details can suddenly become major points in international diplomacy. President Carter allowed the Shah to come to New York. Immediately, the Iranians stormed the embassy in Tehran and grabbed the hostages. How could they do such a thing, Carter wonders.

Rather than deal with complex facts, Carter has decided to fall back on the thing everybody loves most, a false display of muscle. "The United States will never apologize to Iran!" he tells campaign audiences. They cheer. Carter flies off in his big plane. The hostages sit.

And in the Picadilly Hotel in New York, after talking about how usually only the truly strong are gentle, Ramsey Clark was asked, "Some see you as an Iranian sympathizer. What do you say to that?"

"That tells you more about them than it does about me," Ramsey Clark said.

With 'em, not agin 'em

By JACK W. GERMOND
and JULES WITCOVER

WASHINGTON — While Republicans of various stripes are busily creating "independent" committees to raise and spend millions for Ronald Reagan's election, President Carter's political strategists are trying another way to generate more money beyond the $29.4 million in federal funds each major-party candidate will get for the fall campaign.

The Carter approach has the virtue of enabling his campaign to keep a tight rein on use of the additional funds, whereas federal law prohibits any contact whatever between the formal Reagan campaign and such "independent" committees.

The Carter campaign is using state Democratic committees in at least 20 key states to raise and spend money for the Carter-Mondale team locally, but under the direction of hand-picked members of the national campaign staff located at the state committees. The objective is to free up most of the $29.4 million for Carter's own travel and paid advertising.

Amendments to the federal campaign finance law in 1979 lifted a $1000 limit on spending by state party committees. Now they can raise and spend unlimited amounts to increase volunteer participation in campaigns.

About a month ago the Carter-Mondale campaign detached former White House aide Les Francis to the Democratic National Committee to undertake the state parties' project.

The Kennedy campaign squawked loudly when Francis was moved to the supposedly neutral but actually heavily pro-Carter national committee before Carter had a clear majority of convention delegates. Now Carter-Mondale operatives in New York and Michigan, both Kennedy states, have been switched to the DNC payroll and moved in while Kennedy continues to insist the fight for the nomination is not over.

Francis vows that all nine political hands are operating under strict instructions to involve themselves in no pre-convention maneuvering for Carter or against Kennedy, and to concentrate only on party-building for the fall. But Tim Kraft, Carter campaign director, acknowledges that talking to Kennedy delegates and shoring up Carter delegates constitutes "a very limited part of their assignment."

Kraft admits also that the nine have been put on the DNC payroll because the Carter campaign "is approaching the limit" on pre-convention campaign spending under federal law. In that sense, the nine constitute a kind of political "taxi squad" — out of game uniform but on the team just the same.

Still, the DNC's belated efforts within the state parties is the first solid indication that Jimmy Carter, who ran without them in 1976 and ignored them throughout most of his first term, is beginning to appreciate the benefits of running with the establishment instead of against it.

By MARY McGRORY

No more debating — debate

WASHINGTON — President Carter's newest method for coping with John Anderson is to cast him in a freak show.

He might, he said, on his way back from the West Coast, meet in debate with Anderson and other "theoretical" candidates.

In an impromptu news conference aboard Air Force One — and later repeated for television cameras — he allowed that he might give Anderson a chance to appear with his peers, the likes, presumably, of Lyndon LaRouche, who believes the world is set on assassinating him; Edward Clark, the Libertarian, and Barry Commoner, the environmentalist.

Clark and Commoner have already qualified for the ballot in some 30 states. Anderson is just in the foothills of his climb up Ballot Mountain.

Carter understandably wishes to protect what he regards as the main event — a showdown between himself and Ronald Reagan. Reagan gives him an opportunity to pose as a man of peace and compassion — and, of course, reliable information.

He could do worse than agree to a three-way debate. Anderson is a debater of considerable gifts. His information is as precise as Carter's. He is experienced in legislation and civil in manner.

But Reagan's casual approach to government — and facts — rattles Anderson.

Carter is not an adventurous politician. And presently he wishes to convey his irritation with the Illinois challenger — as well as with those Democrats who profess to see no treachery in voting for an independent.

Making a fringe contender of Anderson is what Carter wants to do most. Or at least what he wants to do some days, which is to paint Anderson as an eccentric with no claim on the serious voter. On other days, of course, the President has described him as a "conservative Republican."

Actually this particular line of attack serves Anderson rather well, since he has to count on more than anti-Carter Democrats. Suggesting that he is nothing but a Republican at heart reassures Republicans who might otherwise feel guilty about deserting the Grand Old Party at a moment when its prospects seem brightest.

But the ploy will not work. Anderson will not oblige Carter by appearing with dismissables. Fifty-three percent of those interviewed in an NBC-Associated Press survey said they thought the President should meet Anderson in debate. Their sentiments had been stirred up to some extent by Edward Kennedy's long, futile campaign for a public exchange with Carter.

It's just more evidence that the President is a fretful, compulsive candidate.

If he would stop and think about it, the President would see that the case against Anderson is being made by people most inclined to vote for him. You hear it everywhere: "I'd like to, but I'm afraid I'd just be electing Reagan."

The B that is John Anderson's middle initial might as well stand for "But-he-can't-win," and unless he can overcome the profound pessimism of his likeliest followers, he could fade quickly.

Anderson's strategic problem is circular. He needs a vice-presidential candidate, a Democrat, to make good on his promise of "national unity." He can't get one until he shows higher in the polls. And he can't go up in the polls until he gets a Democrat willing to run with him and prove that his candidacy is not "the fantasy" of White House hope and phrasing.

Anderson insists he is not worried. He is concentrating on ballot access and money-raising.

Names float by. Hugh Carey, the governor of New York. Recently, that of Kevin White, mayor of Boston. They are both, obviously, ethnic Democrats with the big-city following that Anderson, coming out of Rockford, Ill., lacks. Either Carey or White might soften the hostility of labor, the Democratic group which seems unlikely to forgive Anderson his staunchly anti-labor record in the House. The Jews have signified their willingness to let bygones be bygones on the Jesus amendment. The peaceniks can live with his pro-war record; the campuses with his erstwhile pro-nuclear stand.

But labor forgets nothing. Plainly, the unions are not entranced with Carter, but Anderson makes him look like a Democrat.

If the President spent his time in a debate with Anderson simply reciting Anderson's labor votes, he might do himself more good than by refusing to enter a television studio with him.

A sad state: Apologizing for all sins except their own

By JOSEPH SOBRAN

Nobody seems to be terribly shocked that rocks and bottles were thrown at a US President in Miami. The event certainly caused much less agitation than the Venezuelan mob that attacked a Vice President in Venezuela back in 1959. Miami's mayor was even sympathetic about it all: He called the mob's action a "natural" expression of "frustration." So is child abuse, I suppose.

Why should we be shocked? We have gotten used to attacks, physical and verbal, on our leaders, institutions, traditions. The Statue of Liberty gets mugged every fortnight or so. Politicians themselves join the assault. In 1976 candidate Jimmy Carter told us that our war in Vietnam had been "racist" and let on that he would introduce Washington to the wholly novel virtue of veracity. He even named names, and wound up going to Texas to placate Lady Bird Johnson.

Jimmy Carter, born-again anti-politician, was going to make all things new. That approach is good for one term; and now, Jimmy Carter having lowered our expectations of American leadership beneath anything Richard Nixon could have achieved, John Anderson is acting like the 1976 Carter's understudy, ready for the big role.

We have bred a generation of politicians who are ready to apologize for the country's sins, but never for their own. Blacks riot? Apologize to blacks. Iranians seize hostages? Apologize to Iran. But make it clear that it's somebody else's sins you're repenting.

Ramsey Clark has come back from Iran to tell every interviewer available that "we" must admit "our" mistakes. The principal mistake we have made, in my judgment, has been to appoint Ramsey Clark to public office. Clark himself enjoins national repentance without acknowledging that he personally owes anyone the slightest gesture of remorse.

Only Jimmy Carter would have dispatched Ramsey Clark as our representative as late as last December. But the choice was appropriate. Both men are possessed of an enormous humility that applies to everything they belong to — everything but themselves. It takes a special kind of modesty to beat every breast but one.

Carter has been especially modest about all his predecessors. Thus he could modestly attack the Vietnam War, modestly repudiate our ties to allies like Taiwan, modestly deplore our inordinate fear of communism. Clark can be modest about the eloquence of Shakespeare (while he himself misquotes Samuel Johnson, and attributes the butchered mot to Ambrose Bierce).

Have such men any sense of anything they should be grateful for, loyal to? Not conspicuously. It serves Carter right, then, that Clark should embarrass him by defying his feeble attempts to assert the authority he has helped discredit.

But don't expect Carter to do anything about it. An unnamed Treasury official told Lars-Erik Nelson of the New York News why not: "A decision to prosecute a former Attorney General in a Democratic Administration would be a tough one for Jimmy Carter to take — especially if he wants a reconciliation with Teddy Kennedy and the left wing of the Democratic Party. There are a lot of us left-wing Democrats in the government, and for all of us, Ramsey Clark is still a symbol."

Which being interpreted is, don't expect a law-breaking former Democratic attorney general to be prosecuted as fiercely as (say) a law-breaking former Republican attorney general. Never mind that Ramsey Clark and other left-wing Democrats spent the Watergate era intoning the ancient truth that no man is above the law. Edmund Muskie has now told us that this law wasn't meant to apply to people like Ramsey Clark.

The Democratic Party has had a lot to say about the nation's sins, but little to say about the sins of the Democratic Party. The best comment on its record of sustained misgovernment came at Miami, in the form of flying bottles, from the constituency that party has tried to woo and serve.

is surveillance, editorial comment or interpretive coverage is correlation.

3. *Transmission of the social heritage* from one generation to another. This function is essentially educational, taking the intellectual contributions of one generation and passing them on to the next.

4. *Entertainment,* providing amusement and pleasure for the audience. Comics and crossword puzzles entertain, for example. Entertaining content may have other functions, such as providing information, but they are secondary.

The first three of these functions were identified by scholar and commentator Harold D. Lasswell;[1] the fourth was added by communications researcher Charles Wright.[2]

How do these functions relate to the form of a medium? The form of a book gives it a permanent quality; it is therefore most suited for transmitting the social heritage from one generation to the next. It contains words that are meant to be preserved for the future as well as the present. Flimsy, quickly produced newspapers, on the other hand, are well suited for providing the news of the day. We might say that a novel entertains, a newspaper's front page informs, and an opinion magazine correlates.

But the relationship between form and function is not a simple one of cause and effect. The same functions, after all, are served by different forms. Books, newspapers, and radio can all inform, and within each form there is considerable diversity. Most of the print media have multiple functions, although often one function is dominant. For example, most novels mainly entertain, although they may also inform and persuade the reader. Functions change as well. For example, in the nineteenth century newspapers and magazines emphasized entertaining content; they serialized novels and included many humorous columns. At one time 60 percent of the printed matter in popular magazines was fiction, and 40 percent was nonfiction. Now this ratio has been reversed. Why? The functions of existing media change when a new medium is introduced. The introduction of films, radio, and television changed the uses and content of the print media. As the electronic media offered more and more entertainment, the print media reduced their emphasis on this function.

Looking at the relationships among the media, Canadian critic Marshall McLuhan offered an intriguing explanation for their differences and a radical prediction. Whatever their content, McLuhan has said, the print and electronic media make different demands on their audiences. Electronic messages, especially on television, involve several senses at once. Print, on the other hand, makes a dominant demand on the eyes and forces the reader to think in sequence, just as the reader's eyes move in a sequence from left to right on the printed page. The electronic messages, according to McLuhan, are more challenging and engage the mind in different ways than the print media do. This and other ideas led McLuhan to his famous aphorism: "The medium is the message." In other words, the way a medium interacts with people's minds is more important than the content it delivers. To McLuhan, the print media have become obsolete, and he predicted their death as a result of the appearance of electronic media such as television.

Whether or not one accepts McLuhan's extreme position, it emphasizes that technological innovations change the media, that one medium affects the other media, and that there is an important element in communication besides form and function: the audience. To understand the differences between, say, the magazines of the nineteenth and twentieth century, we need to ask who the audience is, what uses people make of the medium, and what gratifications it gives them. The audience is at the heart of any understanding of media functions.

The Audience

There is, of course, no mass communication of any form without an audience. Most forms of print were begun with tiny, discrete audiences in mind. Books at first were produced to be read by learned individuals, either to themselves or aloud to audiences in churches and governmental institutions. Early newspapers carried the political and financial information that was interesting and useful to their elite audience. There was a premium on information, and information was equated with power, which was not to be given indiscriminately to the common person.

To a great extent the rise of true mass media paralleled the decline of political and social control by elites and the rise in power of the common person. As society became more democratic and as literacy spread to the lower classes, the print media had a new potential audience — including workers as well as bosses, for example. Nineteenth-century workers in New York City might not have been very interested in financial news and shipping, but they were interested in news of people like themselves. When newspapers in the 1830s started to offer that kind of news at a reasonable price, they captured a new audience and developed into a mass medium. In books and magazines, too, changes occurred as society, and the audience, changed.

Understanding the development of print thus requires some

understanding of the characteristics of the audience they serve. Furthermore, audiences constantly change. What is popular today, what meets the demands of today's reader, may not satisfy the reader of tomorrow. The growth of the print media has been the story of a changing audience with new expectations and demands. As sociologist Robert E. Park said of newspapers more than a half-century ago:

> The natural history of the press is the history of the surviving species. It is an account of the conditions under which the existing newspaper has grown up and taken form. A newspaper is not merely printed. It is circulated and read. Otherwise it is not a newspaper. The struggle for existence, in the case of the newspaper, has been a struggle for circulation.[3]

Printed words are messages prepared for specific audiences, and their acceptance or rejection of these messages determines the shape and direction of the medium. It is because audiences have frequently changed in degree of literacy, tastes, and interests that all forms of print have undergone almost constant modification since they emerged centuries ago.

Newspapers

The distance is great from the simple colonial newspaper, run by a single printer in a tiny shop, to the complicated operations of a paper like the *Washington Post*. In place of ink-smudged typesetters one finds gleaming computers. In place of the printer who was also essayist, editor, and business manager, one often finds a corporation employing thousands. Approximately 61 million newspapers are sold in America every day. To examine this huge medium, we begin with its definition.

Defining Newspapers: A Dual Identity

Scholars have suggested numerous definitions of newspapers, some focusing on their content, some on their audience, some on how they are published. Police departments and other agencies even decide what is or is not a newspaper when they issue the press credentials that allow journalists to attend various events. In the late 1960s the Los Angeles Police Department decided that the Los Angeles *Free Press* was not a newspaper, and so its reporters were not entitled to press credentials. (The courts eventually overturned this decision.) We define newspapers rather simply: newspapers regularly publish by mechanical processes general news prepared for a general audience.

Obviously, newspapers are different things to different people. As Ernest Hynds said:

The United States Department of Commerce classifies newspapers in business terms. Newspaper publishing is the nation's tenth largest industry and its fifth largest industrial employer. The United States Constitution and its interpreters see newspapers as conveyors of information and opinion vital to the operation of government and the maintenance of freedom. Their responsible operation is protected under the First Amendment. The millions who read newspapers see them in myriad roles. . . . The newspaper is at once a private enterprise struggling in a highly competitive economy and a quasi-public institution serving the needs of all citizens.[4]

Thus newspapers are private, profit-making businesses with a special role. Most political theorists argue that a democratic society depends on a robust discussion of public affairs, and newspapers remain the basic instrument for delivering information to citizens to allow such a discussion. Indeed, many feel that this belief is the justification for the freedom of the press guaranteed by the First Amendment and that this freedom gives newspapers a special responsibility to inform the public.

Newspapers thus have a dual identity: on the one hand, they are quasi-public institutions that claim to serve the public interest; on the other hand, they are profit-making businesses that can be very self-serving. These two identities often clash. As a business, the newspaper seeks to make a profit and is a member of the business community, a major employer, a member of the chamber of commerce. In its role as a quasi-public institution, the newspaper is supposed to be the watchdog of the public interest and often an antagonist of government and other forces in power.

It probably makes little difference how we define newspapers, but how newspaper people define them can make a great deal of difference. If a publisher sees the newspaper as only, or primarily, a business, why bother to investigate a minor scandal that is likely to antagonize advertisers? Why bother to pay the salaries necessary to keep good reporters if your gossip columns and comics and sports section can maintain your circulation and your advertising? Then again, if the publisher does not see the paper as a business, it is not likely to be printing the news or anything else for long.

The conflict inherent in the newspaper's dual role can show up within the newspaper organization as business interests and the professional values of journalism often clash. The advertising and editorial departments, for example, may compete for space, or they may argue over how some stories should be covered. Most experienced newspaper people say this conflict can be minimized by good management and good communication between people.

The Communicators: How Newspapers Are Organized

Although newspapers range in size from the *New York Times*, with a staff of about 6,000 employees, to the country weekly, with a staff of three or four, certain elements are common to all papers. Every newspaper has both business and editorial operations. Generally, the business side manages business affairs and advertising — which generates income and keeps the paper alive — while the editorial side acquires information and produces the paper's editorial content.

The entire organization is headed by a publisher. It was *New York Times* publisher Arthur Ochs Sulzberger, for example, who made the final decision to publish the Pentagon Papers. Under the publisher there is usually a business manager and an editor supervising their respective staffs.

The larger the paper, the more complex the organization. On the business side several essential activities are often organized as separate departments. The advertising department handles both *display advertising* from merchants and businesses and the brief announcements (such as apartments for rent, help wanted) known as *classified advertising*. The production department is responsible for typesetting and printing. Selling the paper and arranging for its delivery by home carriers, mail, or to street sellers is the responsibility of the circulation department. A general business department handles such things as accounting, personnel, and building maintenance.

The editorial side of the paper includes the gathering and writing of stories as well as the selection of what to include and its preparation for printing; photographs, too, are handled by the editorial side. It is headed by an editor, sometimes called the *executive editor*. The executive editor works for the publisher and coordinates operations with the business manager. Reporting to the executive editor is the *managing editor*, who manages the newsroom. The managing editor hires and fires staff members and supervises various subeditors. Among the subeditors may be an editor of the editorial page (sometimes called the *associate editor*) and a *city editor*, who is the direct supervisor of all reporters and of the special editors for entertainment, sports, business, and so on. The city editor also manages the various copy editors and copy desks, where the work of reporters is reviewed, given headlines, and generally readied for publication. These desks (or little departments) include the city desk (where news from the city itself is coordinated), the metropolitan desk, the county desk, and the state desk. In addition there is a news editor, sometimes called the *wire editor* or *telegraph editor,* who edits and coordinates the national and international news coming from wire services such as the Associated Press and United Press International.

Reporters are the people who gather news and write stories. There are basically three kinds of reporters. *General assignment* reporters cover a wide range of news as it happens, regardless of the topic; they also rewrite stories. *Beat reporters* are assigned to particular areas of government, such as the courts, police, and state government. *Specialist reporters* are trained to cover fields such as business, science, and urban problems. Naturally, the size and complexity of a newspaper's organization depends on the paper's circulation, local circumstances, and functions.

Changing Functions

Since colonial days some newspapers have had a special function as a local government's official newspaper. An *official newspaper,* according to Black's law dictionary, is one "designated by a state or municipal legislative body, or agents empowered by them, in which the public acts, resolves, advertisements, and notices are required to be published." For example, the laws of a city or state may require that the government publish a notice of candidates for office, of an auction of property taken over for failure to pay taxes, or of a building contract open for bids. When a local government designates a paper as its official newspaper, it pays the paper to print these notices and advertisements. In many cities and towns the official newspaper is the community's main daily or weekly, but in large cities it is often a specialized legal or commercial newspaper. Since colonial times, local governments have subsidized selected newspapers with legal advertising. Sometimes the subsidy made the difference between survival and bankruptcy for the newspaper.

Looking at a newspaper's functions more generally, we find some changes from colonial times to the present. American papers shortly after the Revolution could be classified into two categories: (1) *political papers,* which were the organs of political parties or factions and argued their point of view, and (2) *commercial papers,* which simply recorded commercial transactions and business matters such as the comings and goings of ships. The newspapers' own definition of their function was limited, and so were their audiences.

Ben Day's *New York Sun* did something else, and along with the rest of the penny press it spurred a revolution in communication in the 1830s. Day offered his readers the news that was nearest at hand — the incidental happenings of New York life.

The *Sun* was filled with news of human interest about common people. In its first issue, Day declared: "The object of this paper is to lay before the public, at a price within the means of everyone, all the news of the day, and at the same time afford an advantageous medium for advertising."[5] The penny press expanded the range of topics that newspapers surveyed and correlated, and it did far more to entertain its audiences than previous papers had. And its audience grew in size. With the growth of American cities came the rise of mass-circulation newspapers.[6] Since the time of the penny press, American newspapers have included diverse content for a diverse, and large, audience.

American newspapers come in all types and sizes, but the *Sun*'s emphasis on New York life points up a characteristic that most American papers have shared, then and now: they are vigorously local papers; few are national papers. In France, Britain, and most other nations, the newspapers emphasize national news and national concerns. They are aimed not at one specific city or area but at a whole country; they are national papers with a national audience. American newspapers, in contrast, are regional papers with a distinctive local stamp. There are exceptions, of course. The *Christian Science Monitor* and the *Wall Street Journal*, for example, are national newspapers. But most American papers are associated with a particular area and give special attention to that area. Both the *New York Times* and the *Washington Post*, are read nationwide, but both give special attention to the news of their area and depend on that area for most of their readers. They frequently have news of their city on the front page and devote a section of the paper to news of their region.

Within their local areas, however, American newspapers appeal to a broad-based audience. Very few American papers are aimed at a particular social class or particular group. Rather they are aimed at the mass of people within their geographical area. To attract this heterogeneous group of people, most American papers try to fulfill many functions simultaneously: to inform, correlate, entertain, and serve as a marketplace for goods and services. Their dominant functions, however, have been to provide information and to serve as a marketplace.

Types of Newspapers

Newspapers are usually classified in terms of circulation, although several other categories are also useful.

Major Metropolitan Dailies. The major metropolitan dailies in the nation's largest cities have circulations in excess of 250,000 and a probable readership several times that. (*Circulation* is the number of copies sold; any copy sold may be read by several people.) They usually publish seven days a week, including a large Sunday paper that devotes considerable space to features on topics such as books, travel, the arts, and personalities. Major metropolitan newspapers, such as the *Chicago Tribune* or *Los Angeles Times,* often reach readers not only in their city or metropolitan area but also in several surrounding states. These papers may have national significance (the *New York Times*) or regional importance (the *Kansas City Star*) or primarily a local readership (the *Minneapolis Star*). They are distributed house to house by carriers or occasionally by mail.

The major metropolitan dailies include news, features, entertainment, sports, and opinions. They rely on the wire services for much of their national and international news, although a few have national staffs (usually based in Washington) and foreign correspondents in important cities around the world. Several have set up special investigative teams that put together detailed stories on local problems or scandals. For example, in 1980 the *Boston Globe*'s Spotlight team won a Pulitzer prize for a series of articles on Boston's transit system. In 1977 several *Chicago Sun-Times* reporters opened a tavern, keeping their identities a secret, and proceeded to document a flood of attempts by health inspectors, fire inspectors, and assorted other officials to extort money from them.

The vast majority of metropolitan newspapers are printed full size — usually approximately fourteen by twenty-two inches with six or seven columns. Some are tabloids — approximately twelve by sixteen inches with five columns. At one time tabloids were usually splashy, sensational newspapers in big cities. They were designed to capture attention for high sales on the street, and often they had large, bold headlines. Today tabloids include the strikingly sensational *New York Post* as well as the more sedate *Christian Science Monitor.*

Medium-sized and Small Dailies. Medium-sized dailies may have modest circulations (say, between 50,000 and 100,000), but they are often physically hefty. They may have fewer of their own editorial resources than the major dailies, but they can use the news and features supplied by the wire services. They may also subscribe to syndicates that provide feature material, comics, and political columns. Some medium-sized dailies have regional circulations, but most try to provide local news not readily available from other sources.

Small dailies have a circulation under 50,000. They are even more localized than medium-sized dailies and sometimes are meant to be read along with a larger, nearby regional paper. Usually physically smaller than other dailies, they use less material from external sources such as the wire services than the medium-sized dailies do.

Weekly Newspapers. Sometimes called the *community* or *grassroots press,* the weeklies were once exclusively rural or suburban publications. They ranged from sophisticated suburban papers that featured lifestyle stories (for example, on apartment living or how to fund a day-care center) to small country papers dominated by local events and country correspondence.

Although most of these papers have survived into the 1980s, an increasing number of new urban weeklies have developed. Some concentrate on their own neighborhood; others are sophisticated, cosmopolitan publications that review such things as politics and the arts. Urban weeklies like New York's *Village Voice,* Chicago's *Reader,* and Boston's *Real Paper,* for example, are mainly supplementary reading for people who are already informed about public affairs from other media.

Most weeklies are local papers in local communities, although there have been some notable national weeklies. The family-oriented feature paper *Grit,* published in Pennsylvania, has been serving people in small towns across America for generations. The *National Observer,* which died in 1977, appealed to Americans nationwide, presenting magazinelike content — feature articles and interpretations about the nation — in a newspaper format.

The Ethnic Press. Since colonial days the ethnic press has been a part of American journalism. It has included both foreign-language papers and papers written in English but aimed at a particular ethnic group.

At one time there was a substantial foreign-language press in America. In the colonial period papers in French were common. Later, during the late nineteenth century, German and Scandinavian papers prospered. But as an immigrant group assimilates into the general population, its foreign-language papers tend to die out. Thus German-language papers are less common today than they once were, while the number of Spanish-language papers is increasing. In the late 1970s a rash of Vietnamese-language papers were started in various cities to serve that newly arrived group of immigrants.

English-language papers serving racial and cultural minorities are more common today than foreign-language papers. The black press in America began in the nineteenth century. From 1827 to 1830 John B. Russworm issued the periodical *Freedom's Journal* to counter the attacks on blacks by New York papers. In 1847 Frederick Douglass began publication of his *North Star,* later called *Frederick Douglass' Paper.* In 1855 Francisco P. Ramirez founded *El Clamor Publico* ("The Public Outcry") to give Mexican-Americans a voice. Today there are more than a hundred black newspapers, including the *Baltimore Afro-American, Bilalian News, The Amsterdam News*, and the *Chicago Defender.* Prominent Mexican-American newspapers include *La Raza* (Los Angeles), *La Guardia* (Milwaukee), and *El Grito del Norte* (Albuquerque). Indian papers include *Cherokee Advocate* (Oklahoma) and the *Yakima Nation Review* (Washington). For the most part these papers are community weeklies that give close attention to local people and local affairs, but they also take on broader issues that affect their readers.

Most black newspapers developed when the white-dominated press ignored black people. Many began to falter in the 1970s, although some, such as the Black Muslim paper *Bilalian News,* gained circulation. The prognosis for the black press by 1980 was uncertain, in part because the white-dominated media were giving greater attention to black Americans. Similarly, black journalists in the 1980s are more likely to find jobs in the conventional press because of affirmative action in hiring.

Other Specialized Newspapers. The list of specialized papers can go on and on. There are many industrial and commercial newspapers; labor newspapers; religious newspapers; hobby, voluntary association, and other special-interest newspapers; and, of course, college newspapers. There are even prison newspapers. Specialized newspapers are aimed at a very specific group of people rather than a general audience, and in that sense they fall outside our definition of newspapers as a mass medium. Some of these papers are supported not by advertising but by membership fees or an organization's profits.

Alternative Newspapers. Yet another type is the alternative newspaper, which is aimed at countering the majority press through unconventional messages. In the 1960s underground newspapers emerged to cater to participants in the counterculture. They were mainly concerned with such matters as psychedelic art, drugs, rock music, and political and social causes. Most had died by the mid-1970s. The few that survived, including the Boston *Phoenix*

el Diario La Prensa — Campeón de los hispanos

EDICION NACIONAL — VOL. XXXI — No. 10074 — NUEVA YORK · MIERCOLES 18 DE JUNIO DE 1980 — 25¢

Guerrilleros de Colombia rechazan oferta de paz

Incluirán en el censo a los indocumentados

Deja de publicarse la revista "Harper's"

El séptimo en cuatro años

Abandona a Koch otro de sus vicealcaldes

RINDEN HONORES A HUSSEIN

combatting racism in the women's movement

THE MILITANT
A SOCIALIST NEWSWEEKLY/PUBLISHED IN THE INTERESTS OF THE WORKING PEOPLE

JUNE 13, 1980 · 60 CENTS · VOLUME 44/NUMBER 22

Upsurge in S. Africa

Students, workers challenge racist regime

Left, Johannesburg students march to protest segregation and discrimination in education. Above, cops attack student demonstrators. Repression has not stopped spread of protests, which include new wave of strikes by Black workers. Page 5.

TOP LEFT. *Minority groups like Hispanic Americans find news of special interest in ethnic papers like this one. A longstanding tradition in American journalism, the ethnic press dates back to the 1790s, when French language papers were published. Today, new newspapers are being published in Vietnamese and Cambodian.*

TOP RIGHT. *This example of the growing feminist press provides information of special interest to women and serves as a voice for feminist causes.*

BOTTOM LEFT. The Militant *is an unabashed advocate for leftist causes.*

and the Los Angeles *Free Press,* are a far cry from their earlier forms. Rather than urging the cause of a counterculture and social change, they now provide some coverage of politics plus a large dose of fairly conventional information on the arts and local entertainment.

The alternative newspapers clearly represented dissatisfaction with the prevailing standards and styles of journalism in America. Closely related to them are muckraking papers like the investigative and scrappy *San Francisco Bay Guardian* and the *Maine Times,* a paper largely concerned with the quality of life and environmental issues in Maine. Another paper, *The Willamette Week* of Portland, Oregon, got a reputation for quality journalism by winning important prizes, much to the envy of the city's major dailies.

Trends in the Newspaper Industry

By 1980 all these newspapers employed nearly 400,000 Americans. Their salaries — as well as all the other costs of the newspapers — were paid principally by advertising. The newsstand price accounts for only about one-fourth of a newspaper's revenues; advertising accounts for about three-fourths. To get these advertising dollars, newspapers today must compete with radio, television, magazines, and direct-mail advertising. This competition has led to some changes in newspapers, but on the whole they are faring pretty well. To put together a profile of the state of the industry, we can ask how many papers are sold, how many are published, who owns them, and how profitable they are.

Circulation and Changes in American Papers. Total circulation of daily newspapers in America has climbed from about 51 million in 1946 to almost 62 million in 1978. Except for declining circulations in 1974–1976, the growth in circulation has been pretty steady. Circulation per household, however, has declined; the American population has grown faster than newspaper circulation. Newspaper circulations may be barely holding out against the competition of other media, both print and broadcasting.

When the appearance of radio threatened newspapers, they began to emphasize the news "scoop" less; radio, after all, could always get the news out faster. Instead, newspapers emphasized the details and the significance of the news, which they could supply better than the radio could. When newspapers in the 1960s and 1970s feared they were losing out to other media, they began to give less emphasis to "hard" news and more attention to lifestyle and consumer issues. Even the *New York Times,* known for its tendency to be staid and serious as well as reliable, now includes special sections each week on the Home, Living, and the Weekend. In a typical newspaper today you might find, in addition to the 60 percent of the space given over to advertsing, 20 percent to features, columns, sports, comics, and so on, and 20 percent to news.

The changes in newspapers were not all negative. For one thing, they confirm pretty well what people will actually read in a newspaper. For another, some changes in news coverage might be beneficial. Educator Todd Hunt has spoken of a trend away from *event-centered news* — such as stories on fires, meetings, or political speeches — and toward *process-centered news* — such as economic analyses, stories on cultural trends, and background reports on political decisions.

Changes in coverage have been aimed at one group especially: the youth market, those in their late teens to late twenties. A few years ago newspaper executives were alarmed by studies showing that young people were not becoming newspaper readers, much less newspaper buyers. The trend portended a bleak future for newspapers and did not please advertisers. People in this age group, after all, are among those whom advertisers most want to reach. As a result, the Newspaper Advertising Council in 1977 urged newspapers to provide more material of interest to young people. The result was special sections and more coverage of entertainment and clothing.

These changes have tended to make newspapers lighter and more like light magazines in their content and have been accompanied by similar changes in format. Some papers once included as many as nine columns of rather small type. By the early 1980s, however, most papers had reduced the number of columns, adding white space between columns and reducing the size of the page. The result looks easier to read. Other changes in design, including greater use of drawings and color by some papers, have made them visually more appealing.

The Number of American Papers. Between 1880 and 1900, the number of newspapers in America more than doubled — from 850 to 1,967. After 1910, however, when the country had 2,202 English-language dailies and 400 foreign-language dailies, the number of papers began to decline. Some papers merged; some dailies became weeklies; others suspended publication completely. The number of newspapers declined from 2,042 in 1920 to just under 1,800 in 1945. Since 1945 the number of papers has stayed fairly constant at around 1,750.

The story is a bit more complicated than these numbers suggest, however. Data on *weekly* newspapers show a steady decline in their numbers since 1960 but a continued growth in total weekly circulation and estimated readership. The number of small dailies (under 50,000 circulation) has generally decreased since the end of World War II, whereas the number of middle-sized papers (between 50,000 and 100,000 circulation) has grown markedly. Especially noteworthy is the fact that the number of all dailies with circulations over 50,000 has grown markedly. The number of dailies with circulations over 250,000 (that is, the major metropolitan papers) has remained rather stable.

These numbers suggest that the economy will support a more or less fixed number of papers. This notion is supported by the large sums that publishers have been willing to pay to buy existing newspapers. If there were a market to support new papers, they would not be willing to pay so much for existing ones.

The Owners of American Papers. While the number of papers has remained pretty stable in recent years, the number of independent papers has declined. The small, individually owned business in America has often been assimilated into giant corporate enterprises. So it is with newspapers. Small, independent, family-owned papers have been sold to newspaper groups or chains.

Chains are nothing new. But in recent years chains have been buying chains, and groups have been gobbling up groups. The media gave considerable attention to the Australian press lord Rupert Murdoch, who came to America and began buying up newspapers and magazines. But the impact of Murdoch, who owns newspapers in Texas and New York (where he bought the *New York Post*, the *Village Voice*, and *New York* magazine) is small compared with that of other takeovers that have occurred with less public fanfare. For example, by 1980 the Gannett Corporation owned eighty daily newspapers, as well as seven television stations and twelve radio stations in thirty-three states; according to *Fortune* magazine, it was one of the nation's 500 largest companies. The Times-Mirror Company, which has even larger financial resources than Gannett, owns the *Los Angeles Times*, *Newsday* (on Long Island, N.Y.), and the *Dallas Times-Herald* as well as several book publishers, magazines, television stations, paper mills, and cable television companies.

Most communications enterprises are owned by companies that specialize in communications; but lately other corporations have moved into the communications field. Media critics like Ben Bagdikian have warned that in a few years a handful of insurance companies, oil companies, and other corporate enterprises might have a stranglehold on the American media, especially newspapers. This prospect is even more alarming than dominance by large communications industries for two reasons: with its far-flung and diverse economic interests, the conglomerate is more likely to have reasons to bias the news; and it is less likely that the managers of a conglomerate will see the newspaper as an institution with special responsibilities to the public as well as a business.

Ownership and Content. Does the trend toward consolidation of newspapers and their ownership matter? What have the economic trends meant for newspaper content and personnel?

In 1945 Justice Hugo Black declared that the First Amendment guarantee of a free press "rests on the assumption that the widest possible dissemination of information *from diverse and antagonistic sources* is essential to the well-being of the public" (italics added).[7] The trend is surely away from "diverse and antagonistic sources" of the news. For example, the Cox Broadcasting Company, which owns newspapers as well as other media outlets, reaches 83 percent of the homes in Georgia. No other organization in the state comes close to matching its influence.[8]

Whether ownership patterns in fact influence content is not altogether clear, however. Some observers say that editors are losing their authority and power and have less influence on the contents of their papers. They become responsible to corporate managers who may or may not understand the special mission and purposes of newspapers. Some feel that the chains and corporate ownership have led to a sameness and blandness in newspaper content. One study of the presidential endorsements of chain-owned newspapers found that papers within a chain tended to endorse the same candidate; generally, the study found less divergence of opinion once a newspaper had become part of a chain.

On the other hand, Ben Bagdikian, who is generally a caustic critic of chain ownership, has said, "I think [the result] varies greatly. Some [papers] were schlock operations before they were bought and they are schlock operations now."[9] Spokespersons for chains tend to say that local papers are autonomous in spirit and that local control of their contents prevails. Allen Neuharth, president of the Gannett group, disputes those who decry the impact on quality. He has noted that group ownership can give a local paper access to a well-staffed Washington bureau and to other resources that enrich its content.

For the staffs, chain ownership may mean absentee management. New people may join the newspaper and may decrease its local orientation. According to Bagdikian, "With notable exceptions I find there is usually less satisfaction among the staff of newspapers that have been bought by chains."[10]

Profits. Whatever the effect of consolidation of newspaper ownership, the trend seems unlikely to change. Newspapers are attractive purchases because newspapers are, by and large, profitable. In spite of publishers' laments, newspaper profits were never higher than in the 1970s. As one commentator wrote, "Except for a handful of big-city dailies beset by problems endemic to metropolitan regions, the newspaper ledger shows blue ink, and lots of it."[11]

Information on newspaper profits is somewhat fragmentary, however, because many newspapers are still privately held companies. But a 1971 report showed that, for those newspapers whose stock was publicly traded, the average return on sales was almost twice the average return for the nation's 500 leading corporations.[12] Similar reports have reinforced this picture of a profitable industry. There is little doubt that today's newspapers—large, small, and medium-sized—are profitable industries.

Criticism of Newspapers

For as long as they have existed newspapers have been criticized. In the 1960s the criticism was fierce. Fueled in part by the general social discontent of the time, press observers and analysts began to criticize all manner of newspaper sins of commission and omission. The press was blasted in the 1960s for poor coverage of issues such as the Vietnam War, student unrest, and race relations and for its failure to cover minorities, the poor, the aged, and others. Hardly an interest group, from black Americans to consumer advocates, was satisfied with the newspapers, and they said so. In the late 1960s and early 1970s, former Vice President Spiro Agnew claimed that the press was controlled by liberals. Then in the late 1970s other conservatives complained that newspapers were not covering adequately the taxpayers' revolt and the campaigns for the death penalty and against abortions. Both the style and the substance of newspapers were targets for criticism.

Objectivity and Its Opponents. At the heart of many critiques of the press was an assault on objectivity, a style of reporting that has been the accepted standard in American newspapers for decades. *Objective reporting* attempts to be impersonal and factual; it is based on the idea that fact and opinion can be separated. Defenders of this style say that by removing emotion and personal involvement from their stories, fairness and a balancing of interests is ensured. Critics claimed that the objective form was not objective — that is, unbiased — at all. Often, they said, it was a cover for repeating the government's line as fact and thus for supporting the status quo. No matter how impersonal the tone of a story, the selection and ordering of what was to be said was subjective and, again opponents claimed, biased in favor of the status quo. Readers would be better informed, they claimed, if reporters did not pretend to be objective but instead let their feelings and opinions be known.

This criticism of objectivity came from the press itself, especially reporters; from groups that demanded a change in the coverage of their activities; and from analysts in universities and critics in government, to name a few. The result was the appearance of new styles of writing. Some journalists practiced what came to be called the *New Journalism*. Found more in magazines than in newspapers, this style allowed color and feeling in newswriting. Some practitioners of the New Journalism used interior monologues (reporting what people said they thought), extensive descriptions, and other methods usually found in fiction writing.

The New Journalism made room for the emotions and personalities of reporters. Other journalists wanted to practice *advocacy journalism*, which made room for their political beliefs. In advocacy journalism the reporter takes a point of view, identifying with a particular cause or purpose. Through advocacy journalism journalists felt they could become participants rather than mere observers.

Interest in the New Journalism and advocacy journalism has slowly faded, but not without leaving a decided mark. Newswriting generally is more creative and flexible today than before they came on the scene, and advocacy pieces continue to appear.

What Is Covered: Deciding the News. New Journalism and advocacy journalism were attempts by reporters to change the way the news is reported; the *media access movement* was an attempt by outsiders to change the content that is reported. It was an attempt to open the newspapers to those outside the industry.

The media access movement was based on what one law professor called a "positive interpretation" of the news. Professor Jerome Barron argued that when the framers of the Constitution wrote the First Amendment, they meant that *all* the people have a right to freedom of the press, not just the owners of the media. Barron claimed that all people should have the legal right to buy advertising and reply to editorials in the print media. The fairness doctrine developed by the FCC grants equal time for people to reply to comments made on television and radio; Barron wanted the fairness doctrine to apply to the print media as well.

Barron pressed his case in speeches and articles and received support from many consumer groups. But newspaper editors were livid. Barron's position amounted to an assault on freedom, they said. Newspapers have a right to decide what is news and what to edit, they claimed.

The debate came to a head when a Florida state legislator discovered a little-known state law that required newspapers to provide space for a reply to a personal attack. He decided to test the law, claiming his right to reply. In 1974 the U.S. Supreme Court decided against the legislator's claim — and against Barron's interpretation of the First Amendment (*Miami Herald* v. *Tornillo*). Citizens do not have a right of access, said the Court, and the Florida law interfered with freedom of the press

> because of its intrusion into the function of editors. . . .
> The choice of material . . . the treatment of public issues and public officials — whether fair or unfair — constitutes the exercise of editorial control or judgment. It has yet to be demonstrated how government regulation of this process can be exercised consistent with First Amendment guarantees of a free press.

No legislature can force a newspaper to be responsible.

The media access movement was only one form of criticism of newspaper coverage. More generally, the way newspapers define what is *news* often seems curious. Those committed to a cause are most likely to question the completeness and fairness of coverage. But even impartial observers can be perplexed by and critical of what is and is not reported. Why is famine in Cambodia on the front pages almost everywhere for a few days and then forgotten for weeks? Was Jimmy Carter's fight with a rabbit or Gerald Ford's stumbling out of planes really news? The significance of events may be secondary in determining what newspapers cover. At least two other questions seem to help determine their coverage: what are other media saying, and what is new and different?

Forums for Criticism. Out of the rumblings of many critics came several instruments for criticism of the press. These are especially relevant to newspapers but they apply to magazines and broadcasting as well. One is the *press council*, a voluntary organization of citizens that is intended to provide a forum for criticism of the press. It has no formal powers in the United States, but by identifying newspaper practices — both good and bad — it can be a moral force.

The roots of the press council movement can be found in several foreign countries and in the 1947 Report of the Commission on Freedom of the Press. Sweden's first press council was founded in 1916; in Britain a press council was first established in 1953. The first American press councils started in small communities like Littleton, Colorado, mainly on an experimental basis. In the late 1960s William L. Rivers started councils in several cities in the West. Other local councils followed, some of which survive today. A statewide press council was begun in Minnesota in 1971, followed by one in Hawaii and another in Delaware. In 1973 the National Media Council, with headquarters in New York, was established. The press councils today are forums where citizens can meet with publishers and voice their complaints, but they have no direct control over the press.

Another result of the new wave of criticism was the *journalism review*. Unlike press councils, journalism reviews are run by the people who work for a newspaper or broadcast station. Their purpose is to criticize their own newspapers or stations and bring about changes. This move by journalists to engage in systematic self-criticism on a regular basis was unprecedented. It was part of the so-called reporter-power movement in which newspaper reporters and others demanded a larger voice in newspaper policy.

One of the first reviews was established in 1968 in Chicago. Before long there were reviews in nearly twenty U.S. cities. Maintaining the reviews required considerable personal sacrifice and enthusiasm, but meanwhile media criticism became fashionable. Major magazines and newspapers began to feature critical articles and explanations of their internal operations. The need for the tiny journalist-run reviews was not compelling. Most simply died, although a few remained in existence in the late 1970s. Indeed, a new review was begun in Washington, D.C., in 1977.

Other instruments of media criticism also emerged in the 1970s. Some newspapers appointed readers' representatives, or *ombudsmen*, to handle citizen complaints. In some cities worker-participation committees gave reporters and other newspaper personnel greater authority in running their own organizations. These moves were a step short of democracy in the newsroom, but they did expand participation in policy making.

A Balance Sheet. By the standards of businesses, newspapers are doing well: they are profitable. We have seen that circulation is increasing as the number of papers holds steady and their ownership is consolidated into fewer and fewer hands. Fearing that they were in danger of losing their audience and their advertisers in the 1970s, newspapers adapted, changing their content and format to be more appealing to the mass of readers.

By the standards of their critics in the 1960s and early 1970s, however, newspapers have not done so well, although they have certainly changed. No one reform movement was able to bring about striking change, but together they had an effect on style and coverage. Newspapers today are less objective; they include more interpretive articles as well as more personal stories. These changes might result from publishers' opinions of what readers like rather than political criticisms of the objective style, but they are changes nonetheless. Coverage of women and minorities is substantially greater than it was twenty or even ten years ago, and there are more ways for the public to criticize newspapers. In becoming more like magazines, newspapers have become better at offering interpretations to their readers. Whether they have become better at what has been their main function for decades — providing their readers the basic news — is questionable at best.

Magazines

Just what is a magazine and how does it differ from a newspaper? Generally, a magazine is published less frequently than a newspaper. It is also manufactured in a different format — usually on better-quality paper, bound rather than just folded, and with some kind of cover. There are exceptions to all these characteristics, but for the most part they satisfactorily distinguish the form of magazines from that of newspapers.

To these differences in form we can correlate differences in the functions and audience of magazines. Because they are published less often than newspapers, magazines can look into issues and situations more carefully. Magazines have less concern for information on the immediate day's events and more for interpreting and correlating topics in a broader context. Historically, according to Roland Wolseley, magazines have appealed to a regional or national audience and have been free of fierce localism of newspapers. Theodore Peterson offered this succinct description of magazines:

> Although the magazine lacked the immediacy of the broadcast media and the newspaper, it nevertheless was timely enough to deal with the flow of events. Its timeliness and continuity set it apart from the book. As a continuing publication, it could provide a form of discussion by carrying responses from its audience, could

FEBRUARY 1902

HARPER'S MONTHLY MAGAZINE

PRICE 35 CENTS

HARPER & BROTHERS
NEW YORK AND LONDON

McCLURE'S MAGAZINE

APRIL, 1904

Enemies of the Republic
By LINCOLN STEFFENS

The Breaking Up of the
Standard Oil Trust
By IDA M. TARBELL

The Negro—Part Two
By THOMAS NELSON PAGE

SEVEN SHORT STORIES

Illustrations in Color

S. S. McCLURE CO. NEW YORK AND LONDON

DAMON RUNYON'S New Humorous Story

FAITH BALDWIN · MARGARET CULKIN BANNING · MARTHA OSTENSO

THE FOUR BOOK MAGAZINE

Cosmopolitan

Early twentieth-century magazines had national circulations and published fiction and nonfiction alike. Their function was to inform, influence, and entertain. Harper's showcased quality fiction and essays from leading authors. McClure's carried the writing of such famous muckraking journalists as Lincoln Steffens and Ira Tarbell. But not all magazines were strictly sober, as this issue of Cosmopolitan indicates.

sustain campaigns for indefinite periods, and could work for cumulative rather than single impact. Yet its available space and the reading habits of its audience enabled it to give fairly lengthy treatment to the subjects it covered. Like the other print media it appealed more to the intellect than to the senses and emotions of its audience. It was not as transient as the broadcast media, nor did it require attention at a given time; it was not as soon discarded as the newspaper; its issues remained in readers' homes for weeks, for months, sometimes even for years. In short, the magazine by its nature met well the requirements for a medium of instruction and interpretation for the leisurely, critical reader.[13]

The Development of American Magazines

In its early years the American magazine was primarily a genteel journal intended for an elite group of people. Magazines around the time of the Civil War were publishing short stories, novels, poems, scholarly essays, and political and social commentary. Several magazines of this period survived into the twentieth century, including *North American Review* (founded in 1815), *Harper's Monthly* (1850), and *Atlantic Monthly* (1857).

As the century was ending, the magazine industry was expanding and diversifying. Advertisers were eager to reach women, and they did so through such magazines as *Ladies Home Journal*, *McCall's*, and *Woman's Home Companion*. The 1880s and 1890s saw the beginning of several new mass-circulation magazines that included both fiction and nonfiction, such as *Collier's*, *Cosmopolitan*, *McClure's*, and the *Saturday Evening Post*. In addition, magazines appealing to every interest, every philosophy, and every profession appeared.

The early years of this century were dominated by the muckraking magazines. The name was given to the magazines by President Theodore Roosevelt to express his disdain. Roosevelt likened the journalist to the "Man with the Muckrake" in *Pilgrim's Progress*, who would not look up from the filth on the floor even when he was offered a glittering crown. As early as the 1870s *Harper's Weekly* had campaigned to oust New York City's "Boss" Tweed; and another nineteenth-century magazine, *The Arena*, had attacked slums, sweatshops, and prostitution and demanded sanitation laws, birth control, and socialized medicine. But at the turn of the century such campaigns became common. Many magazines began to publish thorough exposés of corruption and abuses, and they were widely read. The muckrakers attacked corruption in the cities and bad practices in industry. The names of such reform-minded writers as Lincoln Steffens, Ida Tarbell, and Ray Stannard Baker became household words. Steffens produced the widely praised "Shame of the Cities" series, and Tarbell painstakingly developed her "History of the Standard Oil Company" over several years. Baker crafted a series of articles, titled "The Right to Work," on the problems of the working man and corruption in labor unions. All three of these authors appeared in *McClure's*. Both mass-circulation and opinion magazines joined in the muckraking.

Some magazines tried to push social change in ways other than investigative reports. *Cosmopolitan* had sent a correspondent to Spain to negotiate the purchase of Cuba during the Spanish-American War. The correspondent was ignored, but his dispatches made good copy. *Cosmopolitan* also sent good-will ambassadors to foreign countries, asking that they be allowed to meet with heads of state. It proposed an international language and an international congress and even started a national correspondence university complete with campus. Eventually, it too joined the muckrakers.

By World War I, interest in muckraking had declined, but new classes of magazines soon appeared. One was the *newsmagazine,* a term coined by Henry Luce and Briton Hadden when they founded *Time* in the 1920s. New concepts arose, too, such as the *digest* — a collection of excerpts from other publications. *Reader's Digest* is one of the most successful magazines of all times. The *New Yorker* was also founded in the 1920s. In 1936 the picture magazine *Life* was founded. In 1945 the black picture magazine *Ebony* was founded. For almost thirty years large, general-circulation magazines like *Life, Look, Collier's,* and the *Saturday Evening Post* were a dominant force in the magazine market. Magazines were far ahead of newspapers and books in the effective, sophisticated use of photographs and graphic design.

By the end of World War II magazines were slick and profitable; many were geared to the mass market. Then came television. Like television, magazines depend mostly on national advertising, and, like television, magazines offer both visual appeal and light entertainment. Thus, as television's popularity grew, the general mass-circulation magazine found its audience and its advertising revenues dwindling. Specialized magazines fared well, but many general-interest magazines, such as *Collier's* and *American,* succumbed to economic pressures in the 1950s. In the 1960s many others died, including the large picture magazines *Life* and *Look.*

Some returned in the 1970s, but in their new form they have smaller, more carefully targeted circulations.

By the 1980s mass-circulation magazines were all but defunct. In their place were thousands of special-interest magazines —from *Psychology Today* to *Parents* and *Skiing.* Magazines had become a more specialized medium that had great ability to reach people of selected ages, incomes, educational levels, and so on. There are still a few immensely popular magazines that appeal to the general population, including *TV Guide, Reader's Digest,* and *People.* But most magazines today are directed not to a broad, heterogeneous audience but to a more defined group with distinct interests. Computers help the publishing companies sort out persons into neat, demographic categories; the publishers then refine their products to match the interests of those readers. They target their magazine's content and tone to appeal to their discrete audiences. The specialized audience that magazines offer also appeals to many advertisers, who like to be able to target their advertising to likely consumers.

The Magazine Industry

Like newspapers, many magazines today are owned by chains, large corporations, and conglomerates. The most successful magazine publishers, in fact, are those who produce more than one magazine. If one magazine fails, they still have others to keep their company alive. Like newspapers, most magazines depend on advertising for a large part of their revenue since a magazine's selling price is usually less than the cost of production.

Audience ratings and audience surveys are important in determining the advertising rates that magazines, like other media, can command. But as Philip Dougherty has pointed out, there is an interesting twist for magazines:

> If an editor creates a magazine that is so on target that subscribers refuse to part with it, that's bad. If, however, the editor puts out a magazine that means so little to each individual that it gets passed from hand, to hand to hand, that's good. Reason: the more the magazine is passed along, the higher the total audience figure will be. In that way, the ad agency rates will look more efficient to agency people, who would be more likely to put the magazine on their media schedule. [That is, to buy ads in it.][14]

For magazines a very high reader-per-copy rate is 6 and a low rate is 1.8. Simmons Marketing Research reported in 1979 that the

Drawing by Gretchen Dow Simpson
© 1980 The New Yorker Magazine, Inc.

Increasingly, magazines have become specialized channels of communication, appealing to special interests or special audiences. There are still a few mass circulation general magazines, but they are definitely outnumbered by the scores of magazines devoted to a range of interests — science fiction, sports, fiction, city life, news.

New Yorker had a very high rate (6.1), while the *Saturday Review,* which competes for some of the same audience, had a relatively low rate (2.5 readers per copy).[15] So, although the circulation rates of the two magazines were about the same at that time, the *New Yorker* could charge twice as much for its ads as *Saturday Review* could. The *New Yorker's* popular cartoons were thought to be the main reason for its high pass-along rate. In an effort to be more competitive, the *Saturday Review* added cartoons and features.

Thus, like all other media a magazine must pay keen attention to its audience in order to survive. And many do not survive. In 1978 there were 9,732 periodicals in America, whereas in 1950 there had been just 6,960. But each year many die. American magazines seem to be in a continual process of birth, adaptation, and death. Because magazines rarely own their own printing presses, the initial investment needed to start a magazine is reduced, and so it is relatively easy to start a magazine. Maintaining it is more difficult. By one estimate, you can start a magazine with about $1 million, and in 1979 about 200 new magazines appeared. But only about twenty survived their first year.[16] Most leading observers of magazines agree that many magazines die because the publisher fails to strike a balance between revenue from circulation and revenue from advertising. Some magazines die because their publishers fail to fine-tune their product to meet changing fashions and interest.

Types of Magazines

The American magazine industry today provides a magazine for just about every income level, age, educational level, occupational group, and interest. In 1971 there were still about 600 general-interest magazines, but there were also a host of magazines devoted to particular subjects. A hint of this variety is found in the *Literary Market Place,* which sorts magazines by subject matter. Among its categories are art and architecture; book digests; business and finance; juveniles; adults and child study; fantasy and science fiction; farming and agriculture; and so on to travel, nature and sports; and women's interest, house and garden. *Writer's Market* uses another system of classifying magazines, as follows:

1. *Consumer magazines* These periodicals are purchased on newsstands or subscribed to by the general public at home. The major consumer magazines are also called the *slicks* because of the smooth paper on which they are printed. Slicks include such publications as *McCall's* and *Ebony.* Many are mass-circulation magazines. A subcategory is the secondary

consumer magazine, which concentrates on a specialized topic, such as religion or politics, but is still broadly circulated. Yet another subcategory is the so-called little magazine, a small-circulation journal that usually includes poetry, fiction, and commentary.

2. *Trade journals* Such publications as *Meat Packer Digest, Modern Machine Shop,* and *Publisher's Weekly* are also called the *businesspaper press.* Although aimed at people in a particular trade or commercial area, they speak to a whole industry or trade, not just to one firm or organization.

3. *Sponsored publications* These periodicals are the internal publications of particular organizations, unions, or other groups. They include publications like *Elks* and *American Legion* as well as the magazines that airlines publish and distribute on their flights, such as *Ambassador* (TWA) and *Passages* (Northwest Airlines). Sponsored publications include college and university magazines; customers' publications; magazines aimed at a company's dealers, agents, and franchisers; as well as various employee magazines.

4. *Farm publications* Ranging from *Farm Journal,* a rather general family-oriented farm magazine, to *Southern Hog Farmer,* which aims at Southerners concerned with hogs, these magazines are given a category of their own because of their large number and the degree of specialization within the farm press.

Although these categories are useful, the single category of consumer magazines hides a diversity of types, including the following:

Newsmagazines Serving as national newspapers in America, newsmagazines include *Time,* a Luce publication once known for its Republican bias which recently has become more liberal; *Newsweek,* a less doctrinaire publication with a generally liberal bias, owned by the Washington Post Company; the conservative *U.S. News & World Report,* with a strong pro-business orientation; and such newcomers as *Seven Days,* a radical left magazine that tries to counter the conventional newsmagazines.

City magazines Publications such as *New York, The Washingtonian,* and *New West* exemplify the city magazines, which grew up in the 1960s and tend to concentrate on the activities of a particular city or region. Most major cities and many smaller ones (for example, Albuquerque) now have city magzines that both investigate public affairs and try to sort out the local scene (especially entertainments and restaurants).

Sex magazines With their wide range of sometimes controversial publications, these publications have high circulations and generate high incomes. This group includes such general-interest sex magazines as *Playboy* and *Penthouse*, which have become increasingly respectable over the years. Sex magazines take pride in their fiction and nonfiction articles and interviews as well as in their suggestive photographs. There are also raunchier publications like *Hustler* and *Screw* and others that cater to people with unusual sexual appetites (for example, sadomasochism). Sex magazines are mainly designed for men, but some, such as *Playgirl*, are aimed at women.

Sport magazines Americans are preoccupied with sports of all kinds, and there are scores of magazines to satisfy their interests, ranging from the general *Sports Illustrated* and *Sport*, which cover a variety of sports, to specialized magazines covering just one sport — tennis, skiing, weightlifting, and so on. In fact, a new sports fashion will quickly generate magazines. When racquetball gained enthusiasts in the late 1970s, several racquetball magazines appeared. Sport magazines, like sex magazines, once seemed to be intended "for men only." Now, as women make up more and more of the audience for general sport magazines, some sport magazines designed for women have emerged.

Opinion magazines These include some of the oldest and most respected journals in America. They range from the venerable *Nation*, which has been publishing since the Civil War, to the *National Review*, a conservative magazine founded in the 1950s by columnist William Buckley. Some others are the liberal *New Leader*, *New Republic* and the *Progressive*, which received front-page headlines in 1979 when it clashed with the government over publication of a story describing how an H-bomb is made.

Intellectual magazines Such publications as *Commentary*, *American Scholar*, and *Partisan Review*, are very similar to the opinion magazines, but they usually have denser copy and are aimed at a more intellectual audience. Both the opinion magazines and the intellectual magazines pride themselves on "influencing the influential." They generally have small circulations.

Quality magazines Although these magazines are similar to opinion and intellectual magazines, they usually have slightly larger circulations (say, 500,000) and reach a more general audience than the intellectual journals. Some examples are the *Atlantic Monthly, Harper's*, the *Saturday Review*, the *Smithsonian*, and *National Geographic*.

Men's interest   These publications, such as *True: The Man's Magazine* and *Argosy*, sometimes overlap with sex magazines and sport magazines.

Women's interest magazines   Some of the most successful magazines in the country, with the highest circulations are aimed at women. The first American magazine in the nineteenth century to have a circulation of more than a million was *Ladies' Home Journal*, which continues today. Other magazines in this class are *Better Homes and Gardens, Good Housekeeping*, and *McCall's*. A women's interest magazine that departs from the traditional mold of women's periodicals is *Ms.*, which reflects a moderate feminist viewpoint.

Humor magazines   Taking hold in the 1870s with *Puck, The Comic Weekly*, humor magazines have been with us ever since and include the *National Lampoon, Mad*, and *Harpoon*. The *New Yorker* is not primarily a humor magazine, but its urbane humor has certainly contributed to its success. Closely related to humor magazines are the comic magazines and comic books, which are almost an industry in themselves.

Functions of Contemporary Magazines

We can also classify magazines by function. Some, such as the newsmagazine *Time* and the technical publication *Scientific American*, mainly inform. Others are intended mainly for entertainment, such as *Playboy* and *True Story*. Still others mainly persuade, including opinion magazines like the *New Republic* and *National Review* and those like the *Watchtower*, a religious magazine, that advocate a belief or ideology.

Some historians credit magazines with aiding social change, documenting their case with such evidence as child labor laws, the federal Food and Drug Act, and other political and social reforms that were advocated by the muckrakers and then implemented by government. Present knowledge of the dynamics of public opinion leads us to doubt that the muckrakers were the immediate cause of such changes. But undoubtedly they — and, later, other magazine writers — focused attention on needed changes and activated people to set in motion the forces that eventually delivered the reforms they demanded. Carey McWilliams, for many years the editor of *Nation*, has said that reform journalism is cyclical, rising and falling over time. At the high points of the cycle, magazine influence is presumably most pronounced.

Although television may be the most popular source of daily news, magazines have an interpretive function that can be quite profound. Throughout their history magazines have been at the forefront of fashion, ideas, and style, although no one would claim that their influence operated in isolation. They have clearly been instruments of surveillance, often delivering information ahead of the rest of the media. But they have been interested mainly in what we have called *correlation* — interpreting society and its parts, projecting trends, and explaining the meaning of the news by bringing together fragmented facts. Magazines, in other words, are the great interpreters.

Historian James P. Wood evaluated the role of the magazine:

> The magazine is, and it has been, a vehicle for communication among people, a medium for the transmission of facts, ideas and fancies. An improved vehicle now, it provides more efficient communication among more millions of people than it did over two centuries ago. It transmits more and different facts and more complicated ideas largely because the twentieth century has more of each to transmit than the eighteenth century, and because people today wish and need more knowledge and information. Its social force is greater because it reaches more readers who through their education are more receptive to ideas in print and who have learned, largely through magazines, to live in an extended social, political, and economic environment.[17]

Theodore Peterson has succinctly described the magazines' contributions to American life:

> First, magazines certainly were responsible in some measure for the social and political reforms made during the century. . . .
> Second, magazines not only interpreted issues and events but put them in national perspective. . . .
> Third, the national viewpoint of magazines no doubt fostered what might be called a sense of national community. . . .
> Fourth, magazines provided millions of Americans with low-cost entertainment. . . .
> Fifth, for millions of Americans the magazine was an inexpensive instructor in daily living. . . .
> Sixth, magazines were an educator in man's cultural heritage; and

Finally, one of the most reassuring strengths of magazines was their variety in entertainment, information and ideas.[18]

Magazines have often been ahead of other media in the way they package and present information and in their ability to target a well-defined audience. Other media have repeatedly copied magazines. Newspapers have become more like magazines both in marketing methods and in writing style. Even television has been affected. Various stations have recently developed "evening magazine" shows, and CBS's popular "Sixty Minutes" calls itself a television newsmagazine. These examples illustrate the popularity of the magazine's approach to information.

Books

Books share with other media the functions of informing, persuading, and entertaining, although unlike newspapers and magazines they usually do not include advertising. They differ from the other print media in that they are bound and covered and consecutive from beginning to end. Because books often take a year or more to produce, they are less timely than newspapers and magazines. More than the other media at least, books are made to last, and their form lends itself to the exploration and development of a topic or idea in depth.

These characteristics suit the book to a special role among the mass media. Most books sell only a few thousand copies. Even a national best seller will probably sell no more than 10 million copies — far, far less than the audience for many television programs. Yet the social importance of books can hardly be overestimated. They have promoted powerful ideas and have led to changes in institutions and people, even to revolutions. They are a major channel for transmitting the cultural heritage. Books are seen as delightful, but they are also seen as dangerous. Books have been banned from libraries and burned by dictators. Like opinion magazines, books often persuade the influential, and they have influenced beyond their actual sales and readership.

Between the authors of these powerful messages and the public lies the publishing company. The publisher's role is threefold: to select what will be published; to produce the physical artifact that is a book; and to take the risks involved in investing the money needed to convert the manuscript into a book and to promote and distribute it to the public. Most publishers, however, are private businesses, and they therefore have a fourth role: to make a profit. The industry's changing economics have influenced the way publishers carry out their other roles.

Book publishers seek to appeal to a wide range of audiences. The college audience, for example, provides a huge market for textbooks, which are published by many leading companies.

Trends in Book Publishing: An Overview

Books published early in America's history included religious works, almanacs, and political and social treatises. In the nineteenth century meticulous, scholarly publishers opened their doors, as did religious publishers. Their work was characterized by fine printing and leather binding, and it was aimed chiefly at a refined audience of educated people. Even in the nineteenth century, however, American publishers offered books for large audiences: cheap paperback novels, textbooks, and reference books, as well as works of literature and scholarship.

In the years between the turn of the century and the end of World War II, book publishing took an important turn toward greater commercialism. What it offered the public was determined more and more by a concern for profits. As education increased, so did the sale of textbooks and reference books. In the 1920s the Book-of-the-Month Club and the Literary Guild were founded, expanding the market for books by reaching those who were far from bookstores. Still, publishing was something of a gentleman's profession; it was not the place where one usually found either big money or the sharpest business skills.

It was after World War II that the publishing industry experienced significant change. Returning veterans from World War II, helped by the GI bill, filled colleges and universities to capacity, increasing the demand for textbooks. Larger numbers of children entered school than ever before. Book clubs expanded. The market for paperbacks grew as publishers distributed them in drugstores and newsstands. Technological changes soon allowed faster production of books.

All this resulted in dazzling growth in book publishing. The industry embraced more partners, relying on outsiders for more and more aspects of book production. What was once an industry of small family-owned enterprises went public. Looking for resources in order to take advantage of the new possibilities for growth, companies went public, issuing stock. Banks and investors began to put money into publishing companies. The 1960s began a period in which many publishing companies merged or were acquired by communications corporations or conglomerates. The Times Mirror Company, for example, bought several publishing companies, including New American Library and World Publishing Company. Xerox took over Ginn & Company and R. R. Bowker. As a result of these trends, publishing companies gained financial resources and business and marketing skills, but some publishers also lost autonomy in their decision making.

By 1980 publishing looked less like a craft and an intellectual enterprise and more like a modern industry. Critics feared that neither the meticulous craftsmanship of the traditional publishing industry nor intellectual standards would survive, and in their place would be "uniformity — conformity to the median of popular tastes." [19]

The Process of Publishing

Until recent decades publishers ran their own printing plants, binderies, and bookstores. Publishing companies were known for the quality of their printing and binding, among other things. Then the economics of publishing led publishers to give up these operations; now they contract with outside typesetters, printers, and binders to work on specific books. In fact they often hire people outside the company to design the inside and outside of their books, to draw illustrations, to research photographs, to proofread copy, and to do many of the other tasks that are part of the process of producing a book. Thus, as less of the craft of publishing is done by employees of the companies, publishers to a great extent are orchestrators, hiring and coordinating the work of many people outside the company.

Foremost of these "outsiders," of course, is the author. In most cases authors are not employees of a book's publisher, although some companies have experimented with staff-written books — a few successfully. Either the author or the publisher may initiate the idea for a book. Many authors, especially well-known ones, are represented by literary agents. Agents ferret out book ideas, negotiate with the publisher for authors, and know which publishing houses and which editors within those houses might be interested in a particular idea. The agent gets a percentage (usually 15 percent) of the author's share of a book's earnings. The author supplies a manuscript to the publisher.

The manuscript is processed by editors. Publishing companies have all kinds of editors with all kinds of titles, and their responsibilities vary from company to company. Among the tasks that may be assigned to one or several kinds of editors in a company are: generating ideas for books, finding authors, evaluating the quality of a manuscript or its sales potential, polishing the grammar of a manuscript, coordinating its production into a book, or developing illustrations. Other people design the book and the cover and check proofs.

For setting the manuscript into type, publishers hire outside companies called *compositors*. Publishers also buy paper from paper companies and contract with printers and binders. Sales representatives from the publishing company convince independent booksellers to carry the company's books or convince faculty members to assign their textbooks. (A few publishers also run bookstores of their own.)

Thus the publisher brings together a team that includes authors, editors, compositors, printers, and booksellers. In all this the publisher "is the grand strategist and organizer of the whole undertaking."[20] Through the various stages of book making, publishers try to control the cost, schedule, and quality of all the work done by people inside and outside the company. Their role, in writer Dan Lacy's words, is "somewhat analogous to that of a theater producer, or an independent film producer."[21]

Like producers, publishers — to some extent at least — have styles and reputations. In part these come from how they organize the process of publishing, how they tend to deal with authors, and the physical appearance of their books. Some companies are stodgy; others are bold. Some produce books as quickly and cheaply as possible, publishing books on events like the Jonestown massacre of 1979 while they are still front-page news. Others are known for their craftsmanship. Perhaps even more, however, companies are known by the kinds of books they choose to publish.

Types of Publishers and Types of Books

A few American publishers are known for their political point of view. For example, Devon-Adair is a conservative publisher, as is Arlington House. International Publishers is the official publishing organ of the American Communist party. Beacon Press of Boston is closely tied to the Unitarian Universalist Society and has a liberal political reputation. Other publishers are known for specializing in one subject, such as art or law.

More common is the distinction between *text publishers*, who produce educational or reference books, and *trade publishers*, who produce everything else, whether fiction or nonfiction. *University presses* form a third and smaller category. They are publishing houses associated with a university, and their books are intended primarily for scholars and scientists. Some companies specialize in hardback books, or in paperback books, or in *mass paperback* books, which are cheap and sold through grocery stores, supermarkets, and newsstands.

We can also classify books according to their audience and function, as follows:[22]

1. *Trade books,* including literature, biography, and all nonfiction books for general reading. These books are usually handled by retail bookstores.
2. *Textbooks,* including books for elementary and high schools,

Paperbound books account for the consider-able success of a good many publishers and for the growth of numerous bookstores, especially such chains as Dalton's and Waldenbooks.

colleges, and universities. These books are usually sold through educational institutions or college bookstores, but publishers make their sales pitches to state or local school boards or faculty members.

3. *Children's books,* sold through bookstores or to schools and libraries.
4. *Reference books,* including dictionaries, encyclopedias, atlases, and similar books. These require long and expensive preparation.
5. *Technical and scientific books,* such as manuals, original research, and technical reports.
6. *Scholarly publishing,* which can overlap with textbooks and scientific books.
7. *Law books,* which involve the codification of legal materials and constant updating.
8. *Medical books,* which also require frequent updating.

Trade books account for about 15 percent of book sales and textbooks for about 29 percent.[23] Encyclopedias and book club sales also account for a large share of the books published.

The Economics of Publishing

By 1980 American book publishers were turning out some 40,000 book titles a year. About two-thirds of these were new titles; the other third were reissues of old titles. In addition to these are the uncounted publications of the U.S. Government Printing Office, the nation's largest publisher. Some publishers are subsidized by religious, political, or educational organizations; but for the most part America's books are published by private companies trying to make a profit.

Writer Dan Lacy, commenting on the "essence of publishing as entrepreneurship," noted, "The publisher pays the costs and assumes the risks of issuing each book, and hence he occupies a highly speculative position."[24] Of course, authors also take a risk. Although they may get some money from the publisher before their books are published, almost all their money will come from *royalties* on the book — a percentage of the net sales. If the book does well, authors do well; if it does not, they do not. They don't even receive their royalties from the publisher until several months after the sales have occurred. The size of the royalty and the schedule for paying it are stated in a contract. The amounts vary considerably; a well-known author can often command a handsome royalty. Trade book authors usually get lower royalties than textbook authors.

Another branch of publishing that works very differently is called *subsidy publishing*, or the *vanity press*. In this type of publishing, the authors, not the publishers, pay for the printing of the book, and the authors receive nearly full returns on any sales. But this kind of publishing rarely pays off for the authors. They often end up with printing costs in the thousands and no returns at all. Authors who go to the vanity press have often failed to find a commercial publisher, however, and they have no other way to publish their books. Many books published by the vanity press are family histories, personal reminiscences, or other unlikely sellers. When you see an ad declaring "New York Publisher Seeks Authors," you can bet that it is a subsidy publisher seeking customers.

The vanity press is far outside the mainstream of American publishing. The center of that mainstream is found in the large publishing companies, most of which have their headquarters in New York. Retail sales of books in 1980 have been estimated at nearly $4 billion. Just 3.3 percent of the nation's publishers account for about 70 percent of book sales.[25]

Scattered all over the country, however, are many small publishing houses. In 1972 the R. R. Bowker Company listed more than

6,000 American publishers, but only about 1,000 published five or more titles.[26] A publishing company can begin with only one or two people and little equipment. They do not need printing presses; they hire outside printers and binders on a book-by-book basis. Unlike the small radio station or small newspaper, the small book publisher is not limited to a local audience. It is possible through promotion and advertising to command national attention and sales. Book publishers can thus begin with limited capital, publishing only a few titles until they begin to show a profit.

Many books, however, never turn a profit. Profits may, of course, be very high on a best seller, high enough to pay for other books that lose money or barely break even. Some economists have observed that book publishers would be better off publishing fewer books, concentrating on obtaining higher sales for those they do publish. Some critics attribute the tendency to produce a wide range of titles to optimism. Others say it results from the amount of competition. An author rejected by one publisher can go in search of another and is likely to find one or more who will take the manuscript if there is a chance (even a slim chance) that it could become a modest-to-good seller.

Even this somewhat staid industry uses modern marketing techniques. One method is a special prepublication price. Sometimes, working through book clubs or magazine ads, publishers offer a reduced rate for buying the book in advance of the publication date. A few companies, such as Time, Inc., and Reader's Digest, are mail-order publishers. They send out elaborate brochures describing a book or series of books to prospective buyers, elicit responses, and analyze the responses carefully. After this market research has been completed, the book is written. The replies to the brochure may lead to cancellation of the project or to changes in its proposed content, format, and promotion.

Book publishers operate under a number of limitations. It is said that there are too few retail bookstores. Traditionally publishers have had tiny advertising budgets compared with other consumer product industries. Perhaps more than other forms of print, books depend on other media. For example, they depend on magazines and newspapers to promote books through reviews as well as paid advertising. Authors are frequent guests on television and radio talk shows, where they promote their books.

Books in Perspective   Book publishing is not always as serious as it seems. Who can take seriously books with titles such as *The Non-Runner's Book* or

The Dieter's Guide to Weight Loss During Sex? Even publishers are willing to mock themselves. Workman House published a satire written by Christopher Cerf and several colleagues called *The 1980s: A Look Back at the Tumultuous Decade, 1980–1989.* Released in 1979, the book carried a 1990 publication date. In a spoof of special prepublication prices, advertisements said that the publisher's list price would be $69.95, but that the book was available to advance buyers for a mere $7.95. Publishers can also be unwitting accomplices in jokes on the industry. Several years ago publisher Lyle Stuart brought out a novel called *Naked Came the Stranger.* Supposedly written by a quiet homemaker named Penelope Ash, the book was promoted in ads and on television talk shows. A woman calling herself Ms. Ash even made public appearances. But it was later revealed that the real "author" of the book was several members of the staff of the Long Island Newspaper *Newsday.* They had agreed on an outline for the book, and then each one wrote a chapter.

Still, books are the most permanent and most serious medium, and they provide much of the content for other media. Films are often based on novels; magazines often popularize ideas that books have presented in full. Books are a key to the intellectual process in what is mainly an intellectual medium — print.

The Future of the Print Media

All forms of the print media — newspapers, magazines, and books — are not only channels of communication but also businesses that try to eke out a profit. All, but especially newspapers, are very profitable today, and they have a substantial role in American industry. They are doing battle with the electronic media for advertising dollars and have been more than holding their own. Critics claimed that the public would tire of print; McLuhan predicted the death of the medium. But many disagree. One of them, the distinguished magazine editor Norman Cousins, described the role of print well:

> We are confident that print will not only endure but will continue to be a primary force in the life of the mind. Nothing yet invented meets the intellectual needs of the brain so fully as print. The ability of the mind to convert little markings on paper into meaning is one of the ways civilization receives its basic energy.[27]

There can be no doubt that print remains a powerful force even in the face of the electronic media. Whether in the future words will be printed on paper (a scarce commodity in the contemporary world) or displayed on computer terminals is not particularly important, but most predictors say that print will survive in some form and will continue to give its audience a message with permanence and force.

Summary

In this chapter we have presented a perspective on print, the oldest medium, by looking first at the concepts of form, function, and audience. Print's three forms today are newspapers, magazines, and books. Its functions are to provide information, influence opinion, interpret the environment, transmit the social heritage, serve as a marketplace for goods and services, and entertain. The audience for these media as a whole is large and diverse, although many magazines and books are aimed at a specialized audience.

Newspapers in America are private, profit-making businesses with a special role: delivering the information that citizens in a democracy need. Since the early nineteenth century American newspapers have appealed to a large, diverse audience and have fulfilled diverse functions. Although there is great variety among American newspapers, most are fiercely local, not national, in their audience and perspective. For most of their revenue they depend on advertising. Many are owned by chains and conglomerates. In the 1960s and early 1970s newspapers were fiercely criticized for the style and content of their coverage; in the mid-1970s their circulation declined; and for decades they have faced competition from broadcasting. But newspapers adapted. They increased their coverage of "soft" and process-centered news, included more subjective writing and interpretation, increased their coverage of women and minorities, and brightened their appearance. Most are profitable today.

Like newspapers, magazines depend on advertising for most of their revenue, are often owned by chains and conglomerates, and have had to adapt in the face of competition from broadcasting. One result of this competition has been a decline of mass-circulation, general-interest magazines and an increase in magazines designed for specialized audiences. Magazines lack the immediacy of newspapers, but they often present a broader context and more depth in their discussion of ideas and events. They have often pushed new styles, new policies, and new ideas into the mainstream of American life.

Books have a smaller audience than magazines and newspapers and are less timely, but they are more lasting. They have been powerful instruments both for preserving the social heritage and for changing society. Between the authors of these powerful messages and the public stand the publishers. In recent decades publishers have become primarily orchestrators and risk takers. As orchestrators they bring together the author, the people who produce the physical book, and booksellers. As risk takers they invest the money to turn the manuscript into a book. Most publishers are private businesses; many are owned by large communications companies and conglomerates. Although many publishers now use modern marketing techniques, many books never earn a profit.

Notes and References

1. See Charles R. Wright, *Mass Communication: A Sociological Perspective*, 2nd ed. (New York: Random House, 1975) p. 9.
2. Ibid.
3. Robert E. Park, "The Natural History of the Newspaper," in *Mass Communication*, ed. Wilbur Schramm (Urbana: University of Illinois Press, 1960) pp. 8–9.
4. Ernest C. Hynds, *American Newspapers in the 1970s* (New York: Hastings House, 1975) p. 11.
5. *New York Sun*, September 3, 1833, p. 1.
6. See Edwin Emery, *The Press in America*, 3rd ed. (Englewood Cliffs, N.J.: Prentice-Hall, 1972) pp. 441–442.
7. *Associated Press et al.* v. *United States*, 326 U.S. 1 (1945).
8. Martin H. Seiden, *Who Owns the Mass Media?* (New York: Basic Books, 1974) p. 56.
9. Deirdre Carmody, "More Newspapers Change Hands With the Role of Chains Increasing," *New York Times*, February 15, 1977, p. 16.
10. Ibid.
11. Arnold H. Ismach, "The Economic Connection: Mass Media Profits, Ownership and Performance," in *Enduring Issues in Mass Communication*, ed. E. E. Dennis, D. M. Gillmor, and A. Ismach (St. Paul: West, 1978) pp. 243–259.
12. Ismach, "The Economic Connection," pp. 243–259.
13. Theodore Peterson, *Magazines in the Twentieth Century*, 2nd ed. (Urbana: University of Illinois Press, 1964) p. 442.
14. Philip Dougherty, "Saturday Review's New Drive," *New York Times*, April 12, 1979.
15. *New York Times*, April 12, 1979.
16. Thomas Collins, "Magazine Industry Growing but Mortality Rate Is High," *Los Angeles Times*, May 27, 1980.
17. James Playsted Wood, *Magazines in the United States*, 2nd ed. (New York: Ronald, 1956) p. 378.
18. Peterson, *Magazines*, p. 448.
19. Quoted in Charles A. Madison, *Book Publishing in America* (New York: McGraw-Hill, 1966) p. 402; see also Benjamin M. Compaine, *The Book Industry in Transition* (White Plains, N.Y.: Knowledge Industry, 1978).
20. Datus C. Smith, Jr., *A Guide to Book Publishing* (New York: R. R. Bowker, 1966) p. 7.

21. Dan Lacy, "The Economics of Publishing or Adam Smith and Literature," in *The American Reading Public* (New York: R. R. Bowker, 1965). Based on an issue of *Daedalus*.
22. See Smith, *Guide to Book Publishing*, pp. 128–129.
23. John P. Dessauer, *Book Publishing: What It Is, What It Does* (New York: R. R. Bowker, 1974) p. 23.
24. Lacy, "Economics of Publishing."
25. John P. Dessauer, "Book Publishing," *The ALA Yearbook* (American Library Association, 1976) p. 293.
26. Dessauer, *Book Publishing*, p. 22.
27. Quoted in Roland E. Wolseley, *The Changing Magazine* (New York: Hastings House, 1973).

5 The Broadcast Media

> One of the basic troubles with radio and television news is that both instruments have grown up as an incompatible combination of show business, advertising and news. Each of the three is a rather bizarre and demanding profession. And when you get all three under one roof, the dust never settles.
>
> EDWARD R. MURROW

Our definition of mass communication in Chapter 1 seems made to order for radio and television. The broadcasting industry sends out messages twenty-four hours a day according to detailed schedules, using such complicated technology as communications satellites. Every day it reaches millions of people, whatever their background, level of education, or interest. Radio of course came first, but television has not displaced it. The story of radio's survival and the current status of radio and television illustrate again the impact of one medium on others and the relationships among form, function, and audience.

We look first at the broadcasting industry as a whole, examining the technology that makes it possible, the way its communicators are organized, and the messages it sends. Then we examine radio and television in more detail, looking finally at what the future may hold for cable television.

Approaches to Broadcasting

The twentieth century, said British writer John Crosby, is the age of noise — "physical noise, mental noise and noise of desire — we hold history's record for all of them. And no wonder; for all the resources of our almost miraculous technology have been thrown into the current assault against silence."[1] Broadcasting led this assault. Although motion pictures and radio developed at about the same time, broadcasting brought the "noise" of the modern age right into people's homes and stayed there. Broadcasting enlarged people's reality in a way that film never could because film has been primarily an entertainment medium. Broadcasting brought events from faraway lands and gave people the sounds — and later the sights — by which they could know and understand the world and its people much better.

Mention the word *broadcasting* to a group of people, and they are likely to think of many different images: a television set, a disc jockey playing records, a favorite star, or a stock certificate in a broadcasting company. Broadcasting is all these things and more.

Defining Broadcasting

We are using the term *broadcasting* to refer to a particular type of telecommunication. *Telecommunication* is the general term for communicating over a distance using electromagnetic instruments.[2] In *point-to-point telecommunication* electromagnetic instruments are used for a direct, relatively personal kind of communication; for example, by telephone, teletype, mobile radio, or air-to-ground radio. A second type of telecommunication is *surveillance telecommunication*, which "scans the horizon," such as a search for danger signals. Surveillance telecommunication includes radar, atmospheric pollution monitoring, and weather-scanning devices. We are interested in a third type of telecommunication, *mass telecommunication*, which uses electromagnetic instruments to reach a mass audience simultaneously. This is *broadcasting*, which includes radio and television.

More than any of the other media, broadcasting meets the definition of mass communication set out in Chapter 1: messages are sent out regularly by professional communicators through mechanical media to a large, diverse audience. The broadcast media also fulfill all the functions of the print media outlined in Chapter 4: they are deeply involved in surveillance and correlation of the environment and in transmission of the social heritage. They also provide entertainment and advertising. To see just how broadcasting does all these things, we need to approach it from several angles, looking at broadcasting as a technology, as a production and distribution system, and as content.

Broadcasting as Technology

Broadcasting technology is a subject unto itself, involving everything from the early scientific experiments with radio waves to modern television cameras and global satellites, the theory and practice of information processing as well as engineering feats. Look inside a television station and you will see sophisticated transmitters, control rooms, cameras, videotape equipment, editing devices, microphones, and much more. Even in the home, the technology of broadcasting is becoming varied and complex. There may be not only radio and television sets but also videotape recorders, playback systems, giant screen receivers, and video games.

From this variety of technical devices we can isolate the essence of broadcasting as a technology: a means of transmitting electronically generated radio waves to receiving devices. The broadcasting station is the center for transmission. Basically, the transmitter generates two types of waves that it radiates into space. A lower-frequency wave carries information — that is, the sound or images to be broadcast. But the energy of this *information wave* is not sufficient to go through the air itself; hence it is superimposed on a high-frequency *carrier wave*.[3] It is in the transmitter that the information picked up by cameras or microphones is superimposed on the carrier wave. When the information wave is superimposed on the carrier wave, the carrier wave is said to be *modulated*.

This modulation can occur in two ways: amplitude modulation or frequency modulation. In *amplitude modulation* (*AM*) the height of the carrier wave is altered when the information wave is superimposed on it. In *frequency modulation* (*FM*) the frequency of the carrier wave is changed. AM broadcasts can reach a wide area, but FM is less affected by electrical disturbances and static. In television the video signal is amplitude-modulated and the audio signal is frequency-modulated. At the receiver the carrier wave is converted back to sound and/or images.

The transmitter is the heart of the broadcasting station, but the station may receive as well as send messages. Messages — from a television network, for example — may come to the station via microwave, coaxial cable, telephone wire, or satellite. (These are all point-to-point communication devices.) The broadcasting station then relays these messages.

Technological Development and Social Use

If we look at broadcasting only as a type of technology, much of the radio and television world will remain a mystery. For one thing, technological developments in the laboratory are often far ahead of their actual use in the world. For another, the uses eventually found for the technology often differ from what the inventors and technicians expected in their laboratories. How and when a technology moves from the laboratory to homes, streets, and businesses depends on economics, politics, and culture.

Guglielmo Marconi, the so-called father of radio, experienced this gap between the laboratory and the world. He began his earliest broadcasting experiments by testing his wireless telegraph on his father's estate in Italy. Thinking that his invention probably had great social consequences, Marconi tried to interest the Italian government in helping him finance his work. But the Italian government wasn't interested, and broadcasting lost some valuable time until Marconi took his ideas to England, where he was able to patent his device and obtain financial backing to develop it further.

Why is it that such innovations as Marconi's are not more quickly adopted? There are many reasons: economic realities, government regulation and policy, community interests, cultural habits, and others. It is common in industrial societies for the technological or material aspects of a culture to surge ahead of the society's ability to control and use the technology — a phenomenon called *culture lag*. New discoveries in atomic weaponry, for example, outpace attempts to find ways to control existing weapons. Fantastic advances in medical technology seldom reach the vast majority of people because development of the social systems needed to deliver medical services widely lags far behind.

The history of American broadcasting has also been marked by culture lag. For example, the first experimental televised image was transmitted between New York and Philadelphia as early as 1923; five years later the first regular television schedule was begun. Thirteen years later — in 1941 — the federal government authorized commercial television. By 1948 the great expansion in television was ready to begin, but television did not reach most of the American people until the 1950s. As we saw in Chapter 2, in part the lag in television's development was the result of World War II, when manufacturers turned away from production for consumers in order to make weapons and military supplies. Also, the government put a freeze on television licenses from 1948 to 1952 so that it would have time to develop a system of licensing stations in order to avoid the chaos that unfettered competition for stations might produce. Thus when the technology of television was ready for widespread use, its expansion was delayed while social and political systems caught up with it.

More recently, the federal government's regulations helped slow the growth of cable television. The development of other aspects of broadcasting has also lagged behind their potential. By the mid-1960s some futurists were saying that within ten years

America would be a "wired nation" with a vast system of television channels and information transmission units wired into every home. Arthur C. Clarke even predicted the end of travel and the development of an orbiting electronic post office. In fact many of the devices and uses envisioned by the futurists are technically feasible now, but most Americans do not have sophisticated information storage and retrieval systems in their homes, and old-fashioned over-the-air television still dominates broadcasting. The use of any new technology usually requires not just technological development but also economic, social, and sometimes even political adjustments.

Broadcasting has developed as a partnership of theoretical and applied science, idealists and entrepreneurs, commercial interests and regulations. Such a coalition of interests, working and battling together, has produced a broadcasting system that is neither very rational nor very systematic. The technology and the actual uses of the broadcast media have often seemed out of sorts with each other. Radio, for example, could have taken many directions as a medium. Its technology would have permitted the development of rational, efficient systems of broadcasting for business, education, or economic uses in the home. Indeed, some people predicted that radio would have just such uses. Instead, by the mid-1920s radio had become a medium of popular culture, with entertainment, news, and advertising. Even some of the most far-sighted pioneers of broadcasting failed to see how the business of broadcasting would evolve. They did not foresee the nature of the medium and its potential for massive development — commercially, culturally, and technologically.

The history of radio exemplifies the variety of forces that shape the transformation of technical knowledge into a technology in use. Inventors fought over patents; audiences used the infant medium in unexpected ways (broadcasting music from private transmitters, for example); and large companies and government took an interest in radio's development. Eventually it was a combination of social, economic, and political forces and decisions that gave broadcasting its place as a medium of communication. Three of the most important decisions determining that role were

- the decision to finance broadcasting by the sale of time to advertisers, which was an American Telephone and Telegraph innovation
- the formation of national networks, also inspired by AT&T
- the intervention of the federal government to establish order in the chaos that had arisen as stations competed for frequen-

cies over which to broadcast. The government provided a protective framework that allowed the forces of the private sector to work effectively.[4]

Both economics and politics were thus key forces in determining how the technical knowledge of broadcasting would be put into use. What they gave us is a broadcasting system composed chiefly of profit-making businesses broadcasting to a mass audience under the constraints of some government regulation.

Broadcasting as a Production and Distribution System

Broadcasting is far more than a technological system. We can imagine a broadcasting system that used basically the same technology in use today but with a very different organization and perhaps different uses. Suppose the federal government had established a monopoly on broadcasting for use as a way to keep its citizens informed. We might have only national programming, with live coverage of Congress and diplomatic visits and bulletins on new grants available to local governments. Or suppose that in cities across the nation local merchants had joined together to buy stations to sell their goods. We might have only local programming filled with descriptions of local goods and services for sale. Television and radio would then mean something far different to us. But those systems never developed. Broadcasting is not only a technological system but also a system for producing and distributing the messages that are to be communicated.

In the United States this system has both local and national components. It is mostly made up of private, profit-making enterprises. Although the system also involves public, noncommercial elements and government regulation, American broadcasting was founded on and remains committed to commercialism. Commercialism has been blamed for the quality of programming and for the excessive role of advertising in influencing broadcast decisions. On the other hand, commercialism has also been praised for helping to develop the most diversified system of broadcasting in the world. To understand this system, we look at both its organization and its economics.

The Organization of American Broadcasting. The most visible part of American broadcasting is the local station. Even though they range from tiny fifty-watt radio stations in isolated, rural communities to large metropolitan television operations, all radio and television stations have some similarities. The larger they get, the more complex they are, but they still have many of the same functions and the same departments.

A medium-sized radio and television station, for example, will have four main departments — program, engineering, sales, and business. In the program department a *program manager* supervises announcers, disc jockeys, a music librarian, a news director or coordinator, reporters, and a public affairs director. The engineering department is run by a *chief engineer* who supervises audio engineers, transmitting engineers, and (in the case of television) camera operators, projectionists, lighting directors, and design and maintenance engineers. The sales department is headed by a *sales manager* who supervises a national sales manager, a local sales staff, a traffic manager who handles the scheduling of commercials, as well as public relations and promotion people. Finally, a *business manager* runs the business department, coordinating accounting and payroll personnel and dealing with secretarial pools, purchasing, and janitorial services. Over all these departments and department heads is the *station manager,* whose position is similar to that of a newspaper publisher.

Broadcast news departments are part of the program department, and their personnel differ somewhat from those on a newspaper. The *news director* is in charge and has overall responsibility for what goes on the air. The news director manages people, equipment, and the budget. Then there are assignment editors, who help decide which stories will be covered, which reporters and camera personnel will cover them, and how much equipment will be used. Producers have direct responsibility for the content of a given newscast. Both the producer and the assignment editor work with the reporters, who go into the field to cover stories and then present them on the air, and with writers, who stay at the station rewriting stories and taking material over the phone from reporters. Both reporters and writers work with editors; at television stations the editors edit the film or videotape and put together the audio and video portions of the newscast.

Large radio and television stations may have specialist reporters who cover areas such as science, politics, and consumer affairs. More common are weathercasters, sportscasters, traffic reporters (who sometimes report from helicopters), and entertainment critics. The most prominent members of the news team are, of course, the announcers and anchorpersons.

Important as the local station is, it is only one part of the production and distribution system. Economist Bruce M. Owen and two colleagues have explained the workings of the broadcasting industry as the interaction of several major components, including

1. *Stations* Local broadcasting stations generate an audience, which they offer for sale to advertisers. They also transmit the

broadcast message and develop programs. Although stations may be owned by large nationwide companies, they are associated with a region or even a city, which greatly influences the content and advertising the station broadcasts.

2. *Networks* Many stations are affiliated with a network and give over a large percentage of their time to the network's programming. Others are independent and buy their programming from private production companies. The networks give American broadcasting a national component that supplements the localism of most broadcast stations. They provide a nationwide hook-up for local stations, making possible the nationwide distribution of some programs, technical services, and advertising. The networks are both suppliers, offering their own products to stations, and brokers, buying services and programs from others and then offering them to stations. The stations pay nothing for the programs they get from the networks. In fact, they receive a percentage of the revenue that the networks collect from the advertisers.

3. *Viewers and listeners* Without an audience, of course, there is no mass communication, and the size and composition of the audience determine the effectiveness and profitability of stations and networks. As Owens and his colleagues have said, "TV stations [and radio stations] are in the business of producing audiences. These audiences, or means of access to them, are sold to advertisers."[5]

4. *Advertisers* Commercial broadcasters receive their revenue from advertisements. To keep advertisers, a broadcaster constantly courts them and gives them data to show that his or her station is an effective vehicle for advertising.

The Economics of Broadcasting. Professor Harry J. Scornia is one person who thinks that broadcasting, especially television, is best analyzed as a business. After all, he wrote, "for over forty years broadcasting in the United States has been carried on principally as a business, conducted for profit, by corporation-trained leaders with a sales and business orientation."[6]

As a business, commercial broadcasting is a somewhat smaller industry than newspapers. It generates about $8.2 billion in revenues a year — compared with newspapers' $10.1 billion. But broadcasting's relatively modest place in the marketplace is somewhat deceptive. Besides those working directly for stations and networks, there are technicians who install and repair equipment and consultants who recommend ways to enhance profits. Assessing the full significance of broadcasting as an industry, wrote

Sydney W. Head, means taking into account "the secondary economic activities broadcasting creates or supports: manufacturing, sales, and servicing of receivers and equipment; electric power consumption; trade and consumer publications; advertising, talent, market research, legal and engineering services."[7]

As a business, broadcasting is based on advertising. Both local stations and networks depend on advertising for their revenues. There is local, regional, and national advertising. What stations and networks charge for air time depends on the time and day the commercials are aired and the expected size and composition of the audience. Since stations are selling audience attention, they must take care to offer their advertisers adequate data from rating services to show the number of eyes and ears in their audience. Advertisers want to know what kinds of people their listeners and viewers are, how many of them there are, and how closely they pay attention to the advertisers' messages. It's the job of a station to convince a sponsor that its advertising is more effective on that station than it would be on another station — or in a newspaper or magazine.

The relationship between stations and networks complicates the economics of broadcasting. The radio networks now receive less advertising revenue than local radio stations, but the opposite is true in television. If a television station is affiliated with a network, then its fortunes are closely tied to those of the network since network shows account for more than half of the affiliate's programming. The size of the audience for the network's shows will determine not only how much money the station gets from the network but also how much money it can command from advertisers for the station breaks that the networks leave open to local stations. If belonging to a network is not profitable to a station, it will end the relationship. During the late 1970s many stations shopped around and changed their network affiliations.

If a station manages its time well and finds a good mix of investment, costs, and revenue, it should make a profit. Broadcasting is known for giving excellent returns on investment. Some stations have annual profits of over 20 percent. In 1977 the industry reported profits of $1.6 billion. British media owner Lord Thompson once declared rather cynically that "a broadcast license is a license to print money."

The profitability of broadcasting has not gone unnoticed by large corporations. Stations are often part of chains or owned by national and sometimes multinational corporations and conglomerates. *Cross-media ownership* is common; that is, the same person or company owns both print and broadcast outlets. In fact nearly 30 percent of television stations are owned by newspapers;

in some communities one company owns almost all the principal media.

But the tendency toward the concentration of ownership in the media has not gone unnoticed by government. It has regulated both the number of stations any one company can own and cross-media ownership. In this and other ways, as we shall see, government is an important influence on the broadcast industry.

Noncommercial Broadcasting. Not all stations and networks are privately owned enterprises. There is also what has been called the "fourth network," which includes public broadcasting, stations operating as nonprofit corporations by local groups, communities, religious institutions, and universities. There has been a spectacular growth in Christian broadcasting — the so-called electronic church.

Public broadcasting gets its operating expenses from grants from the federal Corporation for Public Broadcasting and other agencies, state governments, universities, religious organizations, private donors, and others. Many public stations set aside time for pledge drives, when they urge the audience to call the station and pledge money to help support it. In recent years business gifts underwriting the cost of a program or series have been important. Thus public television stations announce that a "grant from Mobil Oil" or some other donor has made a program possible. For the corporation this arrangement means a chance to be portrayed as a public-spirited supporter of culture rather than a self-interested reaper of profits. For public braodcasting the arrangement has been a financial boon, but it has also raised questions about the independence of public broadcasting from their new-found benefactors.

The nation's public television has three main components: the Corporation for Public Broadcasting, which receives and distributes federal funds for the system; the Public Broadcasting Service, which manages the production and distribution of programs and connections among stations; and the local stations. The role of the Public Broadcasting Service is similar to that of the commercial networks, but the local stations have a more independent role than commercial stations. They produce many of the programs that are then shown nationwide. This system has been plagued by financial problems, by bickering between the Corporation for Public Broadcasting and the Public Broadcasting Service, and by controversy over how independent local stations should be.

Public broadcasting is meant to provide programs that commercial broadcasting cannot or will not support. The commercialism of the broadcast industry, it is often argued, has given us not only the ever-present commercial but bad programs. Yet public broadcasting has been slow to develop in America not only because of problems in financing it but because of Americans' belief in private, profit-making enterprise. It has also been stifled by the fear that control of broadcasting by the advertising dollar would be replaced by control by government. But in all broadcasting, public and private, government has played a significant role.

Government Regulation

There can be little doubt that the excesses of commercialism — in any industry — often run head-on into the "public interest." The government's response to this conflict in the broadcasting industry is completely different from its response to the conflict between the print media and the public welfare. Since the 1920s the government has had a hand in regulating individual broadcast stations and the industry generally. In fact, the Federal Communications Act of 1934 requires that broadcast stations serve "the public interest, convenience and necessity"; an attempt to demand the same of a newspaper would be considered unconstitutional.

Why has the government taken such an interest in broadcasting? Looking at British broadcasting, writer Peter Jay said there were two compelling reasons for intervention and regulation by government:

1. The frequency spectrum is limited; that is, there are a limited number of channels over which radio and television can broadcast. There must be some way or someone to allocate these channels. We can call this the "traffic cop" function of broadcasting — deciding who will be on what frequency.
2. A power mythology surrounds broadcasting. This is "the widespread contemporary belief, especially among politicians, that broadcasting — and particularly television — exercises over the public some extraordinary, almost hypnotic, power, which is supposed to be much more sinister and dangerous than anything that the printed word threatens."[8] "Irresponsible" broadcasting thus presents a special threat to the public interest.

These two reasons for government involvement apply equally well to the American system, and the two reasons are related. Scarcity has always been at the heart of government regulation and control of broadcasting. The need to allocate licenses to avoid confusion was the impetus for the Federal Communications

Act of 1934, the basis for our present regulatory system. That Act makes one thing abundantly clear: *the airwaves belong to the people* and licensees (stations) are temporary custodians who must have government-granted permission to broadcast. Moreover, these temporary custodians of public property must serve the public interest — the needs, conveniences, or necessities of the people. Government is the arbiter of whether the public interest is being served.

Almost every branch of government can and does get involved in broadcasting issues. The executive branch suggests policy; the legislature enacts laws and holds hearings to investigate aspects of the industry; both the executive branch and Congress influence broadcasters through their criticisms; the courts resolve disputes. As we pointed out in Chapter 3, most active in regulating broadcasting are the Federal Trade Commission (FTC), which deals with advertising and unfair competition, and the Federal Communications Commission (FCC). These groups have developed a body of laws and regulations that has some influence on most every aspect of broadcasting — from who owns a station, to the technology used, to what is broadcast.

The Extent of Government Regulation. Underlying the government's regulations of broadcasting is the requirement that stations serve the public interest. Just what that means has been hotly debated. Over the years the FCC has set forth various principles that have helped define the "public interest." Some of them are:

1. The right of the public to broadcast service is superior to the right of any individual to use the ether [an old term for the regions of space through which radio waves travel] . . .
2. Broadcasting must be maintained as a medium of free speech for the people as a whole.
3. Television and radio stations have a definite responsibility to provide a reasonable amount of broadcast time for controversial public discussion. . . .
4. Licensees must maintain control over programming of their own stations, and may not surrender their program responsibility by contract or otherwise to networks, advertising agencies, or other program producing organizations.
5. Television and radio stations must be responsive to the needs and interests of the communities in which they are located. . . .

6. Television and radio stations may not be used exclusively for commercial purposes. They must use some of their broadcast time for sustaining programs and must avoid advertising excesses which offend good taste.
7. Television and radio stations are expected to abide by their promises of program service unless exceptional circumstances supervene. . . .
8. The Commission favors diversity of ownership of radio and television stations. . . .
9. The Commission may not censor any television or radio program in advance of broadcasting.[9]

The FCC upholds these principles primarily through its ability to grant and renew licenses. This is no simple procedure. Each license is granted for three years, and community groups can and do challenge stations' requests to renew their licenses. However, they rarely succeed. To apply for renewal a station must submit information on its performance, personnel policies, and programming. Broadcasters are also required to consult with community leaders to be sure that the station's programming is meeting the community's needs. The requirement that programming meet the public interest is often equated with providing news programs and public service announcements, but the FCC also examines whether religious programming, children's programming, and service to minority groups, among other things, are meeting the community's needs.

If a company is shown not to have served the public interest, its request for renewal may be denied. Or the FCC might fine the station, or grant only a temporary license. It can also revoke a license and take stations to court for violations of FCC regulations. Through its licensing procedures, the FCC has not only decided the fate of individual licenses but also shaped new policies.

Performance is not the only criterion for holding a license. The FCC has said that diversity of ownership is in itself in the public interest. No organization is allowed to own more than seven AM and seven FM radio stations or more than seven television stations, including no more than five VHF stations. The issue of cross-media ownership has also long concerned the FCC, as well as the Justice Department, which generally investigates and tries to break up monopolies. But despite the FCC's rules promoting diversity of ownership, when licenses were challenged because of cross-media ownership, the FCC often backed off, failing to take action.

Finally, in 1975 the FCC developed new cross-ownership rules designed to forbid (in the future) common ownership of a newspaper and broadcast station in the same community. But *existing* cross-ownership was allowed to continue, except in sixteen communities in which one owner held the *only* daily newspaper and the *only* television station.

The rules brought an immediate response. Broadcasters said the rules went too far. They also argued that cross-ownership can be beneficial because other, profit-making parts of the organization may keep a weak publication or station alive. Public interest and citizens groups such as the National Citizens Committee for Broadcasting said the FCC's rules didn't go far enough. The rules were challenged in the courts. Finally, in 1978, the Supreme Court in *FCC* v. *National Citizens Committee for Broadcasting* upheld the FCC's rules.

The FCC also deals with technical issues, such as engineering standards for radio stations and the use of color in television, and with the content of broadcasting. Regulations on two types of content are especially noteworthy:

1. *Advertising* The FCC is interested in the total amount of broadcast time devoted to advertising and the number of commercial interruptions per hour. Too much advertising is not in the "public interest." The government has avoided setting rigid standards for how much advertising is too much, but the broadcast industry has set its own limits on advertising under the National Association of Broadcasters and Television Codes. Most stations have an average of fifteen to twenty minutes of advertising per hour.[10]

2. *Discussion of public issues* Through a series of decisions and rulings, the FCC has determined that the public is entitled to hear a reasonably balanced presentation of responsible viewpoints on public issues. As a result of these decisions, which are known collectively as the *fairness doctrine,* stations must sometimes grant equal time to opposing viewpoints on particular issues. The fairness doctrine was extended in 1969 when the Supreme Court ruled that individuals who are personally attacked on the air are entitled to a chance to respond.

In addition, the FCC enforces the *equal time provision* established by Congress. It requires that a station that gives time for one candidate for a political office must give equal time to his or her opponents. Coverage of bona fide news events are exempt from this provision.

Other Regulatory Forces. Besides the regulations of government, the broadcasting industry is subject to pressures from other groups both inside and outside the industry. The National Association of Broadcasters, an industry group, has long urged self-regulation and has developed a code of ethics for radio and for television, including both advertising and programming standards. In addition, professional organizations within broadcasting, such as the Radio and Television News Directors Association, have developed ethical codes to guide their members. Other industry groups set standards, urge responsible performance, and sometimes give awards for exemplary work.

Such codes and standards are a nice idea, but they don't always work. They are strictly voluntary, there is no way to enforce them, and not everyone follows them. But their very existence may be a positive influence on broadcasters. Their real purpose, however, is not to regulate broadcasting but to act as a kind of public relations buffer between the industry and the public and between the industry and government, whose regulation broadcasters fear.

The industry's public relations efforts have often failed to convince private groups that it is acting responsibly. Consumer groups such as Action for Children's Television (ACT) have campaigned vigorously against programming they believe harmful to children. Former FCC Commissioner Nicholas Johnson, an outspoken critic, organized the National Citizens Committee on Broadcasting to push for what it sees as the public interest. It later became part of Ralph Nader's organization. These groups and others representing minorities, women, and the handicapped seek to influence the government regulators, as to industry organizations that oppose government control.

The Future of Government Regulation. How effectively does the FCC and other governmental regulations regulate broadcasting? The answer depends on who is consulted. The broadcasting industry generally feels that there is too much regulation and rails against it. Libertarians argue that the First Amendment's guarantees of free speech and free press are being violated. Consumer groups often feel that the Commission has been reluctant to cancel licenses and enforce its regulations. And the FCC is not immune from politics. Its seven members are appointed by the president for seven-year terms, and its philosophy has changed over the years along with its composition.

Aside from debates about how well the FCC or other groups have done their job, some people argue that the broadcasting industry should be deregulated because the justification for regulation — a scarcity of channels for broadcasting — no longer exists. When the FCC was established, only AM radio existed. When television was first regulated, almost all stations were VHF stations. The expansion of FM and UHF broadcasting and of cable television has multiplied the number of channels available. A bill to deregulate the industry was proposed in 1979, but it died in that session of Congress.

Broadcasting as Content

Put together the technology of broadcasting, the production and distribution system, the pressures from economics and politics, and finally we get the content of broadcasting. Marshall McLuhan has argued that *what* is broadcast is not all that important: what matters is the medium not the message. The medium itself — broadcasting — has an impact, he says, on the nature of human beings and our world.

But the messages of broadcasting do matter to us, and they can be analyzed in several ways. Probably the easiest way is to examine the types of content that are broadcast, which include entertainment, advertising, and news and information.

A second, more difficult approach is to assess the impact of broadcasting messages. Advertisers, for example, want to know whether their commercials are actually selling soap, mouthwash, beer, whatever. In examining its impact, we can look at broadcasting as either an aesthetic or a social force. We may want to ask: Is a program aesthetically good or bad? Does its content enhance or debase a society's taste in literature, the arts, or music? Looking at it as a social force, we might ask whether the messages distort reality. Do they portray blacks or women in a way that perpetuates stereotypes and prejudices? Can violent programs teach children to be aggressive? Can programs instill in children values such as respect or disrespect for authority?

The content of broadcasting, especially on television, seems to draw critics from all quarters — from those who find its quality lacking, from those who fear its effect on their children or their neighbors, from those who object to the lack of coverage the news gives their cause or the way a group is portrayed. Almost everything on television has attracted the ire of one critic or another.

In part the uproar reflects the belief in broadcasting's power — the legacy of fear. It also reflects broadcasting's vast potential to bring beautiful sounds, beautiful images, and a wealth of information to millions of Americans any day the broadcasting industry chooses to do so. Finally, it reflects broadcasting's constant presence in the daily lives of Americans. Perhaps, too, some of the criticism arises from the simple fact that broadcasting is a mass medium, a medium of mass communication, and thus a part of popular culture. It's an easy target for simple snobbery. But in fact the content and quality of broadcasting vary greatly, and there are interesting differences between radio and television. We look next at each medium in more detail.

Radio

Unlike television stations, which are found in urban centers, radio stations broadcast from even the smallest towns across America. In January 1980 there were 8,752 radio stations operating in the United States; 1,038 noncommercial stations, 4,559 commercial AM stations, and 3,155 commercial FM stations. The AM stations operate on medium frequencies (from 535 to 1605 kilohertz) and

Producing sound effects for early radio programs was an imaginative undertaking.

FM stations operate on very high frequencies (from 88 to 108 megahertz). Because they operate on such widely separated frequencies, the two systems do not interfere with each other. AM broadcasts reach farther than FM, but FM broadcasts generate better sound, with less electrical disturbance and static.

Although a single television program like "Roots" may reach more people than any radio program, radio still has the largest composite audience of any medium. It has been estimated that there are 444 million radio sets in the country. Of these, 74 percent are in homes and 26 percent are in cars, offices, stores, and so on. The success of radio in the 1970s was almost as big a surprise as its rapid growth was decades ago.

The Rise of Radio as a Mass Medium

It took less than twenty years for radio to grow from a tiny, experimental enterprise to a great medium of mass communication. The technical equipment that made broadcasting possible moved beyond the wildest dreams of its inventors, and the uses to which it was put were just as amazing. Radio moved into entertainment with dramatic presentations and its own star system. It broadcast music and made bands famous. It presented dramatic news coverage by distinctive commentators and announcers. It expanded the consciousness of average Americans and put them in touch with personalities that were larger than life. As one account put it:

> Powerful personalities who won their followings through the effective use of the broadcast word . . . ranged from Franklin D. Roosevelt, whose fireside chats, delivered in a personal and intimate manner, captured the imagination and loyalty of most Americans, to men like the famous Dr. Brinkley, the patent medicine man who advertised his goat-gland pills over the air, to distraught men anxious to regain their lost youth. In between came firebrands like Louisiana's Huey Long and Father Charles E. Coughlin, the Detroit priest who became a storm center when he tried to build up a political movement through his radio broadcasts.[11]

As America discovered the amazing possibilities of broadcasting, the constant interplay of economic and political, public and private forces shaped it. These forces and the pioneers of radio in the 1920s and 1930s established the structure and operation of much of today's broadcasting industry. Networks developed in the late 1920s and worked out agreements with local stations. Radio did battle with newspapers to claim its share of the advertising market and to define such issues as the "ownership" of the

President Franklin Delano Roosevelt was a brilliant and effective communicator in his famous "Fireside Chats" delivered via radio from the White House.

news. Scared by the competition radio was giving them, newspapers had tried to stop local stations from using the early editions of papers as the source for their news. They claimed that the radio stations were violating copyright laws. But the courts ruled that although the particular expression of a writer can be copyrighted, the factual content of news is in the public domain — no one owns it. Thus radio stations could broadcast news shows even if they could not afford to hire their own reporters.

From 1912 on there had been some government regulation of radio. During World War I the government took over all radio operations. The U.S. Navy operated all ship-to-shore stations, and patent disputes among various radio inventors were set aside for what the government called "the good of the country." After the war, competition for frequencies over which to broadcast was fierce. For a while, the secretary of commerce assigned frequencies to transmitters. After much confusion the Federal Communications Act of 1934 set up a formal system of government regulations, including the FCC, while retaining the status of broadcasting as a private, profit-making enterprise. By World War II, AM broadcasting was a soaring industry, and the government

Radio personalities like Jack Benny (with violin and cigar) became household fixtures during the golden age of radio in the 1930s, when radio brought a considerable diversity of programming — including live performance of music — into the home.

asked for its cooperation in broadcasting messages about the war to the American people. But because broadcasting was now a fixture in the private sector, the government made no move to take over the industry as it had in World War I. Then came television.

Radio Versus Television: Decline and Rebirth

Radio was flourishing as the nation entered World War II. After the war television expanded and took away part of radio's financial support. Radio profits dropped, and it soon lost its prime-time evening audience, which turned to the television set. Some observers predicted the death of radio.

Radio might have died had it not been for its resourceful response to the challenge of television. The content of broadcasts changed sharply. Out went the well-developed radio drama, the soap opera, the quiz program, and other entertainment fare that had been taken over by television. In came the disc jockey, country and western music, frequent spot news, weather reports, and call-in shows. For the most part radio ceased to be a national medium. National programming decreased, and radio became a local medium providing local services to its audiences. Radio tightened its belt for a time and took on advertising accounts that could not afford costly television commercials.

In effect radio changed its functions. It gave more emphasis to information and music and less to its older forms of entertainment. In this way radio survived as a more intimate and local medium.

After its slump in the 1950s, radio came back vigorously with its regenerated programming, and it has continued to grow. Most early radio was AM. Later, numerous FM broadcast stations developed, emphasizing audio quality. In 1961 the FCC allowed FM stations to broadcast in stereo.

Along with these changes in commercial radio came the growth of noncommercial radio. Indeed, the FCC set aside special channels for FM educational stations. Noncommercial stations began to provide leadership in public affairs and cultural programs. It became a medium for a more elite audience. These developments are similar to recent changes in modern magazines, which now cater to carefully targeted audiences.

There is some overlapping between the content of radio and television, but not much. In sports, for example, local radio stations broadcast the games of high school and college teams that do not generate a large enough audience for coverage by television. Because it is portable and can be background listening during other activities, radio became the medium of the beach, the car, the kitchen, and the backyard, as well as a handy source of news, music, and advertising.

Although radio was successful in the 1960s, it seemed to take a decided back seat to television, and no one paid much attention to its growing cultural and commercial influence. It was something of a surprise when by 1980 radio was enjoying a new prosperity. Frank Mankiewicz, president of the public supported National Public Radio, even speculated that we might be entering a "new Golden Age of Radio."

Because radio peaked as a mass medium in 1950, the high point of network radio, advertisers were largely unaware of its capacity for reaching specialized audiences, not just in a local area, but nationwide. It took an obscure radio station in New York City, WKTU, to show that radio has the capacity to draw a large, specialized audience.

In 1979 WKTU introduced a new programming format, playing only disco music. Almost overnight it became the nation's most listened-to station. Some nights it captured 16 percent of New York City's listener market, where it competed with forty-three AM and fifty-six FM stations. Although disco music may not last

The American disc jockey holds a pivotal position in deciding which musical offerings to feature for on-the-air presentation.

long, the success of this station's programming demonstrates the popularity of radio, even with competition from television.

Earlier, CBS radio bought the rights to broadcast the National Football League's "Monday Night Football" — an event staged for television. Immediately the radio broadcasts drew 10 million listeners each week, compared with 45 million television viewers. Audience research showed that many listeners were also watching the game on television — but they turned down the volume and listened to the radio, partly to avoid TV announcer Howard Cosell!

While network sports programming was making a comeback on radio, radio drama returned. During the nostalgia craze of the 1970s, old programs like "The Shadow," "The Green Hornet," and "The Lone Ranger" came back briefly. More important was CBS's "Radio Mystery Theater," a new show that began in 1973. More than 200 stations carry this program, which has been so successful it has been followed by other new radio dramas, on both commercial and public radio. In the late 1970s the British-inspired "Masterpiece Radio Theatre" was launched, and National Public Radio reported impressive audiences for its popular "Earplay" dramas.

The Continuing Appeal of Radio

"Why," asked writer Frank Brady, is "radio drama making a comeback when television is still omnipresent?" The answer, he said, "involves economic, cultural, and psychological factors."[12] Of course, the modest return of radio drama — which does not come close to its popularity decades ago — is only one indication of radio's rebirth. Brady's answer applies to the general upsurge of radio, too.

First, the economic reasons. "Advertisers find they can reach more people with less money through radio than with more costly television commercials."[13] Radio has become attractive to advertisers because its rates have stayed fairly constant while increases in the costs of equipment, labor, and newsprint have brought rate hikes in print and television advertising. Nationally, radio takes in more money than magazines do, although it takes in only about one-third as much as television and less than one-fourth as much as newspapers. Radio is also regarded as a good place for investors to put their money. Compared with a television station or a newspaper, it takes relatively little capital to buy a radio station and a smaller staff — and thus lower labor costs — to run one.

Second, cultural tastes seem to account for the success of such high-quality public radio programs as the news program "All Things Considered" and the dramatization of classics such as "Wuthering Heights." Unimaginative television programs and endless reruns are said to be pushing more discerning viewers back to radio. Radio may be increasingly popular as its programming gets more diversified in the 1980s, moving well beyond the diet of music and news that was standard during the 1960s and 1970s. In other words, radio may be prospering from a sort of backlash against television.

Third, psychological factors have always made radio a fascinating medium, though this was largely ignored after radio drama disappeared in the 1950s. Radio is a medium in which the imagination must come into play. As Brady put it:

> The listener becomes the costumer, set designer, and the makeup man and creates the characters and sets in his mind. The basic appeal of radio has always been that in order to enjoy it, one can't merely *hear* it. It has

to be *listened to* attentively. This process of mental animation is attractive to many people who over the years have been fed on a steady diet of the passive experience of watching television, and who seek a more participatory entertainment.[14]

The humorist Stan Freberg once illustrated radio's power to engage the listener's imagination by creating the world's largest ice cream sundae in the listener's mind. He told the audience how he would scoop out Lake Michigan and fill it with chocolate syrup. Then came a massive avalanche of ice cream, then whipped cream. Finally, the Royal Canadian Air Force placed a huge maraschino cherry on top while 2,500 extras cheered. "Now," said Freberg, "try that on television."

Thus radio has distinctive advantages for its audience and for advertisers. Although television and radio sometimes compete for the same advertising dollars, advertisers are buying different services from the two media. Both radio and television are here to stay.

Television

It has been estimated that 98 percent of American households have at least one television set, and many have several. To reach this vast audience, there were, by January 1980, 988 television stations in the United States — including 514 commercial VHF stations and 221 commercial UHFs, as well as 99 noncommercial VHFs and 154 noncommercial UHFs.

These statistics indicate the staggering dimensions of television's reach. Perhaps even more significant is the fact that on the average American households have a television set on for 6.7 hours each day, about an hour more than in 1960. "Television," said Paula Fass, "confronts most of us regularly as an uninvited dinner guest, the sandman of sleep, often the teacher, and, for many, a daily companion. It's a habit, a sedative, even a social mediator as it introduces us to the facts and fantasies of American society."[15]

Doubtless, there is some exaggeration in Fass's portrait. (Television is, for example, usually an invited — not an uninvited — guest, and that fact is significant.) But the view of television as an intimate part of American life cannot be disputed. On the other hand, just what role it plays in that life — as a directing force or a bit player, for good or for ill — has been much disputed. The sheer size of television's audience makes it an attractive scapegoat for those looking for the causes of society's ills. Before either criticizing or praising its effects, we want to examine the medium more closely — as a technology, as a production and distribution system, and as content.

The Technology of Television

Television personality Steve Allen once mused that "television is a triumph of equipment over people," a statement that points up the importance of the technical aspects of the medium. Just how does television work? How is the action that cameras and microphones record in a studio transmitted to the home? And how does network programming stretch all the way across the country — and sometimes the world?

Television's sound is basically FM radio. Sounds are picked up from a microphone, turntable, or tape recorder. They are then mixed in an audio board and sent to the transmitter, where the waves we described earlier in the chapter are generated, modulated, and sent out the antenna to be received in the home. Of course, since not all television is live, the sound (and the pictures) may be stored on videotape and broadcast or rebroadcast later.

The picture portion of television begins in the television camera, which can focus an image and make adjustments for light. Usually, there are several cameras in a studio, and technicians select one of several pictures to be aired. The picture then goes to the transmitter to be sent out the antenna, much like audio signals, but the video signal is amplitude-modulated rather than frequency-modulated. After they are modulated, the audio and video signals are joined and broadcast from the antenna.

In television transmission there are two basic types of radio waves: very high frequency (VHF) and ultra-high frequency (UHF). Stations using VHF waves occupy channels 2 to 13, whereas UHF stations have channels 14 to 83. Both kinds of waves follow a straight line between the broadcast station and the television receiver, but UHF signals can be blocked more easily by buildings, trees, and hills. They can also be absorbed more easily into the atmosphere. As a result, UHF signals require more power for transmission. They also require more sensitive adjustment, although UHF transmission has the capability of bringing a more technically perfect picture than VHF. VHF stations — the majority of American television stations — require less power to reach a wider geographic area.

Normally, a television signal travels in a direct line of sight from the station's transmitter and antenna to the home antenna and receiver, the television set.[16] But there are other possibilities if the television signal must be sent beyond its normal reach. The networks, for example, use microwave relays. Microwaves are electromagnetic waves like radio waves (and sunlight), but they have a higher frequency and shorter wavelength than radio waves. For microwave relays, the networks use relay stations set about thirty miles apart; these stations are usually on specially built towers or high buildings. At each station the microwave signal is received, amplified, and retransmitted to the next station. Thus the network's signals can be sent across the country beyond the range of regular VHF and UHF transmission.

Signals are also transmitted by communications satellites. A ground station sends the signals to a satellite, which beams the signals to transmitters around the world. Many special events such as the Olympics as well as news reports from abroad are transmitted by satellite, whereas most network programs come through microwave transmission. With the use of satellites a television show can now have a worldwide audience.

Technological Development

By the time television began to reach a mass audience, the mechanisms for government regulation were already in place. The FCC has therefore overseen the implementation of technological innovations in the industry. In particular it has played a major role in determining the use of VHF or UHF transmission and the use of color.

VHF versus UHF. When the FCC began authorizing television licenses, they assigned the VHF channels first. Consequently, manufacturers began building television sets designed for VHF. Later, as UHF stations were established, viewers either had to forego watching UHF programs or equip their sets with a conversion device that cost about one hundred dollars. Thus UHF television grew up in an environment in which the majority of viewers could not receive its signal. While VHF stations prospered in the 1950s, UHF stations often went bankrupt.

Naturally, this situation was a thorny problem for the FCC. It considered several solutions, including the strange idea of reassigning all frequencies, giving VHF one side of the Mississippi and UHF the other. But in the end the FCC decided to ask Congress to require all manufacturers of television sets to build them so that they could receive both VHF and UHF signals. Congress did so in the 1950s.

After a drop in the number of UHF facilities in the late 1950s, they have grown steadily, going from 76 commercial UHF stations in 1960 to 221 in January 1980. In contrast, there were 441 commercial VHF stations in 1960. VHF stations showed steady and remarkable growth until the early 1970s. Then the number began to level off as the available frequencies were used up. Still, today there are more than twice as many commercial VHF stations as commercial UHF stations.

The Coming of Color. Color television got off to a slow start. There was much talk about it as early as the 1940s. The networks and manufacturers struggled to perfect a system for transmitting and receiving color pictures, but the quality of early color transmission was uneven at best. There were other problems as well. Many black-and-white sets could not receive pictures transmitted in color. The FCC insisted that the system for color transmission be such that black-and-white television sets could still receive a picture (though not in color). Add to these problems the need to produce a color television set within the financial means of large numbers of people, and the slow development of color is not surprising.

In 1953 the FCC approved RCA's system of color television. Although the system produced crude colors, it did allow existing black-and-white sets to receive programs. The networks exercised much caution in delivering color broadcasts to American homes. At first they broadcast only a few programs in color. By 1967, though, most network programs were in color, and even local stations began to produce programs in color. All the black-and-white cameras had to be phased out, and new technicians trained. But the industry made the transition to the new technology smoothly. By the late 1970s about 74 percent of those homes with a television set had color television, and it seemed that nearly all American homes would have a color set by the early 1980s.

Subscription Television. Despite its large potential, pay, or subscription, television has developed slowly. Pay television, which is also called *toll television,* is a special method of transmission in which the signal is scrambled at the sender's end. Unless the receiver has a device for decoding it, no image can be viewed.

Whereas regular broadcasting delivers programs for a vast, heterogeneous audience, programs on pay television, like a specialty magazine, can be targeted to limited, homogeneous audiences. First-run movies, leading ballets, and Broadway plays have been part of its programming. It has provided special entertainment in luxury hotels and some homes. In auditoriums and theaters, subscription television has provided direct broadcasts of championship fights and other sporting events that are kept off the air because of agreements between sports entrepreneurs and broadcasters.

In the early 1980s subscription television still has only a small audience. Its opponents are many. Various commercial interests from television stations to movie theaters have fought it vigorously. Critics argue that if pay television succeeds, then "free" commercial television will gradually wither. Those who cannot afford pay television, they argue, will lose access to many programs.

Production and Distribution

The production and distribution of television programs, like other media content, is a business that relies on a variety of managers, specialists, and technicians. Programs are made somewhat differently depending on whether they are network or local programs, their budget, the type of content, and the style of the people involved. Thus it is difficult to generalize about how programs are made, but in the case of a network entertainment program (such as a drama or situation comedy), the process and the division of labor go something like this:

We begin with the producer. The producer is in charge of a program or series and oversees everything from the budget to hiring personnel and arranging facilities where the show will be shot. The producer also works closely with the network, which is commissioning the series and paying the bills.

Producers are rarely network employees. Instead, they are either independent entrepreneurs with their own companies or they work for the major motion picture and television studios, usually in Hollywood. Producers may have an extensive staff working with their company, or much of the staff help (called *talent*) may be contracted on a free-lance basis. Whether the producer is initiating a new series, preparing an episode of a continuing series, or arranging a one-time-only program, the sequence of events involves the following:

1. *An initial story conference* The producer meets with a writer. In some instances the producer has a clear idea of what is desired and tells the writer what to prepare. In other instances there is "give and take" between the writer and producer, a kind of brainstorming out of which comes a story idea that will be developed in the script. In still other instances the writer simply "pitches" story ideas to the producer.
2. *A treatment is prepared* A treatment of a story is a brief presentation, usually five to ten pages long, that tells the plot

of the story. It has no dialogue or camera direction. (An actual script for a one-hour show is about seventy pages long.)

3. *The treatment is reviewed* The producer, executive producer, and writer review the proposed plot. The writer is then either told not to continue or commissioned to prepare a first draft.

4. *A draft is prepared* Once a first draft is done, another conference is held and a story editor joins the discussions. A variety of suggestions are made: the draft may not reflect what the director had in mind or there may be problems in the tone, dialogue, or flow of the story. Once the director, story editor, and writer agree on the first draft, the writer is asked to do a second. This time the visualization is added (that is, directions for camera shots, lighting, and so on). Finally, the writer is paid for the second draft.

5. *The director gets the draft* Now the director, who has authority over the crew during rehearsal and taping, goes to work. The director takes the draft, breaks it down into a shooting script with action notes and an indication of what individual shots will be like, and gives it a "director's polish."

6. *The show goes into production* At this point stage managers, floor managers, camera personnel, and others begin their work, as do the actors. A one-hour show is usually shot in about one week. Motion pictures, in contrast, have been known for legendary delays in production, sometimes involving months or even years.

7. *Rehearsals* The director, producer, and story editor read through the script with the stage personnel and actors present. Changes may be made. Then there is a second rehearsal, in which everyone runs through the script. At about this time musical material is being prepared in sound studios off the set; music will be lip-sung during the show.

8. *The taping or filming takes place*

9. *Editing is done* Film or tape editors go to work making appropriate changes to get the best possible production from what has been captured during the taping.

10. *The program is prepared for the network* This means arranging for its delivery by microwave transmission to local television stations.

Television Content

In the early 1960s Newton Minow, who was then chairman of the FCC, looked at what this complex system produces and delivered a famous verdict. Television, he said, was a "vast wasteland of mediocre programs," delivering a "dulling sameness." Leaving aside the question of quality for the moment, we would dispute the accusation of "sameness." The television networks and local stations transmit content that covers a broad range of topics, formats, and styles.

The type of content you are likely to see when you turn on your television set depends greatly on the time. Different kinds of people tend to watch television at different times, and they make different uses of television depending on the time. Broadcasters aim their programming at the audiences most likely to watch during certain hours. As a result we can distinguish three very general categories: daytime television, prime-time television, and limited audience periods. The audience is largest during prime time, which is from about 8 to 11 P.M. EST. Limited audience periods include Sunday morning and early in the morning and late at night on any day.

To decide what to show during these periods, broadcasters ask themselves, or market researchers, Who is home and awake in the early morning? Who is likely to watch late at night? Who are the key daytime viewers, and how do they differ from the rest of the population? What kinds of programs will these groups respond to, and how do they differ from the rest of the population?

Broadcasters also ask, What is the audience at this time most likely to want out of television? Do they want a light diversion while they go about doing housework? Do they want to know what's been happening around the world? Programs obviously have different functions. Some programs inform; others entertain or persuade; some combine all these functions.

By looking at television programs from the early days of the medium to the present, we can tell something about what kinds of programs people liked and how reality has been portrayed by television. There are sharp contrasts in the portrayal of the American family, for example, from the 1950s to the 1980s. According to programs such as "Ozzie and Harriet" and "Father Knows Best" in the 1950s, the American family was happy, easygoing, and middle-class, with a mother who seemed to have no interests or abilities outside the four walls of her home. None of the family members, in fact, seemed to have any serious concern with the larger world outside their very small circle of friends. The shows were almost pure escapist entertainment. In the 1970s programs such as "Family" showed us instead families with problem-filled lives. The programs were surely meant to entertain, but not by pure escapism, and the reality they offered was harsher than that shown in the 1950s. But one characteristic of American families persisted unrealistically on television until the 1970s: They were

Situation comedies focusing on the American family have long been a staple of television entertainment programs, but the values they convey have shifted over the years to meet new public attitudes and lifestyles. The themes of "Father Knows Best" during the 1950s grew out of a happy, stable family in which problems were usually solved by wise Jim Anderson, played by actor Robert Young. Contrast this proper family setting with the more contemporary activities of "One Day at a Time" (see opposite page), in which a divorcee, her two lively daughters, and a gentle but meddling janitor confront such controversial subjects as birth control.

overwhelmingly white. Programs such as "Good Times" and "The Jeffersons" in the 1970s finally broadened television's portrait of reality by trying to present black families.

Today about 75 percent of all commercial television can be classified as entertainment; the other 25 percent is a mix of news and public affairs, advertising, educational and religious programming, and sports. The following more detailed classification should illustrate the range of content available on television.

Commercial and Other Interruptions. Lodged between regular programming are regular interruptions, of several types.

1. *Commercials* This is paid advertising. Commercials pay for almost everything else you see on television. They are produced both locally and nationally. High-quality technical production characterizes commercials; many are done with more care and precision than some programs. Obviously, they are designed to sell products. Commercials vary greatly in their cost to the advertiser, depending on whether they are broadcast in low-viewing hours or in prime time. To have a commercial carried on the Super Bowl may cost an advertiser many times as much as a commercial on an early-morning farm program.

2. *Public service announcements* A kind of unpaid commercial, public service announcements "advertise" public services

Television gives advertisers a market that includes millions of viewers available instantaneously on a nationwide basis. Inventive advertisers constantly seek new and captivating ways to promote their products. Coca Cola,® one of the most imaginative, ran a commercial featuring football player "Mean Joe Green" and a small, Coke-imbibing fan.

ranging from cultural events to hotlines for emergency health care. The station donates this time as a public service, which counts as part of the service to the "public interest, convenience, and necessity" required by the FCC. Public service announcements often promote government services, such as free booklets on consumer issues.

3. *Program promotion*   Yet another type of commercial is a kind of house advertising in which the station promotes its programs or those of its network.

Entertainment Programs. Most entertainment programs are part of a series and appear weekly or even more often. Included in this broad category is everything from artistic dramas to scores of situation comedies that last less than a season and are, understandably, quickly forgotten. Table 5.1 indicates the popularity of a few kinds of entertainment programs.

Table 5.1 Types of Network TV Shows and Their Audiences, February 1976 (7–11 P.M.)

Type of show	Number of programs	% of average audience	% share of programming
General Drama	10	18.6	14
Variety	5	19.5	7
Western Drama	—	—	—
Situation Comedy	23	21.2	32
Mystery and Suspense Drama	23	19.1	32
Feature Films	7	19.1	10
All Regular Programs	73	19.7	

Source: *NTI/NAC Audience Demographics Report*, February 1976.

4. *Dramas*   Most dramatic shows are fictional presentations. They range from public television's "Masterpiece Theatre" to family shows like "The Waltons," to police-detective shows, medical shows, and many others. Usually these programs are pure entertainment, or nearly so, and their characters and plots are similar to those of motion pictures. They may also seek to instruct or persuade. For example, the "Lou Grant" show, set in a newspaper's city room, has examined issues such as the treatment of Vietnam veterans, alcoholism, the treatment of the mentally ill, and censorship — while providing dramatic entertainment as well.

5. *Situation comedies*   These shows trace the humorous foibles and activities of a regular cast of characters. They have been extremely popular for years. Designed to get laughs, the situation comedy may also take a serious turn now and then. In the 1960s producer Norman Lear pioneered the inclusion of social issues in situation comedies with his show "All in the Family," which later became "Archie Bunker's Place." Lear's show "Maude" also dealt with social issues, including feminism, alcoholism, and abortion. Situation comedies such as the old "Mary Tyler Moore Show" and "Laverne and Shirley" and "Three's Company," along with "All in the Family," have been among the most popular shows on television.

6. *Variety shows*   A revue format with various musical performers, comedians, and other entertainers characterizes the variety show. Usually it includes a host who introduces the

Actor Ed Asner plays a socially conscious and dynamic city editor on the CBS show "Lou Grant," further developing a role that he began years earlier on the "Mary Tyler Moore" show, where he portrayed a television news director.

acts and chats with the entertainers during the program. Although they almost disappeared from television in the late 1970s, some of the longest-running shows on television have been variety shows. The "Ed Sullivan Show" lasted sixteen years.

7. *Talk shows* These programs are somewhat similar to variety shows, but they focus on one or more guests interacting with the host. The guest may be an entertainer, author of a recent book, or public figure. Long-standing talk show hosts include Johnny Carson, Merv Griffin, and Mike Douglas; Phil Donohue and Tom Snyder are more recent hosts. Many local shows imitate the format of these national talk shows. Now and then, talk shows have sparked real controversy. For example, authors Truman Capote and Gore Vidal swapped vicious insults on the "Dick Cavett Show."

8. *Personality and game shows* These feature people chosen from the studio audience (or through a national canvass) competing for prizes or money. They are designed to give a thrill to home viewers, who imagine themselves in the place of the

participants. Some of these programs — "The Hollywood Squares" and "Match Game," for example — use show business personalities to enliven the show and draw a larger audience. Almost since the beginning of television, game shows have been a staple for audiences of limited sophistication.

9. *Soap operas* This type of dramatic show began in the golden years of radio and was eventually transferred to television. Originally, they were sponsored by soap companies and other producers of household cleaning supplies, and they appealed mostly to women who were at home during the day when they were aired. The "soaps" deal with a range of male-female relationships; marital infidelity, premarital sex, mate swapping, and health problems figure often in their plots. Traditionally, they have been characterized by cheap production, maudlin scripts, and marginal acting. But today some critics say that some soaps are superior to some evening fare. Among the best-known soaps have been "The Edge of Night," "Days of Our Lives," "General Hospital," "All My Children," and "The Young and the Restless." So popular are the soap operas that weekly magazines like *Soap Opera Digest* summarize their plots.

10. *Children's programs* Some of the earliest shows were aimed at children, and children's programs are still an important share of entertainment programming. They range from the long-running "Captain Kangaroo" to educational programs such as "Sesame Street," to the children's variety show "Zoom," to violence-filled cartoons. Although most children's programs are shown during after-school hours and Saturday mornings, some like "The Wonderful World of Disney" get prime-time evening spots, as do popular holiday specials like "Peanuts," which are aimed at children and adults.

11. *Movies* Television makes extensive use of movies. Relatively recent releases from the major studios are shown in prime time. They have already run at local theaters and are sold to television by the movie studios. The major studios also make movies for television only. In addition, many old movies are shown, mainly late at night and in the early morning hours.

12. *Specials* The special is simply a program that is not part of regular network programming. It may be a Christmas special — a one-time-only variety show hosted by a famous star — or a one-person special showcasing the music of a popular singer, for example. Specials also include award shows,

beauty contests, and holiday parades. They are usually presented to boost ratings and often take the place of a program that has sagging ratings.

13. *Sports and special events* Virtually every major sport can be seen on television almost every week. There are shows that give play-by-play coverage of professional sports, especially football and baseball; shows like the "ABC Wide World of Sports" that feature a range of sports on the same program, from frog jumping to horse racing to skiing; and specials that cover championship events or worldwide contests such as the Olympics. These broadcasts account for vast chunks of television time.

14. *Docudramas* This hybrid form, which straddles historical fiction and public affairs, has become increasingly popular in recent years. Usually, the docudrama is a fictionalized treatment of a piece of recent history. For example, in 1977 a show called "Washington Behind Closed Doors" was a thinly veiled treatment of the Watergate scandal. One of the most spectacular of all docudramas was "Roots," which attracted the largest audience in television history when it was shown in 1977. In 1980 PBS aired the very controversial docudrama "Death of a Princess" about the execution of a Saudi Arabian princess. It sparked lively international debate.

Other Programs. Most of the content we've discussed so far mainly entertains. There is also television fare that primarily informs and influences.

15. *News and public affairs* This important category includes the network and local news shows, special coverage of important public events — political nominating conventions, visits by foreign dignitaries, and so on — documentaries and news specials, and regular interview shows like "Meet the Press" in which journalists question public figures. Among the most popular shows in the last few years has been CBS's "Sixty Minutes." Television is often criticized for its coverage of the news. What goes on television news, say the critics, is greatly influenced by a search for visual appeal, spectacle, and entertainment. The values of show business overshadow the values of journalism. Mostly the news programs concentrate on covering events, although they include some background reports, interpretation, and editorial comment.

16. *Religious programs* Religious programs, sometimes called "the electronic church," range from the elaborately produced

Every four years, television election coverage holds the attention of millions of Americans. Seen here is Dan Rather of CBS News, reporting from the floor of the 1980 Democratic Convention.

specials of Billy Graham and Oral Roberts to religious talk shows such as the "PTL Club" and regular broadcasts of local church services. All the major religions in America are usually represented on local stations on Sundays, when religious programming is at its most intense. Included are traditional religions and faith healers and interviews with theologians as well as with people who promote spiritualism. Several religious networks produce religious programming and offer it to local stations. Religious programs sometimes cross the fine line into politics. When a religious program deals mainly with social action and political issues, local stations find themselves offering equal time to opposing viewpoints.

17. *Cultural and educational programs* At one time educational

and cultural programming was little more than a dull presentation of "talking heads," panel shows of educators lecturing to their audiences. But in recent years public television programming has become more competitive, especially among the better-educated audience. Much but not all cultural and educational programming appears on noncommercial, public broadcasting. This category overlaps with the other types of content we've described, but it is distinguished by efforts to teach about something or to explicate a cultural theme. The rise in the diversity and popularity of these programs probably began when shows such as "Upstairs Downstairs," "Masterpiece Theatre," and the zany "Monty Python" were imported from the British Broadcasting Company. Often the imported programs were high-quality productions of serialized novels, docudramas, or classics of literature and drama. Today there are also many American-produced dramas of high quality. The programs available range from symphony orchestras, jazz concerts, ballets, and documentaries on great artists, to public affairs programs such as "Washington Week in Review," to "The French Chef" with Julia Child and "National Geographic."

Criticizing Television

In its earlier days television was regarded as beneath the dignity of critical comment by serious writers. Today there is a growing body of criticism of television in both scholarly and popular sources, including newspapers, television, and magazines. Critics differ greatly. Michael Arlen, for example, has earned a reputation for literate and inspired criticism, whereas Cleveland Amory is known for brisk and sometimes searing commentary, almost always very negative. Still others like Rona Barrett are more like gossip columnists.

Besides these professional reviewers the critics of television include a diverse cast of characters — from technical authorities to politicians to social scientists to political activists. They take on a wide range of issues with varying intensity, but the content of television and its effects probably fuel the hottest debates. The diversity that we have glimpsed in that content does not support the claims of some critics that the medium is merely a "vast wasteland." It is, rather, a cafeteria that offers the equivalents of everything from junk food to caviar. It offers different programs for different tastes: simplistic cartoons for the Saturday morning audience, which is made up mostly of children; turbulent soap operas for daytime viewers who are mostly housewives; simple comedies for those in need of diversion; and serious dramas for those who want more demanding fare.

We should not overstate the case for television's diversity, however. The comedian Fred Allen once remarked that "imitation is the sincerest form of television," and many television programs are unimaginative copies from other shows or movies that proved popular. Whether this hurts the quality of programs is open to debate. But it has given us some seasons when police shows kept cropping up in prime time and others when doctors were everywhere. In some communities "Kojak" was appearing not only in prime time but also, in reruns, two other nights a week. Do we really need "Kojak" — or any other program for that matter — three nights a week?

Television news shows have come in for their own share of criticism. "Happy news" shows — with their chatty, personable anchor people, frequently trivial stories, and inane comments—have been sharply denounced. The critics say that serious attention to important issues is being displaced by a search for entertaining stories. They may have a point. Television stations regularly employ consultants who survey the viewing public and then, armed with their survey data, suggest changes in the news show to boost ratings. News shows, like entertainment programs, depend on audience ratings.

To all this criticism, defenders of the industry sometimes answer that they are giving viewers what they want to see, that the American people would not watch more of the higher-brow fare that some critics seem to be looking for. Television, they say, is just a mirror of American values, not their creator.

Those who disagree with this assessment worry not only that the quality of television is poor but also that its effects are harmful. Game shows and "I Love Lucy" reruns, some argue, are not just "brain candy" but also contribute to a kind of mindlessness. Some critics ask whether television is muting the rich, regional accents of America. Will the time come when the people of the deep South sound like Walter Cronkite? The dirt-obsessed women of many commercials do not mirror American women or harmlessly sell a product, critics say; rather, they help maintain a view of women — and an anxiety about housekeeping — that are harmful. As broadcast historian Erik Barnouw said, "One of the most fascinating things about television is the continual overlapping of everything. Drama is inevitably propaganda, it's politics, it's also merchandising. It is continually selling a way of life or a pattern of consumption." [17]

But how effective is it in selling these things? Is television a mirror or a force in itself? Some critics have argued that the effects of television go far beyond responses to the obvious messages it broadcasts. As Richard Adler explained, Marshall McLuhan "insisted that trying to understand television by examining the programs it offers is as futile as attempting to comprehend the impact of the printing press in the 15th century by interpreting the contents of Gutenberg's Bible."[18] In Adler's words, McLuhan has portrayed television "as nothing less than a major landmark in the evolution of human consciousness."[19] To critic Michael Novak, television "is the molder of the soul's geography. It builds up incrementally a psychic structure of expectations. It does so in the same way that school lessons slowly, over the years, tutor the unformed mind and teach it 'how to think.' "[20]

In Chapters 8–11 we will assess the nature of television's influence, as well as that of other media. Here, though, we can offer a very general assessment of the quality of television and how well it has performed its functions by quoting commentator Eric Sevareid. There was a thoughtful expression on Sevareid's face as he looked into the television camera one evening in 1978. Of course, Sevareid was always thoughtful, but on this occasion he wasn't thinking about world affairs but about the medium that had brought his evening commentaries to millions of Americans. He was thinking about television. This was to be Sevareid's final commentary on the CBS Evening News: "Television," he said, "has learned to amuse well; to inform up to a point; to instruct up to a nearer point; to inspire rarely. The great literature, the great art, the great thought of past and present make only guest appearances. This can change."

Cable TV: The Shape of Things to Come

All the broadcasting services discussed so far have a common characteristic: there are a limited number of channels. Beyond a certain point, if you try to broadcast more signals over the air in one area, the signals interfere with each other. This scarcity of channels not only led to government regulation of television but also influences its content. In any area the number of channels is small and each station tries to appeal to all the people in the area; its content is therefore aimed at a heterogeneous, not a specialized, audience.

Cable television differs in a fundamental way. It is characterized not by channel scarcity but by channel diversity. It is the "television of abundance" because its signals are sent not over the air but through coaxial cables stretched from place to place like telephone wires.

The Coaxial Cable and Its Potential

Coaxial cable has several special characteristics. It has two conductors, like two wires, one inside the other. The cable is a mixture of copper and aluminum and is tightly sealed in plastic. Such a cable has the capacity to prevent signal linkage, so it can transmit a very clear picture. In addition it can carry many more signals than a single wire or even a wireless system can. With appropriate technology, cable can bring in signals from cities hundreds, even thousands, of miles away.

These characteristics give cable operators many choices. They can include in their system all the local stations and choose other distant channels to import. They can put together their own programs and still have channels to lease to others. Groups that could not afford to buy time on an over-the-air station might be able to afford time on cable, which is far cheaper.

For consumers, cable also opens the possibility of choices, possibly vast choices. They can receive more than thirty-six channels on cable television. Theoretically, at least, they can mix and match programs from local and distant stations, specialized and generalized programs. Although network television has been ingenious in creating programs for a mass audience and has captured millions of viewers, it has virtually ignored people's specialized interests. Cable television might satisfy those interests.

Futurists considering cable television found its possibilities mind-boggling. Scores of channels were imagined. Some channels might give just business information; others would include cultural programming — operas, ballets, symphonies. Ethnic groups might have their own channels. People making television programs would no longer be restricted by the need to reach the mass audience; they could produce programs for a specific audience with special interests. Two-way communication between the home and the transmission facility is also a possibility. But cable television has been slow to develop and is still far from matching these visions.

A History of Cable in America

Cable television was first used for a very practical reason. In the late 1940s, as television began to reach a large audience, two problems became obvious. First, because the few existing stations were in large cities and were not very powerful, people who lived outside those cities either got no picture at all or got a hazy, snowy image that all but disappeared every time a car drove past their home. Second, because television signals travel basically in a line of sight, bouncing off obstructions, mountains and skyscrapers can block their signals. But cable can solve both these problems.

There is some dispute about just when cable television was first used, but one likely story credits Robert Tarlton with beginning it in 1950. Tarlton owned a radio and television repair shop in Lansford, Pennsylvania. Although Lansford is only sixty-five miles from Philadelphia, a mountain outside Lansford blocked television signals. Tarlton knew that his chances of selling television sets would increase if signal reception in Lansford could be improved. So Tarlton organized the Panther Valley Television Company, placed an antenna on the mountain that was interfering with signals, and strung cable down to the homes of people who owned television sets. The antenna picked up the television signals, and the cable brought them to the homes.

As Tarlton's idea caught hold, cable companies sprang up elsewhere around the country. They brought a sharp picture to distant rural areas and to large cities where skyscrapers interfered with broadcast signals. Thus cable brought television to additional viewers, expanding the television audience, to the delight of the broadcasting industry.

In 1960 fewer than 2 percent of American television households had cable television, and there were only 640 cable companies. Cable was being used only to bring in a clear signal. Then a few cable companies saw the other possibilities for cable; they began to bring in signals from other cities. To local broadcast stations, the cable companies were now unwanted competition, taking away some of their audience and giving it to the distant, imported stations. To the distant stations, the cable companies were thieves, using their programs without paying for them. Under pressure from the broadcast industry, the FCC in 1965 declared that cable television was under its jurisdiction. From then until the 1970s, the FCC slowed the development of cable in order to protect the broadcasting industry.

For cable to offer a diversity of channels and specialized programming, two things were necessary: economic feasibility and favorable government regulations. But at first the FCC's rules were very restrictive. In 1972 the regulations included requirements that the cable company carry all stations licensed within thirty-five miles of the system as well as guidelines for rates, complaint procedures, and construction schedules. Local governments actually grant the franchises to cable systems to operate in their area, and they, as well as state government, can add other rules. The FCC also ruled that a cable system in the hundred largest television markets had to have at least a twenty-channel capacity, to set aside one channel for public access and others for schools and local government, and to have the facilities to originate programs itself. Perhaps most important, the FCC restricted the number of signals that the cable companies could import.

Then the FCC began to loosen its regulations. In 1979 it allowed cable operators to bring in as many signals from distant broadcast stations as they wished. Also in 1979 a Supreme Court decision freed cable operators from the FCC's rule that they must provide public-access airtime to almost any group that put together a show. State and local governments, however, can still require some public service programming as long as their rules do not interfere with the federal government's policies.

By 1979 cable television seemed on the verge of becoming a major medium of communication. Not only were government regulations relaxed but the economic picture for cable television was improving. Advertising agency executives say that a medium must be able to attract 30 percent of the potential audience for national advertisers to find it economically worthwile. It was when over-the-air television reached 30 percent of American households in the 1950s that it became a significant mass medium that could attract sufficient amounts of national advertising, and it was this number that made color television a commercial reality by the 1970s. At the end of 1978 there were over 4,000 operating cable systems, reaching almost 18 percent of American households. By 1980, 20 percent of American households were hooked up with cable systems, and *Time* magazine predicted that that number would jump to 33 percent in 1981. Cable companies were originating more of their own programs and bringing in more specialized programs from distant stations. In 1980 the cable industry seemed on the verge of challenging conventional network television.

| **Cable Television in the 1980s** | Two kinds of cable services were available at the beginning of the 1980s: basic cable and pay cable. With basic cable the subscriber pays a one-time fee, and the local cable company strings a wire to the back of the television set much as Ma Bell puts in a phone. Then the subscriber also pays a monthly service fee. In 1980 the nationwide average fee was about $15 for the installation plus about $7 a month. In return subscribers view multiple channels, compared with the more limited number of channels that a standard in-house or rooftop antenna can bring in. In addition to the local UHF and VHF channels, cable subscribers in many areas can see out-of-town stations, special telecasts of sports events, shows in foreign languages, and special educational programming. They |

often receive programs from the so-called superstations as well — independent television stations that lease space on a communications satellite. There were four superstations in 1979, including WTCG in Atlanta, WOR in New York, WGN in Chicago, and KTVU in San Francisco-Oakland. They provide programming that includes sports events and reruns of old television shows. By 1980 the superstations had produced little programming of their own, but they were responding to criticisms of their poor quality by promising to produce original shows for children and other programs. A 24-hour news network was initiated in June 1980.

Cable subscribers who want more and better programming than basic cable provides can buy it for an additional $8 to $10 per month. For their money they get high-quality motion pictures only a few weeks after they have been shown in local theaters, sports events not available on regular TV or basic cable, and entertainment specials from Las Vegas and other entertainment capitals. Some viewers especially like one aspect of pay cable — no advertising. Also, films are left intact in their original form, not censored for sexual content as they are on network television.

Television critic Nicholas Johnson used to tell TV viewers to "talk back to your television set." Of course, he was not speaking literally but meant that people should find ways to communicate with the networks and the FCC. By the late 1970s, some viewers in the United States really could talk back to their television sets. Some were talking back to their sets by playing electronic games. In an experiment in Columbus, Ohio, Warner Cable Corporation developed a two-way cable system (called QUBE) that allowed viewers to talk back to their sets by pressing buttons on a hand-held console. The programs that viewers saw were mainly local news and talk shows in which questions were asked of the audience. For example, consumer advocate Ralph Nader, on a visit to Columbus, asked QUBE viewers whether they would back a petition to change children's advertising. Viewers could push a "yes" or "no" button. (The yes's won.) The possibilities for greater citizen participation in public affairs and for more rapid marketing research for advertisers are obvious. In Japan a more advanced experiment allowed people to talk back to their sets and be seen through a small camera mounted on the television.

As impressive as cable seems, its content by 1980 was still far from what futurists had anticipated ten years earlier. Cable companies still were not producing much of their own programming. But the future is likely to see the development of special news and opinion channels, public affairs programming, more personal involvement shows, as well as richer entertainment and cultural programming — perhaps including the best of the Broadway stage and opera, ballet, and symphony orchestras. As a result of cable, the average home could also have electronic tie-ins to commercial establishments, stock reports, and connections to libraries. People could make commercial transactions with banks and department stores without leaving their homes. A Canadian system, called Teledon, is already doing these things and more on an experimental basis in several Canadian cities. Teledon can create pictures and graphs through computer graphics, order up information about the economy, help a person pick out a local restaurant, and much, much more.

Cable television could also deliver a wide range of special services to institutions and community organizations. Local communities could expand their sources of public health, educational, and consumer information through cable hook-ups. Much of the activity anticipated by cable operators is not mass communication at all but the communication of specialized information to specific, targeted audiences.

It may not be unreasonable to think that in the future people will create their own shows by selecting certain features and rejecting others. Imagine a news show in which you decide that you want more news about your own neighborhood, less world news, a special feature on cross-country skiing, and a detailed report on a particular stock on the New York Stock Exchange. Of course, some people are already making their own entertainment packages through the use of cassettes. This capability, linked to cable television and computers, conjures up an image of an information-rich future. Critic Alvin Toffler has predicted that cable will contribute to the demassification of the media, encouraging many channels and increasingly fragmented and diversified audiences. Naturally, the national networks fear this development.

Summary

This chapter has reviewed the American broadcasting media, which have both commercial and noncommercial components. Our emphasis has been on commercial broadcasting, with passing reference to the public systems.

Broadcasting can be defined as a technology, as a production and distribution system, and as content. The actual use of broadcasting's great capabilities has often lagged behind technology. The principal components of the broadcasting industry are the local stations, the national networks, the audience, and the advertisers. Commercial broadcasters sell access to their audiences to advertisers. This is the source of revenue in the broadcasting industry, and as a result the industry has been profitable and programming has been influenced by advertisers and interrupted frequently by their messages.

As a result of the scarcity of broadcasting channels, broadcasting is subject to government regulation and to the regulations of the FCC in particular. The FCC licenses stations and monitors their performance to see that, as custodians of the public's airwaves, the stations act in the public interest. Among the factors the FCC has looked for as evidence that the public interest is being served are diversity of ownership and fair coverage of public affairs. In addition, broadcasting must adjust to social pressure and criticism.

Radio was the first of the broadcasting industries, and it survived competition from television by becoming a more specialized and more intimate medium. To the surprise of many, radio is prospering today.

Radio's resurgence does not seem to have hurt television, which Americans watch, on the average, more than six hours a day. Despite its great range of programs, the content of television is frequently attacked for poor quality, imitation, and harmful effects. Yet television unquestionably does much to inform and entertain Americans. It has done less well as a source of inspiration and in appealing to people's specialized interests. The growth of cable television might make up for these deficiencies. Cable offers the possibility of more diverse and more specialized communication, a potential demassification of the media.

Notes and References

1. John Crosby, "The Age of Noise," in *Radio and Television, Readings in the Mass Media,* ed. Allen and Linda Kirschner (New York: Odyssey Press, 1971) p. 183.
2. For a useful discussion of these concepts, see Reed H. Blake and Edwin O. Haroldsen, *A Taxonomy of Concepts on Communication* (New York: Hastings House, 1975) p. 42.
3. Lynn S. Gross, *Hear/See; An Introduction to Broadcasting* (Dubuque: W. C. Brown, 1979) p. 45.
4. Giraud Chester, Garnet R. Garrison, and Edgar E. Willis, *Television and Radio,* 4th ed. (Englewood Cliffs, N.J.: Prentice-Hall, 1971) p. 42.
5. Bruce M. Owen, Jack H. Beebe, and Willard G. Manning, Jr., *Television Economics* (Lexington, Mass.: D. C. Heath, 1974) p. 4. Some of the other material in this section is also derived in part from pp. 6–12.
6. Harry J. Scornia, *Television and Society* (New York: McGraw-Hill, 1965) p. 7.
7. Sydney W. Head, *Broadcasting in America; A Survey of Television and Radio,* 3rd ed. (Boston: Houghton Mifflin, 1976) p. 207.
8. Peter Jay, "The Future of Broadcasting," *Encounter,* April 1977, p. 69.

9. Chester, Garrison, and Willis, *Television and Radio,* pp. 122–123.

10. Mary B. Cassata and Molefi K. Asante, *Mass Communication: Principles and Practices* (New York: Macmillan, 1979) p. 175.

11. Chester, Garrison, and Willis, *Television and Radio,* p. 34.

12. Frank Brady, "Move Over, TV — Radio is Booming," *Parade,* October 7, 1979, p. 5. Also see, "Striking It Rich in Radio," *Business Week,* February 5, 1979, pp. 58–62.

13. Brady, "Move Over," p. 5.

14. Ibid.

15. Paula S. Fass, "Television as Cultural Document: Promises and Problems," in *Television as a Cultural Force,* ed. Richard Adler and Douglass Cater (New York: Praeger, 1976), p. 37.

16. This section draws on the fine introduction in Gross, *Hear/See.*

17. Quoted in Douglass Cater, ed. *Television as a Social Force* (New York: Praeger, 1975) p. 8.

18. Richard Adler, "Understanding Television: An Overview of the Literature of the Medium as a Social and Cultural Force," in ibid., p. 36.

19. Ibid.

20. Michael Novak, "Television Shapes the Soul," in Cater, ed., *Television as a Social Force,* p. 23.

6 The Movies

> Some day someone with an authentic
> movie mind will make a cheap and simple
> motion picture that will arrest the notice
> of the civilized minority [and] when that
> day comes, the movies will split into two
> halves. . . . There will be huge, banal,
> maudlin, idiotic movies for the mob, and
> . . . there will be movies made by artists
> for people who can read and write.
>
> H. L. MENCKEN

From a quick description, movies sound much like television: moving images plus sound. Some of their differences appear at first to be like disadvantages: You have to go to the movies and pay for them rather than having them come to you for free. And, of course, the same movies shown in theaters are often shown on television. Not surprisingly, the movie industry lost a lot of its audience to television. But the dark theater, the large screen, and the uninterrupted film continue to exert a special force and to draw people out of their homes.

Perhaps as television continues to change it will draw even more people away from the movie theater. But today film remains an important and a separate medium. In this chapter we ask what films are, what their functions are, how they are made, and what their content has been. We examine, too, the links between films and economic, political, and social forces and some of the ways film makers receive feedback. As we will see, the movies in America have been marked from their beginnings both by a search for successful formulas that would sustain audience enthusiasm and by a turbulent battle between the profit motive and artistic standards.

Defining Motion Pictures

No other medium of mass communication has enjoyed the glamour and public acclaim of the movies. From *The Birth of a Nation* to *Star Wars*, from Douglas Fairbanks to Dustin Hoffman and Meryl Streep, movies, movie stars, and the intrigue of the industry have been in the public eye. Screaming tabloids, gushing movie magazines, and caustic television commentators pass on the latest Hollywood gossip and speculation to a fascinated public.

The publicity that has been given to movies, however, may do more to hinder than to help our understanding of what they are. Behind the gossip and the glamour lies the reality of the movies. A comment in F. Scott Fitzgerald's *The Last Tycoon* is worth considering:

> You can take Hollywood for granted like I did, or you can dismiss it with the contempt we reserve for what we don't understand. It can be understood too, but only dimly in flashes. Not a half dozen men have ever been able to keep the whole equation of pictures in their heads.[1]

According to Joan Didion, critics are often guilty of forgetting the "whole equation." She denounced them for refusing to acknowledge the economic reality of the movies.[2] Film, claimed Didion, is more of an industry than an art form. We have no precise equation by which we can say that motion pictures are "more" of an industry or "more" of an art form, but certainly they are both. They are also a mass medium of communication and a social force.

The many facets of motion pictures are reflected in the fact that certain names for them do not necessarily mean the same thing. Take the terms *film, cimema,* and *movie.* French film theorists make a clear distinction between film and cinema. To them the term *film* describes the relationship of the medium to the world around it, whereas *cinema* describes its cultural standards and internal structure. Add to this the American word *movies,* and we have a convenient label for a third aspect of motion pictures — their characteristics as an economic commodity.[3] As film scholar James Monaco wrote:

> These three aspects are closely interrelated, of course: One person's "movie" is another person's "film." But in general we use these three names for an art in a way

that closely parallels this differentiation: "movies," like popcorn, are to be consumed; "cinema" (at least in the American parlance) is high art, . . . "film" is the most general term with the fewest connotations.[4]

For this reason we use the word *film* most often in this chapter, recognizing that the term may embrace many things.

As art, film includes the whole spectrum of art forms. Film, like the theater and dance, is a performing art; like painting and literature it is representational; and like music it is a recording art. Thus critics evaluate the performance of actors and actresses in their roles. They also comment on the representational beauty of the photography or the literary quality of the screenplay. Music, sound, and special effects also get their attention.

Evaluating the artistic merit of films, however, is beyond the scope of this book, and film as a social force is the topic of later chapters. Here we are most concerned with film as a medium of mass communication and film as an industry.

Film as a Medium of Mass Communication

For the people who make films, they provide an avenue for expression, an opportunity to practice their craft, a chance to influence and to entertain, and a livelihood. The film itself may be frivolous entertainment, it may make a political or a social statement, or it may have important artistic qualities. For the audience the film may be an escape or a lesson in fashion, language, or human relationships. Throughout their history, however, American films have been primarily, though not exclusively, a medium for entertainment. They have been fantasies, taking their viewers away from the mundane details of everyday life. No matter what the fortunes of the marketplace or to what extent other media such as television have competed for its audience, this medium has held onto the function of entertaining as its main reason for being. Explanations for this emphasis can be found both in the history of film and in the conflicting forces that still shape American films today.

An Overview of American Film History

Film history, according to James Monaco, "is a matter of decades and half-decades." That is, changes are frequent because of the explosive impact of films, the fast development of technology, and the large size of movie audiences.[5] Monaco has distinguished seven periods in American film history:

1. The film has a *prehistory,* which includes all the precursors of the camera/projector as well as other media developments from the rotary press to the phono-

graph and telegraph, all of which contributed to the motion picture, though some indirectly.

2. An important *transition* occurred from 1896 to 1912 when the cinema evolved from a side-show novelty into a full-fledged economic art. At the end of this period came the full-length feature film. With this change of form the movies became entertainment in their own right, not just something to fill out the vaudeville bill.

3. The *silent period* lasted until 1927, when the "talkies" and the star system began and the major studios had become established in Hollywood.

4. The *growth of world cinema* occurred from 1928 to 1932 when filmmakers in other countries got into the act after they recovered from World War I. It was during this same period that sound movies became commonplace.

5. The *Golden Age of Hollywood* lasted from 1932 to 1946. The film was dominated by major American studios and movies had their greatest economic success. During this period color came to the screen.

6. The *assault from television* occurred from 1947 to 1960. The movies suffered severe economic losses during this period. Hollywood lost its grip on the industry and confronted increasing government regulation. Greater international involvements also came.

7. The *period of readjustment* has been from 1961 to the 1980s. Hollywood recovered somewhat; technology advanced again; movie content continued to diversify; new filmmakers and styles had an impact on film.[6]

Styles of exhibition changed through these periods. The rather primitive theaters of the nickelodeon era gave way to gilded motion picture palaces during the 1920s. By the 1930s and 1940s the massive motion picture palace was commonplace. Theater chains, mostly owned by the major studios, erected impressive structures. As use of the automobile increased and the suburbs expanded, drive-in movies became popular. Some drive-ins could handle more than 2,000 cars and were connected to amusement parks, swimming pools, and even laundromats. As the cities declined economically and in population, theaters moved to the suburbs and shopping malls. By the 1960s and 1970s, a combination of audience tastes and television's competition brought about smaller, more intimate theaters. Meanwhile, stricter zoning laws reduced the number and size of the drive-ins.

The form of the movies changed, too, as technology and the art of film making matured. In the late 1920s the first talkies were produced; color appeared in the 1930s. Increasing sophistication with lenses and cinematography allowed a host of innovations. Film makers constantly experimented with their art and craft. Wide-screen movies appeared in the early 1950s; three-dimensional viewing was tried; wrap-around sound systems expanded. Competition of all kinds — artistic, economic, intellectual, and technical — brought about change.

The Functions of Films

Throughout their history films have provided entertainment of all kinds, from tragedy to comedy, from realism to fantasy. Some films, but of course not all, are made to be pure entertainment, to serve as an escape. Others seek to entertain while they enrich or inform or persuade. In some films, such as documentaries, entertainment is at most a secondary function. Especially during wartime, some films have been made as propaganda.

The function, of course, is partly in the eye of the beholder. Most people see Walt Disney films as harmless, perhaps gushy, family entertainment. But others have seen them as ideological statements praising an unrealistic image of America with artificial, antiseptic communities devoid of social problems or racial and ethnic identities. Still, despite some variety and many changes in films, most have been made and watched primarily for the purpose of entertainment. A closer look at the early history of American films helps explain why.

Magazines grew out of newspapers and television from radio; thus their origins were related to media in which providing information and influencing opinion were important functions. But films were related to the traditions of strolling players, the theater, and similar popular amusements. In other words, their origins had little to do with the media of information and opinion but much to do with entertainment.

Early films, however, were not a form of mass entertainment. They were shown as novelties to small audiences. Their transformation into a mass medium early in this century was nurtured by an expansion of leisure time — a "recreation revolution" in the words of historian Garth Jowett. Certainly an increasingly prosperous America at the turn of the century had more leisure time, which led to a growing interest in various forms of recreation and entertainment.

By the early 1920s films "had become the largest and most widespread commercial entertainment form the world had ever seen."[7] It was the coming of the full-length feature film that made a solid place for movies in American entertainment, transforming them into a mass medium. At first film makers believed that audiences would not sit still for more than ten or fifteen minutes. Movies were just one reel long. But producer Adolph Zukor rewrote the rules in 1912 when he imported the four-reel French film *Queen Elizabeth,* starring Sarah Bernhardt. The film was an hour and a half long, and it was an immediate success. Zukor could not provide prints to theaters fast enough. With longer films came better photographic and acting quality which assured audience appeal. With the full-length film, the movies could compete with the stage, opera, and musical comedy.

Movies joined music, drama, sporting events, novels, and popular magazines as part of America's entertainment fare. They all flourished as citizens looked for diversions and amusements to fill their leisure hours. But movies came to have a special place because they could do something better than all the rest: it is said they provide a channel for dreams. As critic Hollis Alpert has written,

> Never in history has so great an industry as the movies been so nakedly and directly built out of the dreams of a people. Any hour of the day or the evening you can go into a darkened theater . . . and as the figures move across the wide screen you sail off on storm tossed seas of sex, action, and violence, crime and death. . . . When you come home to sleep, your dreams are woven out of the symbols which themselves have been woven out of your dreams, for the movies are the stuff American dreams are made of.[8]

How Films Are Made

Making movies is a communal process. They are the product not of one person but of many. As a result, according to Professor John L. Fell,

> The substance of any particular production is likely to change appreciably between its early idea stages and the final release print. These changes may be dominated by some individual's vision, ordered by his own evolving understanding of what the movie *is,* but such a happy circumstance is never altogether the case, . . . even if most of the time someone pretends to be in charge.[9]

Moreover, every film requires the solution of both mechanical and aesthetic problems. The many people that are part of the

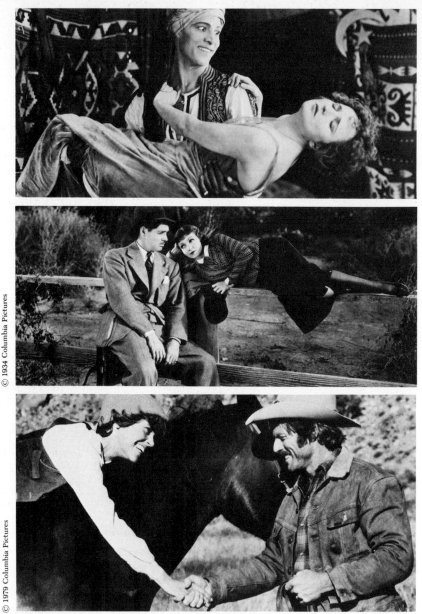

TOP: *Actor Rudolph Valentino, shown here in his famous portrayal as "The Sheik," captivated American audiences in the 1920s and solidified the role of the male sex symbol.*

MIDDLE: *In* It Happened One Night *(1934) Clark Gable and Claudette Colbert gave the public an artful romantic comedy.*

BOTTOM: *Jane Fonda and Robert Redford proved in* The Electric Horseman *(1979) that even westerns are not immune to romantic plots.*

team making the film must have different skills. Just consider the various unions involved in film making: the Writer's Guild of America, American Cinema Editors, Director's Guild of America, Screen Actors Guild, International Association of Theatrical and Stage Employees. Films are put together under chaotic conditions with a variety of artistic, technical, and organizational people.

Fell has identified seven stages or elements in the process of film making:

1. *Conceptualization* The idea for a film may come from any one of various people. Early directors often wrote their own films.
2. *Direction* The director chooses the film script and solves the problems it poses during production.
3. *Visualization* The planning and execution of the actual filming involves cinematographers, lighting technicians, and others.
4. *Performance* Actors must be chosen and their performances calibrated to the script and to other personnel involved in the film.
5. *Editing* This process involves choosing takes from all the film that has been shot and processing a finished film.
6. *Special effects* Everything from camera trickery to monsters to stuntmen and stuntwomen comes under this heading.
7. *Production* To produce a film means to get the money together, organize all the people involved and the schedule, and put the film on the screen.

The producer is a key figure in putting all these elements together. In most cases he or she is part of a film studio that has the space, facilities, and personnel to complete the film. It is the producer who carries the responsibility for most of the central decisions — other than technical ones about acting, editing, and so on. The producer initiates the development of a film by acquiring a story or a script. The producer may merely take an option on a story (that is, an agreement giving one the right to purchase at a later date) until he or she sees if the talent and the money are available to produce the film. If financial backing is available and suitable acting talent can be placed under contract, then a director is found and the rest of the film-making team is assembled. Directors direct the shooting.

The Content of American Films

From this varied group of people with different needs and different interests comes the film. Its content is almost always shaped by conflicting forces. The audience, technology, economics, and the film makers themselves play a part. Producers look carefully at the balance sheet, continually worried about audience interests. They ask, What is technically and economically possible, and what does the audience want? They are seeking, in the words of one film historian, *efficient dreambuilding*.

> *Efficient* means meeting production demands of cost and time while developing an intelligible visual narrative within the prescribed single-double or multi-length reel length. *Dreambuilding* means satisfying audiences' appetites for formula structure in comedy and melodrama with accepted standards of moral and philosophic thought.[10]

What films constitute efficient dreambuilding varies with the times. The search for efficiency led, for example, to standardized lengths for films, though the lengths changed through the decades. Efficient dreambuilding also calls for coherent plot structures. Old westerns, for example, were usually melodramas with a hero, villain, a beautiful girl, and perhaps Indians. The audience had particular expectations of what they would see, and plots were usually standardized to meet those expectations.

Over time what the audience wants to see changes. Anxious to find out more about their audiences, studios hire the services of groups like the Opinion Research Institute of Princeton, which puts together a profile of moviegoers. Today, for example, about 76 percent of moviegoers are under the age of thirty; less than 6 percent are fifty years or older; 31 percent are teenagers.[11]

But often, rather than finding out more about their audience, producers may assume that if one movie is popular then another one like it will be, too. Thus they may take the search for efficient dreambuilding a step further and just repeat a formula or produce a sequel. Because of the success of *The Godfather* (1972), *Jaws* (1975), and *The Exorcist* (1973), we soon had *The Godfather II* (1974), *Jaws II* (1978), and *The Exorcist II* (1977).

But the balance sheet is not alone in determining the shape of films. Directors and actors, and even producers, may also be interested in putting the mark of their own imagination on a film. According to one film historian, "It was this dialectic [working of opposing forces] . . . that drove the Hollywood cinema: the clash between the artist's sensibility and the classic mythic structure of the story types that were identified and popular."[12]

Out of this clash came a broad range of films. We can look at their diverse content in terms of differences in themes, styles, and genres.

The Development of Themes and Styles. The early movies looked to the established forms of drama (comedy, tragedy, musical) for their patterns. They often looked to books for ideas and screenplays. Early silent film comedies relied on the art of mime. But soon American films developed their own forms and traditions. In the silent period figures such as Mack Sennett, Charlie Chaplin, Buster Keaton, and Harold Lloyd created their own forms of acting or storytelling; later, directors such as Eric von Stroheim and Cecil B. De Mille added their mark. These film makers, and later others who created films with a distinctive style, are known as *auteurs*. Eventually, the content and style of the film was less influenced as a dramatic form by material from plays or books and more by its own emerging traditions.

A glimpse at those emerging traditions is provided by the research of Edgar Dale in the 1930s. As part of a famous series of studies on the effects of the movies (the Payne Fund Studies), Dale analyzed the content of 1,500 films: 500 that were released in 1920, 500 released in 1925, and 500 released in 1930. He found that only three major themes — crime, sex, and love — accounted for approximately three-fourths of the movies studied.

In general, directors were the dominating force shaping films until the 1930s. Then in the 1930s and 1940s the studios were dominant. Several studios came to have recognizable styles. MGM was long known for its richly produced, glossy epics aimed at middle-brow tastes. The 1939 film classic *Gone With the Wind* is a splendid example of this style. Paramount was said to give its films a European sensibility. Warner Brothers often shot on location because creating the sets would have been too expensive. Thus Warner developed a reputation for realism.[13]

Today these studio styles have disappeared as the influence of the major studios has declined. But even in the heyday of the studios some individuals marked their films with their own distinctive stamp. Different members of the film-making teams may dominate at any time and in any film. For example, as head of MGM James Aubrey reedited director Sam Peckinpah's *Pat Garrett and Billy the Kid* (1973) and Ken Russell's *The Boy Friend* (1971) at a time when it was becoming popular to see the director as king of the film.[14] On the whole directors have gained greater control over their films in the 1970s, and awareness of their varying styles has grown.

Genres. Balanced against the film maker's desire for individuality is the need to give the audience a message it will understand and accept — the need for efficient dreambuilding. As a result of this

need, plots become more or less standardized. Story types —
genres — develop. Literature developed genres, and so did
American films.

Probably the most popular film genre of all time has been the
western. It was a completely American invention, with brave
men and women moving across the frontier, where they met hardship in battle with the elements, with Indians, and with the law.
The Republic studio in particular made large numbers of early
westerns.

Musicals were also immensely popular in past years, and some
studios like Warner Brothers virtually specialized in this form. It
was Warner Brothers that produced Busby Berkeley's elaborate,
geometrically choreographed dance films of the 1930s, featuring
such stars as Fred Astaire and Ginger Rogers.

Comedies have also attracted wide audiences. They have
ranged from dry-witted, British-inspired parlor comedies to screw-
ball films by the Marx Brothers. Other genres include gangster
films, horror films, historical romances, thrillers, and war films.

Through the years the various forms have been altered to suit
changing public tastes and interests. Popular singers, from Bing
Crosby and Rudy Vallee in the 1930s to Kris Kristofferson and
Peter Frampton in the 1970s, have found their way into musicals.
By the 1970s some westerns were serious dramas and some were
concerned with social issues. Some genres are parodied to suit
changing tastes. For example the Italian-made "spaghetti westerns" (often starring Clint Eastwood) are parodies of westerns and
are best appreciated by those who know and understand westerns.
Producer Mel Brooks created a parody of horror films in *Young
Frankenstein* (1974) and of silent movies in *Silent Movie* (1976).
Occasionally, public taste dictates creation of a new genre, such as
the science-fiction thriller or the black films of the 1970s that depicted black heroes, unity among blacks, and, usually, victory over
the white establishment. *Super Fly* (1972), *Shaft* (1971), and
Buck and the Preacher (1972) are examples of this genre. Although blacks often wrote, directed, and acted in these films, they
were owned and distributed by white-run studios. Recent films
like *The Turning Point* (1977), *An Unmarried Woman* (1978),
Julia (1977), and *My Brilliant Career* (1980) had clear feminist
themes.

Documentaries. Most of the films we have discussed have fictional themes. But nonfiction films, called *documentaries*, are
also important. The term *documentary* was first introduced by
British film maker John Grierson, whose early nonfiction film,

The Drifters (1929), depicted the lives of herring fishermen in the North Sea.

In the purest form of the documentary, the film maker intrudes as little as possible; the director, for example, does not direct actors or set up scenes. The *cinema verité* technique takes this idea further: it is spontaneous, direct filming. To make *Titicut Follies* (1967), for example, Frederick Wiseman wandered through a mental hospital capturing representative snatches of life in the institution; then he edited these snatches into a coherent portrait of what he saw. Some directors feel that it is impossible *not* to intrude on the subject in some way, not to include one's own interpretation, consciously or unconsciously. Others feel that such intrusion and interpretation is necessary if the film is to be coherent.

Through the years documentaries have dealt with people at work, the efforts of nations at war, social problems, and other issues. Some are artful classics like Robert Flaherty's *Nanook of the North* (1922), which depicted Eskimo life. Others like Frederick Wiseman's *Titicut Follies* (1967), *High School* (1969), and *Law and Order* (1970) portrayed the grim reality of institutions in contemporary America. Some documentaries take bits and pieces of a process and weld them into a film. For example, Emile de Antonio and Daniel Talbot's award-winning *Point of Order!* (1963) put together film that others had taken of the Army-McCarthy hearings; he creatively used the work of other film makers and of camera operators not under his direction. Documentaries often carry a powerful message, like Peter Davis's *Hearts and Minds* (1975), which traced the painful relationship between the United States and Vietnam.

An offshoot of the documentary is the *docudrama:* quasi-historical re-creations of recent historical events. A docudrama, in fact, is not a documentary because it uses actors, stages, and sometimes fictionalizes the story. Probably the best-known docudrama is the television production *Roots.* In the 1970s and early 1980s docudramas, ranging on topics from the life of actor Humphrey Bogart to the Watergate scandal, gained popularity as television movies.

Public Preferences. For all their visual power and artistic achievement, documentaries have never been able to challenge the dominance of the fictional, entertainment film. More people want to see entertainment films than want to see documentaries. Tables 6.1 and 6.2 give some indication of public preferences at various times for different film genres. Film critic Bosley

Table 6.1 Film Content Preferences in the United States, 1945

Type	Males	Females
Musicals	35	49
Light comedy	35	42
Serious drama	23	42
Excitement, adventure	39	25
Slapstick comedy	43	18
Army, navy, aviation	40	23
Detective, mystery	36	24
Romance, mystery	9	32
Westerns	16	7

Source: Bosley Crowther, "It's the Fans Who Make the Films," *New York Times Magazine*, June 24, 1945, p. 14.

Crowther found that film audiences around 1945 seemed to prefer musicals and light comedies. Between 1947 and 1954 (a period that embraces both the high point of movie attendance and the beginning of the downslide because of television), the studios seemed to prefer to make westerns.[15] In the late 1970s, a list of top-grossing motion pictures showed that the public still likes comedies (see Table 6.2).

Another view of public preferences is given by the annual list of all-time box office champions compiled each year by *Variety,* the show business trade paper. *Variety's* financial yardstick is the rental fees paid to distributors in the United States and Canada in the years since a film was first released. The champions as of January 1980 were:

Star Wars (1977)	$175,849,000
Jaws (1975)	$133,429,000
Grease (1978)	$ 93,292,000
The Exorcist (1973)	$ 88,100,000
The Godfather (1972)	$ 86,275,000
Superman (1978)	$ 81,000,000
The Sound of Music (1965)	$ 79,000,000
The Sting (1973)	$ 78,889,000
Close Encounters (1977)	$ 77,000,000
Gone With the Wind (1939)	$ 76,700,000

Obviously a range of genres have been popular. Science fiction, adventure-thriller, gangster, supernatural, musical, and historical epic films have scored immensely with the public.

Table 6.2 Classification of the Thirty Top-Grossing Motion Pictures in the United States, 1976

Type	Number
Comedy:	
Farcical or near-farcical	6
Other	3
Cartoon	2
Western	2
Crime/police/suspense	
Based on fact	2
Other melodrama	2
Horror	
Supernatural	2
Romantic	1
Disaster (historical, modern, science fiction)	3
Psychological drama	2
Romantic drama	2
Science fiction	1
Historical costume drama	1
War	1

Source: Motion Picture Association of America.

Many factors influence preferences — trends in morality, popular passions, current events, plus various styles and standards. The 1930s fostered stark realism and grim Depression themes as well as cheerful musicals that helped the public escape from its troubles. Historical and patriotic themes and war films were popular during World War II and after, but so were light comedies. In the 1950s, films seemed to reflect the light-headed mood of the country. Comedies and westerns were increasingly popular, and sexual themes were becoming more explicit. In the late 1960s, during a period of dissatisfaction with prevailing standards and styles, films celebrated the anti-hero and began to take on controversial social topics. Films in the late 1960s and 1970s explored racism, drug use, war, and homosexuality. Still, there was time for the nonsense comedy and the light-headed musical. Films in the 1970s also explored international espionage and organized crime as well as the supernatural and catastrophes.

Although fewer motion pictures are made in the United States today than decades ago, their content may be more diverse as films continue to skirmish with other media for audiences. Film

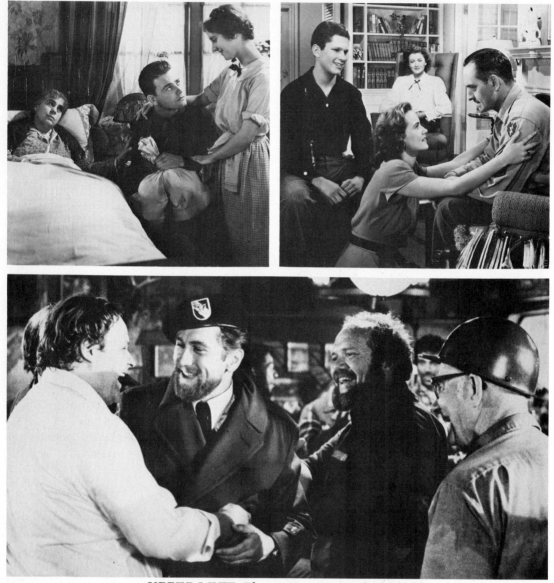

UPPER LEFT: *The great epic novel of World War I,* All Quiet on the Western Front, *has been brought to the screen several times.*

UPPER RIGHT: *The problems of veterans returning from World War II were pointed up in* The Best Years of Our Lives (1946).

BOTTOM: *The grim realities of the Vietnam war and its impact on the inhabitants of a particular American community were the subject of* The Deer Hunter (1978), *which, like many earlier war films, did not glorify war or military life.*

offerings seem as diverse as the people who see them. There are films for small audiences of intellectuals and films aimed at the masses. To fight the competition from television, which attracted the mass general-interest audience, film makers sought first the superhit, but second the specialized audience.

Film as an Industry

Charlie Chaplin, whose "Little Tramp" films are now regarded as art, put it bluntly in 1972: "I went into the business for money and the art grew out of it. If people are disillusioned by that remark, I can't help it. It's the truth."[16] There can be no doubt that film making is a process in which money talks. To sketch a profile of this industry, we will look briefly at its organization — owners, studios, and employees — at the source and size of its revenues — the number of theaters and films and how many people watch them — and at profits.

The Film Makers: Owners, Studios, and Employees

By the late 1920s the movies were a billion-dollar industry employing thousands and claiming a large share of America's entertainment dollar. It was in Hollywood that the early studios created their huge dream factories with back lots that could be made into a western town or a jungle paradise. Hollywood soon became as much an elusive symbol of glamor as a real place. As editor Peter Buckley has written, "Hollywood was synonymous with everything that came out of the U.S. film industry, yet few films were actually made there. . . . Hollywood was a wonderful, fanciful state of mind: the film capital that never really was."[17] From its beginning the film industry in Hollywood made links with Wall Street. It had artistic and production ties with European countries and often filmed on location.

The myth of Hollywood overstated the geographic concentration of the film industry, but concentration of control and ownership was always part of the equation in American film. The studios organized early and gained tight control over the whole production process as well as distribution and exhibition. They had control from idea to camera to box office. It is no wonder that smaller companies had difficulty breaking into the business.

Several major studios (six as of 1973) have been the dominant force in Hollywood since those early days. The big six studios today are Columbia, Paramount, Twentieth Century-Fox, United Artists, Universal, and Warner Brothers. Metro-Goldwyn-Mayer, once a leader, stopped distributing films in 1973, concentrating its financial interests instead on hotels and film rentals from its library. Another major studio, Walt Disney Productions, is in a separate category because it produces mainly children's films and made-for-TV movies. RKO, which was powerful in the 1930s and 1940s, disbanded in 1953.

Founded by legendary motion picture moguls such as Samuel Goldwyn and Louis B. Mayer, the studios bought up theaters and set their huge production plants in high gear producing films. In the heyday of the studios in the 1930s and 1940s, if you wanted to work in the movies you worked for a studio. They had their own writers, directors, actors, and actresses under contract, as well as their own technicians, equipment, and lots. Through a practice known as *block booking*, they forced theater owners to show the studio's bad films if they wanted a chance to show the good ones. The studios also owned their own chains of theaters. Thus they had an assured outlet for their films — good or bad — while other producers found it difficult to have their films exhibited.

Then the federal government stepped in. The courts ruled that the major studios must stop block booking and give up their theaters. Film making was to become a riskier business, and the major studios less powerful. The final appeals of the court decision ended in 1950. By then the studios began to face another economic problem: competition from television.

In the 1960s various corporations bought up studios and theaters, integrating these holdings with other kinds of investments. Large corporations bought up the old major studios: Gulf & Western bought Paramount. Warner Brothers was bought by Kinney National, which also owned funeral parlors, parking lots, and magazines, among other things, and eventually the whole conglomerate became Warner Communications. In the 1970s the trend toward conglomerate ownership of studios abated.

The movie industry is more diverse and scattered today than it was in the first half of the century, with independent producers making many films. But the major studios continue to lead the industry, financing and distributing most films produced by independents as well as producing their own. They collect more than 90 percent of the total income of movie distributors, although they share this income with the independent producers and directors whom they hire for particular services or assignments.

Working for the studios are electricians, makeup artists, property workers, grips, projectionists, studio teamsters, costumers, craft workers, ornamental plasterers, script supervisors, actors, extras, film editors, writers, composers, musicians, cameramen, sound technicians, directors, art directors, and set directors, not to mention the stars. Almost all the technical workers are unionized. The Bureau of Labor Statistics estimated that about 211,000 people were employed in the industry, full time or part time, in 1977, with a total payroll of $213 billion.

In 1975 the average salary in the movie industry was $10,870 — with a wide range of salaries from poorly paid usher to the extremely well-paid superstar. Marlon Brando was said to have made $1.6 million on *The Godfather* and $1.25 million plus 11.3 percent of all gross receipts over $8.85 million for *Missouri Breaks,* not to mention $3.5 million for a few minutes on the screen in *Superman.* But most actors make much, much less. The weekly minimum wage set by the actors' unions was $785 in 1977; at the same time the minimum weekly wage for writers was $821. These wages seem high, but note that people in the movie industry rarely work steadily; they may have months without work between pictures. Their overall earnings over long periods are therefore much lower than the minimum weekly wage suggests.

Revenues

Wages of course are only part of the cost of movies. By one estimate, the stars and cast account for only 20 percent of the costs, whereas sets and physical properties account for 35 percent.[18] *Close Encounters of the Third Kind* (1977) had a production budget of some $19 million, plus a promotion budget of $7 or $8 million. The money that the studios take in to balance such costs obviously depends on the number of films they distribute, the size of their audience, and the cost of admission.

Films Released. From 1917 to 1975 the low for film distribution was just under 400 per year and the high was around 850, according to the *Film Yearbook Daily,* which includes shorts as well as full-length feature films. According to data from the major studios, the number of films they release has gone down steadily from a high of well over 300 films per year during the period 1931–1942. From 1942 to the late 1950s, the number released each year stayed around 250; then it dipped under 200. Since 1975 the major studios have released fewer than 100 films per year.

One reason for these decreasing numbers is the retirement of RKO and MGM from the ranks of production and distribution companies. But in their heyday each major studio produced fifty or sixty films per year; by the 1980s each was producing under twenty per year. For example, in 1976 the major studios released a total of ninety-two films: Columbia released fifteen; Paramount, fifteen; Twentieth Century, nineteen; United Artists, eighteen; Universal, thirteen; and Warner Brothers, twelve.

Inflation and conservative corporate management have helped

Judy Garland got star billing in the MGM movie Meet Me in Saint Louis (1944), *a good example of the genre of musicals that brought lavish song-and-dance routines to the screen in the 1930s and 40s.*

lower the number of pictures produced each year. So has the search for the superhit, a movie that can generate more than $40 million in domestic revenues. Mindful of financial losses in the early 1970s when Hollywood's inventory of films exceeded the capacity of the world market to use them, the industry is making fewer films, but films with massive budgets. These films have the potential for great earnings and for disastrous losses.

Theaters and Theatergoers. In the late 1940s there were 20,000 theaters in the United States. Today there are about 17,000, including about 13,000 indoor theaters; the rest are drive-ins. About 12.5 percent of all theaters are controlled by six major movie theater chains. Whereas in 1950 the average indoor movie theater had about 750 seats, in 1980 the average theater had 500. At any one time America's theaters can seat about 7.3 million patrons.

The average weekly attendance at movies reached more than 90 million in the late 1940s; it was down to under 20 million by 1980. Of course, the price of attendance rose from a low average of 23¢ in 1933 to an average of $2.23 in 1977. (These are averages; admissions to first-run motion pictures were much more expensive.) At least one commentator predicted that the average admission price in the United States would soon be $5 (at the current rate of inflation, it might soon be much higher). Thus Americans were spending more money on movies by the 1980s than they had before, but movies accounted for a much smaller part of their entertainment dollar than formerly. For example, in 1943 Americans spent more than 25 percent of their recreational expenditures on movies. By 1980 this figure had dropped to less than 5 percent.

These numbers, however, and the movie industry's data, do not reflect the growing use of movies by network, independent, and cable television systems. Figures that reflect television audiences would give a better index of the public's total exposure of films and of the studios' activity. For several years the major studios in Hollywood have produced made-for-TV movies for the networks. As the use of cable television increases, there is little doubt that cable systems will bid for more first-run Hollywood movies and for special made-for-cable productions designed to meet the more specialized needs of the cable audience.

Thus we see a trend to fewer films, fewer theaters, smaller and more intimate theaters (some with three screens), and smaller theater audiences, but more exposure on television. For every dollar spent at the box office, the Motion Picture Herald Institute of Industry Opinion estimates that 34.4¢ is paid to the studios for renting the film. These box office revenues give the studios almost $1.5 billion a year, whereas the sale of films to television gives them about half a billion dollars. For every dollar taken in by a movie theater,

24.5¢ is for the house (rent, mortgages, upkeep)
26.6¢ for the staff of the theater
34.4¢ for film rentals

9.0¢ for advertising and publicity
3.5¢ operating profit for the theater (before taxes).

Profits

To be labeled a success, a film must bring in revenue that exceeds its original costs by two and a half times. At that point the film starts making a profit. It was estimated that *Close Encounters of the Third Kind,* for example, had to bring in $40 to $45 million before it turned a profit. (A cartoon in the *New Yorker* spoofed Hollywood's search for the superhit with a cartoon showing a theatergoer looking at a billboard that declares, "See the movie with the fabulous $8,000,000 promotional budget that everyone's talking about.")

In general the major studios' profits declined in the 1950s, when they lost their theater chains and then faced competition from television, but they began to regain ground in subsequent years. The British journal the *Economist* has traced a detailed picture of the studios' profits. From 1932 to 1976, there was a cyclical pattern of boom and slump.[19] In part this pattern resulted from overstocking films as the studios rushed to imitate earlier successes. For example, efforts to imitate the success of *The Sound of Music* (1965) in the late 1960s led to losses in the early 1970s. As commentator Cobbett Feinberg has written:

> Although the industry throughout its history has attempted to find ways to reduce the horrible risks of spending millions of dollars up front without knowing whether a film will succeed or not, none of those ways have been foolproof. The star system has worked often, but not in a consistent and predictable fashion. Studio ownership of theaters was another way to reduce risk, but that policy was declared illegal almost thirty years ago. Stepping up investment to make films noticeably better than television fare has also failed to work regularly. Movie making remains a risky enterprise.[20]

Still, the possibility of making great profits in films exists. This fact has not been lost on the various corporations that have bought studios and theaters. The economic indicators that we have reviewed chart an industry that has seen great glory in a golden past but has suffered hard times and is now back on the mend. The mission of the movies has been refined. Less of the entertainment produced is for the relatively small theater audience, and more is for the massive audience that sits in front of the television set.

From Censorship to Social Responsibility

As movies became a part of American life, they brought problems. They challenged old ways of thinking and gave people new images and concepts to consider. The industry's massive growth in its early years, its ability to reach huge audiences, and the public belief that films are "powerful" led to efforts to control films and film makers. Many people believed the new medium was having too great an impact on their lives. Many civic and religious leaders feared the movies would have negative political and moral consequences for American life. As a result of all these concerns, pressure was placed on the industry to "clean up" its product. Most of the concern has centered on films with "mature" themes — by which people usually mean films that deal with sex.

Sex and the Movies

The film industry responded to mounting pressure in the 1920s by appointing a former postmaster general, Will H. Hays, to head their trade association, the Motion Picture Producers and Distributors Association. Part of Hays's charge was to develop a system of self-regulation and to create a better public image for the movies. Hays and his group cooperated with various religious, civic, and women's groups who had set up motion picture councils. During this early period, Hays's office was a buffer between the film industry and the public. Then Hays developed a tough self-censorship code which all producers had to follow. Without code approval, a film could not be shown in American theaters. Film producers who tried to do so were subjected to costly legal battles. The code restricted depictions of sex in particular. From the mid-1930s until the rise of television threatened the industry, movies avoided direct treatment of sexual themes and sexual behavior.

Meanwhile, a number of local governments screened and censored films. Even through the 1960s Chicago gave this assignment to its police department, which called on a group of citizens to screen controversial films. Among the most active private groups in the efforts to censor films was the Catholic Legion of Decency, which was established in 1934. It developed a list of recommended and non-recommended films, and it promoted the list with both Catholics and the general public. Although the legion's most celebrated activities occurred in the 1930s and 1940s (including a boycott of all theaters in Philadelphia), it could still stir controversy in the 1960s by denouncing *The Pawnbroker*. The legion's ratings carried a special moral force and occasionally were reinforced by bishops who warned Catholics to stay away from certain films on penalty of sin.

Eventually, the Legion of Decency was replaced by the Catholic church's Office for Film and Broadcasting, which published regular newsletters and film guides. Until the office was abolished in September 1980 it continued to promote the following ratings:

A-1: Morally objectionable for general patronage
A-2: Morally objectionable for adults and adolescents
A-3: Morally objectionable for adults
A-4: For adults with reservations
A-5: Morally objectionable in part for all
  C: Condemned

Several Protestant groups have also been active in making recommendations about films.

Efforts like those of the Legion of Decency stimulated the code that Hays developed for the industry, the Motion Picture Production Code. Although the code was not tough enough for some groups, such as the Legion of Decency, others regarded it as harsh, repressive, and highly legalistic. Some film historians think the code hindered the development of American motion pictures.

By the late 1960s the production code had been modified greatly. Numerous legal actions had broken efforts to apply rigid censorship. The industry entered a new era of self-regulation by establishing a movie classification system. Instead of barring certain films from theaters, the new system required that the public be warned of what to expect in the film. The result, after two modifications since it was adopted in 1968, is the following:

G: All ages admitted, general audiences
PG: Parental guidance suggested, for mature audiences
R: Restricted, children under seventeen require an accompanying parent or adult
X: No one under seventeen admitted

The classification was not intended to indicate quality; it is only a guide to parents considering what motion pictures their children should see. The industry, through the Motion Picture Association of America, in effect puts its seal of approval on the first three categories of films and denies it to the fourth. This system won public support and stilled some criticism, but some film producers feel that the system is too restrictive. There has been no active move to overturn it, however.

One of the top-grossing films in movie history, Gone With the Wind *(1939), won special acclaim as "the greatest American film of all time" in a 1977 survey conducted by the American Film Institute.*

Star Wars *(1977), a science-fiction thriller that earned more money than any film in history, spawned a sequel,* The Empire Strikes Back *(1980).*

Censorship and Politics

Although their treatment of sex has been the center of most of the outcry against movies over the years, politics too has been the basis for censorship. Many hard-hitting political films of the 1930s were widely criticized. In the late 1940s and 1950s, as the country was touched by a Red scare and by McCarthyism, actors, directors, and producers (among others) were *blacklisted* — denied an opportunity to get work in the movie industry because of their alleged leftist leanings. This period, when unsupported charges were frequent, is one of the darkest in movie history. Postwar fear of communism was the culprit, and the film industry was hard hit by the informal censorship that resulted.

The groups outside the movie industry exerting influence on the content of films have been many: Congress has summoned actors and directors to public hearings, the Supreme Court has tried to define what is and is not obscene, and church groups and local officials have tried various strategies to shape American movies. The result is a constraint on the artistic freedom of film makers, but not a new level of feedback for them. The groups pressuring the film makers are too small and their interests too narrow for their efforts to constitute effective feedback for a medium intended for mass use. The results of their efforts can seriously distort the communication between film maker and audience. Still, consumers of films have the same First Amendment rights that the film makers do: and this includes the right to protest against content they do not like.

Evaluating Film Quality: Criticism and Awards

Film ratings based on conceptions of morality are only one form of the many assessments that film makers get. A legion of critics working for newspapers, magazines, scholarly journals, and radio and television stations judge films regularly. In addition, there are many awards for films. Some, like the Academy Awards, are given by the industry itself; others are given by various societies, groups, and organizations. Another form of recognition is the film festival. Some film festivals are so prestigious that just being included in the festival is a mark of international approval. Surveys try to ascertain the "best" films of all time, and some wags compile annual lists of the worst films.

All these things — the writings of reviewers and critics, awards, film festivals, and surveys — give the public help in judging films. These assessments might suggest that there are uniform standards of excellence in films, but that is not the case. Although occasionally there may be widespread agreement on which film was the best film this year or this decade, there are about as many standards for criticism as there are critics and awards.

The Critics

Some people distinguish between *reviewers*, who make consumer-oriented assessments for a general audience, and *critics*, who judge a film by more artistic and theoretical criteria and try to ascertain its social importance. The terms are used interchangeably by most people, as they are in this book.

All critics have standards against which they judge a film, although the standards differ. Some critics can state these standards clearly; others present them obscurely. Because the film has gained status as an art form, a good deal of film criticism is based on artistic standards and concerns. Some critics judge a film on the basis of artistic potential and compare it with other films and theatrical productions. They consider factors such as the film's originality and its ability to project universal themes. A critic might be interested in any number of things about a film: the technical aspects such as photography, sound, use of close-ups, and color; the quality of the screenplay as a piece of writing; the performance of the actors; the unity and cohesiveness of the production. Some critics discuss the film in terms of the way it fits into a particular actor's or director's career. For example, a critic might ask whether the direction and acting in the latest Woody Allen film is as good as in his previous films.

Film criticism appears in many places. Specialized film magazines speak mainly to the movie community and to film scholars. Many other magazines have movie reviews and criticisms. *Time* and the *New York Times*, as well as other publications, publish annual "ten best movie" lists. NBC's popular "Today" show has a regular movie reviewer, Gene Shalit. Increasingly, local television and radio stations review films on the air. There are local critics who speak mostly to local audiences, and there are critics with considerable national followings. There are even annual awards for the best film criticism.

The Awards

The granddaddy of all the movie awards is the Oscar. An Oscar is the gold-plated statue about a foot high given each year in a nationally televised spectacle by the Academy of Motion Picture Arts and Sciences. The Oscars are prizes from the industry itself to its honored few, and they are the most coveted of all the movie awards.

The academy makes awards in many categories, including best picture, best director, best actor, best actress, best supporting actor, best supporting actress, best screenplay adaptation, best original screenplay, best cinematography, and best foreign-language film. There are also awards for art direction, sound, short subjects, music, film editing, and costume design as well as various awards for service to the industry, honorary awards, and scientific and technical awards.

The Academy Awards have not been without their critics. Some charge that those giving the awards concentrate on the most popular films rather than on the best or most socially significant. Some of the best films of all time — for example, Orson Welles's brilliant *Citizen Kane* (1941) — did not fare well with the academy (it got only one award, for best screenplay). Still, the list of Oscar winners is a who's who of well-known films and film makers.

Other honors and prizes are less well known. Both the Writers Guild and the Directors Guild give awards, and there are a number of awards by groups independent of the industry. The National Board of Review Awards is given for films that are recommended for children. Both the National Society of Film Critics and the New York Film Critics give annual awards for exemplary films, and the foreign press corps covering Hollywood gives annual Golden Globe Awards. Prizes at film festivals in Venice, Cannes, Berlin, and New York are prestigious; these awards usually honor artistic quality.

Finally, there have been a number of efforts to identify the greatest films of all time by surveying directors and critics. One of the most ambitious efforts to identify the "greatest American film of all time" was carried out by the American Film Institute in 1977. The 35,000 members of the institute across the nation — including academics, critics, and industry people — were asked to select five choices, in order of preference, for the best American film. Some 1,100 film titles were mentioned in the balloting, and the institute compiled a list of the top fifty films. The list was heavily weighted with films produced since 1970, and the silent era in particular was underrepresented. Andrew Sarris, critic for the *Village Voice*, commented, "I suspect that many AFI voters were simply not familiar with many great films."[21]

Nevertheless, the institute unveiled the list of the top fifty films at a dazzling ceremony attended by the President of the United States. The top ten films in their list were:

1. *Gone with the Wind* (1939)
2. *Citizen Kane* (1941)
3. *Casablanca* (1942)
4. *The African Queen* (1952)
5. *The Grapes of Wrath* (1940)

Singin' in the Rain (1952), *another lavish MGM musical, is famous for its music and for the performances of such great dancers as Cyd Charisse and (shown here) Gene Kelly.*

One Flew Over the Cuckoo's Nest (1975), *based on the novel by Ken Kesey, was a brilliantly comic and provocative look at life in a mental hospital. Jack Nicholson starred as the excitable inmate McMurphy.*

6. *One Flew Over the Cuckoo's Nest* (1975)
7. *Singing in the Rain* (1952)
8. *Star Wars* (1977)
9. *2001: A Space Odyssey* (1968)
10. *The Wizard of Oz* (1939)

To balance all the self-congratulation of the movie industry and its friends, the *Harvard Lampoon* presents annual worst movie awards.

Summary

American film has gone through many changes in its short history. For the most part, it has been a medium for entertainment. Despite technological and artistic changes and competition from television, its primary function today is still entertainment.

Every film is a product of technology and artistry, managerial skill and showmanship. It involves a wide range of professionals and craftsworkers. At various times different members of the film-making team have tended to be the dominant voice in shaping films. In early films, for example, directors had the dominant role.

But almost always the content of the film is shaped by conflicting forces: the desire for efficiency, a view of what the audience wants, and an individual's desire to shape the film. The result of this conflict has been a wide range of genres and styles in American films.

After enjoying great success in the 1940s, the American film industry declined in the 1950s. Today conglomerates control some of the major studios, and the studios themselves are less important than they were in the 1940s. Independent producers make more films, although films are usually financed as well as distributed by the major studios. Small, intimate theaters have replaced the old movie theaters, and the young make up a large part of their audience. Although fewer movies are made now and the average weekly attendance at movie theaters is less than a fourth what it was in the 1940s, movie companies today still make a profit because of higher admission prices, an occasional superhit, and revenue from television's use of films.

Film was once a more important entertaining medium than it is today, but the film industry has responded to the demands of new competition, changing technology, and changing audiences. It is a lively and still significant medium.

Notes and References

1. F. Scott Fitzgerald, *The Last Tycoon* (New York: Charles Scribner's Sons, 1941).
2. Joan Didion, "Hollywood: Having Fun," *New York Review of Books*, March 22, 1973, pp. 15–18.
3. James Monaco, *How to Read a Film* (New York: Oxford University Press, 1977) p. 195.
4. Ibid.
5. Monaco, *How To Read a Film*, p. 195.
6. Ibid., p. 196.
7. Garth Jowett, *Film; The Democratic Art* (Boston: Little, Brown, 1976) p. 139.
8. Hollis Alpert, "Sexual Behavior in the American Movies," *Saturday Review*, June 23, 1956, pp. 9–10.
9. John L. Fell, *An Introduction to Film* (New York: Praeger, 1975), p. 127.
10. Thomas W. Bohn and Richard L. Stromgren, *Light and Shadows; A History of Motion Pictures* (Port Washington, N.Y.: Alfred, 1975) p. 170.
11. Opinion Research Institute of Princeton.
12. Monaco, *How to Read a Film*, p. 246.
13. Ibid., p. 208; also see an excellent summary history of the major studios in Cobbett Feinberg, *Reel Facts; The Movie Book of Records* (New York: Vintage, 1978) pp. 376–389.
14. Axel Madsen, *The New Hollywood* (New York: Thomas Y. Crowell, 1975) p. 12.

15. John Cogley, *Report on Blacklisting I: Movies*, p. 282.
16. Feinberg, *Reel Facts*, p. xiii.
17. For an excellent abbreviated analysis of the movies, see Gairth Jowett and James M. Linton, *Movies as Mass Communication* (Beverly Hills, Sage Publications, 1980).
18. Warren K. Agee, Phillip H. Ault, and Edwin Emery, *Introduction to Mass Communications*, 6th ed. (New York: Harper & Row, 1979) p. 301.
19. See *The Mass Media, Aspen Institute Guide to Industry Trends,* Christopher Sterling, ed. (New York: Praeger, 1978), pp. 184–185.
20. Feinberg, *Reel Facts*, p. 392.
21. Andrew Sarris, "The Night They Left Garbo Alone," *Village Voice*, December 12, 1977, p. 51.

7 The Auxiliaries

> *There is no more important question to be considered by the American people than the question, Is the Associated Press fair? Does it transmit the news?*
>
> UPTON SINCLAIR in *The Brass Check* (1919)

Both newspapers and the broadcasting stations have important help from outside their organizations, from groups we call the *auxiliaries:* the wire services, feature syndicates, ratings services, and various research organizations. If you doubt the importance of auxiliaries, take a newspaper, clip all the stories that come from wire services and feature syndicates, and put the clippings aside. You'll probably be left with a few local stories, advertisements, and little more.

The auxiliaries are flourishing today, partly for economic reasons. But they also serve an important function as the media's windows on the world, links between media organizations and outside events. In this chapter we examine the nature and scope of each type of auxiliary service, their origins, and their present status.

The Role of the Auxiliaries

Except for the national broadcasting networks, the American news media are fiercely local. But they depend on national organizations for much of their content and for other services. *Wire services* (or *press associations* as they are sometimes called) such as the Associated Press (AP) and United Press International (UPI) bring national and international news to local papers and broadcasting stations; *feature syndicates* bring cartoons and comic strips, columns, and crossword puzzles; *rating services* monitor radio and television audiences; *pollsters* and *market researchers* provide data that help media executives make decisions. These are some of the auxiliary, or supportive, services that link the local media with the outside world and influence their content and direction.

The advantages of these services are many. They allow even the smallest newspaper or broadcast station to

- be linked with a worldwide network of news reporters
- enjoy the keen insights of a brilliant commentator or the biting wit of a great cartoonist
- bring readers and viewers a wide range of entertainment
- provide intelligence about the public pulse through major polls
- find out what its audience is reading or watching through the services of a marketing research firm

Thus, rich resources that would otherwise be very expensive are put within the reach of many organizations. As a result, the auxiliaries probably help many newspapers and broadcasting stations to survive.

More importantly perhaps, some commentators argue that these auxiliaries foster what Harold Lasswell called a "transmission of the social heritage." That is, because these services are used all across the nation, they provide the American people with a wide range of *shared* information. This effect is increased by the fact that the wire services deal with both print and broadcast media. Furthermore, the information provided by the auxiliaries helps set the media's agenda. That is, what appears on the front pages of newspapers throughout the country is largely determined by the recommendations of the wire services.

The wire services' blanketing of papers and broadcast stations across the country means that news reports have little regional diversity. From Maine to southern California, publications and newscasts are similar. Standardization of communication results. A dramatic example is the fate of editorial cartoons. In the late nineteenth and early twentieth centuries, most daily newspapers had their own cartoonists. But with the coming of the feature syndicates, papers relied on a few syndicated cartoonists. The local cartoonist drifted out of sight on almost all but the larger papers. Critics say that the free flow of ideas requires diversity of communication and that the near-monopoly on international and national news that is held by a few wire services endangers freedom of expression.

As always, there are answers to the critics. Others say that within the wires there is much diversity of information. Moreover, newspapers and broadcast stations are not just passive recipients of the auxiliaries' services. Years ago, Walter Lippmann marveled at the rich offerings of American newspapers when he wrote, "The range of subjects these comparatively few men [editors] manage to cover would be a miracle, indeed, if it were not for a standardized routine."[1] Part of that routine involves managing the material from outside sources as well as contracting with various consultants. The people within the media organizations still decide what to use from the auxiliaries and how to use it; they are important *gatekeepers*.

These and other arguments about the auxiliaries have made for continued controversy almost since they first appeared on the American scene in the nineteenth century. The wire services were the first to appear.

The Wire Services

If anyone ever wondered how the country's news organizations would fare if the wire services shut down, they came close to finding out in the summer of 1977. On a Wednesday evening in July of that year, New York City suffered a massive power outage. Not only did the lights go out, but so did the computer systems that link the wire services to the nation's news media. Imagine the surprise of copy editor Bob Kraft at the *Cincinnati Post.* Kraft sat down at a video display terminal and requested transmission of a story from United Press International that was stored in UPI's New York computer. Instead of the story, Kraft got "a series of flickering green checks, dots and other symbols."[2] As Richard L. Gordon wrote in *Editor and Publisher:* "It was 9:34 P.M. Wednesday, July 13. He lifted the emergency phone and called UPI in New York. He listened briefly to a distraught voice and, turning to Assistant Managing Editor Laura Pulfer, he said, 'Jesus Christ — there's a blackout in New York!' "[3]

Although regional systems continued to send copy around the country, for several hours no news was sent from the nation's communications center. While technicians worked on an emergency backup system, UPI staffers telephoned stories to Washington, and the nation's capital became a makeshift national headquarters. Twenty hours passed before all service from New York was restored.

The Associated Press, the largest and most powerful of the press associations, also had problems and shifted some of its operations to Washington. But AP had better backup systems, and it was able to get its New York wires running again three hours after the

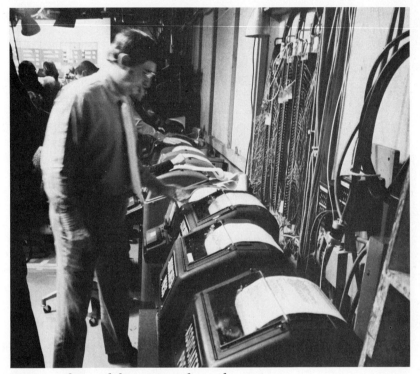

Wire machines deliver news from the various press associations or wire services to newspapers and broadcast stations. They run continuously, and reports are regularly updated or modified.

breakdown. The blackout was an inconvenience for the wire services, but it demonstrated their widespread and decentralized nature.

Organization of the Wire Services

Although the wire services rely on New York as a transmission point for national and international news, they also have strong operations in Washington, Chicago, Los Angeles, and other major cities, as well as foreign capitals. Virtually every state has wire service bureaus in its major cities and state capital, offices where reporters and editors produce copy for the wire. They are also receiving points to which correspondents send their stories. And, importantly, they are two-way communication centers linked to thousands of newspapers and broadcasting stations that subscribe to and contribute to the around-the-clock coverage of the wire services. The office, whether a large bureau in a major city or a one-person operation in a small state, is linked to computers that tie the whole system together.

Thus, the wire services, as well as supplementary services run by major newspapers, are a kind of central nervous system for the American news media. Their circuits send and receive news, reprocess it, and channel it to appropriate outlets. The New York blackout was like a minor heart attack. It short-circuited the system and slowed it for a time, but the system soon recovered.

The role of the wire services is basically twofold: to gather and to distribute the news and interpretive material. For this service newspapers and broadcasting stations pay rates that are set on a sliding scale, from as little as $50 per week for small papers and stations to as much as $6,000 per week for larger organizations.

In gathering the news, wire service reporters work much like other reporters, although the news they assemble transcends the interests of a local area; naturally, reporters are always looking for stories that have national or international significance. The wire

Wire service reporters work both in their headquarters offices in various cities and in the field. These reporters are covering the World Series and are preparing stories for deadline.

service reporters give their copy to editors, who send it along to regional centers. For example, in the Far West news from small California cities flows to Los Angeles, the regional center, where editors decide whether to edit and redistribute the story to the region only or to pass it on to the national offices in New York. Thus news moves up the chain toward New York. Items of regional or narrow interest are picked off along the way.

Once the news gets to New York (or to a major regional center, such as Los Angeles, Denver, Seattle, Chicago, Kansas City, Dallas, Atlanta, Miami, New Orleans, Boston, Philadelphia, or Washington), the distribution process begins. The news is sorted out and rechanneled across the country either to all wire outlets or to selected ones, depending on the story. Once, trusty Morse Code operators distributed the stories by sending dot-and-dash messages over telegraph lines. Later they were replaced by electronic teletypesetters, which have now been connected to sophisticated computer systems. By 1980 the wire services were transmitting the news via satellite.

Origins of the "Wires"

The complex, computerized news-gathering and distribution systems of the contemporary wire services stand in dramatic contrast to their simple beginnings in the mid-nineteenth century. It all began in the 1840s when several rival newspapers pooled their resources in order to provide faster, cheaper, and more comprehensive coverage of the Mexican War. This temporary but innovative link-up of newspapers in New York, Baltimore, and Philadelphia set a precedent. In 1848 six New York newspapers signed an agreement to share the costs of telegraphing foreign news from Boston, where ships first arrived from Europe. This agreement was the forerunner of the modern AP. The papers were members of a cooperative association, and they elected their own board of directors.

At first the AP was mainly an organization linking Eastern newspapers. But as Americans moved westward and railroads grew, AP began to cover the nation rather than just the East. During the Civil War, the AP newspapers covered the great battles and troop movements with considerable detail.

Increasing dependency on the "wires" led to changes in the writing style of newspapers. The telegraph seemed to demand clarity and precision. The correspondent in the field had less time for the flowery language and elongated sentences common to nineteenth-century newspapers. Before long, reporters and editors began to distinguish between "telegraph" and "newspaper" stories. Telegraph stories were rather like bulletins. This style eventually evolved into AP's famous lead of "who, what, where, why, and how"; stories were organized into an *inverted pyramid style,* in which the most important elements were first, the next important second, and so on. In a desire to appeal to newspapers in various regions and with various political persuasions, AP avoided opinionated and controversial interpretations of the news. In fact, AP pioneered what would later be called the *objective report.* Thus, almost from the beginning the wire services broadened the content of news (allowing more newspapers to have a wide range of coverage from distant points) and narrowed its style.

After the Civil War various cooperating and competing AP groups sprang up around the country. Some groups died; others eventually consolidated in a reorganization of the Associated Press in 1900. But the competitive undercurrent pointed up a problem: newspaper membership in AP was very controlled and closed. In some cities rival newspapers had difficulty holding readers unless they had the advantages of AP membership and news coverage.

Not everyone was happy with the content that AP provided. Edward Wyllis Scripps, the owner of the Scripps chain of newspapers, complained that "at least 90 percent of my fellows in American journalism were capitalistic and conservative."[4] Scripps's answer was to found the United Press Association (UP): "I knew that, at that time at least, unless I came into the field with a new service, it would be impossible for the people of the United States to get correct news through the medium of the Associated Press."[5] On July 15, 1907, the first "By United Press" byline appeared over a dispatch from New York that began: "The completion of an important press association consolidation was announced this morning."

Two years later, another press lord, William Randolph Hearst, formed his own press association, the International News Service (INS). From that time until 1958 the United States was served by the three rival services, although AP always outdistanced the other two. In 1958 UP and INS merged into UPI, which led to more vigorous competition with AP.

Originally, both UP and INS had newspapers owned by Scripps and Hearst as their chief clients, but they later expanded to include other papers. Whereas AP had "members" and only members received their stories, UP and INS sold their reports to "clients." Even today AP has "member" papers and stations and UPI has "users" or "clients." But this distinction is now rather academic because both AP and UPI are responsive to boards of directors linked to members and clients, and papers and stations using either wire pay a fee.

Since the early 1960s several supplemental wire services have been organized. The New York Times Service, the Washington Post/Los Angeles Times Service, the Copley News Service, the Knight-Ridder News Service, and other provide a variety of news and feature material.

AP and UPI: Similarities and Differences

At a glance the two major American wire services seem much the same. Both AP and UPI cover a wide range of news, national and international as well as state and local. Both provide a steady flow of the news — from sightings of Bigfoot to earthquakes in major cities — as well as interpretive and background articles. Both have special sports and business wires, and both have a photographic service. But there are also differences between them.

Size and Economics. By early 1980 about 11,000 newspapers and broadcast stations were getting AP news and picture services, whereas UPI reported about 6,000 subscribers worldwide. AP had 119 domestic (U.S.) bureaus and 66 foreign bureaus in late 1979, whereas UPI claimed 99 news bureaus and 40 picture bureaus in the United States and 62 news and picture bureaus overseas. About 45 percent of America's daily newspapers get only AP; 30 percent get only UPI; and 25 percent get both. It is estimated that AP has well over 3,000 full- and part-time employees whereas UPI has about 2,500. The performance of AP and UPI during the New York blackout indicates that there are also some technological differences between them.

The rates charged by the two services are somewhat different: UPI's rates for big papers are lower than AP's, but in broadcasting the situation is reversed. AP's revenues for 1979 totaled $112 million; UPI's were about $80 million. But the essential differences go well beyond these revenue figures. AP was a money maker for most of the last decade while UPI was losing money, reporting after-tax losses of $2.5 million in 1979. Between 1961 and 1979, UPI reported losses of about $17 million. Until late 1979, UPI was owned jointly by the E. W. Scripps Company (95 percent) and the Hearst Corporation (5 percent). But in 1979, UPI could no longer sustain its losses and invited several American publishers and broadcasters to become financial partners; however, the plan was not successful.

By 1980 UPI had expanded into the home computer business,

supplying information to the Telecomputing Corporation of America. UPI's vice president and editor, H. L. Stevenson, observed, "We think of ourselves as an information service, not just a news agency." The extent to which UPI can succeed in this area may determine its financial health and survival.

Style, Content, and Reputation. UPI started as a Midwestern wire and was the first wire service to serve the broadcasting industry. These differences had been blurred by the mid-twentieth century, but other differences in the images of the two wire services persist. AP is seen as a somewhat conservative but reliable service; UPI has a reputation for less attention to accuracy and more colorful writing. But these images don't always match reality. UPI has made its share of errors over the years, no doubt, but its reputation for inaccuracy is regarded by many critics as undeserved. It may stem from a massive error in 1918 when UP reported the Armistice four days early. As late as the 1970s Roger Tartarian, a former UPI president, complained, "We're still living down the premature Armistice."[6]

Several leading journalism texts persist in perpetuating the UPI's image of inaccuracy even though evidence refutes it. J. Richard Cote, in a study of the accuracy of the two wire services in 1970, looked for errors of fact and errors in interpretation. His findings: "On the basis of the sample drawn, . . . the difference between the number of errors overall between the two services is not significant. Similarly, neither is the difference between the number of stories indicated by the sources as totally accurate significant."[7]

Yet the perceptions of those who use the wire services are very important because they decide which service will enjoy greater financial security. Clearly AP is the most popular service among U.S. newspapers. Journalism professor Richard A. Schwarzlose tried to find out why. Three factors seemed to account for AP's popularity: (1) the reputation — true or not — for reliable and accurate coverage; (2) AP's organizational structure, which gives the impression that newspapers are part owners of AP and that the wire is an extension of the dailies' own news gathering; and (3) AP's image as a newspaper wire because of UP's early entry into broadcasting, a decision that angered many publishers. But, wrote Schwarzlose, "UPI's brighter writing style and its somewhat faster handling of news stories make it a desirable resource for competitors, particularly those subordinate competitors seeking to increase circulation rapidly."[8]

Although the attitudes of editors using the wires may change,

B. H. Liebes found another indication of the perceived differences between the two services. In a study of decision making by newspapers' telegraph editors, Liebes asked them to rate the AP and UPI in five broad categories — Washington news, international news, general news, news analysis, and color stories. He found, "Although the consensus favored AP in Washington and international reporting, UPI rated outstandingly high in reporting news from the White House and the Soviet Union. . . . UPI also scored high in reporting Latin American and Caribbean news.[9]

The ratings of the wire services at any given time probably depend largely on who is covering a particular beat. In large part the reputation of the service is linked to the reporter. For example, Merriman Smith, as UPI's White House correspondent, was widely respected for very competent reporting and graceful writing under pressure. Smith won the Pulitzer Prize for his dramatic account of the Kennedy assassination in 1963. The thorough analysis and detailed coverage of the 1976 presidential campaign brought a Pulitzer Prize to AP's Walter Mears. UPI's Charlotte Moulton was the dean of correspondents at the U.S. Supreme Court and was regarded as gifted in her handling of that most difficult assignment, and Alton Blakeslee of the AP (like his father before him) was a respected science writer. The major point is that the quality of the wire service personnel, the consistency and reliability of their reports, and the speed with which the news is delivered build a wire service's reputation.

The reputations of the two wires are really undeserved, said editor Gordon Pates. "Both have tried to correct their weaknesses," he noted.[10] The most significant difference between the two services, some observers believe, is that they provide two points of view, two perspectives on the news, and this, of course, gives editors a choice. This choice, Judge Learned Hand believed, is healthy for the American public. In a Federal Court opinion, Judge Hand overturned two bylaws of the AP that he said created a monopoly in the news: one prohibited AP members from selling news to nonmembers; the other gave each AP member almost a veto over the application of nonmembers to join AP. In his opinion on the case, Hand wrote:

> In the production of news every step involves the conscious intervention of some news gatherer, and two accounts of the same event will never be the same. . . . For [this] reason it is impossible to treat two news services as interchangeable, and to deprive a paper of the benefit of any service of the first rating is to deprive the

reading public of means of information which it should have.[11]

This now-famous opinion was later upheld by the Supreme Court.

The Wire Services in Perspective

The importance of the wire services, both in this country and worldwide, greatly exceeds their monetary worth and other statistical measures. But the statistics do give some clues. About 95 percent of the nation's daily newspapers subscribe to either AP or UPI or both. The wires supply about 75 percent of the state, national, and international news in American newspapers and on radio and television. Without doubt, the wire services blanket the American news media. Even when large newspapers and broadcasting stations send their own reporters to the scene, the wires still set the tone and provide a backstop. As Russell Baker of the *New York Times* has written of Washington coverage:

> After the wire men comes a profusion of reporters working for individual papers, networks, news syndicates, and trade journals. These men concentrate on specific "beats," thus duplicating much of the work of the "wires," but looking for special "angles" to suit their peculiar audiences.[12]

The American wire services have an importance that stretches far beyond this country's national boundaries. They are worldwide organizations with operations in many national capitals and the ability to dispatch personnel to almost any spot in the world. By the same token, the American wire services are used not only by newspapers and broadcasting stations in the United States but also by those abroad. Of course, abroad the American wires run into pretty stiff competition from the British service, Reuters, and from the French wire, Agence France Presse. Many of the major nations of the world have their own press associations — Tass in the Soviet Union and the New China News Service in China, for example. Wire services are found mainly in rich, industrial nations, but the developing nations are moving to set up their own press associations. In Latin America, for example, major daily newspapers have organized a press association, Latin. African journalists and government leaders have taken steps to form their own press associations.

Because wire services cover the globe and monitor the world's news systematically, they have tremendous influence on the content of the world's press. Each day they give updated reports on

These advertisements from the trade journal
Editor & Publisher *illustrate the range of
services that the various syndicates and press
associations offer their clients and users.*

the important stories of the day, providing a kind of running priority list called *budgets*. The budgets set the agenda for the press; that is, the wire services' priorities influence the amount of attention that newspapers and broadcast stations give to stories.

If anything, the influence of the wire services has increased since the end of World War II as fewer newspapers and broadcast stations today use more than one wire. The trend has been away from diversity and toward reliance on just one wire service. Wire service personnel argue, however, that their reports are neither

The Auxiliaries 249

rigidly standardized nor prepared by people with a single point of view. Indeed, the wire services get their content not just from wire service reporters but also from newspapers. AP, for example, has the option of using news reports from any of its member newspapers. "In theory," wrote A. Kent MacDougall of the *Wall Street Journal*, "the AP gets exclusive use of these stories, even if the paper is also a UPI client. But in practice, UPI staffers in many cities freely lift local stories from papers that have AP ties as well as from other papers and from broadcasters."[13] In addition, newspapers use various supplemental services.

The Supplemental Services

As the competition between AP and UPI increased in the 1970s, the leaders of the two giants looked worriedly at the extraordinary success of the relatively new *supplemental* services. The supplemental services make no effort to match the exhaustive coverage provided by AP and UPI. Instead they present special reports, features, and other material that supplements the work of the newspaper, AP, and UPI.

For years various specialized news services have covered science, religion, and financial news, but another type of service became important in the 1970s. Especially noteworthy was the growing use of the New York Times Service, which allows subscribers to use a selection of stories from the *Times*. These stories are transmitted electronically at the same time they appear in the prestigious New York daily, linking a number of newspapers, large and small, with the impressive worldwide sources of the *New York Times*. Between 1960 and 1973 the Times Service increased its clients from 36 to 150. Another specialized service, the Los Angeles Times/Washington Post Service, boasted of overseas bureaus and strong coverage of Washington, D.C., and southern California. It grew from 77 subscribers in 1970 to 105 by 1973.[14] Michael W. Singletary in 1975 reported that the New York Times and Los Angeles Times/Washington Post services "by 1973 accounted for 62 percent of all reported supplemental news service subscribers."[15] Somewhat similar supplemental services include the Chicago Daily News Service (known for its national and international reporting), the North American Newspaper Alliance, and the Newspaper Enterprise Association.

Several supplemental services started by serving the members of a particular newspaper chain. Many of these have expanded and now sell their services to other newspapers and broadcast outlets. They include the Copley News Service, Newhouse News Service, and Knight-Ridder News Service. Other news services are more specialized, offering reports of a particular kind such as the Dow Jones wire, which offers superb financial coverage, and the Women's News Service, which provides enthusiastic coverage of women's news and problems. During the 1960s several "alternative" news services arose to provide an antiestablishment viewpoint on the news, including the Liberation News Service, Underground Press Syndicate, Pacific News Service, and Earth News Service. Few were financially successful.

In more specific terms, what can a supplemental news service offer? An advertisement for the Los Angeles Times/Washington Post Service answered succinctly: "For less than the cost of one good reporter the Los Angeles Times/Washington Post News Service offers exclusive world-wide live wire coverage of the best journalists in all news centers of the globe."[16] The service claims to bring together the resources of the two papers based on what they describe as "two epicenters of movements that shake people." It carries contributions from *Newsday*, the Long Island newspaper; the *Dallas Times-Herald* in Texas; Los Angeles *Times* bureaus in Chicago, Atlanta, Houston, New York, Sacramento, and San Francisco; *Washington Post* bureaus in Los Angeles and New York; plus a traveling corps of specialists. To this they add material from 30 foreign bureaus of the *Post* and the *Times*, 40 correspondents of the *Manchester Guardian*, and 160 bureaus of Agence France Presse. The Los Angeles Times/Washington Post News Service boasts of its Washington coverage, which included the work of investigative reporters Bob Woodward and Carl Bernstein during the Watergate scandal. Other nationally important journalists cover national politics, economics, fashion, science, and technology, as well as cultural affairs and books, gardening, and sports.

Clearly, local media benefit from such links to other journalists. But no one is yet claiming that the supplemental wires can replace AP or UPI for immediate coverage of fast-breaking news or for the vast range of news that they carry. For all their richness of content, the supplementals are just that — *supplemental* sources of interpretation, analysis, interviews, and other information. The growth of the new supplemental wires may eventually change the role of the major wires, which have tried to expand their interpretive coverage in recent years. Clearly, the supplementals signal more diversity of content for American readers, listeners, and viewers.

The Syndicates

The feature syndicates, like the wire services, trace their origins to the mid- and late nineteenth century. Enterprising editor-publishers recognized the importance of entertaining their readers. They surmised rightly that a profit could be made by offering newspapers a package of ready-to-print features including opinion columns, poetry, cartoons, short stories, and other entertainment fare. They formed companies to provide such material.

The earliest syndicate was organized by two Wisconsin newspapermen just after the Civil War. Others quickly followed suit, and by the late nineteenth century such figures as Irving Batchelor and S. S. McClure, who later became famous as magazine publishers, organized feature syndicates. By the early 1900s syndicates were bringing editors opinion pieces, political cartoons, and comic strips as well as columns on fashion, personal problems, politics, and other topics. There was considerable competition among the syndicates. William Randolph Hearst, whose papers were lively centers for feature material, organized his King Features Syndicate in 1914. Almost from the beginning, the syndicates played an important role in making the work of particular writers and artists popular among millions of readers.

At first the syndicates directed their appeals to small papers that could not afford to produce their own material, but eventually they sold to larger papers, too. Some syndicates were tied to a particular group of newspapers; others sought clients throughout the country. At first they provided printed pages that had feature material on one side and blank pages on the other so that local papers could fill in local advertising and news. Later, syndicates circulated copy that could be photographed and used by offset presses. Today syndicates number more than 300, and they range from those with billings of more than $100 million per year to small firms that represent one or two writers.

Unlike the wire services, which distribute their wares to both print and broadcast media, the syndicates aim almost exclusively at the print media. But material from the major broadcast networks (ABC, CBS, NBC, and PBS) as well as some independent companies is to local television and radio stations what syndicated material is to newspapers and magazines. Local radio and television news and the evening magazine programs often include material that comes from the networks, a kind of syndicate of the air.

What the Syndicates Provide

The offerings of a syndicate are often seen as valuable commodities. For example, newspapers have occasionally fought vicious court battles to retain a particular columnist or cartoonist. In 1977 two Philadelphia newspapers went to court to determine who had the contractual rights to the popular comic strip "Doonesbury" by G. B. Trudeau. The strip, represented by Universal Press Syndicate, had appeared in the *Philadelphia Bulletin,* but the syn-

Gary Trudeau's highly topical and often political strip "Doonsbury" pokes sophisticated fun at contemporary lifestyles and preoccupations. Its liberal political bias and irreverent treatment of such public figures as Henry Kissinger have made this strip controversial.

dicate was switching it to the competing *Philadelphia Inquirer*. The *Bulletin* cried foul, and got a court injunction to prevent the syndicate from taking the strip away. In a statement to the court, the *Bulletin*'s management charged that "each of the subject features [including "Doonesbury" and several other items] is unique, irreplaceable and of peculiar value and economic worth . . . and the loss thereof will result in irreparable damage to the *Bulletin*." [17] The *Bulletin* left no doubt that loss of the popular strip could affect circulation. The *Inquirer* won and was running the strip in the 1980s. The various syndicates are proud of their offerings, often with good reason, and they compete to convince newspapers and magazines of their value.

The syndicates mostly provide entertainment and opinion material for newspapers, including serializations of popular books, columns by noted political commentators, comic strips, and editorial cartoons. Some of the key syndicates are the Chicago Tribune-New York Daily News Syndicate, Publishers-Hall Syndicate, King Features Syndicate, the Los Angeles Times Syndicate, the Newspaper Enterprise Association, and the Des Moines Register and Tribune Syndicate.

King Features Syndicate claims to have the greatest array of comic strips for the Sunday pages, including such favorites as "Blondie," "Beetle Bailey," "Buz Sawyer," "Inside Woody Allen," "The Heart of Juliet Jones," "Rip Kirby," and many others. Among the famous columnists carried by the syndicate are Jim Bishop, Jeffrey Hart, Marianne Means, Nicholas von Hoffman, and Sam Shulsky. They cover such diverse subjects as astrology, automobiles, books, bridge, politics, gossip, consumer advice, human relations, music, religion, television, and women's features. The syndicate has many old favorites that go back a couple

Cartoonist Chic Young's "Blondie" has depicted family life in the Bumstead family for decades, adapting over the years to new trends and values.

254   *The Communication Industries*

of generations, but they also syndicate material from *Rolling Stone*, the rock magazine. In addition subscribers have access to various puzzles and game columns.

Chicago Tribune-New York Daily News Service offers "Dear Abby," the nation's most widely read advice column, columnists such as Rex Reed, Omar Sharif, Eliot Janeway on finance, Elizabeth Post on etiquette, and gossip columnists Suzy Knickerbocker, Liz Smith and "The Ear." Its comics include "Moon Mullins," "Dick Tracy," and "Little Abner." Along with crossword puzzles and other amusements the syndicate carries editorial cartoonists Jeff MacNelly and Wayne Stayskal, as well as a "Youthpoll," which keeps watch on the pulse of America's young people.

Washington Post Writer's Group claims to offer "bylines that build readership." Among its services are political commentary by George F. Will and David S. Broder, economic analysis by Hobart Rowen and Jane Bryant Quinn, and media criticism from Sander Vanocur and Charles Seib, as well as Pulitzer-Prize winning columnist Ellen Goodman. It also provides illustrations by Geoffrey Moss and editorial cartoons by Tony Auth, as well as the Book World Service.

The syndicates promise that their material will bring circulation gains, something every newspaper covets, and readership studies indicate that the syndicates are sometimes right. For example, "Dear Abby" and "Ann Landers" often head the list of the most-read items in a newspaper, and the comics also have strong appeal.

How the Syndicates Work

A former syndicate editor, W. H. Thomas, wrote, "Of all the outlets available as a market for creative talent, none is so little understood or so ill defined as the newspaper syndicate, that insular and elusive shadow-organization which exercises so much power within the various communications media."[18] True, little is written about syndicate organizations, although even the largest of them are modest in size and complexity. But in spite of this lack of publicity and the variations among the syndicates, we can make some generalizations about how they work.

First, the syndicates must acquire material. To do so they maintain regular contacts with writers, artists, designers, and others. Acquisition can be complicated and secretive, as in the negotiations for Richard Nixon's memoirs. Or it may result from opening the morning mail. Writers and artists who free-lance frequently send material to syndicates. The syndicates often serve as representatives for their writers and artists, much as literary agents represent authors.

Once material is acquired, it is edited (in the case of written matter and comic strips) and sent to production. A production staff gets it ready for distribution to various media outlets. Some syndicate sales people call on newspapers and magazines to urge them to try a new column or cartoon.

Syndicates must manage and market their wares like any business that produces a product. New items are added and marketed; unsuccessful columns and cartoons are dropped. The syndicates usually work on a contract basis, offering a newspaper a variety of materials for a specified time at a specified cost. Like the wire services, the syndicates have a sliding scale of fees; papers with small circulations pay less. Some syndicates make it financially attractive for a newspaper to take several of their offerings, but most often newspapers take material from several syndicates. Sometimes, as in the Doonesbury case, there is vigorous competition for a feature.

Sometimes syndicate personnel must coordinate many talents. For example, in 1917 John F. Dille was a creative businessman with experience in advertising when he founded the National Newspaper Syndicate. Through the syndicate Dille popularized the commentaries and other creative efforts of several prominent persons by making their work available to newspaper clients at a relatively low cost. At the same time Dille made a handsome profit.

Although Dille was neither an artist nor a writer, he is credited with originating adventure comic strips as an entertainment medium. The most notable accomplishment of Dille's syndicate was no doubt the "creation" and development of the science fiction comic strip, "Buck Rogers." Dille got the idea for "Buck Rogers" from a science fiction article in a magazine. He talked the author into writing for a comic strip based loosely on the story. Then he hired an artist to work with the writer, and "Buck Rogers" was born. Dille's involvement with the strip didn't end there. He knew scientists at the University of Chicago and often talked with them and reported their ideas about the future to his artist and writer. Perhaps more important, though, Dille convinced newspapers to buy the futuristic new strip. The strip prospered, appearing in some 287 newspapers at the height of its popularity.

Syndicates coordinate many elements, including contracts between the creators of syndicated material and the syndicate itself and contracts between the syndicate and subscribing newspapers. They also handle the flow of money from the newspaper to the syndicate and the payment of royalties to the writers and artists.

Science fiction strips have long been popular subjects for the comics. "Buck Rogers" gave readers in the 1930s and later a preview of future space exploration.

Additionally, they promote and market the syndicate's products through personal contact, advertising, and other means.

Thus syndicates are multifaceted organizations that link a wide variety of creative energies to potential outlets. Syndication can be carried out by large organizations or by the self-syndication effort of a writer or artist. Syndicates are brokers, but they can also be quite creative, as John Dille was.

Measuring Services

Although there is increasing consolidation of media outlets in America, competition between and among different media can be intense. They are competing for audiences and for advertising. One important tool in this competition is information about the audience. With the right kind of information, media managers gain feedback that tells them if they're communicating effectively. Research on their audience can tell them how to reach more people. Or they can use data on their audience to convince advertisers of their effectiveness. Newspapers, magazines, and radio trumpet the advantages of their medium for reaching particular audiences, nationally or within a market area.

For most of this information on audiences, the media turn to ratings services and companies that specialize in market research. Professional rating services measure the size, characteristics, and behavior of audiences. They may use data from government agencies such as the Department of Commerce on the characteristics of market areas (for example, the number of households or the average age, education, and income of people in the area). Market researchers provide information about the effectiveness of advertising. Some trade organizations and media organizations conduct research themselves and offer data about the advantages of a particular medium or a particular outlet. Some of this research is conducted by neutral organizations that report their findings objectively, much as academic researchers do. But most of the data come from self-serving groups that use research as a weapon to point up the advantages of a particular medium. This does not mean that the research is never conducted rigorously; sometimes it is. But in many cases the questions in interviews are phrased or arranged to emphasize the advantages of one medium over another.

Ratings, polls, and market research data have an important influence on the health of media outlets. They may chart the rise and fall of a publication or program or lead to changes in content. Within a single market area radio and television stations fight ratings wars to show advertisers who has the greatest share of the market and degree of audience attention at particular times of the day. Losers may find themselves financially strapped. Sometimes ratings indicate impending death, as they predicted the fall of slick mass-circulation magazines in the 1960s. Such magazines as *Life* and *Look* faltered in the 1960s when the rating services revealed that they could not compete with television for large, diversified audiences, and their advertising revenues declined. Program ratings often bring rapid changes to the television networks. A new series may disappear from the air in midseason, or a network may announce major changes in its management, all as a result of ratings. The ratings game and market research form a bizarre battlefield that merits close scrutiny.

Measuring Circulations

The basic rating for a newspaper is its circulation. There was a time when newspapers and magazines made exaggerated claims about their audience. Some would increase the figures to impress the advertisers. To end this practice and promote reliable, impartial circulation reports, a group of advertisers, advertising agencies, and publishers formed the Audit Bureau of Circulation (ABC) in 1914. ABC checks and verifies circulation figures and other marketing data on periodicals and newspapers. It sets standards for circulation (such as solicitation methods and subscriptions) and requires a publisher's statement of circulation and other data every six months. The statements are checked, processed, printed, and distributed by ABC. Once a year an ABC auditor goes to the offices of the newspaper or magazine and examines all records and materials necessary to verify the claims of the publisher's statement of circulation. Information provided by ABC in its semiannual reports includes audited, paid circulation figures for the six-month period, with breakdowns for such things as subscriptions versus newsstand sales and data on regional, metropolitan, and special edition circulation. The report also includes an analysis of a single issue of the publication in terms of the market area it reaches and much more.

Today most daily newspapers and magazines in the United States and Canada are ABC members. Several other organizations and groups provide basic circulation data for the print media and audience figures for broadcast stations. Among them are Standard Rate and Data Service, which reports audited audience/circulation figures and lists advertising rates, policies, and practices. Still more audience data are available from the Association of National Advertisers, the American Newspaper Publishers Association, the Magazine Publishers Association, and others. Sagging circulation figures in the 1970s led newspapers to add sections such as "Lifestyle," "Weekend," "Trends," and "Leisure."

Measuring the Broadcast Audience

The paid circulation of a magazine or newspaper can be audited rather easily. A physical object — a newspaper or magazine — arrives at a household and is read by a given number of people. But getting reliable information about the audience for a broadcasting station or a network is more difficult. Broadcast messages can occupy long periods of time and reach their audiences in different ways and with varying levels of intensity. Consequently, wrote broadcast historian Sydney Head, "no single universally accepted way of measuring broadcast consumption has evolved. Instead, several research companies using rival methods compete in the audience measurement field."[19] They use different procedures to chart audience size, characteristics, and behavior. Over the last twenty or thirty years they have frequently changed these methods in order to keep pace with new techniques for using surveys and statistics.

Types of Ratings. One way to measure the audience in an area is to relate the number of receivers in working order to the total number of households; the result is the relative *saturation* or *penetration* of the broadcast medium in a particular area.[20] Obviously this figure is not a precise measure of the audience because it says nothing about the viewing habits of people, who may or may not be using their television sets regularly. Penetration or saturation measures the *potential* audience.

The search for more precision in calculating the broadcast audience led to systems in which the relative audience size for a particular time slot or program is calculated. Various measures are used in this approach: *Instantaneous* rating reports indicate the audience size at a particular moment; *cumulative* reports give figures for a period of time, say thirty minutes.

Three measures frequently provided by the rating services are rating, share, and homes using television (HUT). The differences between these forms are subtle. They can be expressed as follows:

Rating = homes tuned to station ÷ total TV homes ($\times 100$)

Thus, the *rating* is the percentage of people who are watching or listening to a particular station.

Share = homes tuned to station ÷ homes using TV ($\times 100$)

A *share* is the percentage of households watching a particular program in relation to all programs available at that time.

HUT = sets turned on ÷ total TV homes ($\times 100$)

HUT is thus the percentage of homes that have television sets tuned to any station. Each of these measures tells us something different, and they are helpful to the station in sorting out its exact audience at any given time.

Obtaining Ratings. More than fifty companies conduct research that leads to ratings of some kind. Their first step is to define the people or the area of interest. A firm called Arbitron developed one method for defining the areas of interest in the television industry. Arbitron divides the United States into about 210 market areas called *areas of dominant influence,* or *ADIs.* Each of the nation's 3,141 counties is assigned to one of the areas, and the markets are ranked according to the number of television households. The ADIs range from New York, with more than 6 million television households, to Pembina, North Dakota, with just over 6,500. The information is used by media buyers to try to capture specified audiences.

In all audience research some more or less representative set of people — *a sample* — must be contacted and data recorded. Various techniques may be used: telephone interviews, in-person interviews, listener/viewer diaries, or receiver meters. The two major broadcast rating services are Arbitron and Nielsen, which provide national and local ratings.

Arbitron, which conducts research for both radio and television, asks a sample of listeners or viewers to keep a weekly diary of their viewing/listening behavior. Radio listeners, for example, are asked to indicate the amount of time they listen and the stations they are listening to, including the specific program and the place they are listening (for example, at home or away from home, including in a car). Samples are drawn from each market area and are weighted to provide a representative picture of the viewing or listening habits of the people who are asked to keep diaries.

As a result of the upsurge of interest in radio in the late 1970s and early 1980s, research on the radio audience has prospered. With both stations and advertising agencies eager for more data, two new firms entered the field of radio research and provided a serious challenge to Arbitron, which once held a near-monopoly. The two firms, Trac-7 and Burke Broadcast Research, conduct telephone surveys, using large samples to impress their potential clients.

The famous Nielsen ratings, from which the television network programs are ranked, are based on data accumulated from meters attached to television sets in a sample of about 1,200 American homes. A meter known as an Audimeter records how long the set is on and to what channel it is tuned. The device then delivers the information to a central computer through a telephone wire network. This allows rapid daily processing of data, which are analyzed for the national prime-time ratings. For ratings of local programs, Nielsen uses diaries.

All rating services have problems in gaining acceptance in homes. Some people simply refuse to cooperate; others do so half-heartedly. These responses distort the ratings somewhat, although the rating services say they try to correct for these distortions. No one (outside these very secretive and competitive organizations) really knows for sure how severe these problems are because they do not readily share information about their methods and procedures. An exception is Arbitron, which publishes a book explaining its methodology. The rating services seem inadequate, complained historian Paula Fass, who wrote, "The Nielsen ratings . . . are not only vulnerable in their sampling techniques, but tell us little about the number of people watching, how long they watch, how much attention they pay. Many of these things we do not and possibly cannot know."[21] But the ratings are generally regarded as sufficiently reliable, and the industry pays close attention to them. Indeed, these ratings sometimes cause major shifts in programming.

Ratings and the News. News programs have not been immune to the probes of researchers and rating services. In fact, broadcast news consultants link audience ratings and perceptions of news programs with specific advice designed to boost ratings. Of

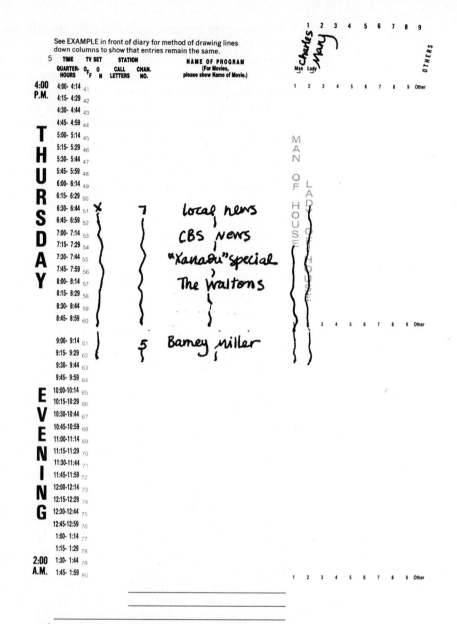

Selected television viewers complete viewing diaries like this one for the Nielsen Company, which evaluates the results and compiles ratings that have great influence on television programming.

course, better ratings means a bigger share of the market and thus greater profits. The most visible sign of the news consultants' work has been "happy talk" news in which anchor people deliver the news in chatty fashion with frequent friendly asides. Other evidence of the consultants' advice is the "action news" format, which includes more stories of shorter length. This format is the result of the consultants' conviction that viewers do not pay attention for long.

The news consultants, firms like Frank N. Magid Associates and McHugh and Hoffman, are really marketing consultants concerned mainly with packaging the news to achieve the greatest possible audience. Their recommendations often have little to do with journalism. As two educators have written:

> Few [of the consultants' suggestions] deal with the complexities of news writing, best uses of resources, lines of communication, controversial reporting, or other journalistic topics. They have traditionally convinced station managers that the anchorwoman needs to convey more warmth on the air, the sportscaster needs to have silver teeth fillings replaced with more telegenic porcelain fillings, the weathercaster needs to practice getting rid of his lisp.[22]

Outrageous and superficial as these examples seem, they do reflect the kinds of recommendations that the consultants make. They urge the station to build new and better sets, suggest more elaborate weather-forecasting equipment, and tell the anchorman to get a new hairpiece.

Station managers take these recommendations seriously, although many news directors have resisted them. In some places the consultant's recommendations have virtually dictated major changes; in others the information is used advisedly in reshaping the format of a program. Some critics admit that the consultants do have an instinct for boosting ratings. In any event, the use of these consultants shows clearly that news programming on radio and television, like entertainment programming, competes vigorously for an audience.

Probing Consumer Behavior

In recent years the ratings services have tried to break down the broadcast audience in terms of such categories as age, occupation, income, ethnic background, and geographic location. Precise knowledge of such characteristics of the audience has become increasingly important as broadcasters try to attract specific kinds of audiences. For example, it must have been determined that people likely to buy records are also likely to watch television late at night, since the airwaves are full of such advertising late at night and very early in the morning. Various kinds of nonrating research probe the size and stability of the audience, seasonal variations, the hours spent viewing, and other factors. A number of market research firms look at audiences as potential consumers. The Axiom Market Research Bureau, for example, uses a large national sample (25,000) and probes people's use of products and the media. Axiom collects information to learn how people make their buying decisions for different products and services. It offers its subscribers information about some 450 products and services, 120 magazines, 6 newspaper supplements, the nation's major newspapers, network television, and television usage as well as radio usage by type of program. The resulting data can help an advertiser decide which medium to use to sell laxatives, perfume, beer, or some other product.

Readership or viewership and product data are also correlated by W. R. Simmons & Associates Research, which studies and describes the audiences of magazines, newspaper supplements, national newspapers, and network television programs in terms of selective markets. Other firms, like Opinion Research Corporation, provide selective market information about the reading patterns of such groups as executives and teenagers. Still another firm, Lee Slurzberg Research, focuses on the black consumer and black media.

Other types of market research firms collect and disseminate information about advertising rates and mechanical specifications, advertising volume, and advertising effectiveness. One such firm, Daniel Starch & Staff, Inc., conducts studies of the readers of consumer magazines, general business and trade periodicals, daily newspapers, and other publications. They also note reading intensities or the reactions of readers to particular typographical devices and approaches.

Individual newspapers or broadcasters sometimes hire firms to probe their audience in more detail. The circulation losses of American newspapers led to a good many of these studies in the 1970s. One such study, commissioned by a large metropolitan newspaper, examined what was in the paper and what people read. As the confidential report described the study's recommendations,

> The prescription outlined here is surgery: It points out what kinds of things might be cut out of the paper to

improve readership, and also what kinds of things readers seem to want more of. It points out how differences in readership are related to such things as the subject of a story, its orientation, where it takes place, where it appears in the paper, the writing approach used in the story, the length of the story, the size and quality of its headline, the size of the newshole and the number of items on the page where the story appears, and the size of any photographs used to illustrate the story.[23]

Clearly, recommendations were offered that would alter the newspaper, in the hope of gaining a larger and more dedicated audience. Thus the various rating services and market researchers do not provide static indicators of audience preferences but information that can be used to change the content or format of a program or publication.

Most of the information gathered by the various firms and agencies we have been discussing is somewhat secret. It is gathered mainly for internal use by advertisers and media organizations. Sometimes, as in the case of the Nielsen ratings, the information is published widely in the press, but still its main use is internal. The public sometimes sees the consequences of the ratings but rarely knows much about how the ratings were determined or why particular decisions were made. On rare occasions a disgruntled Nielsen employee has revealed anecdotes about the internal operations of the firm. Beyond this kind of insider's view, however, little is known about these groups, which have so much influence on the media.

Measuring Public Opinion

In contrast to ratings and market research on the media, public opinion polls are designed for public display and public consumption. The various media are interested in them for two reasons. First, the media are thought to influence public opinion. Second, and more important, public opinion on current topics can be important news.

Some polling groups — such as George Gallup's American Institute of Public Opinion, the Louis Harris polls, and various state and regional polls (Field in California, the Iowa and Minnesota polls in the Midwest) — produce regular reports on the public pulse. These polls have been conducted with ever more precise methods through the years. They measure popularity of the president, public views of political and social issues, and reactions to a

*"And don't waste your time canvassing the whole building,
young man. We all think alike."*

This jibe at polls and pollsters is one of many
similar gag cartoons for which The New
Yorker magazine is famous.

particular policy. The response of the American people, or a segment of them, to such questions is news and is treated as such.

As polls became more common and probed more aspects of American life, they also became controversial. Although the belief that polls influence voters to vote for the front-runner in the pollster's horse race has subsided, polls and pollsters are often criticized for interfering in the electoral process. Congressional committees have probed the question: Do polls have an undue influence on American politics? The pollsters say no, they are merely "photographing" public opinion at a given moment in time. But politicians persist in claiming that the polls influence voting behavior. There is little data to support this claim.

From time to time interest in the pollsters' methods rises. How accurate are the polls? Can they call a close election? What if they are wrong? These questions and others have occupied commentators for years. Much of the concern goes back to hazy memories of the famous *Literary Digest* poll of 1936. The *Literary Digest*, then a popular weekly magazine, mailed 10 million ballots to American citizens. They got 2 million back, and predicted that Alfred Landon would defeat Franklin D. Roosevelt in the presidential election by a substantial margin. Landon suffered an overwhelming defeat, and the magazine was mortified. Later (for this and other reasons), it went out of business.

Why had the *Digest*, which had been accurately forecasting elections since 1916, made such a colossal error? It happened because they had mailed their ballots to those people who were on auto registration and telephone lists. In the middle of the Great Depression of the 1930s, these lists excluded many voters with low income, people who were likely to vote against Landon and for Democrat Roosevelt. In the jargon of polling, the sample was biased.

The *Literary Digest* poll taught the pollsters a lesson and led to more refined and sophisticated methods of both drawing a sample and interpreting the results. Pollsters have continued to alter their methods since then for more accurate prediction.

The major pollsters work in somewhat different ways, but generally they use a national sample of, say, 2,500 people. This sample is sorted and weighted to take geographical differences and differences in neighborhood (and thus social class) into account. The pollsters try to measure carefully the degree of accuracy to predict variation from their results, and they try to control for errors that might creep in. For the most part they have been successful in doing this and in building confidence in their results among media executives (who buy the polling services) and among the public.

If a poll says that only 30 percent of the public favor national health insurance or that 60 percent of the public approve of the president's handling of his job, what does that mean? It is important first to know who paid for the poll, especially if it was a candidate for office or a special-interest lobby, and to know the exact wording of the questions used in the interviews. Information about the sample size and possible percentage of error provides useful insights into the meaning of the findings. How the interview was conducted might also influence the results. Was it conducted in person or on the phone? Did it include only registered voters or those likely to vote? Finally, the timing might be crucial. If, for example, a poll commenting on the president's popularity was taken just before an unpopular presidential decision, it may not reflect the current state of thinking. During the presidential election of 1980, the importance of timing was strikingly evident in polls regarding the race between President Carter and Senator Edward Kennedy for the Democratic nomination. At first, Kennedy ran far ahead of Carter in the polls. Then American citizens were taken hostage in Iran. The country rallied behind the president, his ratings in the polls rose dramatically, and Kennedy's fell.

To help the public interpret polls intelligently, the National Committee on Published Polls has set minimal standards of information that should accompany any published poll. The following information should be provided in all news stories about public polls:

1. The identity of the sponsor of the survey.
2. The exact wording of the questions asked.
3. A definition of the population sampled.
4. The sample size and, where the survey design makes it relevant, the response rate.
5. Some indication of the allowance that should be made for sampling error.
6. Which results are based on part of the sample, e.g., probable voters, those who have heard of the candidate or other subdivisions.
7. How the interviews were collected: in person in homes, by phone, by mail, on street corners, or wherever.
8. When the interviews were collected.[24]

These standards are important because they give the public enough information to evaluate a poll. The major national polls have usually provided most of this information to their readers, although some editors delete parts of it, thinking that their readers won't be interested. Not all public polls are released by respectable and reliable firms like the Gallup organization. Politicians seeking partisan advantage and various special-interest groups pressing their cause often trumpet polls that make them look good. Sometimes such polls are worth examining; sometimes they are not. Information on how the poll was obtained can help readers make that decision. Well-conducted polls have the advantage of taking readers beyond their own experience and that of society's authorities (public figures and others) to the grassroots, to the people.

Summary

In this chapter we have examined the auxiliary organizations that serve, support, or supplement the mass media of communication. The wire services, feature syndicates, and public polls provide content and in the process bring some standardization of media fare. Other auxiliaries monitor and measure audience reaction to the mass media. Although these auxiliaries — rating services, market research, and others—do not provide content for the media directly, they have an indirect influence on the shaping of that content.

AP and UPI are the dominant wire services, providing exhaustive coverage of national and international news. They gather and distribute the news, and both what they cover and how they cover it have a major effect on the content of papers all across the nation. About 95 percent of America's daily newspapers subscribe to AP or UPI or both. In addition, many now subscribe to one of the supplemental services.

The wires serve both the print and the broadcasting media; the syndicates serve just the print media, although the networks act rather like "syndicates of the air." Much of the interpretation and entertainment in newspapers comes from the syndicates. From editorial cartoons to political columns, comic strips to advice to the lovelorn, the syndicates have much to offer newspapers. They most often act as brokers between the writers and artists and the print media.

Ratings, market research, and polls help the media to keep in touch with their audiences and to sell themselves to advertisers. Although these evaluative tools frequently influence the content and format of programs and publications, the methods used and the results are often secret.

Notes and References

1. Walter Lippmann, *Public Opinion* (New York: Free Press, 1965) p. 214, originally published in 1922.
2. Richard L. Gordon, "Cincinnati Post Copes with New York Blackout," *Editor & Publisher*, July 30, 1977, p. 29.
3. Ibid. See also, "News Computers Go Dead During NY Power Outage," *Editor & Publisher*, July 23, 1977, p. 7.
4. Victor Rosewater, *History of Co-operative News-Gathering in the United States* (New York: Appleton-Century-Crofts, 1930) p. 354.
5. Ibid.
6. A. Kent MacDougall, "Wire Services: AP and UPI," in *The Press; A*

Critical Look from the Inside, ed. MacDougall (Princeton, N.J.: Dow Jones Books, 1972) pp. 109–110.

7. J. Richard Cote, "A Study of Accuracy of Two Wire Services," *Journalism Quarterly*, Winter 1970, p. 666.

8. Richard A. Schwarzlose, "Trends in U.S. Newspapers' Wire Service Resources, 1934–66," *Journalism Quarterly*, Winter 1966, p. 637.

9. B. H. Liebes, "Decision-Making by Telegraph Editors — AP or UPI?" *Journalism Quarterly*, Autumn 1966, pp. 441–442.

10. MacDougall, "Wire Services," p. 110.

11. *United States* v. *Associated Press, et al.*, 52 F. Supp. 372 (1943).

12. Russell Baker, *An American in Washington* (New York: Alfred A. Knopf, 1961), p. 197.

13. MacDougall, "Wire Services," p. 118.

14. Michael W. Singletary, "Newspaper Use of Supplemental Services, 1960–1973," *Journalism Quarterly*, Winter 1975, pp. 750–751.

15. Ibid.

16. See advertisement, pp. 28–29A, *Editor & Publisher*, July 31, 1976.

17. Leona Williamson, "Publisher Takes Syndicate to Court to Keep Features," *Editor & Publisher*, August 6, 1977, p. 8.

18. W. H. Thomas, ed., *The Road to Syndication* (New York: Fleet Press, 1967) p. 12.

19. Sydney Head, *Broadcasting in America*, 3rd ed. (Boston: Houghton Mifflin, 1976) p. 227.

20. Ibid., p. 228. See, generally, Head's excellent discussion of audience measurement, pp. 226–255.

21. Paula S. Fass, "Television as Cultural Document: Promises and Problems," in *Television as a Cultural Force*, ed. Richard Adler and Douglass Cater (New York: Praeger, 1976).

22. Julius K. Hunter and Lynn S. Gross, *Broadcast News: The Inside Out* (St. Louis, Mo.: C. W. Mosby, 1980) p. 280.

23. From a confidential report prepared by a market research firm for a large metropolitan daily newspaper.

24. For an excellent discussion of criteria for public polls, see Phillip Meyer, *Precision Journalism*, Second ed. (Bloomington: Indiana University Press, 1978).

The Impact and Consequences of Mass Communication

8 The Media's Influence on Individuals

[The penny papers] are willing to fan into destroying flames the hellish passions that now slumber in the bosom of society. The guilt of murder may not stain their hands; but the fouler guilt of making murderers surely does.

HORACE GREELEY, *The Tribune*, 1841

Research on human communication is complex, perplexing, and often frustrating. New techniques and new ideas appear constantly. It is therefore very difficult to evaluate the generalizations that have emerged from research on communication. Nevertheless, it is from research that knowledge about the effects of the mass media will come. Such understanding will not result from the pronouncements of preachers, the opinions of politicians, the claims of the PTA, the untested views of critics, or any other form of debate. Like it or not, we are stuck with research — with all its problems and limitations — as our best source for understanding the effects of the media.

This chapter examines one aspect of those effects: the media's influences on individuals. We look first at the legacy of fear of mass communication that underlies both public attitudes and most of the research on the subject. We ask why people are quick to blame the media for all kinds of harmful influence. Second, we ask, what are the facts as we know them about the media's effects? To answer this question we examine six studies that have been milestones in the search for scientific understanding of the media's influence.

The Legacy of Fear

If a time machine could transport the generation of the 1920s into the present, the attitudes, sexual conduct, and values of today's youth would probably shock them out of their wits. There is little doubt they would blame it all on mass communication. In fact, since the mass media first emerged, people have accused them of exerting a powerful negative influence on the opinions, attitudes, and conduct of individuals. The ink was scarcely dry on the first mass newspapers of the 1830s before a host of critics rose to denounce them. Educators, jurists, the clergy, and other concerned citizens believed the mass press provoked crime by reporting so much about it. Of perhaps equal concern were fears that people would turn away from books and that, as a result, literary standards would be lowered.

When the movies, radio, and television appeared, they too became objects of fear, scorn, and accusation. In the 1920s the movies were charged with destroying moral values and leading the nation's youth into crime. As radio became popular it was said to be helping to erode musical taste, and, after radio commercials became commonplace, radio was charged with shamelessly exploiting the public for the sake of profits. More recently, television has been blamed for almost every problem that plagues American society. In 1977 a youngster in Florida robbed and killed an elderly woman. His lawyer argued at the trial that he was innocent and television was guilty. The young man, said his lawyer, had viewed so many murders and other violent acts on television that he could not distinguish right from wrong. The jury did not agree, found the young man guilty, and sent him to prison.

Defenders of the mass media deny that they cause personal and social problems. They point to the benefits of the media: that millions now hear serious music, at least occasionally; that ballet and opera are available to the masses for the first time in history; that news analyses make citizens better informed; that educational broadcasts are available daily; that the press, as an adversary of government, can help root out corruption even in the presidency; and so on. Obviously, there is much truth in these claims.

How, then, can we gain a balanced perspective on these issues? Are the media blameless benefactors that improve life for us all? Or are the media responsible for corrupting individuals? Without question, answering yes to either question would oversimplify reality. To understand the media influences better, we first look at why people think they have such awful power and harmful effects.

Public Beliefs About the Media

Anything new generates fear. This dictum has held true in every age and every society. It is valid for almost every advance in science, technology, and thought that has occurred in Western civilization for centuries. Like dozens of other social changes, the growth of mass communication stimulated widespread anxiety. This anxiety was given much publicity as the media themselves published the charges against first the penny press, then movies, then radio and television. As a result, belief in the great power of the media became a part of our society's shared system of beliefs about mass communication.

The events of the Spanish-American War and World War I, in particular, reinforced the belief that the media could shape and mold the opinions, attitudes, and behavior of the masses. Publisher William Randolph Hearst was even accused of starting the Spanish-American War in 1898. To an employee who asked to return from Cuba because nothing was going on there, Hearst supposedly sent a telegram saying, "Please remain. You furnish the pictures and I'll furnish the war." Many historians dispute the idea that Hearst's role in the war was important, but the story became a part of American folklore. However, shortly before war did break out, many newspapers and magazines inflamed public opinion against the Spanish. During World War I extensive propaganda was used to marshall American support for the war, to try to sway public opinion in neutral nations, and to try to confuse the enemy powers. Stories were published in British papers claiming that the Germans had committed atrocities, that they were barbarians and butchers. People believed them even though truths were often badly distorted, blatantly denied, or simply ignored. After the war the revelations of expropagandists made sensational reading — and more fodder for critics of the mass media's power.

These experiences of society as a whole, plus many that would follow, established among the general public a conviction that mass communication is dangerous. The public developed a contradictory orientation toward the mass media, loving and hating them simultaneously. Each new medium was eagerly adopted by waiting hordes. But, at the same time, citizens could easily tick off a list of complaints about their effects.

The belief that mass communication is powerful and dangerous has persisted in our society for a century; we call it the *legacy of*

Striking illustrations on posters like this one
were a central feature of the propaganda
campaigns of World War I. Both sides in the
war used posters, songs, newspaper stories,
and other forms of communication to influence
public attitudes and secure the unflinching
loyalty of their citizens.

fear. It has been and will be passed on from one generation to the next. We can therefore call it a *culture complex:* a related set of beliefs and behaviors that is shared by a group of people and passed on from parent to child. Denouncing the media for their awesome power and bad effects is as American as apple pie.

Social Scientists and the Legacy of Fear

The general public has not been alone in its fear of the media. "Experts" have often reinforced that fear. Scholars joined the public in the outcry against the mass press in the nineteenth century. Gabriel Tarde, an outstanding nineteenth-century criminologist, blamed newspapers for the sharp rise in juvenile delinquency that he observed in France between the 1860s and 1890s. Noting the growing popularity of the mass press, with its emphasis on reports of crime, during the same period, he concluded: "It is the trashy and malicious press, scandal mongering, riddled with court cases, that awaits the student when he leaves school. The little newspaper, supplementing the little drink, alcoholizes his heart."[1] Tarde denounced the press not only for stimulating juvenile delinquency but also for encouraging immorality, crime, and alcoholism among adults. "Pornography and slander," he concluded, "have become the two breasts nourishing the newspaper."[2]

Tarde's belief in the media's power was consistent with the social science of his time. Indeed, the term *mass media* came out of a view of society, people, and the media that supported fear of the media's power. As we noted in Chapter 1, early in this century intellectuals believed that the new emerging urban society was composed of diverse individuals without strong social ties; they called such a group of people a *mass*. In the view of these observers, such people would be especially easy to influence because social ties would not soften the impact of the media. These were thought to be characteristics of the audiences for the media that were developing early in this century — which were therefore called *mass media.*

Early research in the 1920s and 1930s also tended to reinforce the legacy of fear. It seemed to show that the media had powerful effects on their audiences. Later research, we shall see, did not support this view. But as scientists shifted from a conviction that the media have great power to the conclusion that their power is clearly limited, the public did not follow. Thus the legacy of fear is alive and well, flourishing in the dark suspicions of the majority of Americans concerning their mass media.

Early Research: A Belief in Maximum Effects

The legacy of fear prompted much of the research that has been done on mass communication. Public anxiety has been a significant factor in determining which research projects the government and private foundations have been willing to finance. As a result, most of the research has ignored the positive contributions of the mass media.

Research on mass communication did not begin until early in the twentieth century. The social sciences have ancient origins and were established as separate fields of knowledge in the nineteenth century. But the capacity to do rigorous research in social science lagged far behind the ability to theorize and speculate about human behavior. It was not until the 1920s that statistical research techniques were sufficiently developed to permit investigation of the effects of mass communication.

The first large-scale study of a mass medium was published in 1933. By the mid-1940s and early 1950s important discoveries had been made — some by accident. As television became a significant medium, it too came under scientific scrutiny.

In this fifty-year accumulation of research there have been thousands of investigations on every conceivable aspect of mass communication and a few key studies that shaped scientific thinking about the mass media. In this and the sections that follow we review six of these milestone studies. The earliest studies show a view of human behavior, research techniques, and conclusions quite different from those that prevail today.

The Movies and Children: The Payne Fund Studies

Social scientists interested in the effects of mass communication first turned to the movies to apply their new techniques of research. There were clear reasons for this choice. During the first decade of the new century, movies were a novelty. During the second decade they became one of the principal media for family entertainment. By the end of the 1920s, feature-length films with sound tracks were standard, and the practice of going to the movies once a week or more was widespread.

Meanwhile, the public had become particularly uneasy about the influence of the movies on children. In 1929 an estimated 28 million minors — including more than 11 million children under the age of fourteen — went to the movies weekly.[3] Critics raised alarming questions about what the movies were doing to the nation's children. Were they destroying parents' control over their children? Were they teaching immorality? Films with themes that were thought to be unwholesome — such as horror, crime, immoral relationships, and the illegal use of alcohol (during Prohibition) — were especially troubling.

In the midst of this public concern, there was no established system for bringing research to bear on the issue. No government agency existed to give money to investigators who wanted to assess the impact of films on children. But a private agency was formed to seek data in order to develop a national policy concerning motion pictures. This agency in turn called together a group of educators, psychologists, and sociologists to plan large-scale studies to probe the effects of motion pictures on youth, and a private foundation called the Payne Fund was persuaded to supply the necessary money. The resulting Payne Fund Studies were the first large-scale effort to assess the effects of a major mass medium.

When they were published in the early 1930s, the Payne Fund Studies were the best available evaluation of the impact of motion pictures on children. The approaches used in the studies ranged from collecting and interpreting anecdotes to experiments measuring and analyzing responses to questionnaires. But by today's standards of research many of these studies seem quaint and naive. The way data were collected and analyzed limits the usefulness of the conclusions the Payne researchers reached for interpreting the effects of movies today. Still, these studies are worth examining for two reasons: they represent a monumental assembling of data on the impact of the movies during the 1920s, and by their failures they illustrate some of the essentials of good research. To illustrate the approaches, data, limitations, and conclusions of the studies, we will summarize two of them. They dealt with two perplexing questions: how did the movies influence the everyday behavior of children, and can movies change children's attitudes?

Influences on Everyday Behavior. One of the most interesting, if least scientific, of the Payne Fund Studies was done by sociologist Herbert Blumer.[4] Blumer wanted to provide a general picture of how viewing films influenced children's play, their everyday behavior — such as dress, mannerisms, and speech — their emotions, their ideas about romance, their ambitions and temptations, and their career plans. His method was simple. He had adolescents and young adults recall and record influences from films that had occurred in their childhood.

As a first step, Blumer asked two groups of university students to describe in detail their memories of the way movies had affected their ideas or behavior from as early an age as they could remember. The students were assured that the descriptions would remain anonymous and were asked to be as natural, truthful, and detailed as possible. The reports were studied, and recurring types of experiences and influences were identified (for example, influences on play, mannerisms, fantasies, and emotions). From these recurring categories a list of such general topics was compiled. This list served as a guide for the main body of subjects for preparing additional autobiographies.

Eventually, accounts were collected from more than 1,200 persons. Most were college and university students, but some were office and factory workers. The result was an immense number of recollections about how people thought that seeing films had influenced their daily behavior. Blumer attempted to draw inferences and conclusions from these accounts, but he did not subject them to quantitative or statistical analysis. He preferred to "let the facts speak for themselves" by quoting liberally from the autobiographies to illustrate his conclusions. The movies were, he said, a source of imitation, unintentional learning, and emotional influence.

According to Blumer, the movies appeared to have a powerful impact on children's play. Youngsters impersonated cowboys and Indians, cops and robbers, pirates, soldiers, race drivers, and every conceivable hero and villain they had seen in films. Reenacting movie plots, children battled each other with wooden swords, spears made from broom handles, and shields from washboiler tops. They rode horses made of scraps of lumber, shot rifles and pistols made of sticks, and flew airplanes built with apple crates. They dug trenches in their back yards and assaulted forts in vacant lots. They became Dracula, Cleopatra, the dreaded Dr. Fu Manchu, Tarzan, the Red Baron, and Mary Queen of Scots.

The people in Blumer's study generally recalled these experiences with pleasure and warmth. In spite of a few harmful incidents and a number of accidents, most of it was fun. For the most part, these activities seemed to have little lasting influence on later life.

Generally, Blumer concluded that children and teenagers copied many mannerisms, speech patterns, and other behaviors from the people portrayed on the screen. There were hundreds of accounts of how youngsters had tried to imitate the way a favorite movie star smiled, leered, smirked, laughed, sat, walked, or talked. Such attempts were usually unsuccessful and short-lived, but they often perplexed and mystified parents. Although it would seem harmless for children to adopt hair and dress styles from film characters, remember that the 1920s were the age of "flaming youth" and "flappers." The movies showed speakeasies, easy money, powerful cars, and fast women. Parents were accustomed to books and magazines that followed the strict standards of the Victorian era. But by the time of World War I, Victorian morality began to fade, and the automobile was being used for more than just transportation. When they saw movies mirroring the new styles and the new morality, many people believed the movies were the cause of the changes. Blumer, in showing that children copied the behavior they saw in films, gave some support to this view.

Blumer's data revealed another facet of the movie experience. Movie viewing was often an intensely emotional experience. His

Children have for decades imitated the behaviors of the heroes of movies and comic books. This youthful pair from the 1920s shows the style of a Jazz Age romantic couple.

subjects reported that often while watching films they experienced what he called *emotional possession.* As the plot unfolded, they had intense feelings of terror and fear, sorrow and pathos, thrills and excitement, or romantic passion and love. They often left the film emotionally drained, in a state of anxiety, or sexually stimulated — depending on the film. The impact of these experiences was difficult to assess, but the findings testified to the powerful emotions that the movies of the time could generate.

Blumer's procedure was clever, and it permitted some insights into the experiences of the people he studied. It reveals a more innocent time. But his subjects were the first movie generation, and it is scarcely surprising that he concluded that this new and widely used medium had influence. But what can we learn from Blumer's study, and what can we do with his conclusions? His data do reveal a fascinating and detailed picture of how his subjects *thought* the movies had influenced them as children. Since the movies did offer young people a panoply of gods and goddesses to imitate, it seems reasonable to think that the films reinforced certain behaviors copied from the stars. But that is only speculation — and we certainly do not need Blumer's study to suggest it. Can Blumer's study tell us whether the films caused certain behaviors? Can it give any objective measure of the influence of films on children, or even just on Blumer's subjects? Can it tell us whether any influence they might have had lasted?

The answer to each of these questions is no. First, whatever Blumer found out about the first generation of moviegoers may or may not apply to today's youth, who have a great deal of experience with various media. Second, the methods of Blumer's study are not adequate to answer these kinds of questions. Notice first that Blumer's sample — the subjects who wrote the autobiographies — might have been unrepresentative, or biased, in many ways. Perhaps his sample included an unusual number of very intelligent people, or an unusual number of males or wealthy people. Perhaps the requirement that people write down their experiences kept less literate people from responding. Blumer made no attempt to see that his subjects were representative of the larger population. We therefore don't know what, if anything, his study might tell us about other youths, even of that time. Furthermore, although Blumer reinterviewed some subjects six months later to check for consistency, it is difficult to tell how faithfully such recollections reflect events that actually occurred years earlier. Blumer's study may or may not be a true picture of the actual influences of movie going even on his own subjects.

Stated in more technical terms, Blumer's study falls short in meeting two fundamental criteria for scientific research: validity and reliability. A study is *valid* if it measures what it claims to measure. In this case, the study is valid if it actually shows the influences movies had on the children under study and others like them. A study is *reliable* if a repetition of the study using the same techniques would yield similar results. In other words, if Blumer repeated his research, would his findings be the same? Or if another researcher duplicated Blumer's study, would the conclusions be parallel?

Blumer did not give us precise measures of behavior or conclusions that we can apply to children in general. He gave us interesting, informative anecdotes rather than the "hard data" that have become customary in the social sciences. Another study in the Payne Fund, however, did attempt to use more precise methods.

Changing Children's Attitudes. Ruth C. Peterson and L. L. Thurstone focused on the question of how movies influence children's attitudes toward social issues.[5] In its research design and precision of measurement, the Peterson-Thurstone study resembles social science research today more closely than does Blumer's study. First they reviewed hundreds of films to select a few that dealt clearly with specific issues. To be included in the research, a film had to meet three criteria: it had to be recent, acceptable to school authorities, and clearly focused on attitudes toward one of the issues under study. Eventually, Peterson and Thurstone selected thirteen films that depicted attitudes toward (1) the Germans and World War I, (2) gambling, (3) Prohibition, (4) the Chinese, (5) punishment of criminals, and (6) "the Negro." In some experiments they assessed the ability of one film to change attitudes; in others they measured attitude change resulting from viewing two or even three films.

Each of the eleven experiments had four steps. First, the subjects' attitudes toward an issue under study were measured using specially designed questionnaires. Then they were given a free ticket to see one of the selected films at the local theater a day or two later. The day after they saw the film, their attitudes were measured again. In some cases, the subjects were tested yet again from 2½ to 18 months later to see whether any effects of the films had persisted.

The subjects in these experiments were some 4,000 junior and senior high school students from small communities near Chicago. For any given experiment, the subjects were just those students who were at school on the day the study began, who went to the movies according to plan, and who were at school the next day, when their attitudes were retested.

Peterson and Thurstone used sophisticated attitude scales that had only recently been developed, and their results were subjected to careful statistical analysis. But notice several weaknesses in the design of their study. To begin with, they took no precautions to see that their sample was not in some way biased. Also, they made no attempt to study those students who did *not* complete all stages of the study. Perhaps those students who completed the study were more interested in films or in school than those who did not; perhaps their responses to films were different from the responses of the students who completed the study.

Notice, too, that Peterson and Thurstone did not follow one procedure that is now commonplace. They did not use both a control group and an experimental group. They used only an experimental group. A *control group* is a set of subjects that is as similar as possible to those in the experimental group but is not given the crucial manipulation that is being studied in the experimental group. Thus the experimental and control groups can be compared to see whether the experimental manipulation made a difference. In this study, for example, a control group would have been treated just like the experimental group *except that* it would have watched a neutral film, one with no relationship to the attitudes being studied. Then the two groups would have been compared. Simply put, if the experimental group then showed a change in attitude and the control group did not, the researchers would be more confident in saying that the attitude change was the result of the film and not the result of some other undetermined factor. Since Peterson and Thurstone did not use a control group, we can speculate about factors other than the films that might have caused changes in attitudes. For example, perhaps some event in the news caused a change.

Despite these weaknesses in the study by today's standards, its findings were influential. Thurstone and Peterson concluded that films could change children's attitudes, sometimes dramatically. In one experiment, for example, the subjects saw a movie called *Son of the Gods*, which told the story of Sam Lee. It showed Sam Lee as a fine young man who was not accepted by his non-Chinese neighbors, and it portrayed Chinese people and their culture in a positive way. After watching the film, the 182 teenagers in this study showed more positive attitudes toward the Chinese.

From a statistical point of view, the shift toward more positive attitudes was significant.[6]

Other youngsters in another town watched *Birth of a Nation* (1915), a classic silent film to which a sound track was added. The movie is clearly antiblack and sympathetic toward the Ku Klux Klan. In this case questionnaires showed that the subjects' attitudes toward blacks became considerably more negative after seeing the film. In tests of the same subjects five months later, the shift toward negative attitudes persisted. (Such research provoking negative attitudes would violate the ethics of scientific research today.) Still other experiments by Peterson and Thurstone concluded that attitudes toward war, gambling, and punishment of criminals could be altered with a single film. They found that two or three films dealing with the same general topic could shift attitudes even if any one of the films alone could not. In other words, the influence of movies appeared to be *cumulative*.

With their impressive statistical graphs and experimental format, the Peterson-Thurstone studies were regarded as very important. They not only stimulated others to study attitude change but also supported a kind of *magic bullet theory* of mass communication. This view has also been called the *hypodermic needle theory* or the *stimulus-response theory*.[7] Basically, this theory sees the movie as a stimulus that is received in more or less the same way by each subject and brings about an essentially uniform effect in each. The characteristics of persons are unimportant in this theory, and the stimulus — in this case, a film — is seen as immediately and directly changing the person's attitudes. Moreover, a change in attitude was thought to be equivalent to a change in conduct. As W. W. Charters, chairman of the Payne Fund Studies, explained: "Because a close relationship between the attitudes of an individual and his actions *may be assumed,* the study of the effect of motion pictures upon the attitude of children toward important social values is central in importance."[8] (Italics added.)

We shall soon see how social scientists outgrew such a simple and mechanical view of human behavior. But in the 1930s the magic bullet theory had considerable support, and it reinforced the legacy of fear. The entire Payne Fund series, in fact, seemed to support the strongest critics of the media, who argued that the media were both powerful and harmful. Today the technical shortcomings of the Payne studies are glaring. They offer us few guides to understanding the impact of movies — or any medium — on today's communication-saturated youth. Even when the studies were published, experts criticized their technical shortcomings. But to the public such criticism sounded like debates over navigation while the ship was sinking. The Payne studies reinforced the belief that the movies were responsible for bad ideas, bad morals, and bad behavior among the nation's youth. That belief was soon applied to the broadcasting media as well.

The Great Panic: Reactions to the Invasion from Mars

If there had been any doubt that radio could have a powerful impact on its audience, that doubt was dispelled one evening in 1938. On October 30, 1938, horrible creatures from Mars invaded the United States and killed millions of people with death rays. At least, that was the firm belief of many of the 6 million people who were listening to the CBS show "Mercury Theater of the Air" that evening. The broadcast was only a radio play — a clever adaptation of H. G. Wells's science fiction novel *War of the Worlds*. But it was so realistically presented as a newscast that hundreds of thousands of listeners who tuned in late, missing the information that it was only a play, thought that Martian monsters were taking over. Among those who believed the show was a real news report, tens of thousands went into mindless panic. They saw the invasion as a direct threat to their values, property, and lives — as the end of their world. Terrified people prayed, hid, cried, or fled. A high school girl later reported:

> I was writing a history theme. The girl upstairs came and made me go up to her place. Everybody was so excited I felt as [if] I was going crazy and kept on saying, "what can we do, *what difference does it make* whether we die sooner or later?" We were holding each other. Everything seemed unimportant in the face of death. I was afraid to die, just kept on listening.[9]

Among those who believed that the Martians were destroying everything and that nothing could be done to stop them, many simply abandoned all hope:

> I became terribly frightened and got in the car and started for the priest so I could make peace with God before dying. Then I began to think that perhaps it might have been a story, but discounted that because of the introduction as a special news broadcast. While enroute to my destination, a curve loomed up and traveling at between seventy-five and eighty miles per hour, I knew I couldn't make it though as *I recall it didn't greatly concern me either.* To die one way or another, it made no difference as death was inevitable. After

FCC was analyzed. Finally, some 12,500 newspaper clippings related to the broadcast were reviewed.

The result was a sensitive study of the feelings and reactions of people who were badly frightened by what they thought was the arrival of Martians. (Our earlier quotations of reactions come from this study.) The study also yielded a hypothesis about the effects of the broadcast. The researchers concluded that critical ability was the most significant variable related to the response people made to the broadcast. *Critical ability* was defined generally as the capacity to make intelligent decisions. Those who were low in critical ability tended to accept the invasion as real and failed to make reliable checks on the broadcast; for example, they did not call authorities or listen to other stations. Especially vulnerable to misconception of the nature of the program were those with strong religious beliefs, who thought the invasion was an act of God and the end of the world. Some thought a mad scientist was responsible. Others were disposed to believe in the broadcast because war scares in Europe, where World War II was about to begin, made catastrophe seem more plausible.

Those high in critical ability tended not to believe the broadcast was real. They were more likely to be able to sort out the situation even if they tuned in late. These people tended to be more educated than those low in critical ability. In fact, statistical data obtained from CBS revealed that amount of education was the single best factor in predicting whether people would check the broadcast against other sources of information.

Notice that the conclusions of the Cantril study were a departure from the magic bullet theory. According to that theory, the broadcast should have had about the same effect on everyone. But the Cantril study isolated characteristics of the listeners that strongly influenced their response: critical ability and amount of education. The *War of the Worlds* broadcast reinforced the legacy of fear of the media among many, but some researchers were beginning to suspect that the magic bullet theory had flaws.

Beyond the Magic Bullet

The magic bullet theory had assumed that a given message reached every eye or ear in the same way and provoked essentially uniform responses. Whose eye or ear didn't much matter. This view followed the approaches to human behavior that prevailed in social science early in this century. Psychology, for example, was dominated by a fascination with stimuli and responses. Stimuli were seen as evoking responses automatically. Moreover, the relationships between stimuli and responses were thought to be governed by inherited biological mechanisms, or instincts.

People were thought to inherit basically the same instincts, so differences between people seemed rather unimportant.

Around the end of the 1920s, however, psychology and sociology developed new theories that eventually influenced research on mass communication. *Individual differences* became a focus of psychological studies. These studies showed that individual differences in needs, attitudes, values, intelligence, and other personal factors played key roles in shaping the behavior of individuals. Meanwhile, sociologists gave increased attention to the importance of *social categories*. They were most concerned with the nature of social structure, how it changed, and the characteristics of various categories of people who had different positions in that structure. Comparisons of the behavior of categories of people — such as racial and ethnic groups, social classes, rural and urban people, age groups, and males and females — became a focus for research.

Concern with both individual differences and social categories inevitably was brought to the task of studying the effects of mass communication.[15] New formulations then began to replace the magic bullet theory. In fact, Cantril's study already shows this change; it looked to individual differences in critical ability and to social categories based on amount of education to account for differences in the effects of mass communication. We next review two studies that were milestones in replacing the magic bullet theory: one examining soldiers in training during World War II, and the second analyzing the presidential election of 1940. Both studies helped build a new way of understanding the power of the media to influence ideas, opinions, and behavior.

Persuading the American Soldier: Experiments with Film

By World War II social scientists had developed fairly sophisticated techniques of experimentation, measurement, and statistical analysis. The military therefore felt that social scientists could contribute to the war effort. In particular, the Army formed a special team of social psychologists to study the effectiveness of films that were specially designed to help teach recruits about the background of the war and to influence their opinions and motivation.[16]

The chief of staff, General G. C. Marshall, had decided that the troops needed a common core of beliefs. When America entered the war in 1941, many citizens were ill-informed about all the reasons for America's participation. Everyone knew about Japan's attack on Pearl Harbor, but not everyone knew about the rise of fascism, Hitler's and Mussolini's strategies, or the rise of militarism in Japan. Moreover, the United States is a nation with diverse regions, subcultures, and ethnic groups. The newly drafted soldiers included farmers from Nebraska, ethnic males from big-city slums, small-town youths, and young men from the ranches of the West. All were plunged into basic training, and many understood only dimly what it was all about. They needed to be told why they had to fight, what their enemies had done, who their allies were, and why it would be a tough job that had to be seen through to unconditional surrender by the Axis powers.

General Marshall thought that special orientation films could give the diverse recruits the necessary information and a shared set of beliefs. A top Hollywood director, Frank Capra, was hired to produce a series of films both to instruct the recruits and to help shape their opinions. This use of films testifies to the fact that the media were seen as powerful forces capable of creating clear effects among their audiences. But the Research Branch of the U.S. Army's Information and Education Division was also aware that social scientists believed that, because of individual differences, the types or degrees of effects would vary among people.

To social psychologists the Army therefore gave the job of studying the effectiveness of four of the films in this *Why We Fight* series. Their principal questions were how well the films could provide draftees with factual information and how well they could alter their specific and general opinions. The researchers also asked if the films could foster the following:

1. A firm belief in the right of the cause we fight.
2. A realization that we are up against a tough job.
3. A determined confidence in our own ability and the abilities of our comrades and leaders to do the job that has to be done.
4. A feeling of confidence, insofar as is possible under the circumstances, in the integrity and fighting ability of our Allies.
5. A resentment, based on knowledge of the facts, against our enemies who have made it necessary to fight.
6. A belief that through military victory, the political achievement of a better world order is possible.

The Experiments. Four films in Capra's *Why We Fight* series were studied: *Prelude to War, The Nazis Strike, Divide and Conquer,* and *The Battle of Britain.* (*The Battle of Britain* was the most famous in the series. Many commercial producers later used parts of the film to show scenes of World War II air combat.) The procedures used in many of the experiments can be summarized rather simply. Several hundred men who were undergoing training were given a "before" questionnaire. It included two types of

In a series of documentaries entitled Why We Fight, *produced by Hollywood director Frank Capra, the United States Army attempted, with mixed success, to provide information about World War II for newly drafted American soldiers and to shape those soldiers' attitudes toward the war.*

items: questions of fact and questions that measured opinions. These questionnaires had been carefully pretested on at least 200 soldiers to minimize ambiguities. Then the men were divided (by company units) into an experimental group and a control group. The companies designated as the experimental group saw one of the films in the *Why We Fight* series. The control group saw a film that did not deal with the war. After they had seen a film, all

Table 8.1   Percentage of Items Learned by Subjects of Different Educational Levels

Difficulty of material	Educational level		
	Grade school	High school	College
Least	35.1	60.7	75.3
Medium	11.6	30.3	49.9
Greatest	2.6	14.3	31.7

Source: Adapted from C. I. Hovland, A. A. Lumsdaine, and F. D. Sheffield, *Experiments on Mass Communication in World War II* (New York: John Wiley, 1965).

subjects in both groups answered an "after" questionnaire. It measured the same knowledge of facts and the same opinions as the first questionnaire. The questions, however, were rephrased so that repeated exposure to the test could not account for changes in responses. Thus, by comparing the amount of change in the experimental group with the change in the control group, the effect of the film could be assessed.

The Results: Minimal Effects. The films did produce changes in their audiences, but the changes were limited. For example, seeing *The Battle of Britain* increased the recruits' factual knowledge about the air war over Britain in 1940. It also changed specific opinions about many issues treated in the film. But it produced no broader changes, such as increased resentment of the enemy or willingness to serve until the Axis powers surrendered unconditionally.

The results were much the same for the other films studied. All increased the subjects' factual knowledge and modified their opinions on specific items but failed to achieve broad changes in orientation. The researchers also found that seeing two, three, or four films in sequence was somewhat more effective than seeing any one film alone.

Generally, the researchers concluded that the *Why We Fight* films were modestly successful in teaching soldiers about events leading up to the war. They were also modestly effective in modifying rather specific opinions related to the facts covered. But they had no great power to fire soldiers with enthusiasm for the war, create lasting hatred of the enemy, or establish confidence in the Allies. Moreover, the effects were different for soldiers with low, medium, and high levels of education. Generally, soldiers

The Media's Influence on Individuals   293

with more education learned more from the films (see Table 8.1).

Thus the effects of the film were clearly limited. This finding did not confirm earlier beliefs in all-powerful media. And the finding that variations in education modified the effects of the film contradicted the old notion that communications were magic bullets penetrating every eye and ear in the same way and creating similar effects in every receiver. Thus the studies of training films and their effects provided an important link in the evolution of theory concerning the effects of the media.

The Media in a Presidential Campaign

After World War II, research on mass communication blossomed. Social scientists were armed not only with new theories of the nature of human beings but also with increasingly precise techniques. Some researchers tried to sort out the factors in communication through laboratory studies. Professor Carl Hovland, for example, launched a large-scale research project involving anthropologists, sociologists, and political scientists.[17] He and some thirty associates explored several broad issues, including the nature of the communicator, the content of communication, and the responses of the audience. More specifically, they studied the communicator's credibility, the organization of the messages, the effects of group conformity, and the retention of changes in attitudes and opinions. But real-life media campaigns and mass communication were not part of this research. It used mostly laboratory situations and student subjects. The result was a gain in the development of theory, but the applicability of the program's findings to the real world was not clear.

One major study first published in the mid-1940s did focus directly on the real-life media. Professors Paul Lazarsfeld, Bernard Berelson, and Hazel Gaudet probed the web of influences within which voters made up their minds during the 1940 presidential election. In *The People's Choice* they reviewed what their research had revealed about the role of mass communications.[18] Their conclusion was that the media play only a minimal role in directly influencing the intentions and behavior of voters. (Note that this research was conducted before television was a major mass medium.)

This study is a landmark for two reasons. First, its scale was large and its methodology was sophisticated. In fact few later studies have rivalled it in these respects. Second, the findings revealed new perspectives on both the process and the effects of mass communication.

Improvements in Methodology. Lazarsfeld and his colleagues interviewed some 3,000 people from both urban and rural areas of

Erie County, Ohio. Interviewing began in May and ended in November of 1940, when Franklin D. Roosevelt defeated Wendell Willkie in the presidential election. In May all 3,000 subjects were interviewed, and they agreed to give further interviews as the election campaign progressed. This represented a new type of research method: the researchers randomly divided 2,400 of the subjects into four "panels" of 600 people each. One panel was the main panel. These people were interviewed each month from May to November for a total of seven interviews. The other three panels were control panels, each of which was interviewed only one more time. One control panel was given a second interview in July, another in August, and another in October. These interviews were compared with those of the main panel. This procedure allowed researchers to see how repeated interviews were affecting the main panel. They found that the repeated interviews had *no* measurable cumulative effect. Thus the researchers could feel confident that their findings were meaningful and not an artificial result of their procedure.

Some respondents decided whom to vote for early; some late. Some shifted from one candidate to another; some fell back into indecision. Always the interviewers tried to find out *why* the voters made these changes, and they noted the changes carefully. They also focused on the characteristics of the subjects. Rural and urban dwellers were compared; people at various income levels were contrasted. People of different religious backgrounds, political party affiliations, and habits of using the media were studied. Using complex methods, the researchers found that these characteristics could be used with fair success to predict voting intentions and actual voting behavior.

Through these efforts the researchers were able to reveal in an elaborate and detailed way how voters shifted around and finally made up their minds in a presidential election. Personal and social characteristics as well as the media played a role in their decisions. We review here some of the researchers' most important findings.

The Influence of the Media. Much of a political campaign is waged in the media, both through paid advertising and news reports. But Lazarsfeld and his colleagues did not find an all-powerful media controlling voters' minds. Instead, the media were just a part of a web of influences on voters. Their families, friends, and associates as well as the media helped people make up their minds. Nor did the media affect all voters in the same way. When the media did have an effect, three kinds of influences were found: activation, reinforcement, and conversion.

Activation is the process of getting people to do what they are predisposed to do, of pushing people along in ways they are headed anyway. For example, for almost fifty years most well-to-do Protestant farmers have usually voted Republican; most Catholic, blue-collar, urban workers have usually voted Democratic. That is, many voters tend to have certain socially based predispositions for and against the political parties. Yet as the 1940 campaign progressed, many voters were undecided about whom to vote for. The media eventually helped activate voters to follow their predispositions through four steps:

1. The political propaganda presented in newspapers, magazines, and radio broadcasts *increased interest* in the campaign among potential voters.
2. This increased interest led to greater *exposure* to campaign material.
3. But the exposure was *selective.* Background characteristics such as religion and occupation led persons to read or listen to the output of just one party. For example, rich Protestant farmers tended to pay attention mainly to Republican material whereas poor Catholic workers in the city turned to Democratic material.
4. As a result of increasing interest and selective exposure, the voters' intentions eventually *crystallized* in directions that were generally predictable from the voters' characteristics.

Thus, activation by media influences changes no one's mind, but it can affect an election's outcome.

Fully half of the people studied, however, already knew in May how they would vote in November. They made up their minds early and never wavered. Does this mean that the media had no effect on such voters? Not at all. The media were also important as *reinforcers* of the voters' intentions. Political parties can ill afford to concentrate only on attracting new followers. Much of their effort must focus on preventing the loss of supporters. The intentions of the party faithful must be constantly reinforced through campaign materials that show partisans they have made the right choice. The media can be used to provide some of this reassurance. Clearly, reinforcement is not a dramatic effect. It merely keeps people doing what they are already doing.

Finally, the campaign in the mass media did *convert* a few voters from one party to the other. However, most people had either made up their minds in May, or went with the party they were predisposed toward, or paid attention only to the campaign of their own party. But a very small number of voters who were weakly tied to a party and who thought of themselves as "dispassionate" political decision makers were persuaded from one party affiliation to the other.

Perhaps the major conclusion emerging from this study is that the media were very limited in their influence on voters. When people talk of the media's power, the ability to convert is what they usually have in mind. But Lazarsfeld and his colleagues found that of their subjects approximately

16 percent showed no effect of the media
 9 percent showed mixed effects
14 percent were activated
53 percent were reinforced
 8 percent were converted

The media activated the indifferent, reinforced the partisan, and in a very few cases converted the doubtful.

Thus *The People's Choice* opened a new era in thinking about the mass media. It seemed to deny flatly the old hypothesis that the media have great power. Instead it seemed to support a new hypothesis: that the *media have minimal consequences* and are only one set of influences among many. Although some earlier studies had suggested much the same thing, the large scope, sophisticated methods, and impressive findings of *The People's Choice* set it apart as a major milestone in media research.

The Two-Step Flow. One totally unexpected, but extremely important, finding emerged from *The People's Choice*. It occurred almost by accident, in a way that scientists call *serendipitous*. About halfway through the study, the researchers began to see that a major source of information and influence for voters was *other people*. Individuals turned to other individuals to obtain information about the candidates and the issues. Inevitably, those who provided the information also provided interpretation. Thus the flow of information between people also seemed to include a flow of influence. The researchers called this *personal influence* (in contrast with *media influence*).

Those who served most often as sources of information and influence had several important characteristics. First, these opinion leaders had given great attention to the media campaign. Second, their socioeconomic status was similar to the status of those whom they influenced. In other words, voters were turning for information and influence to people who were like themselves but whom they regarded as knowledgeable.

To summarize their findings, the researchers described what they called a *two-step flow of communication*. Basically, they said, content moves from the mass media to opinion leaders, who then pass it on to others whom they inevitably influence. Since *The People's Choice* presented these findings, hundreds of other studies have tried to understand the nature and implications of personal influence as part of mass communication. It has been found to play a major role in spreading innovations and bringing about technical and cultural change.[19]

Thus, in less than twenty years, the view of the mass media's influence presented by social scientists had changed drastically. No longer were the media compared with a magic bullet. Instead their influence was shown to be clearly limited. The media are more likely to provide information than to shape opinions; and they are more effective at activating the indifferent than at converting people. Moreover, the media's influence depends on personal and social characteristics. In addition, often that influence is not direct. Instead the media may first influence opinion leaders who in turn influence other people.

Television and Children

The 1950s saw the rise of television as the dominant mass medium in America. By the end of the decade Americans owned more than 50 million sets. Television was reaching almost every corner of the country, and only one in eight homes did not have a television. Just as the public grew alarmed over the movies during the 1920s, they saw television as a threat in the 1950s. What was it doing to them, and, most of all, what was it doing to their children? Is television, as critic Michael Novak said, "the molder of the soul's geography"?

A trickle of research in the early 1950s did little to quiet the public's fears about television. Several social scientists had found in small studies that the arrival of television had changed the lives of children in several ways. For example, it reduced the time they spent playing, postponed their bedtime, and modified what they did in their free time. Children spent less time watching movies, reading, and listening to the radio.[20] No one knew, however, whether television limited or broadened children's knowledge, raised or lowered their aesthetic tastes, modified their values, created passivity, or stimulated aggression. Research was needed to clarify the influence of the new medium.

In the last thirty years a huge literature has developed on the subject of children and television. Two studies stand out as landmarks. The first was a comparison of television viewers and nonviewers. The second was a series of studies on the relationship between portrayals of violence and aggressive conduct by children.

Children's Uses of Television: Viewers Versus Nonviewers

In 1960 Professors Wilbur Schramm, Jack Lyle, and Edwin Parker published the first large-scale American investigation of children's uses of television.[21] The study was concerned mostly not with what television does to children but with what children do with television. The researchers looked at the content of television shows, the personality of young viewers, and the social setting of television viewing. In eleven studies they interviewed nearly 6,000 children, along with 1,500 parents and a number of teachers and school officials, in both the United States and Canada. They used in-depth interviews and standardized questionnaires, with statistical analyses of the results. In the end they had an impressive mass of quantitative data plus detailed insights about children's viewing patterns and their uses of television.

Patterns of Viewing. Very early in the life of the children studied, television emerged as the most-used mass medium. By age three children were watching about 45 minutes per weekday, and their viewing increased rapidly with each additional year. By the time children were five years old, they watched television an average of 2 hours per weekday, and by age eight the average viewing time had risen to 3 hours. In fact, from ages three to sixteen children spent more time watching television than they spent in school. About one-sixth of the waking hours of the children studied were devoted to television. Only sleep and perhaps play took up as much or more of their time.

Of course, some children watched television much more than these average numbers of hours and some much less. Compared with light viewers, the *heaviest* viewers had a characteristic profile:

They were in grades six through eight (that is, they were about eleven to thirteen years old).
They were less intelligent (this pattern was reversed until about age ten to thirteen; that is, for children under ten, brighter children tended to watch television more).
They were poor.

Children's tastes in television programs varied with their age, sex, and intelligence, but their families were the chief influence on taste. Middle-class children tended to watch realistic, self-betterment programs. Working-class children viewed more programs that provided sheer entertainment or fantasy.

Does television educate or corrupt its spell-bound audience of children? Does it stimulate young minds to explore and inquire, or does it induce a passive blankness? The findings of researchers suggest that television's influence is complex, indirect, and related to other factors in children's lives.

Uses of Programs. The researchers were most interested in finding out how children used what they saw on television. Children, they concluded, used television primarily in three ways: as fantasy, diversion, and instruction.

Fantasy was one of the most important uses, for several reasons. It gives the passive pleasures of being entertained, of identifying with exciting and attractive people, and of getting away from real-life pressures. It provides pleasurable experience free from real-life limitations. Fantasy, in other words, provides both escape and wish fulfillment.

Children often turned to television for diversion, but in fact they often received instruction. This teaching was neither formal nor planned, nor did the youthful viewers intend to learn anything. Such unplanned, unintentional learning is called *incidental learning*. What is learned is related, of course, to the child's abilities, needs, preferences, and patterns of viewing. The lessons of television are not necessarily either objective or correct. Television portrays the world — sometimes realistically, sometimes not. But whatever their merits, television's portrayals of reality are a source of instruction for young viewers.

The occurrence of incidental learning supports one argument of television's defenders: it broadens our knowledge. The researchers found specific evidence for this claim. They compared children in an American community (which they called Teletown) that received television signals with a similar Canadian community (called Radiotown) that had no television. Compared with children in Radiotown, Teletown's children had higher vocabulary scores and knew more about current events. This held true even among those with low mental ability. The researchers concluded that television accelerates a child's intellectual development during his or her early years.

Other Findings. Schramm and his colleagues also found that children's social relationships were related to their use of television. Children who had conflicts with their parents, they found, sought escape through watching television. They also discovered a three-way relationship among conflict, viewing, and aggression; the more severe the child-parent conflict and the higher the child's score on several measures of aggression, the more likely he or she was to turn to fantasy programs on television.

The study reached other conclusions, but in general it revealed no truly dramatic problems arising from television viewing. Although the researchers found that children were preoccupied with television, they did not find that children were passive receivers of evil influences from it. Instead the effects of television depended on factors such as the child's family, mental ability, group ties, age, sex, needs, and general personality.

Although the study had some flaws in its methods, its findings remain important. It offered no support whatever for the magic bullet view that television is an all-powerful stimulus achieving uniform responses in all viewers. On the contrary, it offered evidence that the medium has limited effects, not the awesome ones feared by its critics. Finally, it showed that these effects differ from child to child and from one category of children to another.

**The Impact of
Televised Violence:
The Report to the
Surgeon General**

The legacy of fear in modern dress was the source of the largest research effort ever aimed at understanding the effects of mass communication in America. We have seen that, as each new medium appeared, vocal critics pronounced it to be a major factor in society's mounting ills. The fact that these ills are rooted in the long-term trends of urbanization and industrialization is not readily accepted by most of the public. The media are visible targets to blame for these ills. Thus it is not surprising that many people linked the rising crime and violence and changes in values that occurred in the late 1960s directly to the rise of television in the 1950s and 1960s.

This public concern brought pressure on Congress to "do something." In March of 1969 Senator John Pastore said he was "exceedingly troubled by the lack of any definitive information which would help resolve the question of whether there is a causal connection between televised . . . violence and antisocial behavior by individuals, especially children." With Pastore's urging, Congress appropriated $1 million to the Department of Health, Education and Welfare to conduct research into the effects of television.

HEW, defining the issue as a "potential hazard to public

*In the late 1960s Senator John Pastore of
Rhode Island introduced legislation that authorized the Office of the Surgeon General to
undertake an intensive study of the relationship between television watching and social
behavior.*

health," turned over the task of organizing the project to its Public Health Service, which turned it over to the National Institutes of Mental Health, which in turn appointed a committee of distinguished social scientists to design the project and a staff to do the day-to-day work. All the social scientists on the committee, however, were first approved by the networks. The surgeon general charged the committee with two goals: to review what was already known about television's effects, and to launch new studies on the subject.

Eventually some sixty studies plus reviews of hundreds of prior investigations were published in 1971 in five volumes plus a summary volume, all under the title *Television and Social Behavior*.[22] Many issues were studied, including the impact of advertising, activities displaced by television, and the information learned from television. The focus, however, was on televised violence and its influence on children. We review here some of the main findings on this topic.

Media Content. Just how violent are television shows? Volume 1 of the study presented some striking answers. For example, Professor George Gerbner studied one week of prime-time television in the fall of 1969. He found that eight of every ten programs contained violence. Even more striking, the hours during which children viewed most were the most violent of all. Violence was carried out mostly by men who were free of family responsibilities. About three-fourths of all leading characters were male, American, middle- or upper-class, unmarried, and in the prime of life. Killings occurred between strangers or slight acquaintances, and few women were violent. In fact, in real life most killings involve people who know each other. Overall, television's portrayals of violence are very frequent and very unrealistic.

Television professionals who were interviewed defended their portrayal of violence. Violence, they said, was necessary in order to hold the audience's attention. Additionally, they claimed, it was used not for its own sake but mainly when it was essential to develop a plot or a character. They claimed, too, that televised violence reflects real life and that watching it tends to reduce a child's propensity to act aggressively. Finally, they argued that parents should monitor their children's viewing.

These defenses are pretty weak. Research has shown that television's portrayal of violence is unrealistic in both the amount and the kind of violence it shows. Furthermore, the *cathartic hypothesis* that watching violence reduces aggression has not been well supported by research.

Social Learning. However violent television may be, does the violence change children's behavior? To answer this question volume 2 of the report reviewed prior work on what is called *observational learning*. In this kind of learning a person changes a pattern of behavior, knowledge, attitudes, or values as a result of seeing and then imitating the behavior of others. The classic work was done by Albert Bandura and his associates in the early 1960s. (We will review the idea in detail in the next chapter.)

Bandura had children watch a live or filmed model perform aggressive acts against a large inflated Bobo doll. One group saw the model rewarded for this behavior. A second group saw the model receive no consequences for the aggression. A third group observed the model being punished.

The children were then left in a room full of toys, including a doll like the one the model had beaten. The groups who had seen the model rewarded or receive no consequences showed a great deal of direct imitation: they too beat up the doll. Those who had observed the model being punished for aggression were much less likely to be violent.

Later, to check to see if the subjects had understood the actions of the models, the children in all three groups were asked to show the experimenter what the model had done. They were able to do so without difficulty. In other words, observational learning had taken place regardless of whether the model had been rewarded or punished.[23] However, imitation was clearly linked to the consequences of being aggressive.

Psychological research of many kinds has shown that imitation occurs, and most people believe that modeling is an important factor in personality development. Still, Bandura's study and others like it have become controversial. The question is, Do they adequately represent reality? British social scientists Dennis Howitt and Guy Cumberbatch maintain they are merely scientific "metaphors."[24] The behavior they demonstrate is like real-world behavior, but it is not the same. And the differences could be as important as the similarities. Real-life social constraints, critics say, are absent in the lab. For example, no authority figures known to the child are present in the laboratory. Furthermore, the aggression is only against a doll, and children understand that it does no real damage. Thus the aggression of both the child subjects and the model has no long-term consequences for either them or their "victim," the doll. Children may beat up a doll in an experiment after watching a model do so, but they would not beat up their mother after watching a violent television program. The relevance of demonstrations such as Bandura's to the question at hand — the influence on televised violence on children — remains to be clarified. At the same time, as we show in Chapter 10, modeling theory is an important contemporary approach to studying other influences of mass communication.

Adolescent Aggression. Other studies in the report to the surgeon general did look at attitudes and behavior in real-life settings. In volume 3, *Television and Adolescent Aggression*, eight projects are reported that attempt (1) to measure adolescent use of television, (2) to measure adolescent aggressiveness, and (3) to relate use of television to violent behavior. Perhaps the most interesting of these studies is one by M. Lefkowitz and his associates.

Lefkowitz's study was a ten-year *longitudinal* project; that is, it covered one set of subjects over a period of time. This kind of study is somewhat unusual in social science; more often, studies compare different children of different ages, rather than the same children at different ages. Children in Columbia County, New York, were tested in their third-grade classrooms and again ten years later. The researchers asked the children to rate each other on aggression, and they interviewed the children's parents.

The interviews yielded some interesting results. For example, a child who was unpopular in the third grade tended to be unpopular ten years later, and an unpopular child in the third grade tended to watch television more as he or she got older. More to the point, the television habits of eight-year-old boys were related to their aggressive behavior through their childhood and adolescence. The authors concluded that the more violent the programs preferred by boys in the third grade, the more aggressive their behavior — both in the third grade and ten years later. They saw the effects of television violence as being *cumulative*.

Lefkowitz and his colleagues also found that the greater the child's preference for violent programs, the more likely he or she was to think that these programs were a realistic depiction of life. Furthermore, the more violence a child viewed, the more time he or she was likely to spend watching television overall. Also, the greater the *total* amount of television viewing, the lower the child's IQ and level of educational accomplishment. A preference for violent programs, however, was unrelated to IQ and educational accomplishment.

In summary, these studies found that specific kinds of adolescents were more likely both to watch televised violence and to be aggressive. These were males, younger adolescents, those of lesser intelligence, and those in lower socioeconomic levels. In short, among youths in these categories, viewing violence on television and aggressiveness went together. But the relationship between these behaviors was *not* strong enough to imply that television *caused* the aggressiveness. To show that two things tend to occur together is not the same as showing that one of those things causes the other.

Television in Day-to-Day Life. The fourth volume of the report provided an overview of the kind of television that people watched in 1970. Both laboratory and field studies were reported. Surprisingly, diaries and interviews showed that families did not necessarily prefer violent programs, as the rating services claimed they did. Also, only one-third of the programs seen were likely to be watched all the way through! People thought they watched more than three hours a day on the average, but the diaries revealed that they were viewing less than two hours. Most programs were watched simply because they came on.

One fascinating study by R. B. Bechtel used cameras mounted on top of the television set. For three hours each day the cameras recorded the viewing activities of twenty Kansas City families. While watching television, these people did many other things. They looked out the window, picked their noses, scratched themselves (or others), rocked, untied knots, threw objects at each other, mimicked the television actors, paced around, or crawled on the floor. In other words, although people may spend a great deal of time in front of their television sets, they may or may not be giving the programs their full attention. Television is part of a pattern of relaxation that includes many elements. It may or may not be watched closely.

Conclusions. A fifth volume in this project reported on thirteen research projects that were unfinished. Under study were such issues as facial expressions while viewing (an attempt to assess emotions) and the potential influence of violent television on sleep and dreams. Because the research was incomplete, no definitive conclusions were reported.

The report of the advisory committee, *Television and Growing Up*, contains a summary of the first five volumes. It also presents the committee's recommendations concerning further research and public policy, plus a "definitive" statement about the relationship between televised violence and aggressive behavior. Essentially, the advisory committee complained about the "narrowness" of the studies and advocated further research. First, they

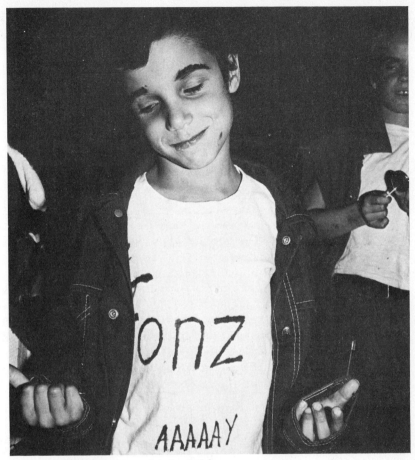

One colorful way in which children react to television is shown in this young man's emulation of "The Fonz."

said, television should be studied in the context of other media. Isolating the influence of television from the influence of other media, they noted, is difficult. Second, television viewing needs to be studied in the context of the total environment of the child, with special emphasis on the home. Third, they suggested that all aggression is not bad. Viewing vigorous competition may be beneficial. Also, any antisocial influence that television may have on a child might be balanced by its prosocial effects. Perhaps, for example, television encourages children to care for their friends and show affection toward their parents.

Nevertheless, the committee concluded that televised portrayals of violence could be harmful to some children. As they put it, the issue posed a potential public health problem:

> Thus the two sets of findings (laboratory and survey) converge in three respects: a preliminary and tentative indication of a causal relation between viewing violence on television and aggressive behavior; an indication that any such causal relation operates only on some children (who are predisposed to be aggressive); and an indication that it operates only in *some* environmental contexts. Such tentative and limited conclusions are not very satisfying (yet) they represent substantially more knowledge than we had two years ago.[25]

The research findings created a storm of controversy. Senate hearings were held in 1972 to explore what it all meant. The public, disregarding all the hedges, limitations, and qualifications of the scientists, focused on the idea that television causes kids to be aggressive. The television industry, seizing mainly on the shortcomings of the research and the tentative nature of the conclusions, declared the findings to be of little importance. Many media critics were outraged; a number of the researchers charged that their work had been misrepresented. Perhaps the final word went to J. L. Steinfield, the surgeon general:

> "These studies — and scores of similar ones — make it clear to me that the relationship between televised violence and anti-social behavior is sufficiently proved to warrant immediate remedial action. Indeed the time has come to be blunt: we can no longer tolerate the present high level of violence that is put before children in American homes."[26]

In other words, the surgeon general of the United States came away from the project believing that *televised violence may be dangerous to your health!*

Emerging Perspectives on Media Effects

The legacy of fear still shapes the attitudes of many people toward the mass media, but research on mass communication has not supported this interpretation. As research became more sophisticated, old theories about the media's great power were questioned, and social scientists came to view that power as very limited. In 1969 British sociologist Denis McQuail summarized the situation in the following terms:

For those who want a simple answer about the power of the mass media, it would have to be in the negative. Such an answer, although in many respects misleading, would fit most of the available evidence. The most careful experiments have failed to substantiate the wide claims on behalf of media or the fears of critics of mass communication.[27]

But a half-century of research has shown that the media have *some* effects on individuals. Studies of children's uses of television have shown that television modified their play, use of other media, homework, and even vocabulary. Research on televised violence has found that particular groups of children both watched more televised violence and were more aggressive than control groups.

Through this research much has also been learned about the process of communication. It is now clear that audiences are not passive, isolated individuals. Each person has predispositions and selects media content on the basis of needs, attitudes, values, and other cognitive and emotional characteristics. Each person is also linked to others in social networks, and these ties influence a person's exposure to the media and his or her interpretations of the media's content. Each person is also a member of various social categories based on race, ethnicity, education, religion, income, and sex. All these modify an individual's behavior regarding mass communication and its effects.

Since the time of the research reported in this chapter, social scientists have continued to study the question of the media's influence on individuals, building on the research of the past. They are sensitive to the role that individual characteristics, social categories, and the receiver's setting might play in determining the media's influence. They have also begun to look more closely at the possible beneficial aspects of the media's influence. No simple laws have emerged from this research, but it has yielded interesting leads about what factors may account for differences in the media's influence. On the question of the effect of televised violence on children, for example, Howard Gardner summarized the state of research through the mid-1970s as follows:

If televised aggression has effects, they are most likely on younger children whose ability to distinguish between reality and fantasy is not yet well established, whose tendency to imitate is most pronounced, and whose understanding of the causes prompting aggression is less well developed. . . .

The studies also suggest that televised aggression may affect children who are already predisposed toward aggression—but in different ways. Whereas younger aggressive children may become more aggressive, older children may become less so. What may have a strong effect on a four-year-old may have little effect, or perhaps even the reverse effect, on an adolescent.

. . . We simply do not know whether the children are simply imitating or are becoming genuinely more aggressive. Nor, in the absence of systematic longitudinal studies, can we evaluate the long-term effects of watching television.[28]

It is clear that occasionally the media can trigger dramatic behavior. For example, in the late 1950s the television program "The Doomsday Flight" featured a mad extortionist who placed a bomb on a plane and demanded a huge sum of money to prevent an explosion. After the show was aired here and abroad, there were sixteen bomb-extortion attempts in various parts of the world. On September 23, 1973, a gruesome "Sunday Night Movie" was aired. It portrayed sadistic teenagers who doused tramps with gasoline and set them on fire. Two days later, a young woman in Boston was dragged by a gang of vicious youths to a vacant lot, beaten, and burned with gasoline. She died in a few hours. Three weeks after the film was shown, a group of youngsters in Florida poured lighter fluid on three sleeping derelicts and set them on fire. They laughed when the men screamed. One man died. And in 1980 two teenagers who, after reading *Illusions* by Richard Bach, had talked of committing suicide in order to be reincarnated on a "higher plane of existence" smashed a car through a concrete wall; one died.[29]

Do these events indict the media? Perhaps. But no more so than any other stimulus that can trigger outrageous conduct by demented or dangerous persons who are already disposed to such acts. Through the ages spectacular crimes have been triggered by every conceivable source, from the scriptures to the comics. One should not be lured into the illogical conclusion that if one disturbed individual, or a vicious gang of youths, imitates a pattern portrayed in the media then the media must have great power over the majority of normal people. The spectacular events must be left to psychiatrists to deal with; they do not characterize the impact of the media on the majority of people. Overall, we must still conclude that the direct impact of the media on individuals has not been shown to be particularly powerful.

Summary

Debates about the power of newspapers to cause unwanted effects, the influence of propaganda during World War I, and the rapid growth of movies after the war all contributed to the growth of a legacy of fear of the mass media. This fear plus the development of better research methods helped lead to attempts to apply scientific techniques to the study of mass communication in the late 1920s. These first efforts to study the effects of the media reinforced the public's fears. The Payne Fund Studies reported that the movies were having powerful effects on children's learning, attitudes, emotions, and general conduct. The panic that followed the radio broadcast of *War of the Worlds* in 1938 further reinforced the belief that the media have great power.

As research became more sophisticated in the 1940s, however, the old magic bullet theory came under increasing attack. Studies of the effectiveness of the Army's *Why We Fight* films showed that the films added somewhat to soldiers' information and modified some specific opinions, but they did not produce major changes in attitudes. It was the research on the presidential campaign of 1940, however, that dealt the death blow to theories about direct media power. The research reported in *The People's Choice* showed that the newspapers and radio did activate some voters to follow their predispositions, and they did reinforce the positions of other voters, but their power to convert people from one position to another was slight. The study also demonstrated that personal influence is an important factor in political campaigns.

In the 1950s television became the major focus of research on the media. The earliest studies seemed to suggest that the medium might have a powerful influence on children, but later studies showed no dramatic effects. In the late 1960s a massive effort was mounted to assess the influence of television, especially its portrayal of violence, on children. The findings were complex. There seemed to be some evidence that children readily imitate what they see and that adolescents watch a lot of violence. Adolescents who had below-average intelligence and were in lower socioeconomic classes were more likely to watch a lot of violence on television and were more aggressive. Although the research could not show that televised violence caused aggression, the surgeon general concluded that the evidence was sufficient to indicate that there might be a causal relationship between the two.

Research on the effects of mass communication on individuals has not given us a set of simple principles capable of describing or predicting the relationship between the media and individual behavior. But it has brought about a transformation in scientific thinking about the relationship. The early view was that the relationship was direct, universal, immediate, and causal. This view was abandoned for more complex theories in which the influence of the media is seen as selective, indirect, and long-term and individual differences and social categories are seen as important determinants of that influence.

Notes and References

1. Gabriel Tarde, *Etudes de Psychologie Sociale* (Paris: Giard and Brier, 1898). See especially pp. 195–204 and 209–225.

2. Ibid.

3. Edgar Dale, *Children's Attendance at Motion Pictures* (New York: Arno Press, 1970) p. 73; originally published in 1935.

4. Herbert Blumer, *The Movies and Conduct* (New York: Macmillan, 1933).

5. Ruth C. Peterson and L. L. Thurstone, *Motion Pictures and the Social Attitudes of Children* (New York: Macmillan, 1933).

6. Speaking more technically, this conclusion emerges from comparisons of the distributions, their central tendencies (averages or means), and the probable error of the difference (between means). The results were

$\text{Mean}_1 \text{ (before)} = 6.72 \qquad \text{P.E.M.}_1 = .073 \qquad \sigma_1 = 1.46 \qquad \tau_{12} = .57$

$\text{Mean}_2 \text{ (after)} = 5.50 \qquad \text{P.E.M.}_2 = .077 \qquad \sigma_2 = 1.54$

$\text{D}_{\text{M}_1 - \text{M}_2} = 1.22 \qquad \text{P.E.}_\text{D} = .0698 \qquad \text{D/P.E.} = 17.5$

7. For a review of this theory, see Melvin L. DeFleur and Sandra Ball-Rokeach, *Theories of Mass Communication*, 3rd ed. (New York: David McKay, 1975), pp. 202–206.

8. W. W. Charters, *Motion Pictures and Youth: A Summary* (New York: Macmillan, 1933) p. 11. For a review of the current view of the relationship between attitudes and behavior, see Timothy Plax and Melvin L. DeFleur, *An Axiomatic Theory of the Relationship Between Attitudes and Behavior With Implications For Persuasion Research* (forthcoming).

9. Hadley Cantril, *The Invasion from Mars: A Study in the Psychology of Panic* (Princeton: Princeton University Press, 1940) p. 96.

10. Ibid.

11. Howard Koch, *The Panic Broadcast: Portrait of an Event* (Boston: Little, Brown, 1970).

12. "The Men From Mars," *Newsweek*, November 27, 1944.

13. Koch, *Panic Broadcast*, p. 111.

14. The full account of the study and its findings can be found in Cantril, *The Invasion From Mars.*

15. DeFleur and Ball-Rokeach, *Theories of Mass Communication*, pp. 202–206.

16. C. J. Hovland, A. A. Lumsdaine, and F. D. Sheffield, *Experiments on*

Mass Communication, Vol. III of Studies of Social Psychology in World War II (New York: John Wiley and Sons, 1965).

17. C. J. Hovland, I. L. Janis, and H. H. Kelley, *Communication and Persuasion* (New Haven: Yale University Press, 1953).

18. Paul Lazarsfeld, Bernard Berelson, and Hazel Gaudet, *The People's Choice* (New York: Columbia University Press, 1948).

19. Everett M. Rogers, *Diffusion of Innovations* (New York: Free Press of Glencoe, 1962).

20. Eleanor E. Maccoby, "Television: Its Impact on School Children," *Public Opinion Quarterly*, 15 (1951), 421–444; also Paul I. Lyness, "The Place of the Mass Media in the Lives of Boys and Girls," *Journalism Quarterly*, 29 (1952), 43–54.

21. Wilbur Schramm, Jack Lyle, and Edwin Parker, *Television in the Lives of Our Children* (Palo Alto, Calif.: Stanford University Press, 1961).

22. Each volume has this title with a different subtitle; the subtitles are *Media Content and Control* (Volume 1), *Television and Social Learning* (Volume 2), *Television and Adolescent Aggression* (Volume 3), *Television in Day-to-Day Life: Patterns of Use* (Volume 4), *Television's Effects: Further Explorations* (Volume 5). The various reports were prepared by George A. Comstock, John P. Murray, and Eli A. Rubenstein. They were published by the Government Printing Office, Washington, D.C., in 1971. The summary volume, *Television and Growing Up*, appeared in 1972.

23. A. Bandura and S. A. Ross, "Transmission of Aggression Through Imitation of Aggressive Models," *Journal of Abnormal and Social Psychology*, 63 (1961), 575–582.

24. Dennis Howitt and Guy Cumberbatch, *Mass Media, Violence and Society* (New York: Halsted Press, 1975).

25. *Television and Growing Up*, p. 11.

26. J. L. Steinfield, "TV Violence is Harmful," *The Reader's Digest*, April, 1973, pp. 34–40.

27. Denis McQuail, *Towards a Sociology of Mass Communication* (London: Collier-Macmillan, 1969) p. 45.

28. Howard Gardner, *Developmental Psychology* (Boston: Little, Brown, 1978) p. 362.

29. *New York Times*, May 15, 1980.

9 Effects of the Media on Society and Culture

Please don't uplift me when I go
to see a moving-picture show.
I don't pay cash, or chisel passes
to hear about the toiling masses.

MARY CAROLINE DAVIES, *Saturday Evening Post*, 1930

Mass communication can affect not only individuals but also a society or culture as a whole. It can influence a group's shared beliefs and values, its choice of heroes and villains, its public policies and technology. In particular, the continuing flow of information from the media can have a truly profound influence on social change.

Unfortunately, less is known about the media's effects on society and culture than about their effects on individuals, for at least two reasons. First, social and cultural effects are more difficult to study because they occur over long periods of time and are not easily observed in the laboratory or through surveys. Second, because the public has been less concerned about social and cultural change, financial support for studies of these processes has been more difficult to come by.

Nevertheless, there has been an accumulation of research on the media's social and cultural influences, and in this chapter we set forth three of the major ways in which the media exert such influence. First, the media can help bring about and spread social change. A special case of this influence is found in developing nations. There the media are sometimes deliberately used to help in the task of modernization. Second, the media influence the public's perception of reality, of what current public issues are about and what importance they have. The media also influence the public's definition of which conditions are social "problems" requiring action. Finally, the media are vehicles of popular culture. They bring to millions a constant flow of unsophisticated music, drama, and media-created personalities. The quality and effects of popular culture, we shall see, have been hotly debated.

Social Change: The Spread of Innovations

Rapid change is familiar to Americans. We are constantly confronted with *innovations* — new technologies, new ideas, new fads and fashions, and new standards of behavior. Whether large numbers of people adopt an innovation can have significant consequences for individuals and for society as a whole. For example, Americans are now confronted with the need to use less energy. To reduce energy consumption significantly, however, we must change many specific behaviors; we must change our collective lifestyle. The shape of our future — of our economy, environment, and international relations — depends to a great extent on whether Americans accept or reject sources of energy besides oil and gas, decreased consumption of gasoline, and less comfortable temperatures indoors.

Obviously, people do not always adopt a new idea or new form of technology, even if adopting it is logical and in their best interest. Decades ago, for example, seat belts for cars were introduced. It was shown that many thousands of lives could be saved by using them. They were not particularly expensive, and they were not much of an inconvenience. Yet the vast majority of Americans simply ignored them. The federal government tried many media campaigns to increase use of seat belts, and federal legislation required that all new cars have them. Today virtually all cars have the devices, yet only 14 percent of American drivers use them regularly.[1] Thus the seat belt is an innovation that by and large has failed, at least so far.

But for each such failure dozens of other innovations have been adopted with enthusiasm: the small electronic calculator, the digital display wrist watch, instant breakfast bars, microwave ovens, hot tubs, and so on. In other parts of the globe many traditional societies have been replacing their customs with modern ways and modern devices. This process of social and cultural change has fascinated scholars and scientists for decades, and research has shown that the media can play a significant role in it.

The Process of Adoption

Studies of the spread of social change go back at least to the nineteenth century, when Gabriel Tarde said that imitation explained the spread of new social forms.[2] Later, sociologists made quantitative studies of the spread of ham radios, hybrid seed corn, new teaching methods, and public health measures.[3] By the 1950s research on this process was an established tradition in all the social sciences.

In order to spread through a society, an innovation must be taken up, or *adopted*, by individuals. Everett Rogers has summarized many theories and research reports on how innovations come to be adopted.[4] He has discussed the process in terms of the following five stages:

1. *Awareness stage*   The individual learns of the existence of the new item, but lacks detailed information about it.
2. *Interest stage*   The individual develops an interest in the innovation and seeks additional information about it.
3. *Evaluation stage*   The individual mentally applies the new item to his or her present and expected future situation and decides whether to try it.
4. *Trial stage*   The individual applies the new idea on a small scale to determine its utility.
5. *Adoption stage*   The individual uses the new item or idea continuously on a full scale.

Obviously, these stages cannot apply perfectly to every individual and every innovation. Some things, for example, cannot be tried out on a small scale; others may be adopted temporarily but then abandoned.

An innovation can be something borrowed from another society or an invention. *Invention* is the process by which an individual or group puts together elements that already exist in the culture into some new pattern. When many individuals decide to adopt the innovation and it comes into common use in a society, we say that *diffusion* of the innovation has occurred.

Where do the media fit into this? Rogers's stages suggest that the spread of information via the media and the adoption and diffusion of innovations are closely related. In older societies innovations came to people's attention by word of mouth and were adopted in the absence of mass communication. And today information about an innovation can spread without adoption occur-

In May 1980 the volcano Mount St. Helens in Washington state blew its top. This spectacular photograph appeared in newspapers and magazines around the world.

Effects of the Media on Society and Culture   317

ring. However, as Rogers pointed out, the first stage in adoption is learning about an innovation. Obviously, then, wide diffusion of a change requires first that news of the innovation be available. Mass media can facilitate the fast and widespread availability of that information and thus stimulate social change. In America today the mass media present information on a great many possible innovations to large numbers of people, and person-to-person communication supplements this diffusion of information. As a result, Americans adopt many innovations over short periods of time. Thus, studying the diffusion of information is one step in understanding social change. One way that this process has been studied is to investigate the spread of news.

Diffusion of Information

Some news reports spread through the population in minutes; others take days to reach more than a small minority. Some reports have eventually reached close to 100 percent of adult Americans; others remain forever unknown to all but a few. To find out what's behind these differences in the diffusion of news, dozens of studies have been done on topics such as Alaskan statehood, the Soviet Union's launching of the first Sputnik satellite, President Kennedy's assassination, and many more recent events.[5] Typically, when the diffusion of news is plotted over time, the percent-

The diffusion of information through the media can foster a trend or a fad. The revival of rollerskating in the late 1970s was spurred by television interviews with young skaters in such places as New York's Central Park.

Figure 9.1

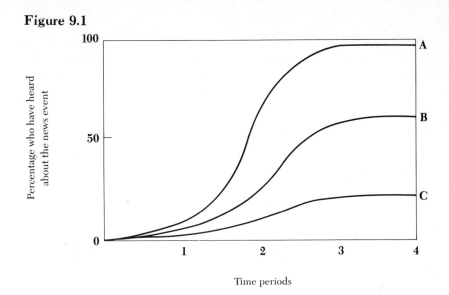

Time periods

age of the relevant population that learns about the event at any given time shows a characteristic pattern: an approximately S-shaped curve. This pattern has been called a *curve of diffusion*.

Figure 9.1 shows what diffusion curves look like for the spread of news through a population. The diffusion curve for very dramatic and significant news might look like curve A. That is, news of a vital event typically spreads rather quickly and reaches a high percentage of the population. For example, a study by Paul Sheatsley and Jacob Feldman showed that within thirty minutes after President Kennedy was shot, 68 percent of the adult population of the United States was aware of the event.[6] In this case, within a few hours almost everyone in the country learned of the event, either directly from the media or by word of mouth. Curve B in Figure 9.1 would be typical of the diffusion of less dramatic news. Curve C represents the pattern for a news event of minor significance. Such news typically spreads more slowly and eventually reaches only a part of the population.

Why does some information diffuse more rapidly and reach a higher percentage of the population (that is, a higher level of saturation) than others? The level of people's interest is obviously very important. News stories of obscure events of little inherent interest diffuse slowly and reach only a few people. News about vital events that may affect many people spreads quickly and reaches large portions of the population. Two other factors, however, are worth discussion: the amount of attention that the media give to the event, such as the number of repetitions of the message, and person-to-person communication.

Repetition of Messages. How does the diffusion of information relate to the attention that the media give it? DeFleur and Otto Larsen predicted that as *stimulus intensity* — defined as the repetition of a message — increases, the percentage of a population that receives the information will also increase. The increase, however, will not match the number of repetitions. Instead, they predicted, it will follow a curve of *diminishing returns*.[7] That is, as we add equal increases in stimulus intensity, the increase in the number of people receiving the message diminishes. Doubling the number of messages, for example, will increase but not double the number of people who learn the message. To see how the curve of diminishing returns works and how well the theory matched reality in an experiment, we examine one study in a project called Project Revere.

Project Revere was a large-scale examination of the diffusion of information conducted in the 1950s. Its objective was to find out how to spread vital messages to large populations during a civil defense emergency. Because newspapers and broadcast stations might be shut down in such an emergency, Project Revere spread information by dropping leaflets from aircraft and by word of mouth.

To test their theory, DeFleur and Larsen conducted one of the sixteen studies in Project Revere.[8] In eight communities with similar characteristics, they dropped varying numbers of leaflets carrying a civil defense message. The media cooperated by not publicizing the event in any way. Four days after the leaflet drop, a sample from each community was carefully polled.

The percentage of people in each community that learned the message varied with the number of leaflets dropped per inhabitant. In the community that received only one leaflet for every four inhabitants, only about 25 percent of the population learned the message. When the ratio was doubled, so that one leaflet for every two inhabitants was dropped, 37.4 percent of the population learned the message, an increase of more than 12 percent. When the ratio was increased fourfold, to two leaflets per inhabitant, 44.1 percent learned the message — an increase of less than 17 percent, or only slightly more than the increase achieved by a doubling of leaflets. When thirty-two leaflets per person were dropped, 87 percent of the inhabitants learned the message.

Overall, the results showed a pattern predicted rather accurately by DeFleur and Larsen's theory. That is, as stimulus intensity

Figure 9.2

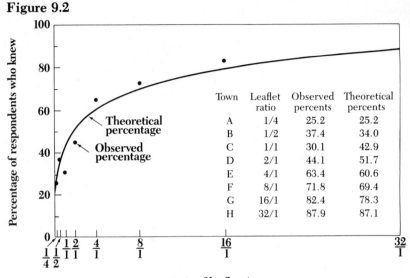

Town	Leaflet ratio	Observed percents	Theoretical percents
A	1/4	25.2	25.2
B	1/2	37.4	34.0
C	1/1	30.1	42.9
D	2/1	44.1	51.7
E	4/1	63.4	60.6
F	8/1	71.8	69.4
G	16/1	82.4	78.3
H	32/1	87.9	87.1

Ratio of leaflets/person

(the number of leaflets per person) increased, the percentage of people learning the message also increased, but the increase showed diminishing returns. Figure 9.2 shows both the results of the experiment and the results predicted by the theory. The match is close — much closer than can be accounted for by chance. If the repetition of a message and the number of people who learn the message are related in this way, then important implications follow for communicators who try to use repetition to get their messages across. Repetition can help diffuse information. But presenting a commercial or a political announcement over and over can be expected to have diminishing returns in terms of the percentage of the audience who learn the message.

Interpersonal Communication. The Project Revere studies had another important finding: the people in the towns played an active role in spreading the messages that were on the leaflets. Thus the study verified the importance of interpersonal channels in spreading information. In place of the two-step flow described in *The People's Choice*, however (see Chapter 8) the study found a *multistage flow.* Even persons who had not seen a leaflet helped spread the message. The information presented to some people through the leaflets was passed on and on through chains of residents, much like a rumor being passed from person to person (and with many of the same distortions).[9]

Person-to-person communication played a dramatic role in the diffusion of information when President John F. Kennedy was assassinated in 1963. Millions of Americans followed the continuous, three-day news coverage of the aftermath of the assassination. This famous photograph records the solemn moment when Lyndon Baines Johnson was sworn in as President as he, his staff, and Jacqueline Kennedy (right) flew back to Washington.

The flow of information after the assassination of President John F. Kennedy provided a dramatic example of the role that person-to-person communication can play in the diffusion of news, especially if the news is of immense importance. Almost half the population first heard about the assassination from other people, not from the media. Then, after hearing about the assassination, they rushed to the media for confirmation and further information.[10]

Thus information is spread through a population by the media, by people who have heard the message from the media, and by people who have heard it only from other people. The time pattern by which the information reaches the population depends on many factors — including the importance of the information, the number of repetitions of the message, and the degree to which the original receivers of the message pass it on to others.

The Media and National Development

Diffusion of information is the first and a crucial step in social change. Traditional societies, which have only limited mass communication, tend to change slowly. Many countries have found that when mass media are introduced numerous changes take place, even changes disliked by the country's leaders. For example, blue jeans, rock music, comic books, and other elements of American popular culture have been widely adopted in various parts of the world. Often such changes occur after content produced in the United States, such as television programs and films, have penetrated the country. To traditional societies, the American media may be seen as a corrupting influence.

Nonetheless, bringing newspapers, radio, and television to these societies does not automatically bring social and cultural change. In fact, leaders in Asia, Africa, and Latin America have often been frustrated in trying to force change on their developing societies. Many of these nations are seeking what is called modernization, or *national development* — a moving away from their customs toward the methods of Western industrial nations. Specifically, national development may include mechanizing agriculture, increasing literacy, raising public health standards, spreading information about nutrition, introducing Western legal systems, and reducing population growth through birth control.

To modernize, a country's leaders must influence the decisions of ordinary citizens. It is the farmer who must decide whether to take up improved agricultural methods. It is the villager who accepts or rejects new techniques of rodent control, water purification, or food preservation.

In some cases the adoption and diffusion of these changes can be influenced by mass communication. The mass media, in other words, can be important agents of deliberate social change.[11] Indeed, they have been used in all parts of the world to help bring innovations in such matters as health, education, and family planning to millions of people.

Just bringing news of a change and urging it on people through the media, however, may not be enough. One of the most interesting examples of the deliberate and sophisticated use of television to foster social change occurred recently in Mexico. Although Mexico is a developed society in many respects, it lags far behind many Western nations in some ways. In particular, it has chronic undereducation. On the average its citizens have only three years of education. The Mexican government allocates from 15 to 20 percent of its annual budget to education (compared with only 3 percent in the United States). But the population grows so fast that it constantly outstrips the country's efforts to provide new schools. With half the population under fifteen years old, many receive no education at all. Illiteracy is widespread, and the low educational attainment of the majority of adults results in serious problems for a country that is trying to raise its citizens' standard of living.

In an effort to provide educational opportunities for adults, the Mexican government developed the National System of Open Education (NSOE). Adults enrolled in the program receive both books and assistance toward achieving literacy and basic education in general. But in 1975, despite attempts to publicize the NSOE programs in the media and elsewhere, fewer than 100,000 adults were participating in the program. Clearly a new approach was needed to persuade people to enroll. So the Mexican authorities decided to experiment with the soap opera as a medium of persuasion. Mexicans, like Americans, avidly view daytime television serials.

Miguel Sabido, general director of the Mexican Institute of Communications Studies, designed and directed a special soap opera called "Come With Me." It was broadcast regularly over government television and radio for more than a year. Mexico has both government and private television stations. The government channels are carried to most population centers through a national network, and a radio network serves rural areas where a TV signal is not available.

"Come With Me" was designed to interest adult viewers in NSOE, to provide them with information about its goals, and to make clear its benefits and procedures. The project attempted to use the theory of modeling developed by Albert Bandura (Chapter 10).[12] That is, as the plot unfolded, actors in the drama who would be attractive "models" for the viewers enrolled in NSOE. Moreover, characters in the serial who enrolled in NSOE and completed their training received benefits. Those who did not, or who scoffed at the idea, were shown as losers. Viewers were also shown how to enroll and how NSOE worked. All this was skillfully woven into the drama.

The program was very popular, but did it achieve its objectives? Before the soap opera was broadcast, enrollment in NSOE was 99,800. During the year that "Come With Me" was shown, enrollment rose to a high of 839,000. Then, a year after the soap opera was terminated, enrollment declined to 398,700. To evaluate whether the program accounted for these changes, Ana Christina Covarrubias studied a sample of 600 adults through detailed interviews.[13] Various controls were built into the study to determine what factors in addition to viewing "Come With Me" might have played a part in leading people to enroll in NSOE. For example, the study found that those who had already completed some years of school were more likely to enroll in NSOE than those with less schooling. Still, Covarrubias found that the soap opera did have a substantial influence in persuading viewers to continue their education. Even a year later its impact was evident. Clearly, this attempt to use mass communication to achieve national development was a success.

It is interesting to note that an experiment of this kind would not be possible in the United States. Although close to 30 million Americans watch the soap operas each day, their production and distribution are controlled by private corporations for profit. No systematic attempt has ever been made in America to use this type of content as a means of formal instruction or persuasion toward prosocial goals. Even so, American soap operas include numerous incidental "lessons" on a variety of issues, from the use of alcohol to the meaning of mental illness.[14]

"Come With Me" succeeded because it was carefully designed by people intimately aware of the culture in which they were working. When outsiders come with plans to make life better for local people in seemingly logical ways their plans often backfire.

> Campaign after campaign [using communication media] had failed, in developing countries, because the campaigners misjudged or misunderstood the local situation. In a South American country, for example, there was a major effort to introduce a new maize which seemed in every way superior to the old variety. The new maize was hardier, had more food value, produced a higher yield, and so forth, and there were high hopes that it would improve the diet and health of both humans and animals. There was only one flaw in the plans. The maize (because it was so hardy and disease-resistant) was too hard to grind by hand, and villagers did not want to haul it to the mill in town. But it proved to make excellent commercial alcohol, and thus the campaign resulted not in improving diets but promoting alcoholism.[15]

Not all attempts to use media deliberately to promote change are as dramatic as the Mexican example, and the majority do not fail as badly as the attempt to bring in new maize. Literally thousands of instances can be cited in which media campaigns have promoted changes in health practices, farming procedures, domestic activities, and other forms of behavior. For the developing society, mass communication can be an important agent of deliberate social change.

Setting the Agenda

For decades Walter Cronkite typically closed his evening news program with the assertion "And that's the way it is, on Tuesday. . . ." The *New York Times* masthead proclaims that it publishes "All the News That's Fit to Print." Similarly, Richard Salant, former president of CBS News, maintained: "We don't make the news; we report it."[16]

The problem with all these claims is that they blatantly ignore the realities of the news industry, and the people who make them are fully aware of this fact. Such claims can lead people to conclude that they are being fully informed about events, or at least that the news media are presenting unbiased accounts of the events covered. If they come to either conclusion they are mistaken. The news media do not just tell us how things are; they do not and cannot tell us everything; and they are not and cannot be totally unbiased. The news media cannot reflect reality perfectly.

Does the discrepancy between the real world and the world presented by the media matter? Decades ago Walter Lippmann noted that people cannot possibly experience most of the events of the world firsthand. Yet those events often require some response. Lacking firsthand access to reality, Lippmann said, citizens must make their choices in response to the pseudoenvironment created by the press. Using more contemporary sociological terms, we would say that people must respond to the *social construction of reality* created by the media. As a result of this dependence on the media and the media's distortions, many problems, said Lippmann, arise because of the lack of correspondence "between the world outside and the pictures in our head."[17]

Many of these same ideas are currently being developed in terms of the agenda theory of the importance of public issues, which studies the relationship between "the world outside," the media, and "the pictures in our heads." An *agenda* is a selection of news items about current issues that assigns those items varying degrees of exposure. *Agenda theory* says that the news media present the public not with a picture of the world as it is but with an agenda of its own — a selection of reports about what is happening in the world. Agenda theorists try to describe and explain (1) how stories are selected, packaged, and presented — a process known as *gatekeeping;* (2) the resulting agenda; and (3) the influence of this agenda on the public in terms of what people think concerning the relative importance of the issues presented.

The News Media and Reality: Gatekeeping

There is little doubt that some news media deliberately slant their content to reflect the biases of those who own or control them. Most newspeople, however, try to be balanced, objective, and thorough. The fact is, though, even the most objective and thorough newspeople are faced with an impossible task: sometimes there is too much news; sometimes too little. They cannot simply reflect the world's events; they must select events and assign relative importance to them.

Should the audience be informed about the latest pronouncements of the candidates for mayor, or what about the hint of scandal in the governor's cabinet? Then there is the road bond issue and the recent disclosures about police payoffs. In international news, there is the mob that stormed the embassy in El Salvador, the ferry boat that sank in the Caspian Sea, the bombings in Ireland, and the plane crash in India. What about the instability of the rupee in Sri Lanka, or the unrest in Jamaica? And there is always a congressman whose sex life is indiscreet and the latest activities of Jacqueline Kennedy Onassis. Which stories out of all these are most important? Which can be dropped, or at least buried in a small paragraph in the back pages somewhere? And what if nothing much has happened? The newspaper and the newscast must still be filled. If nothing has happened that will truly interest the audience, then a selection of events must be made to appear important.

In short, the news media do not just tell us how it is. They select which stories to cover, which details of a story to include and emphasize, and how much space or time to give to a story. *Gatekeeping* is the name given to this process. It results in some stories being in the news and some not, in some being given strong emphasis and others being buried. Thus gatekeeping results in a news agenda presented by the media to the public.

The study of gatekeeping has a long tradition in the study of the media. A whole series of factors — cultural, social, psychological, and so on — operate at various stages to influence what is presented and how. One of the most important is commercialism. A number of journalists maintain that economic considerations often outweigh conceptions of the public interest in determining what is reported.[18] In accordance with the law of large numbers (Chapter 3), the media present what people will find interesting in order to attract the largest audience possible: "I say television news is entering the beer and pizza era. Give them what they want, not

TODAY
Sunny, mid 70s

TONIGHT
Clear, mild, low 60s

TOMORROW
Partly cloudy, low 70s
Details, Page 2

NEW YORK POST

METRO
TODAY'S RACING

TV listings: P. 31   WEDNESDAY, JUNE 18, 1980   30 CENTS

© 1980 News Group Publications Inc.   Vol. 179, No. 181
LARGEST-SELLING AFTERNOON NEWSPAPER IN AMERICA

AVERAGE
DAILY
SALES
EXCEED 650,000

Yeshiva link: How stolen tests were leaked

By MIKE HUREWITZ

THE REGENTS scandal — in which tests are being sold around the city for as much as $1000 — has been linked to a mysterious Yeshiva Connection which funnels the stolen exams through students in private Jewish schools.

The Post, which broke the story by obtaining test copies in advance, has now traced those exams to members of the Orthodox Jewish community in Brooklyn.

Dozens of callers said that the stolen tests originally came from the Orthodox or Conservative Jewish schools in the area.

The pattern parallels the 1974 scandal in which regents examinations were stolen from the Solomon Schechter High School in Brooklyn, part of a nationwide chain of Conservative Jewish schools.

A spokesman for the yeshivas said it was "inconceivable" that the 1980 tests now widely available could be coming from the yeshivas, the less-orthodox Hebrew Day schools or the Conservative private schools.

"We are very concerned about the security of regents exams, and in 1974 we held meetings, consulted with each other and tightened security," said Rabbi Joshua Fishman of the National Conference of Yeshiva Principals.

But, in an apparently typical pattern, the social studies exam obtained in advance by The Post was bought by an intermediary from a former Yeshiva student. He, in turn, purchased it in the heart of the Orthodox Jewish community in Borough Park, Brooklyn.

Traced through a license plate number, the Yeshiva student admitted going back to Borough Park, where he used to live, last Thursday because he heard rumors

Continued on Page 22

THE
REGENTS
SCANDAL

5 O.D. IN TEEN PARTY HORROR

Post Photo by Joe De Maria.
The parents and sister of one of the victims outside Montefiore Hospital this morning.

By CY EGAN and LESLIE GEVIRTZ

FIVE youths, one of them a 16-year-old girl, were felled by drug overdoses last night during a wild party at a park in the exclusive Riverdale section of the Bronx.

The five — all from middle-class families in the area, in Westchester and upstate — were rushed to nearby Montefiore Hospital by some 60 other youths at the party.

All five of the victims were confined to the intensive care unit this morning — four of them in critical condition.

The tragedy came shortly before midnight as the youngsters were partying in the playground section of Seton Park, between 233d and 235th Sts. and Independence and Palisades Avs.

The park serves 100,000 residents.

Continued on Page 22

The size and placement of headlines and stories reflect something of the values of editors and the newspapers they work for, and are also intended to attract the attention of different audiences. The New York Post directs its appeal to people on their way home from work, many of them commuting by bus or subway.

The editors of The Wall Street Journal *have rather different ideas about the kinds of news their audience wants to read.*

what's nutritious. What is good for them and what's attractive and tasty are not always the same.[19] Numerous other factors affect gatekeeping at various stages, including the following:

- the ethics of individual journalists
- the policies of editors or publishers[20]
- a desire to get ahead, to protect one's job, or to avoid conflict
- time and space limitations
- dependence on handouts from government or from public relations offices as the source of news
- fear of a libel suit

In addition, Daniel Boorstin has noted that the media are under constant pressure to fill their pages or time slots with *something*. Many publicity agents, campaign managers, and leaders of protest

Effects of the Media on Society and Culture   329

organizations have learned to use the media to gain publicity. They stage press meetings, stunts, and confrontations to make news. Because the news media are notified of these events in advance and can therefore schedule them, the media tend to cover them. Boorstin refers to these as *pseudoevents* and maintains that a larger and larger part of what we see and hear is this type of manufactured "news."[21]

Out of this welter of pressures and limitations, the daily agenda of the news media emerges. (In Chapter 12 we look at these factors and the process of deciding what's news in more detail.) Clearly news reports don't just mirror the world. The world outside is only loosely correlated with this pseudoenvironment of symbols and images created by the press.

The Media's Agenda and the Audience

Does the agenda of issues presented by the news media actually influence the audience? More specifically, does it affect their agenda — their awareness of issues and their evaluations of the relative importance of issues? We saw that the experiment by De-Fleur and Larsen supports the idea that repetition of a message in the media will increase the number of people learning the message. The agenda-setting hypothesis, however, goes beyond this idea. Its central hypothesis, according to Jack McLeod and his associates, is that "an audience member exposed to a given medium agenda will adjust his or her perception of the importance of issues in the direction corresponding to the amount of attention devoted to those issues in the medium used."[22] That is, presumably, the public's agenda will come to match the media's agenda.

Campaign managers and political commentators often seem to be among the most fervent believers in this hypothesis. Thus, the early months of the campaign for the 1980 Democratic presidential nomination were often explained in terms somewhat like the following, simplified version: Senator Kennedy wanted President Carter's alleged failures as a leader and, later, the poor state of the economy to be the primary issues in the public's mind. President Carter's forces hoped to make the candidate's character a primary issue. Carter was widely thought of as a decent and honest family man whereas Kennedy's car accident at Chappaquiddick — in which a young woman drowned — and his attempts to explain the accident had raised questions about his morality and judgment in a crisis. Once Kennedy entered the race, the media focused attention on him, his character, and Chappaquiddick. These issues, according to this analysis, became top items on the media's agenda and so, too, on the public agenda. Carter's performance and the economy were far lower on the list. When hostages were taken in

Iran, the presidential campaign fell far down on the media's agenda of news — and in the public's agenda of concerns. As a result, for months Kennedy's criticisms of Carter and positive views of Kennedy were kept off a prominent spot on the media's agenda — and the public's. When people voted in the primaries early in 1980, the issues likely to be on their minds were the hostages in Iran and questions about Kennedy's character. The media's agenda set the public's agenda, which determined how people voted.

But is such an analysis valid? Does the public's agenda come to match the media's agenda? The pace of research on the agenda-setting hypothesis has quickened in recent years. An example is the work of Donald L. Shaw, Maxwell E. McCombs, and several associates.[23] They studied the presentation of political issues by the media during the 1972 presidential elections and the responses of voters in Charlotte, North Carolina. They carefully recorded the agendas of issues set by the local newspapers and by the three television networks. They measured the audience in terms of their reading and viewing habits, attention to specific issues, and judgments about the importance of issues.

Maxwell and his associates did not find a simple match between the agendas set by the media and the public's beliefs about the importance of the issues. Members of the audience, they found, had different sets of beliefs depending on their social categories.[24] That is, young people had different perceptions of the importance of issues than older people, and men's patterns were different from women's. Differences in attention to issues and evaluations of their importance also varied among people with different income levels and different political preferences.[25]

But the authors did find some support for the agenda-setting hypothesis. Among their specific conclusions were these:

> "There is a progressive increase in the use of mass communications during a presidential campaign. In fact, the major political role of the mass media may be to raise the salience of politics among the American electorate every four years."[26] (This finding supports the idea that the media activate voters, as discussed in Chapter 8.)

> The influence of the media's agenda on an individual's concern with issues is directly related to how much he or she is exposed to mass communication. Those individuals most frequently exposed to mass communication

show higher levels of agreement between personal agendas and mass media agendas.

Thus the study did not "prove" the agenda-setting hypothesis. The researchers concluded that the influence of the media's agenda must be interpreted in long-range terms and conclusions must take into account social categories, changing patterns of media use, and frequency of media exposure. Do people adopt the agenda set for them by those who select, package, and present the news? Do these issues spread through the society to become the dominant topics that decide elections or influence other decision-making processes? At present research has not yielded complete answers to these questions, but there is considerable suspicion that agenda setting is one indirect way in which the media can change society over a long period of time.

Social Problems and the Media

The media deal not only with specific events and political conflicts but also with general conditions, some of which they define as problems. Thus part of the agenda of issues they present is a list of social problems. In the early 1960s hunger, poverty, and racial discrimination were prominent items on the agenda. By 1970 draft evasion, runaway children, the "generation gap," drug abuse, and ecological issues made the list. In the 1980s toxic chemicals, inflation, energy shortages, and the abuse of children and of the elderly have risen to the fore.

Sociologists have long debated whether some conditions are inherently troublesome or pathological — whether the public recognizes them or not.[27] Some people say the answer is no, that social problems are just a set of conditions that large numbers of people say are troublesome.[28] In any event, out of a large number of conditions that we could worry about, a few become widely known and objects of deep social concern. We could, for example, be as concerned with the ravages of fire as with those of crime, or as worried by infant mortality as we are about the health of the elderly.[29]

In fact, public attention to social conditions comes and goes, often passing through several stages. First, some individual or group identifies a condition as a threat to society. They point out to others that the condition is a problem that should concern everyone and that should be remedied by collective action. If enough people become convinced that a social problem exists, agencies and programs are established and supported to deal with it. Media attention then dies away and the public usually begins to lose its earlier high level of concern. But those whose job it is to deal with the problem (and whose careers depend on the continued existence of agencies and programs to deal with it) fight this loss of concern with a flow of reports to the public and the media concerning the frequency and continued dangers of the problem.

In this natural history of social problems, the media often have significant effects at two stages: in raising public consciousness and concern about a condition so that it comes to be defined as a social problem requiring some action, and in keeping the problem alive in public concern as part of the ongoing agenda.

Defining Problems. The "creation" of a social problem is a complex process.[30] Those who believe that a condition is a serious social problem may not be heard by the majority, even if what they say makes sense. For example, for years a small number of scientists and environmentalists maintained that insecticides were harmful. They received little attention. Then a specific medium — a book on the problem by Rachel Carson called *Silent Spring* — won a broad audience, and public concern began to grow. Seeing the public's interest, other media gave the issue wide coverage, and the unrestricted use of insecticides came to be defined as a social problem. Legislation and government programs to deal with the problem followed.

Similarly, the plight of whales was decried for years by a handful of environmentalists. As time went on, the media gave more and more attention to the topic. Now, many citizens see the fate of whales as a problem, even though they have never had, nor are likely to have, personal contact with a whale.

Automobile safety, child abuse, property taxes, wife beating, the killing of eagles, and carcenogenic food additives have all become matters of widespread concern recently, although all these conditions have existed for decades. Only after they received widespread publicity were they defined as problems. Responsibility for doing something about the issues was then delegated.

Sometimes a crisis or dramatic event helps put a condition on the public agenda as a problem to be dealt with. Thus, when the parents of Karen Quinlan went to court for permission to stop the machines that were keeping her alive, the debate about the wisdom of using machines to prolong life versus "death with dignity" suddenly received publicity. The "problem" had not suddenly increased. But what had been an abstract debate of medical ethics had become a personal drama that the media covered with

The media can help set the public agenda by devoting special attention to a particular subject in order to evoke significant public reaction. A nuclear accident at the Three Mile Island reactor in Pennsylvania in the late 1970s received extensive media coverage that initiated a continuing debate about the wisdom of constructing nuclear power plants (opposite page) and the hazards of disposing of nuclear waste (above).

enthusiasm, and a new social problem appeared. Similarly, many people have recognized for years that the dumping of toxic chemicals poses serious hazards, but such dumping gained widespread publicity only after toxic chemicals at Love Canal, New York, provided an especially dramatic illustration of the hazards.

If no dramatic event has caught the public's eye, those concerned about a condition may, in effect, use the media to create one. Not only protest groups but also political extremists, terrorists, and disturbed individuals often do outrageous things so that the media will draw attention to them or their cause. Dissident groups often stage public events to attract the media because they believe publicity will help to get the problem solved.

Are these people right in ascribing such power to the media? Relatively little research exists on *how* the media create public conceptions or awareness of social problems, although it is widely believed that they do. In an early study F. James Davis focused on the role of newspapers in "creating" crime waves.[31] He studied cases in which newspapers created the belief that a community was experiencing a serious increase in crime by deliberately increasing their coverage of certain types of crimes in a disproportionate way. Thus the newspapers raised public consciousness about the extent of crime as a social problem. More recently Bob Roshier found a similar situation in England.[32]

We can hypothesize that the media's role in creating an agenda of social problems, defining what is and is not a problem, is similar to its role in shaping the public's agenda of issues generally. But additional research on the media's role is clearly needed.

Public Beliefs About Relative Incidence. To cope with social problems, Americans have created a host of federal, state, and local agencies. Examples include the Social Security Administration, juvenile courts, public health services, and welfare programs. Even the police and prisons are agencies designed to "do something" about specific conditions that have disturbed many people. How well an agency does in the competition for funds and job security may depend in part on the public's beliefs about the continued importance and frequency of the problem with which it deals. Relative incidence (or frequency compared to the frequency of other problems) may be one measure of a problem's significance.

Agencies themselves usually produce a flow of reports describing the particular problems they deal with and their incidence. Of course, the media report on these social conditions as well. Thus an interesting question arises: Once an agency assumes responsibility for a problem, what role does it play in shaping citizens' beliefs about a problem, and what role do the media play? A recent study probed the role of the media versus the role of agencies in shaping public beliefs about the relative incidence of a set of established social problems.[33]

The research was conducted in Spokane, Washington, a community of approximately 175,000 inhabitants with two local dailies and three major television stations. The researchers used two criteria to select the ten social problems to be studied: first, the problem had to be widely recognized in the society, and, second, it had to be possible to obtain official data on its frequency. Then they studied and compared (1) public beliefs about the relative incidence of these problems; (2) relative emphasis on the problems by the local media; and (3) the relative incidence of each problem according to the files of official agencies.

Public beliefs were determined by interviewing 150 residents of Spokane, who were selected carefully to represent three socioeconomic levels. Specially constructed questionnaires were used to assess the beliefs of these citizens regarding the relative frequency of the ten problems. The media's presentations of the problems were judged by the relative amount of attention given to each during an eighteen-month period immediately prior to the community survey. The total amount of space or time devoted to news accounts of incidents representing each of the problems was defined as its *relative emphasis*. To determine the agencies' view of relative incidence, the researchers reviewed the files and other records of social agencies in the community, such as the city and state police, juvenile courts, the State Department of Mental Health, and the State Board Against Discrimination.

Table 9.1 presents the basic findings of the study. Each column represents one view of the relative incidence or numerical importance of the problems. The main questions that can be raised are

1. Do public beliefs concerning the relative prevalence of the problems reflect the ranking given those same problems by the media?
2. Does the relative emphasis given by the news media

Table 9.1 Prevalence Rankings for Ten Social Problems

Social problem	Rank		
	Community survey	Media exposure	Agency records
Unemployment	1	4	1
Crime	3	1	2
Transportation mishaps	6	2	4
Juvenile delinquency	2	6	5
Drug abuse	4	5	8
Alcoholism	5	10	3
Mental illness	7	8	6
Discrimination	9	3	9
Sexual deviancy	8	7	7
Suicide	10	9	10

Source: Jeffrey C. Hubbard, Melvin L. DeFleur, and Lois B. DeFleur, "Mass Media Influences on Public Conceptions of Social Problems, *Social Problems*, (October 1975), 29.

to these problems parallel their position in official agency records?

3. Do public beliefs concerning the frequency of problems parallel the rankings in agency records?

Thus, the basic question is whether public beliefs about the occurrence of problems are closer to official agency rankings or to the emphasis that the media give them. Obviously, this question is related to the agenda-setting hypothesis that the media's treatment of issues creates parallel public beliefs about the importance of the issues. In this case, the hypothesis to be tested is slightly different: that the public derives a belief about the relative frequency of the problem from the relative emphasis given it by the media.

As it turned out, the overall relationship between the media's emphasis on the problems and citizens' beliefs about their prevalence was *statistically insignificant*. The media's attention to a problem had no noticeable influence on what people believed about its relative prevalence. The relationship between media emphasis and prevalence as indicated in official records was also statistically insignificant. Thus, the media's attention to a problem neither shaped public beliefs nor reflected official data on the frequency of the problems. On the other hand, a fairly high relationship was found between the frequency of the problems revealed by official records and citizens' beliefs regarding their prevalence.

One hypothesis that can be derived from these findings is that the agencies themselves provided information shaping public beliefs to protect their budgets and jobs. In any event, these data contradict the agenda-setting hypothesis. Media attention to these ten issues did *not* seem to influence people's perceptions of their prevalence.

Some Tentative Conclusions

These findings underline the conclusion reached in Chapter 8: the old magic bullet theory is mistaken; the media do not have simple uniform influences that are the sole causes of individual and social behaviors. The agenda-setting hypothesis is based on a similar kind of thinking, and it needs some reworking. We have seen evidence that the media's agenda is not, in the short term, immediately matched in the public's ranking of the issues presented. We have also seen evidence that the public does not translate the media's emphasis on established social problems into beliefs about the frequency of these problems. Since we saw in Chapter 8 that the media's influence on individuals depends on many factors, including individual differences, social categories, and other channels of communication, we should not be surprised that the media's role in shaping the public agenda and view of social problems is similarly complicated.

Obviously, however, our review of these issues does not imply that the media have no role in shaping public beliefs. In particular, the media are likely to be important in the early stages of defining a social problem. Dramatic media stories may be especially influential in raising public awareness and focusing concern on specific conditions. By showing that white middle-class children, not just poor or minority children, are involved in the problems of drug abuse and alcoholism, for example, the media raise the level of public concern about these problems. Once a problem has been turned over to an agency, media interest and influence appear to decline. But the media also seem to have some long-term influence on the public agenda in general, although that influence is greatly affected by individuals' membership in social groups, their political preferences, and their exposure to the media.

Overall, the influence of the media appears mainly in identifying emerging social problems and in modifying from time to time people's levels of concern about specific problems closely related to their values. We can conclude that the media play a part in creating demand for new problem-oriented programs and agencies and in modifying priorities regarding problems. This appears to be one way that the media promote social change.

Debates About Popular Culture

One of the most controversial (and most fascinating) social and cultural effects of the media is the invention and spread of a constant deluge of such products as popular songs, cheap paperback novels, formula TV drama, low-grade film thrillers, comic strip characters, and other unsophisticated content. Such material often reaches large portions of the population and becomes a part of people's daily lives. People hum the latest popular tunes, suffer the latest problem of the soap opera heroine, exchange analyses of the latest big game based on news reports, and organize their activities around the weekly television schedule. This media output is often called *popular culture*.

The artistic merits of media-produced culture and its impact on society have been debated for generations.[34] Media critics and media defenders have disagreed hotly about whether deliberately manufactured mass "art" is a blasphemy or a blessing. These analyses of mass communication and its products as art forms take place *outside* the framework of science. Media criticism is an arena of debate where conclusions are reached on the basis of personal opinions rather than carefully assembled data. Nevertheless, those who praise or condemn the content of mass communication perform an important service. They offer us contrasting sets of standards for judging the merits of media content. We may choose to accept or reject those standards, but by exercising *some* set of criteria we can reach our own conclusions about the artistic merits of popular music, the soap operas, spectator sports, and so on.

The sections that follow discuss two significant issues: the merits of various forms of popular culture manufactured and disseminated by the media, and the various levels of cultural taste that characterize segments of the American population. These discussions are based on strong opinions, clear biases, and specific sets of values drawn from the writings of a number of critics. You may find these admittedly biased opinions consistent with your own views, or you may disagree violently. In either case, they illustrate the types of analyses found in debates over popular culture and should help you clarify your own views.

Effects of the Media on Society and Culture   339

Folk Art, Elite Art, and Kitsch

Critics tell us that prior to the development of the mass media there were essentially two broad categories of art: folk art and elite art.[35] Both, it is said, are genuine and valuable.

Folk art develops spontaneously among people. It is unsophisticated, localized, and natural. It is a product of many anonymous creators and users. It is a grassroots type of art *produced by its consumers* and tied directly to their values and daily experiences. Thus, villages or even regions and nations develop characteristic furniture styles, music, dances, architectural forms, and decorative motifs for articles of everyday use. Folk art never takes guidelines from the elite of the society. It emerges as part of the traditions of ordinary people. It does not consist of artistic classics that are widely known.

Elite art, on the other hand, is "high culture." It is deliberately produced by very talented and creative individuals, who often gain great personal recognition for their achievements. Thus, elite art is technically and thematically complex. It is also very individualistic; its creators aim at discovering new ways of interpreting or representing their experience. Elite art includes the music, sculpture, dance forms, opera, and paintings that originated mainly in Europe and are given acclaim by sophisticates from all parts of the world. Although it has its great classics, it is also in continuous innovation. Novelists, composers, painters, and other creative artists constantly experiment with new forms and concepts.

But in modern times, some say, both folk art and elite art are threatened. The arrival of the media brought radical change. With the advent of cheap newspapers, magazines, paperback books, radio, movies, and television, a new form of art made its debut, catering to the undeveloped tastes of massive, relatively uneducated audiences. Its content, say its critics, is unsophisticated, simplistic, and trivial. Its typical literary forms are the "whodunit" detective story and the true confession magazine; its typical musical composition is the latest popular tune; its typical dramatic forms are the soap opera, the comic strip, and the western movie. A term that has been widely used to label such mass-mediated art is the German word *kitsch.*

Criticisms of Kitsch. In manufacturing kitsch, critics charge, its producers often "mine" the other categories. They do so "the way improvident frontiersmen mine the soil, extracting its riches and putting back nothing."[36] As Clement Greenberg put it: "The precondition of *kitsch* . . . is the availability close at hand of a fully matured cultural tradition, whose discoveries, acquisitions and perfected self-conscious *kitsch* can take advantage of for its own ends."[37]

But why do the critics see kitsch as such a problem? Essentially they maintain that the older separation between elite art and folk art once corresponded to the distinction between aristocracy and common people. Although they do not necessarily approve of the aristocracy, they believe that such groups were critical to the existence of the most developed forms of art. Prior to the development of mass communication, the critics claim, these two art forms could coexist because they had clearly defined constituencies. Then came the dramatic spread of the media to all classes of society. The result was a deluge of inconsequential kitsch, which had an impact on all levels of society and all forms of art because kitsch competes for the attention of everyone. Its constant presence and attention-grabbing qualities are the sources of its popular appeal. Thus, critics conclude, those who earlier would have read Tolstoy now turn to Ian Fleming; those who might have found entertainment at the symphony, ballet, or theater now tune in on "Laverne and Shirley"; those who would have gained political wisdom from modern versions of Bryce and de Tocqueville now listen to Cronkite or Walters. In other words, say the critics, bad culture drives out good culture as bad money drives out good money. In the words of Dwight MacDonald:

> It is a debased, trivial culture that voids both the deep realities (sex, death, failure, tragedy) and also the simple, spontaneous pleasures. The masses, debauched by several generations of this sort of thing, in turn come to demand trivial and comfortable cultural products. Which came first, the chicken or the egg, the mass demand or its satisfaction (and further stimulation) is a question as academic as it is unanswerable. The engine is reciprocating and shows no signs of running down.[38]

Furthermore, it is charged, kitsch represents a double-barreled form of exploitation. Those who control the media not only rob citizens of a chance to acquire higher tastes by engulfing them with less demanding media products but also reap high profits from those whom they are depriving.

Thus, the condemnation of kitsch by media critics is based on three major assumptions. First, kitsch presumably diminishes both folk and elite art because it simplifies their content and in using them exhausts the sources of these arts. Second, it deprives its audiences of interest in developing tastes for more genuine art

One of the most pervasive forms of popular culture in America is the fast-food chain, and one of the most successful of these is McDonalds. Some McDonald's restaurants feature not only the "golden arches" but also huge representations of the clown Ronald McDonald and, of course, the famous hamburger.

forms. Third, it is mainly a tool for economic exploitation of the masses.

If true, these are serious charges. To examine them further, we look at one specific aspect of popular culture: the heroes of the media. Does the presence of media-created personalities tend to diminish the stature of genuine heroes, as the criticism of kitsch suggests? Does a fascination with media-created heroes lessen interest in meritorious accomplishments in real life? Is economic exploitation a real factor?

The Heroes of the Media. In an earlier America, the critics say, heroes and heroines were extraordinary individuals with rare personal qualities who performed admirable deeds.[39] The list of heroes admired by eighteenth- and nineteenth-century Americans included George Washington, Robert E. Lee, Sacajawea, Sojourner Truth, Daniel Boone, Harriet Tubman, Geronimo, Davy Crockett, and Harriet Beecher Stowe. Such men and women

Alistair Cooke, host of public television's Masterpiece Theatre, *seems to many viewers to be the very voice of culture. His informal, reminiscent, and highly articulate introductions to the British-produced dramas shown serially on* Masterpiece Theatre *have long instructed and delighted American audiences.*

were real people who did real things. Their deeds had a significant impact on history. The critics point out that they did not win acclaim because they were pretty or entertaining but because they had powerful determination. They faced great danger or confronted situations that required courage, dedication, and self-sacrifice.

Even as the media were rising in the twentieth century, the tradition of heroes lingered. Alvin York and Eddie Rickenbacker emerged as the great heroes of World War I. But perhaps the last great individualistic hero, and one of the most adulated of all time, was Charles A. Lindbergh. His solitary flight across the vast Atlantic in a frail single-engine aircraft required steel nerves and an iron will. In his single deed were focused all those qualities that Americans admired in their heroes up to the early decades of the present century.

Are the days of such heroes gone? Some people feel that they may be. As the media gained ascendancy, their critics maintain, a new figure began to replace the hero and heroine of the deed. These new objects of public adulation are not individuals with extraordinary personal qualities. Instead, they are media heroes known for their profiles on the movie screen or the appeal of their throbbing voices, the skill with which they strike a ball with a stick or the sincerity with which they portray characters in films or television dramas. Media heroines are cut from similar cloth. And endless parade of "awards" presented by the media reinforces the idea that these are the people who count.

Thus, contemporary pseudoheroes are media creations made famous on pulp paper, movie celluloid, microgrooves, and electronic images. Some are real people who sing, act, tell funny stories, or play games. Others are pure inventions — imaginary characters of the soap opera or the prime-time drama. There is ample reason to believe, say the critics, that for at least some people, fantasy merges with reality.

We can identify several categories of media-created heroes. First, there is the hero of ball and stick. A long list of athletes have been made into celebrities by the attention of the media, from Ty Cobb and Babe Ruth to Red Grange, Jack Dempsey, Joe Louis, Joe Di Maggio, Ted Williams, and Lou Gehrig, to today's athletes such as Julius Erving, Muhammad Ali, Billie Jean King, and O. J. Simpson. These individuals clearly demonstrate well-developed athletic skills, and they have commanded extraordinary financial rewards. Yet, say the critics, it would be difficult to account for their immense popularity on any other grounds than the status conferred by the media.[40] Striking a ball skillfully with a bat, racket, or club contributes little to the national destiny. Athletic skill is scarcely the stuff of which advances in civilization are made.

Another significant category is the hero of the titillating tune. Their voices are instantly recognized by millions of fans. Not many members of the older generation in the United States would fail to identify the voices of Bing Crosby, Frank Sinatra, or Elvis Presley. More recently the sounds of Blondie and Dolly Parton receive instant recognition. The hits that these and other popular singers have made famous through the media constitute an important part of popular culture. Here, the dependence of what the critics call kitsch on the folk and elite art is especially clear. Many songs that have made the Top Ten have been based on either classical music or American folk traditions, including early American ballads and grassroots jazz.

Of even greater interest to those critical of mass media culture are the heroes of superhuman power. Characters of the imagination have long intrigued people. For example, one could easily speculate that the various "supermen" of today's media are the counterparts of ancient myths about deities with fantastic powers who appeared in human form. There is a timeless attraction to fantasies of power and success. Millions have been entertained for decades by the unusual deeds of a long list of fictional characters with truly extraordinary capacities. For generations audiences have admired and coveted the powers of such fantasy creatures as Superman, the Shadow, Wonder Woman, Batman, and Spiderman; today they can marvel at the Incredible Hulk.

Other contemporary media characters have more human limitations, but they are remarkably capable of combatting the forces of evil. Here the critics include the police heroes of screeching tire, the cloak-and-dagger heroes of international spydom, and the all-seeing private eye. The list would not be complete without mentioning the heroes of legal ploy and the venerable heroes of suture and scalpel. What hard-working private eye measures up to Barnaby Jones? Who can defeat James Bond — or even Charlie's Angels? The capacities of real people in the real world are pale and flabby by comparison.

Even this brief look at media heroes suggests that the enemies of kitsch may have a point. Their charge that popular art draws from elite culture can be substantiated in many cases. Whether this should be condemned is an open question. Their charge that the public is forced to pay for popular culture also seems to have some basis. Ultimately, it is the public that pays the high salaries of media heroes and heroines when they are added to the costs of advertising and marketing the products of sponsors. Whether this truly represents "economic exploitation of the masses" is, however, another matter. Finally, the charge of the critics that media heroes diminish interest in accomplishments in real life may have some basis. Most of the significant accomplishments in science and medicine that make the news do so in the back pages of the paper, while gossip about media heroes often makes headlines.

Overall, then, the critics of popular culture seem to be making an important argument. However, the degree to which these aspects of popular culture represent a threat to more serious art forms — or to the public as a whole — remains debatable.

| **The Media's Dependence on Popular Culture** | Why, one must ask, do the media continue this outpouring of kitsch? The answer is that popular culture is as necessary to the media as water is to a fish. It is the critical element in the process that keeps the media functioning. We pointed out in Chapter 3 that the media in the United States are privately owned, profit-making enterprises. To make a profit, the media must capture and sell consumer attention. Sponsors, who must pay huge prices for media time and space, demand the largest possible audiences for |

their advertisements. This economic base brings pressure to produce and disseminate content that will attract the largest possible number of listeners, viewers, or readers. It is this law of large numbers that brings popular culture, geared to the taste levels of the majority of the consuming public, to mass communication. Thus, both media needs and audience needs are served by what the critics call "kitsch." The law of large numbers, the production of popular culture, and the taste levels of the consuming public are all closely related parts of the basic system supporting the media in the United States.

One must recognize, however, that the vast public that chooses and consumes the products of the mass media is divided into many categories. Some are well educated, some are only partially literate; some are rich, some are poor. Media audiences could be classified into dozens of categories. Many of these categories are important in determining what kinds of tastes characterize a given segment of the public. For example, people who have been educated at an excellent college or university, who have always enjoyed wealth, and who live in a large city are likely to have tastes very different from those of people who have less education and a lower income and who live in a small rural community. In other words, the media audience taken as a whole can be divided into a number of *taste publics* in terms of the kinds of artistic products and media content that they enjoy. The analysis of such taste publics gives additional insight into popular culture, the reasons why the media produce and disseminate a great amount of unsophisticated content, and the probable economic consequences of changing this pattern.

Taste Publics

The analysis of taste publics, like debates about the merits of popular culture, is outside the framework of science. It proceeds from individual opinions and standards. Judgments must be made about whether enjoying a particular artistic product represents "high" or "low" taste, or something in between, and judgments about good and bad taste depend heavily on subjective values rather than on scientific criteria. Nevertheless, such analyses focus our attention on significant factors in the basic support system of American media.

Because of the difficulty of the task and the risk that others will disagree strongly, not many scholars have tried to analyze taste publics in the United States. Sociologist Herbert Gans, however, identified five major levels of taste in American society.[41] In the sections that follow, these taste publics and the content they prefer are described. The description is based largely, but not exclusively, on Gans's analysis. The factor that seems most important in defining the taste levels is education, but many other social categories and factors are also involved.

High Culture. The small segment of the public preferring this type of art and entertainment product consider themselves an elite and their culture exclusive. This is the culture of the "serious" writers, artists, and composers. It is found in the "little" magazines, in off-Broadway productions, a few art-film theaters, and on rare occasions on educational television.

High culture tends to change its styles often. In art, for example, various forms have dominated at one time or another — expressionism, impressionism, abstraction, conceptual art, and so

The debate about the virtues of high art versus popular art raises questions about the role of the media in serving or pandering to the public. Sometimes the boundaries blur, and items of popular culture — such as comic strips and soup cans — become the subjects of serious artists whose work is shown in galleries and museums. This comic-strip lithograph is the work of Roy Lichtenstein.

forth. High culture values innovation and experimentation with such elements as form, substance, method, overt content, and covert symbolism. In fiction it emphasizes complex character development over plot. In modern high culture psychological and philosophical questions are explored; alienation and conflict have been frequent themes. Clearly, this form of culture would have little appeal to the majority of the media's usual audience. For this reason, it is seldom found in mass communication.

Upper-Middle Culture. This type of cultural product is preferred by the American upper middle class, which is composed mainly of professionals, executives, managers, and their families. These people are well educated and relatively affluent, but they are neither creators nor critics. For the most part they are consumers of literature, music, theater, and other artistic culture that is accepted as "good." Their fiction stresses plot more than characters or issues, and this group prefers stories about people like themselves who develop careers, are successful, and play important parts in significant affairs. The film *Kramer vs. Kramer* seems made to order for this group. It shows likable upper middle-class people in an upper middle-class setting. Although the characters are well portrayed, they are not explored in depth, and the plot itself holds much of the film's interest.

The upper-middle taste public reads *Time* or *Newsweek* avidly, as well as the kind of popularized social science that appears in *Psychology Today*. They are familiar with standard symphonic works and traditional operas but dislike contemporary or experimental compositions. They purchase hardcover trade books, support their local symphony orchestra, and occasionally attend the ballet. They subscribe to such magazines as *Harper's*, the *New Yorker*, *Ms.*, and *Vogue*. Yet, although this group is fairly numerous, its influence on media content is very limited. Although some plays on television, public affairs programs, and FM music represent the upper-middle level, most media content is at the level below it.

Lower-Middle Culture. This type of cultural content is the dominant influence in mass communication for two reasons. First, the category who consume it is the most numerous; and, second, it has sufficient income to purchase media-advertised products. The people of this level are mostly white-collar workers. Many are in the lower professions (for example, public school teachers, accountants, government bureaucrats, druggists, and higher-paid clerical workers). A substantial number are college-educated.

Often, their degrees are in technical subjects. This public often consciously rejects the culture preferred by the taste levels above it, but occasionally it uses some of their forms, especially when they have been transformed into popular culture.

The lower-middle public continues to support religion and its moral values. Thus, it does not approve of positive portrayals of gays, loose heterosexual relationships, or other "deviant" life-styles. In other words, this taste public likes books, films, and television drama in which old-fashioned virtue is rewarded. John Wayne was their idol; the lower-middle public likes heroes who accept the traditional virtues and clear plots. Neither complexity of personality nor philosophical conflicts are dominant themes. People of lower-middle tastes read the *Reader's Digest*, condensed books, and McCall's. They purchase millions of paperbacks with fast-action plots. They happily view "Happy Days" as well as cop-and-crook dramas. They like family and situation comedy, musical extravaganzas, soap operas, and quiz shows. They also followed "All in the Family" faithfully (many support Archie's racial and ethnic biases). In music Lawrence Welk has considerable appeal for the older members of this group, as do such figures as John Denver for the younger. These types of music make few intellectual demands, and, like other forms of kitsch, they are often derived from classical sources.

Low Culture. This type of art and entertainment appeals to skilled and semi-skilled blue-collar workers in manufacturing and service occupations. Earlier, their education was likely to consist of vocational high school or less. Recently, younger members of this category have been attending vocationally oriented community colleges. Although still numerically large, this taste public is shrinking as more blue-collar families send their children to four-year colleges.

It was this taste public that dominated media content in the 1950s, and it still plays an important part. But because its purchasing power is somewhat less than that of the lower-middle level and its numbers are declining, it is being replaced by the lower-middle public as the dominant influence on the media. But the media continue to produce a substantial amount of unsophisticated content for this level.

This taste public likes action — often violent action — in film and television drama. Thus, to please this public the media resist efforts to censor the portrayal of violence. This group likes simpler western and police dramas and comedy shows with a lot of slapstick (older examples were the Lucille Ball and Jackie Gleason shows). They like "The Dukes of Hazzard," "Hee Haw," "Mork and Mindy," wrestling, and country-western music. For reading they like the *National Enquirer,* confession magazines (for women), and the sports page (for men).

Quasi-Folk Low Culture. This type of art resembles that of the low culture level. Its taste public of consumers is composed mainly of people who are very poor and have little education and few occupational skills. Many are on welfare or hold uncertain and unskilled jobs. Many are non-white and of rural or foreign origin. Although this group is numerous, it plays only a minor role in shaping media content, primarily because its purchasing power is low.

These people read mainly comic books and occasional tabloids. They like simpler television shows. In many urban areas foreign-language media cater to the needs of this segment of the public. Finally, elements of the older folk culture are found in this group. For example, they hold religious and ethnic festivals and social gatherings; religious artifacts and prints are often found on the walls of their homes; and colorful wall paintings adorn the streets of some ethnic neighborhoods.

Overall, popular culture as media content must be understood in terms of the purchasing power and taste preferences of various segments of the public. Regardless of the protests, charges, claims, and counterclaims of the critics, the media will continue to produce content that appeals to the largest taste publics because it attracts attention that they can sell to sponsors. There is little likelihood that the media will bring about a major cultural revolution by emphasizing high or even upper-middle culture. The obvious prediction for the future is that lower-middle and lower tastes will continue to dominate American mass communication.

Summary

Media researchers have been less concerned with the effects of the media on social and cultural processes than on individuals. Research on their social and cultural effects is more difficult, of less interest to the public, and harder to fund, although it is certainly important.

One way in which the media influence societies and cultures is by helping to spread information about new ideas and new techniques. How fast and how far news spreads depends on its importance, its inherent interest, and other factors. In Project Revere, researchers found that increasing the number of repetitions of a message increased the percentage of the population that learned the message, but the increase followed a curve of diminishing returns. Researchers also found evidence of a multistage flow of communication.

In developing countries governments have often used the media to spread information about new ideas and technologies. That is, they have tried to use the media as deliberate agents of social change in their efforts to modernize a country. In Mexico, for example, information and positive attitudes about an educational program were skillfully woven into a specially produced soap opera; the result was an increase in enrollments. Attempts to diffuse innovations have often failed, however, sometimes because the efforts were not attuned to local beliefs and values.

The agenda-setting hypothesis proposes another effect of the media: that people judge a topic to be significant to the extent that it is emphasized in the media. The agenda for concern about public issues is said to be set by the media when they select and present certain items and ignore others and when they give varying emphases to news reports. At least one experiment suggests that the media's agenda does not have an immediate and direct effect but a long-term influence contingent on other factors such as a person's exposure to the media.

Related to this agenda-setting hypothesis is the claim that the media play a key role in creating social problems, that is, in identifying a condition as troublesome and in need of correction. Once a problem is identified and a system is established to deal with it, the media's role in shaping beliefs about the importance of the problem seems to be reduced.

By manufacturing and disseminating a continuing flow of art forms, the media also influence culture. Many critics refer to mass-mediated popular culture as "kitsch," meaning trashy and trivial. They claim that the manufacturers of kitsch (1) imitate both folk art and elite art without contributing to either; (2) keep media audiences from developing tastes for better forms of art; and (3) force consumers to pay for popular culture.

To understand the media's continued production of popular culture, one must see American society as consisting of distinct taste publics. The lower-middle taste public is the great consumer of popular culture. Its large numbers and high purchasing power make it the most significant target for advertisers who pay the bills for the media. Because other taste publics have less purchasing power, their influence on the media is less.

Generally, then, the media are significant forces in modern society that alter social arrangements and bring new cultural forms. They spread information and innovations, help modernize traditional societies, influence the agenda for public concerns, shape the public's awareness of social problems, and provide a continuing flow of popular culture.

Notes and References

1. *Consumers Reports*, 45 (April 1980), 226.
2. Gabriel Tarde, *The Laws of Imitation*, trans. E. C. Parsons (New York: Holt, 1903).
3. Everett M. Rogers and F. Floyd Shoemaker, *Communication of Innovations: A Cross Cultural Approach* (New York: Free Press, 1971), pp. 52–70.
4. Ibid., p. 100.
5. Ibid., p. 67.
6. Paul B. Sheatsley and Jacob J. Feldman, "The Assassination of President Kennedy: A Preliminary Report on Public Reactions and Behavior," *Public Opinion Quarterly*, 28 (1964), 189–215.
7. The predicted curve was derived from a well-known generalization in classical psychophysics called the *Weber-Fechner Function*.
8. Melvin L. DeFleur and Otto N. Larsen, *The Flow of Information: An Experiment in Mass Communication* (New York: Harper and Brothers, 1958). See especially Figure 10, p. 130.
9. Melvin L. DeFleur, "Mass Communication and the Study of Rumor," *Sociological Inquiry*, 32 (Winter 1962), 51–70.
10. Bradley S. Greenberg and Edwin B. Parker, eds., *The Kennedy Assassination and the American Public* (Stanford, Calif.: Stanford University Press, 1965).
11. Wilbur Schramm, *Mass Media and National Development: The Role of Information in Developing Countries* (Stanford, Calif.: Stanford University Press, 1964) p. 114.
12. Albert Bandura, *Social Learning Theory* (Englewood Cliffs, N.J.: Prentice-Hall, 1977); see pp. 39–50.
13. Ana Cristina Covarrubias, "Social Change and Television: The Experience of 'Come With Me,' " Unpublished report of the Mexican Institute of Communication Studies, Mexico City, 1978.
14. A variety of these issues will be discussed in Chapter 10.
15. Schramm, *Mass Media*, p. 123.
16. David L. Altheide, *Creating Reality: How TV News Distorts Events* (Beverly Hills, Calif.: Sage, 1976) p. 17.
17. Walter Lippmann, *Public Opinion* (New York: Macmillan, 1922). See chapter 1 "The World Outside and the Pictures in Our Heads," pp. 1–19.
18. Altheide, *Creating Reality*, pp. 20–21.
19. M. T. Malloy, "Journalistic Ethics: A Rainbow of Gray," *National Observer*, July 26, 1975.
20. Warren Breed, "Social Control in the News Room," *Social Forces*, 33 (May 1955), 326–335.
21. Daniel J. Boorstin, *The Image: A Guide to Pseudo-Events in America* (New York: Atheneum, 1961).
22. Jack M. McLeod, Lee B. Becker, and James E. Byrnes, "Another Look at the Agenda-Setting Function of the Press," *Communication Research*, 1 (April 1974), 137.

23. Donald L. Shaw and Maxwell E. McCombs, *The Emergence of American Political Issues: The Agenda-Setting Function of the Press* (St. Paul, Minn.: West, 1977).

24. For a discussion of the social categories perspective, see Melvin L. DeFleur and Sandra Ball-Rokeach, *Theories of Mass Communication,* 3rd ed. (New York: David McKay, 1975) pp. 206–208.

25. Shaw and McCombs, *American Political Issues,* pp. 40–42.

26. Ibid., p. 153.

27. Robert K. Merton and Robert A. Nisbet, *Contemporary Social Problems* (San Francisco: Harcourt, Brace and World, 1966).

28. John I. Kitsuse and Malcolm Spector, "Toward a Sociology of Social Problems: Social Conditions, Value Judgements, and Social Problems," *Social Problems,* 20 (Spring 1973), 407–419.

29. Robert L. Lineberry, *Government in America: People, Politics, and Policy* (Boston: Little, Brown, 1980) p. 300.

30. Howard S. Becker, *Social Problems: A Modern Approach* (New York: Wiley, 1966).

31. F. James Davis, "Crime News in Colorado Newspapers," *American Journal of Sociology,* 57 (July 1952), 325–330.

32. Bob Roshier, "The Selection of Crime News by the Press," in *The Manufacture of News,* ed. Stanley Cohen and Jack Young (Beverly Hills, Calif.: Sage, 1973), pp. 28–39.

33. Jeffery C. Hubbard, Melvin L. DeFleur, and Lois B. DeFleur, "Mass Media Influence on Public Conceptions of Social Problems," *Social Problems* 23 (October 1975), 23–34.

34. The term *culture* is being used here in an aesthetic sense rather than in the way anthropologists and sociologists use the term because in the literature on popular culture the term is used consistently to refer to art, music, drama, and other aesthetic products.

35. Michael Real, *Mass-Mediated Culture* (Englewood Cliffs, N.J.: Prentice-Hall, 1977) pp. 6–7.

36. Dwight MacDonald, "The Theory of Mass Culture," *Diogenes* (Summer 1953), 2.

37. Clement Greenberg, "Avant-Garde and Kitsch," *Partisan Review* (Fall 1939). Reprinted in Bernard Rosenbery and David Manning White, *Mass Culture: The Popular Arts in America* (New York: Free Press, 1957) p. 103.

38. MacDonald, "Mass Culture," p. 14.

39. For an interesting analysis of popular heroes, see Ray B. Browne, Marshall Fishwick, and Michael T. Marsden, *Heroes of Popular Culture* (Bowling Green, Ohio: Bowling Green University Popular Press, 1972).

40. Paul F. Lazarsfeld and Robert K. Merton, "Mass Communication, Popular Taste and Organized Social Action," in *Mass Communications,* ed. Wilbur Schramm (Urbana: University of Illinois Press, 1960) p. 497.

41. Herbert Gans, *Popular Culture and High Culture* (New York: Basic Books, 1974) pp. 69–94.

10 Indirect Effects of the Media

I must confess, Lone Ranger, that lately I have been having some uneasy feelings about you and what you did to me. You were the creation of a commercialized image, an image that made us both believe that reality was something other than what we experienced.

RICHARD QUINNEY, *The Insurgent Sociologist*, 1973

If one generalization stands out clearly from the previous two chapters, it is that we do not yet understand fully the effects of the mass media. Overall, the application of scientific techniques to the study of mass communication has been only modestly successful. One strategy for advancing our understanding is to look at the media in new ways. The media may have influences that cannot be readily detected by the research strategies of the past. For example, their effects may be less direct than we have imagined. Their influence both on individuals and on social and cultural processes may be long term, indirect, and subtle.

This chapter is concerned with the media's indirect effects. It presents two distinct theoretical frameworks within which to study the effects of long-term exposure to media content: modeling theory and meaning theory. These theories explain different kinds of media influence, but both assume that the media are unwitting teachers of adults and children, providing long-term, cumulative lessons that guide their audiences' overt behaviors and interpretations of reality. Each theory looks to the content of the media to explain their influence; so after examining the theories themselves we will look briefly at methods for analyzing the content of the media. Finally, we will review research that is based on each of these theories. But first, it will be helpful to illustrate the potential indirect influence of the media with a specific case.

Media Portrayals as Representations of Reality

In 1977 a group of scientists filed complaints with the Federal Communications Commission and other authorities against both NBC and the *Reader's Digest*. NBC had aired "quasi documentaries" dealing with subjects such as Bigfoot, a legendary hairy monster said to walk like a man and roam the forests of the Northwest; and the Bermuda Triangle, a supposedly dangerous area of the ocean near Florida, where it is claimed that many ships and aircraft have vanished under unnatural circumstances. The *Reader's Digest* had published an article entitled, "What Do We Really Know About Psychic Phenomena?" which implied that such events are real. The scientists complained that the broadcast misrepresented reality and that the article was based on hearsay evidence and anecdotal claims that were unacceptable as proof.[1]

There is little doubt that the mass media have catered in recent years to the public's continuing fascination with such themes as witchcraft, UFOs, huge animals, star wars, possession by demons, ancient astronauts, clairvoyance, communication with the dead, levitation, and similar phenomena. The media often present these topics in such a way that they seem to offer "proof" that the phenomena are real.

But what possible effects could result from such exciting presentations? Clearly, Bigfoot and the Bermuda Triangle are hokum, but they are exciting to hear about. The current situation is not new; the media have done this sort of thing since their beginnings. For example, in the 1830s, Benjamin Day hired a writer to increase the circulation of his newspaper, the *New York Sun*. The writer invented a professor in South Africa who was supposedly building the world's largest telescope. The instrument, reported the *Sun*, was so powerful it would be possible to see the surface of the moon as though it were only a hundred yards away. Periodic reports about progress aroused great reader interest. Finally the *Sun* reported that the work had been completed. The first accounts mentioned strange and exotic plants. Then the professor reported that he could see a human footprint! By this time a rival paper exposed the whole thing as a hoax. But what was the reaction of the public? Mainly they felt that even though the telescope was a fake it was a lot of fun to read about. And the hoax did increase the *Sun*'s circulation.

Scientists and other commentators have questioned whether the media behave responsibly in reporting such matters as the sighting of the legendary "Bigfoot," shown here in what one observer claimed was a photograph of the monster.

The complaining scientists today, however, do not see the present situation as a harmful spoof. Calling themselves the Committee for Scientific Investigation of Claims of the Paranormal, they maintain that by pouring a steady torrent of claims about paranormal phenomena into the marketplace the media are creating "cults of unreason." They say that many people cannot distinguish the "evidence" advanced in quasi documentaries from the evidence that scientists require before accepting a claim as true. The result, these scientists claim, is to lead people away from valid sources of truth and reliable procedures of assembling evidence toward a world of unreality.

The scientists may be right. Perhaps the media are influencing both what the public believes is real and what the public believes is sufficient evidence for a "fact." The media may have long-term, indirect, and subtle effects of this type. More intelligent people will probably not believe a lot of nonsense just because the *Reader's Digest* and NBC have discovered that it will sell soap. But it is not difficult to accept the idea that at least some people will be misled by "documentary" accounts of little green men, large hairy monsters, or even things that go bump in the night.

But what about the rest of the content of the media? Do they faithfully represent reality? In other words, is it possible that equally serious misrepresentations occur in the daily soap operas, commercials, comic books, prime-time television dramas, or even children's books about Dick and Jane? If the media do indeed misrepresent reality, what difference does it make? What kind of impact do portrayals of reality of any kind have on people's beliefs and behaviors?

Theories of Indirect Influence

We noted earlier that popular thinking about the influence of the media on individuals remains at the level of the magic bullet theory. Many people still assume that there must be immediate and direct linkages between specific content (such as portrayals of violence on television) and clearly identifiable forms of behavior (such as acts of youthful aggression). We have already pointed out that researchers have not been able to demonstrate such a one-to-one correspondence between the media and behavior.

The formulations of modern scholars differ from such older views in several ways. For one thing, contemporary theorists seldom assume that the media can motivate us to act as a result of a single exposure to some content. Instead, they assume that it is the *accumulated* effects of many similar exposures that will eventually increase the probability that a person will act or think in a given way. In addition, contemporary theorists believe that many variables or factors *intervene* between the media's content and responses to such stimulation. For example, we have seen in Chapter 8 that such factors as education can increase critical ability and can lead people to check the authenticity of a news program. Similarly, religion, rural versus urban residence, and type of occupation can influence voting preferences. Thus, these theorists try to explain outcomes or consequences that are *contingent on* the presence or absence of intervening circumstances or conditions.

Both of the formulations to be discussed in this chapter — modeling theory and meaning theory — assume that the influence of media content depends on intervening circumstances and is accumulative. They are far more complex than the old magic bullet theory. Each assumes that a variety of psychological, social, and cultural conditions are part of the sequences by which the content of the media produces effects.

Media Portrayals as Models for Behavior

Modeling theory derives from a larger formulation called *social learning theory*. This perspective is largely the work of the psychologist Albert Bandura and his associates.[2] It is a general theory that tries to explain the acquisition of behavior from almost any social source. In its application to mass communication, its main idea is that specific patterns of behavior portrayed by actors can serve as models for those who view them. More specifically, under certain conditions people will imitate these models and adopt their patterns of behavior.

Stages in the Adoption of Modeled Behavior. Acquisition of new responses from the media by modeling is said to involve three stages. First, the individual is *exposed* to a portrayal of a behavior that the viewer interprets as a problem-solving behavior. Second, the person attempts more or less successfully to *reproduce* the behavior in a relevant situation. Last, the behavior is *adopted* on a lasting basis as a means for coping with repetitions of the situation.

Much controversy has centered around the third stage, and it is the least understood. Under what conditions will a person imitate and then adopt a form of behavior modeled in the media? The first condition is suggested by the description of the first two stages: the individual must be confronted with a situation to which some response must be given but for which he or she lacks an appropriate previously learned response. Under these conditions the viewer may attempt to use a behavior that was modeled in the media. But if the pattern is to be adopted as the way in which the viewer *habitually* handles that type of situation, an additional condition must be met. Some sort of reward, or *reinforcement*, must occur in order to link the modeled behavior more firmly to the situation. Such reinforcement can come from several sources. For example, people may provide approval, or the individual may provide self-rewards for being able to handle the situation. Finally, if the viewer is to adopt the modeled behavior, he or she must *identify* with the model.

The concept of *identification* is slippery, but in general it refers to circumstances in which (1) the observer approves of the portrayal and (2) either wants to be like the model or already believes that he or she is like the model. In some cases we can add another possibility: that the viewer finds the model attractive, although different from self. Under these circumstances the observer is said to see the modeled behavior as a suitable guide to his or her own actions.

Thus the modeled behavior will be adopted if (1) an individual identifies with the model; (2) an appropriate situation rises in which the individual needs a guide for behavior; and (3) the imitated behavior is reinforced.

Identification with Media Characters. The most controversial concept in this formulation is that of identification, but there is little doubt that audiences identify with characters portrayed in the media. Sociologist Shearon Lowery has reviewed this issue and has concluded that audience identification is widespread, not only in the United States but in other countries as well.[3] Researchers Wilbur Schramm, Jack Lyle, and Edwin Parker found that children readily identify with characters, real or fictional, and that "there is no doubt that the child can more easily store up behaviors and beliefs which he has imaginatively shared with characters with which he can identify."[4]

The process of identification appears to be common enough among children. But what of adults? Lowery believes that adults may be more likely to identify with the characters in the daytime soap operas than with characters on other types of shows because the soap operas are broadcast every day. Thus viewers who follow them faithfully see the characters on a continuing basis, which makes identification truly accumulative. Each week the networks receive thousands of letters addressed to these fictional characters — evidence, says Lowery, of strong accumulative identification. For example, when Julie on the serial "Days of Our Lives" mulled over the problem of having an abortion, viewers who opposed abortion sent pictures of fetuses to the actress playing her part. Another actress, playing the part of a woman who had a mastectomy, was swamped with letters regarding the operation. "It's creepy," she said, "I almost feel I had the mastectomy."[5] CBS has eliminated some soap opera characters who were portrayed as very poor because the network was receiving many packages of food and clothing.[6]

Such bizarre confusion between fantasy and reality illustrates that the strong feelings for fictional characters built up by cumulative exposure can serve as a powerful basis for identification. When identification is coupled with the belief that the modeled actions have social utility, adoption of the behavior becomes more likely. The study of models presented in the media is thus important in its own right.

Media Content and Shared Meanings

Modeling theory explains the effect of the media in terms of linkages between stimuli — that is, media events — and responses, or individual behavior. In contrast, the meaning theory of mass communication sees behavior as a product of inner understandings; that is, it is a product of our personal meanings for the symbols, images, or events to which our culture gives shared interpretations.

Personal structures of meaning are shaped by many forces. Through participation in a variety of communication processes, our meanings are shaped, reshaped, and stabilized so that we can interact with others in predictable ways. These processes take place in our families, among peers, and in the community and society at large. Each of these processes has its own characteristics and special impact.[7] In modern society the mass media are one important part of these communication processes. Thus the content presented by the media plays an indirect part in forming our habits of perception and interpretation of the world around us. It is in this significant but *indirect* way that the media's portrayals of reality can ultimately influence our behavior. In this section we attempt to develop this idea and to set forth a *meaning theory of mass communication effects* in brief terms.

The media have played a major role in establishing America as a nation of consumers.

Media Constructions of Reality. In Chapter 1 we showed how the meaning for our every word and grammatical pattern can be understood as consisting of subjective experiences imprinted in neural cells in the brain; these imprinted experiences we called *traces.* One implication of this imprinting is that the language that we create and use together separates us in many ways from the real or objective world. That is, every word in our culture for which we have imprinted trace configurations (see Chapter 1) tends to separate us from the detailed and objective characteristics of the thing or situation for which the word stands because no word or other kind of symbol can capture *all* aspects of the objective reality to which it refers. But we become accustomed to the word and follow the shared rules concerning the subjective experiences that it is supposed to arouse in each of us. We use the word not only to communicate with each other but also to perceive and think about the reality for which it is a substitute.

In other words, *the word itself becomes far more important to us in many ways than the objective reality for which it is a substitute.* In fact, most of us have never had any firsthand contact with the realities to which the majority of the words in our language refer. For example, only a few of us have ever put on scuba gear and dived to a tropical coral reef. Yet we feel that we have a reasonably good understanding of what "scuba diving" would be like. We have this feeling because we have communicated about coral reefs and scuba diving with others or have seen representations of them on television or in the movies. The fact is, though, it is to these *representations* in words or in media portrayals that we respond rather than to the objective realities of an actual coral reef. In a similar way we share conventions of meaning about such things as army life, ancient Greece, marriage, physicians, and homosexuals. We "know" what these are because we participate in the process of communication, even though we may never have served in the army, visited Greece, been married, gone to medical school, or been a homosexual.

Thus the meaning configurations we share for symbols of all kinds constitute the world to which we adjust. We cannot relate accurately to the objective world of reality itself because our access to that world is limited. We create both our cultural and private worlds of meaning through communication with others. It is through these shared representations that we perceive, think, and shape our responses to what Walter Lippmann called the "world outside."

But how are these principles related to the mass media? The obvious answer is that the process of mass communication is an important part of the way in which we collectively shape our social constructions of reality.

The Meaning Functions of Media Portrayals. The term *portrayal* refers to the representation through symbols, images, or actions of some aspect of social life or some other event or situation to which labels and meaning can be attached by shared rules. For example, television often shows women doing domestic chores — such as cleaning, cooking, and raising children — or acting in superficial ways — such as gushing over detergents, mouthwash, or underarm deodorants. Such portrayals can provide meanings for the somewhat abstract concepts of woman or the female role. A television commercial for Arrid deodorant that was shown in the early 1970s provides another example. A burly, hairy, and very dirty Mexican bandit was about to spray his armpits with Arrid when a voice in the background proclaimed, "If it can help *him*, think of what it can do for you!" The portrayal implied, of course, that Mexicans (the label) are the dirtiest, and presumably smelliest, people imaginable (the meaning). Needless to say, the commercial offended many people, and it was hastily withdrawn.

Through such portrayals, the media can modify the relationship between a symbol and a set of trace patterns. In other words, the media can shape new meanings for people exposed to their content and establish similar meanings among large audiences. The media may not intend to do this, any more than we intend to be influenced by them when we enjoy their content.

The influence that the media have on our meanings may be simple or complex. For example, by viewing the daily soap operas, viewers unaccustomed to using alcohol can learn that there is a drink called a Brandy Alexander and that it is appropriate to order and drink it in a cocktail lounge when having a discussion with a friend. At a more complex level, viewers can learn from news reports that there are substances called *carcinogens* in foods and other products that cause cancer. They can also learn such terms as *biodegradable, ecological,* and *geothermal* that were once highly technical words known only to people in specialized fields of science. Today, such words arouse more or less parallel configurations of traces in the memories of millions of television viewers.

There are at least four ways in which media portrayals can play a part in shaping the process whereby we achieve social constructions of reality. These can be referred to as *establishment, extension, substitution,* and *stabilization.* Each term refers to a relationship between a symbol and the imprinted subjective experiences of meaning to which that symbol refers.

Through exposure to media portrayals of a given aspect of reality, new individuals are brought into the cultural conventions (rules) regarding a language symbol. That is, people acquire meanings for symbols that they were not familiar with earlier (such as carcinogens). We refer to this as the *establishment* function of such portrayals. This idea was discussed as the "expansion" function of the press by Charles Horton Cooley shortly after the turn of the century.[8] By establishing meanings, the media not only expand the number of people who share a meaning for a particular symbol but also expand the understandings of each person who shares the experience.

People can also learn additional meanings for words or other symbols with which they are already familiar. For example, a child accustomed to his or her own friendly dog can learn from media portrayals that dogs can also be dangerous. Thus the media's portrayals can *extend* the meanings of symbols.

Media portrayals can also displace existing meanings. This process can be called *substitution*. For example, in recent years the news media and the film industry have been giving increasing attention to the problems of Vietnam veterans. In the spring of 1979 CBS ran a three-part series on the evening news showing the plight of several veterans who were having problems adjusting to postwar civilian life. Some were in prison for common crimes, several were psychiatric cases, and one had captured several hostages in a bank and shot it out with the police. Recent Hollywood films have also portrayed Vietnam veterans who were in the throes of complex psychological difficulties. The result has been to provide the public with alternative meanings for the term *Vietnam veteran*. Instead of being defined as courageous young people who served their country well in a difficult time, they are being defined as a bunch of potential psychos who would probably be dangerous as prospective employees, husbands, friends, and so on.

The media can also reinforce established meanings. In this case, individuals attending to a medium already share a more or less similar set of meanings for symbols in the portrayal. By repeatedly showing the accepted meanings for these symbols, the media more firmly establish the conventions regarding their interpretation. This can be called the *stabilization* function of media portrayals. For example, the public now holds a number of beliefs about the nature of juvenile delinquents. Generally, they are thought to be dangerous and aggressive. Conventions concerning the expressions we use to refer to such delinquents — "punk," "hood," and so on — link these symbols to inner experiences of potential danger and apprehension. When the media show delinquent youths engaged in vandalism, muggings, theft, and other deviant acts, they reinforce and stabilize these conventions.

Media portrayals that establish, extend, substitute, or stabilize our meanings are important at two closely related levels. At the personal level, inner meanings and the symbols we use to activate them govern our perception, understanding, and response to the physical and social world. At the collective or cultural level, changes in meaning systems are at the heart of social and cultural change.

Despite their importance, the effects of changes in meanings, and their influence on behavior, are not detected easily by the methods that have characterized communications research for decades. The media's influence on our subjective meanings is undoubtedly a long-term and accumulative process. Thus, the link between media portrayals that establish, extend, substitute, or stabilize our symbolic constructions of reality and the specific actions that we take in coping with our external world are undoubtedly very indirect.

Analyzing Media Content

Both meaning theory and modeling theory indicate that it is important to study the *content* of media portrayals with great care. We may not be able to show direct one-to-one correspondences between the components of their content and the details of overt behavior, but the representations of reality in the modern print, film, and broadcast media are an important source from which models for behavior are provided and from which individual meaning structures are formed. They are also a source from which shared cultural definitions are established and maintained.

In other words, *portrayals are the lessons the media offer us.* Unwittingly, they teach us: (1) what society is like; (2) how we should behave toward each other; (3) what others expect of us; (4) what the consequences of an action can be; (5) how we should think about the physical and social world around us; and (6) how we should evaluate ourselves. The lessons may be confused, contradictory, and distorted. Nevertheless, they cannot be ignored. For these reasons, understanding the lessons that the media provide can best be based on *systematic content analyses* of their presentations. By studying the portrayals of the physical and social world in print, film, or broadcasts, we can assess the exact manner in which they provide models for behavior or play a part in the social construction of reality.

Technically, *content analysis* refers to a range of procedures and techniques for assessing what is presented in any form of communication. These procedures may be quantitative, qualitative, or a combination of both. The analyses are usually based on some defined unit or set of units. A *unit* can be almost any attribute of a printed account, a film, or a broadcast message that can be carefully defined and assessed. The units can be specific words, qualitative themes, types of action, and so on. Usually units are assessed by counting the number present in a message. Researchers assess how often such units appear in the content per given amounts of space or time.

Content analyses of printed material often use units such as the number of column inches of print devoted to a particular theme or idea. Film and television content is more difficult to analyze. The frequency with which a topic occurs can be a convenient unit of analysis. Also, the amount of time devoted to a topic or theme is often used. For example, in a news broadcast one might determine the relative amount of time given to local versus national or international events.

In studying television, the portrayal is another way of analyzing the content. DeFleur's study of the world of work as portrayed on television illustrates this approach.[9] The unit was the portrayal of an actor shown carrying on the duties of a recognizable job or occupation for a period of at least one minute. By this means DeFleur found that in the mid-1960s television concentrated heavily on professional and managerial occupations and largely ignored blue-collar work. Most of the people shown working were involved with either the criminal justice system or the medical profession. In reality, only a small part of the labor force worked in those occupations.

Systematic content analyses reveal concentrations and trends that are not apparent to audience members. For example, some years ago the biographies of popular heroes in *Colliers* and the *Saturday Evening Post* from 1900 to 1940 were subjected to an elaborate content analysis.[10] It was discovered that the kinds of people presented as heroes changed dramatically during this period. Early in the century the magazines concentrated on "idols of production" — leaders in business, the professions, and political life. In later decades attention shifted to "idols of consumption." These were mainly singers, actors, and other representatives of the popular arts. Many other trends were discovered that reflected changes in both public interest and editorial policy.

But the major point for our purposes is that it was only through this careful and systematic analysis that these trends could have been accurately described. Thus content analyses provide clear and unbiased descriptions of what is contained in communications.[11]

Content analyses have many important uses, but there are a number of cautions to observe in interpreting them. First, one cannot assume that readers, listeners, or viewers respond to any particular element of content in a direct way. Second, it cannot be assumed that what one finds is there because the communicator deliberately intended it to be there to stimulate some thought or action. For example, although DeFleur found that work portrayals on television concentrated on professional and managerial jobs, it would be silly to assume that the networks were trying at the time to convince viewers that those jobs were more important. In some cases, the intent of the communicator may be obvious (for example, in advertising, information campaigns, or political propaganda); but, in most cases, intent cannot be inferred from the content analysis. Content analyses are important, however, in helping us to understand both the *models* for behavior and the meanings providing social constructions of reality that a medium presents.

Research on Media Models

Modeling theory and meaning theory provide a background for understanding the significance of certain types of content analyses. In this section we summarize two studies done within the perspective of modeling theory. Recall that this approach implies that there are linkages between specific elements of media content and particular forms of behavior. The first study focuses on sex-role models that presumably influence children's self-concepts. The second study focuses on the lessons about drinking behavior that are presented to viewers of soap operas. These two studies are important not only because they focus on socially significant topics but also because they examine models that millions of Americans confront each day.

Sex-Role Models

Learning to be a male or female is one of the most important aspects of early childhood. Becoming either masculine or feminine is not simply a product of one's biological sex. Masculinity and femininity are behavior patterns and self-concepts that must be learned from contact with people. There have been many cases in which a baby's sex has been misclassified at birth. When the error is corrected later, reclassified people must undergo a

Sex-role stereotyping — dainty little girls in frilly dresses, sturdy little boys playing with toy trucks — has often been reinforced by such media as children's books and television programs. A growing number of publishers, producers, and individuals are aware of the problem and are taking steps to correct it.

very difficult learning process in order to match their behavior and psychology to their biological sex.[12]

But how do people learn to be masculine or feminine? For generations of Americans this learning began when the infant boy was placed on a blue blanket and the infant girl on a pink blanket. In other words, until very recent times, society responded very differently to the two sexes even at birth. From the start of a child's life, society demanded different behavior from girls and boys, and it trained them to think differently about themselves. Girls were given dolls, little tea sets, miniature ranges, washing machines, and mops to play with. They were taught to be clean, pretty, and demure. Boys were given toy trucks, cowboy hats, and little machine guns. They were taught to be tough and active. Thus, by the time the child was ready for kindergarten, he or she was very aware of his or her sex role. Each learned to behave in ways that society deemed appropriate; and each developed a self-concept as a male or female. Although the treatment of the sexes has been changing, many of these traditional patterns remain.

The mass media have long offered a rich set of role models to help children learn their sex roles. These models range from the fantasies of Saturday morning cartoons to the deliberate lessons of *Sesame Street*. Models of many kinds show the child what little girls and little boys are made of. In spite of the effects of the women's movement, by the time they are four years old, most children can explain that the major activity of women in America is housekeeping and that the primary expectation of males is to provide for their families.

Depictions of Children in Picture Books. How the media helped children achieve these definitions in the recent past is illustrated by a content analysis of picture books for preschool children by Lenore Weitzman and her associates. They critically examined several hundred books published between 1938 and the early 1970s but concentrated on prize-winning books published from 1965 to 1970. (Many of today's college students used some of these picture books when they were preschool children.) The study's authors maintained that picture books have long been important in the lives of preschool children. They are widely used, and parents often read the stories to the children over and over, thereby reinforcing the values and interpretations that are portrayed.

> Picture books play an important role . . . because they are a vehicle for the presentation of societal values to the young child. Through books, children learn about the world outside of their immediate environment; they learn about what other boys and girls do, say, and feel; they learn about what is right and wrong; and they learn what is expected of children of their age. In addition, books provide children with role models — images of what they can and should be like when they grow up.[13]

Children's books that have received prestigious awards are especially important. There are several major prizes given in the industry, and the books that receive them are widely sold. Another important category are the mass-circulation books (for example, the Little Golden Books) that are sold cheaply in supermarket chains and discount houses. Sales of these books can exceed 3 million per year. Thus the content analysis focused on books to which American children are widely exposed.

The analysis was largely qualitative. The authors gave some numerical data, but they emphasized the qualitative way in which males and females were shown and described in the pictures and stories. One of the more significant quantitative findings was that relatively few females appeared in the books at all. Females make up more than half of the American population, but they were all but invisible in the children's books. For example, of the eighteen books that had won or been nominated for the Caldecott Prize during the five-year period, there were 261 pictures of males. There were only twenty-three of females. Even the animals shown in the pictures were overwhelmingly male, by a ratio of ninety to one.

In the few pictures that did show female children, they were portrayed as *passive* rather than active. Boys were pictured and described as active, vigorous, and even boisterous. Most of the girls were shown sitting quietly in the corner or merely looking on. The few girls shown in some sort of activity were performing domestic chores. They were helping mother cook, sew, sweep, or feed babies. Boys, on the other hand, were pictured mowing lawns, marching in parades, hammering wood, playing baseball, and so on. Even the clothing shown in the books suggested that females have a passive-dependent role. Girls were usually shown in frilly long dresses, with ribbons in their pretty and neatly arranged hair; boys usually wore clothes suitable for action and adventure.

Adult Role Models in Picture Books. Adults also provide role models for children. As Weitzman and her associates noted:

> By observing adult men and women, boys and girls learn what will be expected of them when they grow older. They are likely to identify with adults of the same sex, and desire to be like them. Thus, role models not only present children with future images of themselves but they also influence a child's aspirations and goals.[14]

The adult models in the picture books followed very traditional lines: women were passive; men were active. Women performed domestic chores; men were the breadwinners. By these portrayals the books departed from reality. At the time of the study, about half of the women in the United States were in the labor force, and that fraction has continued to grow. The picture books provided no hint of this fact. In the sample of Caldecott books, for example, not one woman had a job or profession. The books stressed that a woman's highest aspiration is to be a mother. Thus, whereas "mommies" were shown wearing aprons and doing the housework, children were instructed that

Daddies drive the trucks and cars,
The buses, boats and trains,
Daddies build the roads and bridges,
Houses, stores and planes,
Daddies work in factories and
Daddies make things grow,
Daddies work to figure out
The things we do not know.[15]

In general, then, the preschool children's books studied gave clear and forceful role models for both children and adults. Boys were instructed that they were expected to train for a job or profession for theirs would be the breadwinner's task. With few exceptions, girls were given a different set of messages: they were expected to be clean, pretty, and passive. Their main aspiration would be to a life of cooking, cleaning, and raising babies.

Thus a careful content analysis of children's picture books revealed that the models placed before the very young of a particular generation concerning what boys and girls should be like were not appropriate for the world into which they would grow. In a society in which the division of labor in the family followed traditional lines, these models would have prepared children for their activities as adults. In today's America, they may have done both sexes a disservice by creating false expectations that many of the current generation of young adults will have to modify.[16]

Models in the Soap Operas

The daytime serial has been part of American popular culture for about fifty years. The first soap opera was broadcast sometime during the late 1920s or the very early 1930s on radio. In 1947 the first televised soap opera appeared, "A Woman to Remember." It failed for lack of viewers. By 1960, however, the last episode of the final radio soap opera was broadcast, and the soaps moved totally to television.

At first the television soap operas were almost identical to their radio forebears. The plots, characters, problems, and themes were the same ones that radio listeners had heard for years. In some ways, contemporary soap operas are like the early ones. That is, they are played out against a white, middle-class background, and they emphasize both personal and social problems. In recent years, however, the soap operas have become "liberated." They now deal with themes that were taboo in earlier decades — rape, abortion, venereal disease, and incest, to mention only a few of the problems faced by the characters.[17]

The soap operas present many kinds of models — occupational,

Soap opera characters evoke sometimes strong responses and imitative behaviors from viewers who identify with the lives and stories they see in these serial dramas. Some viewers have carried this identity so far as to write letters to a soap opera character, giving or asking advice. This typical scene is from "As the World Turns."

sexual, and romantic, among others. They also present such behaviors as the use of alcohol. A systematic review of a research project dealing with the modeling of alcohol use can help reveal the nature and utility of modeling theory.

Modeling Influences on the Use of Alcohol. Do people actually imitate others in their use of alcohol? The answer seems to be yes. There is reasonably clear evidence that a person's consumption of alcohol can be increased or decreased by modeling. In several kinds of controlled studies in which confederates were used to influence the subjects, people increased their drinking in the presence of models who drank heavily. Similar results have been obtained in a real-life tavern, a simulated tavern, and many laboratory settings. Likewise the drinking rate of heavy consumers have been reduced by the presence of models who drank lightly.[18]

But the important question for our purposes is whether the mass media provide such models and, if so, what they are like. What patterns are shown that could influence the drinking behavior of the many millions of viewers? One study cannot answer this question in terms of *all* media content. For this reason Shearon Lowery singled out the soap opera for study. Her content analysis focused on the nature of models for the use of alcohol that are presented by the daytime soap operas.[19]

Drinking as Depicted in Soap Operas. Lowery's content analysis tried to ascertain: (1) the frequency with which alcohol use was shown on the soap operas, and (2) the qualitative patterns depicted for its use. That is, how much alcohol was consumed, for what purpose, under what circumstances, and with what portrayed effect? To answer these questions, specially trained analysts systematically studied fourteen soap operas, encompassing 172 hours of programming. Accounts were prepared of each scene in which alcohol was used, including detailed information about the plot, characters, social relationships, and other relevant factors.

During the 1,801 scenes viewed, there were 520 incidents involving alcohol use, or about three incidents for each hour of programming. Clearly, the soap operas frequently model the use of alcohol. But more important than the numbers are the qualitative patterns that were modeled. The researcher classified the drinking incidents into three broad categories: social facilitation, crisis management, and escaping reality. Table 10.1 lists the frequency of each category.

Social facilitation is a pattern in which alcohol is served and consumed as a more or less incidental part of the ongoing social interaction. It is a background factor, not a focus of attention. In such portrayals people seldom became intoxicated, and alcohol contributed only incidentally to the action. This was the largest category of drinking shown in the soap operas, with 243 portrayals, or 46.7 percent of the incidents.

Within the social facilitation category, all the portrayals could be classified into two subcategories: ritualistic and tension-control drinking. Over half of the social facilitation drinking was *ritualistic*. This subcategory includes such action as serving cocktails as part of entertaining at home. In *tension-control* drinking the models were shown using alcohol to help deal with a problem. For example, when a couple needed to discuss a proposed divorce, having drinks was shown as making the interaction simpler. Still, drinking was a background factor, not the main focus of the action.

Crisis management accounted for 22.9 percent of the drinking incidents. Here alcohol was portrayed as a temporary measure to aid in the immediate management of a crisis. The crisis in some cases was a distressing physical experience, such as an auto accident or a narrow escape. The idea that "a drink will help" was

Table 10.1 Drinking Patterns Portrayed in the Daytime Television Serial

Drinking pattern	Frequency	Percentage
Social facilitation	243	46.7
Ritualistic drinking	(157)	——
Tension control	(86)	——
Crisis management	119	22.9
Escaping reality	158	30.4
Total	520	100.0

Source: Shearon A. Lowery, "Soap and Booze in the Afternoon: An Analysis of the Portrayals of Alcohol Use in the Daytime Serial," Ph.D. diss., Washington State University, 1979, p. 95.

initiated sometimes by the individual suffering the trauma, sometimes by friends, relatives, or others. In some cases it was not even verbalized. The model simply poured a stiff drink on hearing the bad news. Such actions led to intoxication in some cases, but this was by no means the rule. In any event, the use of alcohol was definitely shown as a means for coping with sudden problems on a temporary basis.

The pattern termed *escaping reality* involved 30.4 percent of the total. In these incidents the problems were chronic rather than sudden or temporary, and alcohol was used as a continuing means of dealing with a problem too difficult to face. Examples of these problems included death of a loved one, interpersonal conflicts, financial difficulties, broken romances, and loss of status. For the most part, the characters shown were identified as alcoholics, with the implication that they had been driven to drink by ill fate, ill fortune, or personal weakness.

Clearly, the soap operas suggest that drinking alcohol is a normal part of life and that there is no question that it is acceptable. In over 70 percent of the cases in which models used alcohol, they suffered no negative consequences. Even when alcohol was used to escape reality, it was not always clear that the habitual drunk suffered very much. In a few cases the alcoholic lost a wife or lover, or even a job. But the alcoholics of soapland seemed to be much easier to rehabilitate than those in real life. Usually, when the problem that touched off the drinking was resolved, the addiction ended. Needless to say, this view departs considerably from reality.

We cannot estimate the degree to which this modeling will

stimulate behavior on the part of viewers — if it stimulates behavior at all. Inferences from content analyses to behavior are treacherous. At the same time, we have seen that there is considerable research evidence that models in real life can and do influence people's drinking behavior. Lowery's study clearly shows that the daytime soap operas present a considerable number and variety of portrayals of the use of alcohol. These episodes are followed daily by millions of women, a category among whom alcoholism is on the rise. Whether the televised portrayal of drinking is one of the causes of this increase has not yet been established.

Both the study of preschool children's picture books and the study of soap operas are excellent examples of content analyses within the tradition of modeling theory. They show very clearly the kinds of lessons that are available for audiences. Other kinds of research can determine the degree to which the models have stimulated similar behavior among the people exposed to the communications. Whether there are point-by-point correspondences between the activities portrayed by the models and behavior in real life is an open question. The main point, however, is that without such systematic content analyses the "hidden curriculum" contained in mass communication could not be adequately understood.

Research on Meaning Theory

The assumptions of meaning theory differ sharply from those of modeling theory. Recall that meaning theory assumes that the media play an important part in shaping social constructions of reality in modern society by shaping the trace configurations of individuals, the meanings of specific language symbols. Thus they establish, extend, substitute, and stabilize both personal and cultural meanings through their portrayals of reality. How meaning is influenced by the media could be studied in many contexts. To understand better the implications of meaning theory, we turn to a study of how the mentally ill are portrayed on evening television.[20] There is no assumption that under certain conditions people will imitate the behavior of the mentally ill as portrayed in these programs. The analysis is intended to illustrate some of the ways that *meaning* is linked to particular symbols by the portrayal of overt action in mass communication. It should be kept in mind, however, that the discussion is intended to show how meaning theory helps us understand a particular set of behaviors in society (rejection of the mentally ill) as those behaviors are influenced by the content of mass communication.

Traditional Meanings of Insanity

In order to understand the general pattern of social rejection of the mentally ill, we need to note the long history of stigmatizing those classified as "mad." Media portrayals that show mentally ill people as dangerous are extending into modern times the stigmas related to madness that have come down to us through the ages.

The Ship of Fools. In medieval times, attitudes toward what we would now call the "mentally ill" were far more benign than they are today. But during the Renaissance, a new practice developed that was to have a special impact on the definition of the mentally ill in Western society. The insane were often confined on ships that moved from place to place, exhibiting the "crazies" to people who would pay a small price:

> "Ships of Fools" crisscrossed the seas and canals of Europe with their comic and pathetic cargo of souls. Some of them found pleasure and even a cure in the changing surroundings, in the isolation of being cast off, while others withdrew further, became worse, or died alone and away from their families. The cities and villages which had thus rid themselves of their crazed and crazy, could now take pleasure in watching the exciting sideshow when a ship full of foreign lunatics would dock at their harbors.[21]

By such procedures the meaning of madness began to be stabilized in Europe. It became a repulsive state — a curse to be concealed, a condition to be punished and dreaded.

As time went on, slow changes took place. A few humanitarians agitated for better treatment of the insane. Toward the end of the nineteenth century, the belief spread that they should be placed in "hospitals" rather than dungeons. Late in the century, psychoanalysis began to provide a view of insanity as a "sickness" rather than as a curse, possession by demons, or inherited bad blood. Early in this century, this *medical model* was widely accepted by professionals. Thus the deranged were seen as "ill," capable of being cured by treatment, and able to return eventually to normal social roles. Unfortunately, public attitudes have lagged far behind these developments in the medical profession.

Although the meanings associated with madness are greatly different today from what they were in earlier times, many elements of the older beliefs persist. Not all segments of the public believe that the mentally ill can be cured or that after treatment they are "just like everybody else." Thus those who have been mentally

The eighteenth-century physician Pinel is shown releasing insane inmates from their manacles. The mentally ill — called "lunatics" in Pinel's time — have generally been portrayed with fear and misunderstanding by the media.

ill suffer a considerable stigma along with those who are still afflicted. Public attitudes and beliefs about the mentally ill continue to focus on the likelihood that they will exhibit bizarre and unpredictable behavior and above all that they are dangerous. In reality, the mentally ill as a whole are no more dangerous than citizens in general, in spite of the few who make headlines.

How the Stigma Is Reinforced Today. What forces reinforce the idea that mentally ill people are dangerous? What are the modern counterparts of the "ship of fools" that continue to teach us that the mentally ill are mindless lunatics, only a hair's breadth away from serious forms of deviant and dangerous behavior?

One important factor is the way the news media report on mentally ill killers. Even though they are very rare, the press gives them great attention. The tradition was established as early as the 1880s, when the relatively new mass newspapers gave great attention to Jack the Ripper. The public was both fascinated and horrified, but, above all, the reports sold newspapers. In fact, we are

THE NEMESIS OF NEGLECT.

"THERE FLOATS A PHANTOM ON THE SLUM'S FOUL AIR,
SHAPING, TO EYES WHICH HAVE THE GIFT OF SEEING,
INTO THE SPECTRE OF THAT LOATHLY LAIR,
FACE IT—FOR VAIN IS FLEEING!
RED-HANDED, RUTHLESS, FURTIVE, UNERECT,
'TIS MURDEROUS CRIME—THE NEMESIS OF NEGLECT!"

Society's tendency to link mental illness with criminal activity has a long history. This cartoon appeared in a London newspaper in 1888, at the height of public alarm over the legendary murderer "Jack the Ripper."

Indirect Effects of the Media   377

NEW YORK POST
METRO
TODAY'S RACING
MONDAY, AUGUST 1, 1977   25 CENTS   Vol. 176, No. 215   © 1977 The New York Post Corporation   DAILY PAID CIRCULATION 2D QUARTER 1977   609,390

'NO ONE IS SAFE' FROM SON OF SAM

Killer outfoxes cops

1: MOVES OUTSIDE QUEENS
2: STRIKES AT SHORT HAIR
3: STRIKES AT BLONDE HAIR
4: SPOTTED BY FEW WITNESSES

Dowd: City in danger
12 suspects ruled out
Cops at square one

The New York Post *used sensational headlines to warn the public against "Son of Sam," another alleged killer who was said to be insane.*

still interested in the case a century later. Cases like the Boston Strangler, Charles Manson, Richard Speck, the Son of Sam, and John Gacy receive intense attention from the modern media. This handful of men seems to represent, for many people, about all one needs to know about the mentally ill.

Yet all the blame for the stigma attached to the mentally ill cannot be placed on journalists. Our daily use of language also plays a part. Colloquial expressions describe irrational behavior as "nuts," "kooky," "kinky," "freaky," "wacky," "looney," and so on. In addition, our common vocabulary for daily behavior that has nothing to do with mental illness helps reinforce the negative meanings associated with insanity. We speak of running "like crazy," being "absolutely nuts" about a new dress, "mad" about a new boyfriend, "insanely jealous" about a friend's new car. Many people judge as "sick" any behavior of which they do not approve. The list could go on and on. The point is that *anything* that departs from the normal — anything that is alien, irregular, or merely inexplicable — is described in the terms that we use for the mentally ill. Thus, by repeatedly emphasizing the connection between the symbols for mental illness and the bizarre, we stabilize our meanings for madness.

But the mass media also play a part in their presentations of entertainment in popular culture. Books, movies, the comics, and especially television frequently portray the mentally ill in very negative ways. Their stories and depictions are meant to amuse us, but unwittingly they are influencing our social constructions of reality.

Television's Portrayal of the Mentally Ill

To understand more fully precisely how the mentally ill are portrayed on evening television drama and to show how meaning theory aids us in understanding the implications of such portrayals, we will review a recent study which focused on the portrayal of the mentally ill in all crime-adventure dramas broadcast by the major networks in a Southwestern city during four months of 1978. A pilot study had established that few other types of television programs had content related to mental illness. A few news stories were found, and there had been a recent documentary and a movie (*One Flew Over the Cuckoo's Nest*) dealing sympathetically with mental illness. But the overwhelming concentration of depictions of mental illness were found in the evening police and detective shows. For this reason, the study focused on the following programs: "Adam 12," "Baretta," "Barnaby Jones," "Charlie's Angels," "Hawaii Five-O," "Kojak," "Police Story," "Police Woman," "Quincy," "Richie Brockleman," "Rockford Files," "Sam," and "Starsky and Hutch."

Overall seventy-five dramas were analyzed in which official or unofficial representatives of law and order took action against wrongdoers or forces for evil. Thirty-one of these programs (41 percent) had content in which persons portrayed as disturbed openly committed serious, deviant acts. A total of thirty-four such portrayals were identified and analyzed. (Several programs had more than one portrayal.) Twenty-one programs depicted serious deviance but not mental illness. These programs served as a kind of control. The number and quality of negative labels used to describe their villains were carefully analyzed in order to see what level of dangerousness was implied for deviants who were

Table 10.2 Television's Labels for the Mentally Ill

Word or phrase	Frequency	Word or phrase	Frequency
Crazy	25	Lunatic	1
Sick (mentally) or sickie	10	Loony	1
		Strange bird	1
Nut or homicidal nut	9	Crippled mentally	1
Creep or creepy	7	Modern-day Franken-stein	1
Needs help (psychiatric)	7	Jekyll and Hyde	1
Weird or weirdo	6	Looking at a full moon	1
Maniac	5	Nuttier than a pecan pie	1
Aggression (displaced, etc.)	4	Should be in a cage	1
Psycho	4	Needs her shrink	1
Psychotic	3	Fugitive from mental hospital	1
Wacko or el wacko	3	Escaped from hospital for mentally insane	1
Disturbed	2	Released from psychiatric institution	1
Freak or dumbbell freak	2		
Insane	2	Crashed out of local funny farm	1
Paranoid	2	Was pushed out of hospital six months too soon	1
Psychopath or psychopathic	2		
Schizophrenia	2	Bomb waiting to explode	1
Screwball or screwy	2		
Animal	1	Delusions (person with)	1
Going bananas	1		
Conversion symptoms	1		
Demented	1		
Flipped out	1		

not mentally ill. Thus the researchers could see if mentally ill villains were portrayed in a more negative way than just plain crooks. As Table 10.2 shows, this was clearly the case.

One or more trained monitors viewed each program and made several kinds of records. These were (1) a lengthy audio-recording of the details of the plot, the characters, and so on; (2) detailed descriptions of the way in which the mentally ill were shown; and (3) a complete list of labels, words, and phrases used to describe or communicate about the mentally ill. For the comparison or control programs a similar procedure was followed. In addition the programs were studied as whole plots so that the meanings of actions, labels, and incidents could be interpreted within their context.

To assess the level of dangerousness implied by each portrayal of wrongdoing, a somewhat subjective scale was devised. That is, for each overt depiction of a mentally ill person, the behavior shown was rated as: (0) "not at all dangerous," (1) "slightly dangerous," (2) "moderately dangerous," or (3) "very dangerous." Although such ratings are not precise, they allowed numerical comparisons of the actions of the mentally ill with the behavior of the non–mentally ill villains.

The programs were classified into several categories according to how mental illness was depicted or described. For example, some of the programs clearly identified people *verbally* as "crazy," "sick," "psycho," "nuts," and so on, as they were shown carrying out deviant acts. A second category of programs used only *nonverbal cues* to indicate that a character shown in deviant activity was "nuts." These cues included such actions as inappropriate laughter interrupted by screaming, unusual facial expressions, close-ups of strange-looking eyes, fixed grins, odd twitching of facial muscles, or other forceful hints to the audience that the character was not normal. Still other programs made extensive use of the *vocabulary* of madness but did not show mentally ill people acting in deviant ways.

Overwhelmingly, these portrayals were definitely *not* sympathetic. The mentally ill were very clearly being used by the writers as "the bad guys." They were murderers, rapists, slashers, snipers, and bombers. In other words, the cues, either verbal or nonverbal, that identified the actors as mentally ill were linked to activities that were extremely harmful to others. Moreover, by comparison with the (presumably sane) regular crooks, the mentally ill were shown as more dangerous. On the scale described, the mean level of dangerousness for the thirty-four portrayals of mentally ill offenders was 2.56. This average is midway between "very dangerous" and "moderately dangerous." For non–mentally ill crooks, the average rating was only 1.54, halfway between slightly and moderately dangerous. These portrayals were vivid and powerful lessons that the meaning of mental illness includes elements of severe danger to others.

The mentally ill offenders were not only shown to be dangerous but also portrayed in ways calculated to arouse fear in the audience. While the mentally ill were shown in deviant acts extremely harmful to others, they grimaced strangely, had glassy eyes, or giggled incongruously. Some laughed strangely and sobbed or cried. Others mumbled incoherently or screamed irrationally. Another bared his teeth and snarled as he jumped on his victims to suck blood from their jugular veins. Still another was shown squeezing raw meat through his fingers and rubbing it on his gun as he prepared to kill his next victim. These scenes were often accompanied by unusual music to enhance the effect. In some shows actions were timed to startle the audience. Such portrayals provide far more intense lessons about the meaning of madness than were ever possible by merely exhibiting the "loonies" on the ship of fools.

In addition to showing the overt behavior of the mentally ill in very negative terms, prime-time television makes abundant use of the popular vocabulary of madness. This goes beyond labeling characteristics of the mentally ill in action. Any kind of behavior that was unusual, eccentric, or merely difficult to explain with the facts at hand was likely to be categorized by the actors as that of "kooks," "chuckleheads," "fruitcakes," "cuckoo-birds," and so forth. More technical terms for neurotic or psychotic conditions, such as *schizophrenic* and *paranoid*, were used far less frequently.

The content analysis revealed many additional nuances and connotations concerning the meaning of insanity, but the essential conclusions are that scriptwriters for crime-adventure shows in prime time use the mentally ill to represent evil, against which the forces for law and order fight and win to protect society. Since the heroes and heroines of popular culture are virtually invincible, the mentally ill never get away with their foul deeds. They are hauled off night after night to "hospitals for the criminally insane," where they will presumably remain for life. The audience breathes a sigh of relief; the ratings go up; products are sold; actors and writers make money; the networks prosper; and stockholders smile. As a byproduct, millions of people who are or once were mentally ill suffer discrimination and rejection as we continue to reinforce the trace configurations that are the basis of our ancient stereotypes. Thus the media serve as a modern ship of fools.

Although these data do not forever "prove" that television causes people to fear or reject the mentally ill, they clearly show the linkage between television's vocabulary for mental illness and depictions of deviant actions that are extremely harmful to others. By offering such portrayals repeatedly, night after night, the medium is probably playing an important role in the long-term shaping of the meanings we associate with mental illness. We can hypothesize with some conviction that television is *establishing* new stigmatizing meanings among some categories of people (such as children who know little about mental illness), *extending* such meanings to include more implications of danger for many viewers, *substituting* new meanings for members of the audience who may entertain more benign interpretations, and certainly *stabilizing* the meanings of madness that have come down to us from earlier times.

Much remains to be done to understand fully the implications of meaning theory. Yet this perspective — like that of modeling theory — leads us to suspect that the media may have powerful but very indirect influences on the way we think, talk, interpret the world around us, and respond to situations and people. Older approaches to research on the effects of the media, through surveys and experiments, are not appropriate to study these long-range and indirect influences.

Summary

The most important influences of mass communication may be long-term, indirect, and difficult to uncover by the techniques of social science research. These influences include modeling behavior and the shaping of meanings that are important to both individual and collective definitions of reality.

Modeling theory holds that people may adopt behaviors that they have seen depicted in the media. The probability that an individual will adopt the modeled behavior on a lasting basis is increased if the imitated behavior is reinforced and if the individual identifies with the model.

The influence of mass communication on meanings is a part of the processes by which people construct and use shared conceptions of reality for thinking and for interacting with others. The meaning theory of media influence is an extension of the trace theory of human communication. The media construct reality by using symbols and providing portrayals — in sounds, images, or words — of the referents of those symbols. Such representations provide shared meanings for the members of the audience. By this means, the media provide us with "pictures in our heads" (specific trace configurations) of "the world outside" (objects, issues, or situations as they exist independent of media portrayals). By so doing, the media establish, extend, substitute, and stabilize the meanings that members of the audience share with others.

To study both the models and the meanings offered in mass communications, systematic analyses of their content are important. *Content analysis* is a term applied to a variety of techniques and procedures for quantitative and qualitative assessment of what is presented in any form of communication. Content analyses cannot reveal in a direct way the intent of communicators or the influence of messages on receivers. However, they can show trends and emphases that are unlikely to be detected by members of the audience. Moreover, they show the models and the meanings in media content that may influence people's behaviors and beliefs.

Content analyses of children's picture books and alcohol use in soap operas provide specific examples of models in media content. Many factors influence the learning of sex roles; the passive role models for girls and the active models for boys shown in picture books for young children are one important source for this learning. For adults the soap operas provide attractive models that show how alcohol may be used.

The meaning theory of media influence is illustrated by a recent analysis of the portrayal of the mentally ill in crime dramas on prime-time television. These programs use a rich colloquial vocabulary to label the mentally ill and they show mentally ill villains committing very deviant and dangerous acts. By this means, it can be hypothesized, television perpetuates ancient stereotypes about madness (stabilizes meanings) and teaches new generations that the mentally ill are very dangerous people (establishes meanings). Since the mentally ill as a whole are not particularly dangerous, the media appear to be creating false pictures in our heads of this particular aspect of the world outside.

Overall, the models and the meanings provided by the media may be far more significant than the information or opinions on specific issues that they present. Such indirect, long-term influences are contingent on many conditions that need to be sorted out by future research.

Notes and References

1. Associated Press, New York, August 11, 1977.

2. Albert Bandura, *Social Learning Theory* (Englewood Cliffs, N.J.: Prentice-Hall, 1977).

3. Shearon A. Lowery, "Soap and Booze in the Afternoon: An Analysis of the Portrayals of Alcohol Use in the Daytime Television Serial," Ph.D. diss., Washington State University, 1979. See especially chapter 1.

4. Wilbur Schramm, Jack Lyle, and Edwin B. Parker, *Television in the Lives of Our Children* (Stanford, Calif.: Stanford University Press, 1969) p. 78.

5. See "Soap Operas: Sex and Suffering in the Afternoon," *Time*, January 12, 1976, pp. 46–53.

6. Ibid.

7. Marshall McLuhan, for example, has developed numerous speculations concerning the special impact of each medium. Marshall McLuhan, chapter 1, "The Medium is the Message," in *Understanding Media: The*

Extension of Man (New York: McGraw-Hill, 1964) pp. 7–21. See also an older research literature on the special effects of each medium. For example, several classic studies are reprinted in Wilbur Schramm, *Mass Communications* (Urbana; University of Illinois Press, 1960) pp. 487–582.

8. Charles Horton Cooley, *Social Organization* (New York: Charles Scribner and Sons, 1929), originally published in 1909.

9. Melvin L. De Fleur, "Occupational Roles as Portrayed on Television," *Public Opinion Quarterly*, 28 (Spring 1964), 57–74.

10. Leo Lowenthal, "Biographies in Popular Magazines," in *Radio Research, 1942–43*, ed. Paul Lazarsfeld and Frank Stanton (New York: Duel, Sloan and Pearce, 1943) pp. 507–548.

11. For more detailed discussions of content analysis procedures and techniques, see Bernard Berelson, *Content Analysis in Communication Research* (Glencoe, Ill.: Free Press, 1952); Ithiel de Sola Pool, ed., *Trends in Content Analysis* (Evanston, Ill.: Northwestern University Press, 1963); George Gerbner, et al., *The Analysis of Communication Content* (New York: Wiley, 1969); and Ole Holsti, *Content Analysis for the Social Sciences and Humanities* (Reading, Mass.: Addison-Wesley, 1969).

12. For example, see the account of Jan Morris, who lived until mid-life as James Morris, a well-known British journalist. After undergoing surgery to clarify sex identity, the transformation involved in becoming a woman in a behavioral sense proved to be a trying experience. Jan Morris, *Conundrum* (New York: Harcourt Brace Jovanovich, 1974).

13. Lenore Weitzman, et al., "Sex Role Socialization in Picture Books for Pre-School Children," *American Journal of Sociology*, 77 (May 1972), 1125.

14. Ibid., p. 1139.

15. Lonnie C. Carton, *Daddies* (New York: Random House, 1960).

16. A recent unpublished study (1980) showed that a sample of over fifty children's picture books sold in major book stores in a Southwestern city *still* contained many of the role models and portrayals of the earlier study. Although women's groups have exerted pressure for changing children's reading materials, those efforts have not been particularly successful.

17. Madeline Edmondson and David Rounds, *The Soaps* (New York: Stein and Day, 1973).

18. Barry D. Caudill and G. Alan Marlatt, "Modeling Influences in Social Drinking: An Experimental Analog," *Journal of Consulting and Clinical Psychology*, 43, No. 3, pp. 405–415.

19. Lowery, *Soap and Booze in the Afternoon*, p. 95.

20. Brigitte Goldstein and Melvin L. De Fleur, "The Television's Portrayals of the Mentally Ill," Unpublished manuscript, University of New Mexico, 1980.

21. Michel Foucalt, *Madness and Civilization* (New York: Random House, 1965) p. 11.

11 Ongoing Concerns in Mass Communication Research

There is nothing especially esoteric about research. It is simply the best way we have yet found to gather information systematically, accurately, and with safeguards that permit one to estimate how reliable the information is.

WILBUR SCHRAMM, *The Role of Information in National Development*, 1965

Researchers continue to study the elusive principles behind the operation of the mass media and their effects. Because of the research efforts of the past, we know more about these principles today than we did even a decade ago. There is much that is new in these ongoing research efforts but their main paths are extensions of those along which researchers have already traveled a considerable distance. In this chapter we give an overview of those paths. Our purpose is twofold: to see how social science works, and to sketch some of the continuing directions of research done in recent years.

We begin by outlining two main issues: what are the long-term questions that have concerned communications researchers, and what are the central characteristics of scientific research in general. Then we discuss these issues in a context of studies of communicators, the content of mass communication, its channels, audiences, and effects.

A Framework for Studying Mass Communication

More than thirty years ago Harold Lasswell stated that communication could conveniently be described by answering the following question:

Who
says what
in what channel
to whom
with what effect?[1]

We can classify much of the research of the past decades in terms of this complex question, and in many ways it still captures the primary concerns of contemporary research on mass communication. To study the "who" in Lasswell's question, researchers look at issues such as ownership trends in the newspaper industry, the process of decision making in television programming, and the division of labor in the film industry. The "what" factor is the focus of content analysis. Studies of the agenda of topics presented to the public, the amount of violence shown on television, children's advertising, and portrayals of women, minorities, and social problems all fall into this category. To study the "channels" of communication, researchers compare the effectiveness of various media and examine the implications of new channels such as cable television and satellites. Researchers also study audiences, their composition, and the uses and gratifications that various groups find in the content provided by the media. Finally, we have seen that the influence of the media continues as a major topic of research. Studies of the effects of mass communication on public opinion, shared beliefs, personality development, patterns of aggression, and so on remain the focus of much research.

Each year literally hundreds of research reports on these and other issues are published. Many appear in the scientific journals, such as those listed in Table 11.1, which are concerned almost exclusively with research on communications. There are, of course, other outlets. Journals in sociology (for example, the *American Sociological Review*, the *American Journal of Sociology*, and *Social Forces*) and psychology (including the *American Journal of Psychology*, the *Journal of Applied Social*

Table 11.1 Professional Journals Devoted Mainly to Research on Communication

Audio-Visual Language Journal
Central States Speech Journal
Communication
Communication Arts
Communication Education
Communication Monographs
Communication Quarterly
Communication Research
Communications
Human Communication
Human Communications Research
Journalism Monographs
Journalism Quarterly
Journal of Applied Communication Research
The Journal of Communication
New Mexico Communication Journal
Ohio Speech Journal
Pennsylvania Speech Annual
Public Telecommunication Review
Quarterly Journal of Speech
Southern Speech Communication Journal
Speech Activities
Studies in Public Communication
Western Speech Communication

Psychology, and the *Journal of Experimental Social Psychology*) also publish reports of research on mass communication. In fact, journals in many fields carry articles on media research. Examples are the *Public Opinion Quarterly* and journals of education, linguistics, journalism, psychiatry, and political science. Still other research is reported in books and monographs.

This research, for all its diversity, has a common framework: the principles and methods of science. There are many kinds and levels of good scientific work, but they share a few very important attributes. And, while science, unlike the proverbial crooked poker game, is *not* the only game in town, these qualities justify our concentration on the scientific approach to understanding mass communication.

Infallibility is not one of the characteristics of science. Researchers and theory-builders often make mistakes, study obscure topics, or otherwise bark up the wrong tree. Thus at least some of today's scientific truths may become tomorrow's obsolete explanations. But science is the only procedure for gathering knowledge that systematically *polices itself* and tries hard to disprove its own claims through the use of both logic and controlled observation. Moreover, science insists on *accumulation* — on following up, testing, and retesting leads that seem to survive researchers' initial screening. It is characterized too by *innovation* — by the exploration of new ideas and possible explanations. Thus science is the cutting edge of understanding, moving forward, correcting its own mistakes, but usually following directions guided by the past.

As a result of accumulated research, we know a great deal more about mass communication than we did a half-century ago, when the scientific study of mass communication had just begun. It is impossible in one chapter to summarize all the noteworthy studies that have contributed to that accumulation. Therefore we restrict this discussion to examples from the last decade that either are particularly significant or illustrate important points. To organize this overview, we rely on the categories Lasswell set out thirty years ago, beginning with questions about the communicators themselves.

Mapping Constraints on Communicators

Those who control and operate the media play the key role in determining their content. In doing so they are constantly aware that they are manufacturing a product designed to capture and hold the attention of audiences. Thus, the "who" in Lasswell's question is made up of those professional communicators who lead the continuing struggle for readers, listeners, and viewers from whom income can be obtained.

In their search for maximum attention, communicators operate within powerful constraints. These include the limits on the economic resources of their company or corporation, the potential profit for a particular form of content, and the creative talent that they can command, as well as boundaries set by public values and tastes, legal restrictions, journalistic or artistic traditions, and the bureaucratic structures within which they work. All these limitations have provided fertile ground for research and analysis for many years.[2] One of the most thorough studies of these constraints done in recent years is David L. Altheide's detailed analysis of the factors that affect the selection and dissemination of news on television.[3] It backs up with research evidence many of the points we have discussed in other sections of the present text. It pulls these points together in an important real-life setting.

Altheide's work builds on approaches that Walter Lippmann pioneered shortly after World War I.[4] For three years Altheide studied the day-to-day selection, editing, and presentation of the news. After lengthy studies of the newsrooms of three local television stations that were network affiliates, he made more limited observations in other stations. Later he also studied central managers in the news-making industry.

Altheide followed carefully the way in which several major stories were handled, including the presidential campaign of 1972, the Vietnam War, and Watergate. He used in-depth discussions and interviews plus many hours of detailed observation on a daily basis. His findings were complex, but essentially they reveal the details of what Altheide calls the *news perspective*. The news perspective, according to Altheide, is a set of systematic constraints that distort the news. Among the significant contributors to these distortions are (1) commercialism, (2) ratings, (3) bureaucracy, (4) lack of real news, (5) journalists' views of the audience as essentially stupid, and (6) competition with other media.

Commercialism implies that television news, like any other content in the media, must make a profit. Time for commercial announcements during a news program is sold in the same way as space in a newspaper. The price per minute depends on the number of eyes and ears that the news can attract to the sponsors' advertisements.

The ratings measure the number of eyes and ears and the types of heads to which they are attached. Advertisers want to aim their messages at their relevant market. If a news program is not attracting enough potential buyers of a particular type — such as women between eighteen and forty-nine for a manufacturer of cosmetics — then the sponsor will look for other programs on which to advertise. A drop in ratings is a signal to the newspeople that the audience does not like their version of the news; it threatens their jobs, the organization's profits, management's success, and the owners' satisfaction. Thus the fate of the communicator rests with the audience.

All this implies that the audiences for television news do not receive an accurate picture of what is happening. Instead, they receive entertaining accounts of what news personnel hope will capture and hold their interest. Beating the competition in the numbers game is the most important definition of doing a good job. Thus "good news" is equivalent to "good numbers" from the rating services. The numbers are what interest management, the numbers define success or failure. This principle was summed up very nicely shortly after the turn of the century by Will Irwin, writing about the newspapers of the time: "We will give the public what it wants, without bothering to elevate the commonwealth. If we find that people prefer murders, then murders they shall have."[5]

Other factors also introduce bias into the local news. For example, news reports reflect the bureaucratic nature of the organization that produces them. Even the most interesting stories must be produced in a limited time, according to a fixed schedule, and at the least cost. Thus news stories — like refrigerators, blue jeans, and canned soup — have production cost limitations. These constraints limit the activities of all newspeople, from camera operators to on-the-scene-reporters to top management. The result is a reduction in the fidelity of news accounts through the process of gatekeeping.

Yet another factor that frustrates local news communicators is that on many days nothing particularly interesting is going on. It is difficult to capture and hold the attention of an audience when nothing of real significance has happened. One of the great skills that can make the difference between competing newsrooms is the art of making something out of nothing — producing pseudo-events. As Altheide reported, "From this perspective, any event is newsworthy if it is treated properly. During my research I have seen stories about defecating dogs, fifteen cent robberies, treed cats, and pie-eating contests."[6] Clever newspeople can provide an interesting treatment of almost anything.

Some of these constraints also affect national news programs, but there are differences. The competition is intense, the talent is far greater, and the resources are far more abundant. Still, numerous biases creep in. Events are wrenched from their context in order to make an interesting story. Themes are imposed in subtle ways that transform people and events by focusing on only part of the situation. For example, during the presidential campaign of 1972, George Wallace was never taken seriously by the network news. He was displayed as a phenomenon rather than a potential president. Broadcasts centered on his redneck constituency, his stand against busing, and other racial issues. Little or no attention was given to his broader political ideas.

Overall, Altheide's central finding was that "events become news when transformed by the news perspective, and not because of their objective characteristics."[7] His work probes and reveals the host of factors that shape this set of constraints. This research, like the pioneering insights of Walter Lippmann more than half a century earlier, raises important questions about whether we can rely on advertising-dependent media in a democratic society. It presents a serious challenge to those who maintain that we have a free press. When the news must be shaped and presented for the purpose of focusing attention on messages that sell girdles, deodorants, and beer, it is difficult to claim that citizens are receiving accurate and objective accounts of the events that may be shaping their lives. Altheide's research findings reveal in the day-to-day world of TV news almost all of the concepts and generalizations that have been set forth in a more abstract way in previous chapters. In other words, those claims are supported by evidence.

Assessing Content

Contemporary efforts to analyze the content of the media have looked at almost every conceivable topic and theme. Studies continue to be conducted on how males and females are portrayed, what images of minorities are presented, the relative emphasis of political issues, the amount of violence, the use of drugs and alcohol, the content of advertising directed at children, and dozens of other topics. All these efforts are valuable. Indeed, any question concerning the media's influence on individuals, society, or culture must begin with studies of content. Today, when people often express anxiety about the influence of the media's portrayals of violence and sex, it is not surprising that many studies have analyzed the presence of these themes in media content.

Some observers say that the presence of these themes is the result of society's influence: The media are giving the public what it wants. Thus we have the old chicken-or-the-egg problem: Which came first, the media's emphasis on certain themes or the public's taste for them?[8] Under certain conditions studies of content can point to the possible influence of society on the media. For example, when in the late 1970s groups such as the Parent and Teachers Association pressured the networks to reduce the level of violence on television, the networks reevaluated, rescheduled, and in some cases changed program content. Critics charged that the networks then increased the sexual content of programs in order to attract viewers. So here is one possible influence of society on the media. Did the networks reduce the violence on television, and are programs now "sexier" than they were five years ago? If so, what impact will such content have on young people and sex norms in the future? While studies of "what" is presented cannot answer all these questions, researchers have used the methods of content analyses described in Chapter 10 to understand what the media are presenting.

Table 11.2 Types of Sexual Behavior Portrayed on Prime-time Television

Behavior	Frequency per hour	Intensity Casual	Intense
Kissing	3.74	3.70	0.04
Embracing	2.68	2.64	0.04
Heterosexual intercourse	0.04	0.04	0.00
Homosexual behavior	0.00	0.00	0.00
Rape and other sex crimes	0.28	0.25	0.03
Touching—aggressive	5.48	1.64	3.84
Touching—nonaggressive	68.11	67.62	0.49
Flirting and seductiveness	1.38	1.38	0.00
Innuendo (with canned laughter)	0.27	0.27	0.00
Innuendo (no canned laughter)	0.41	0.41	0.00
Total innuendos	0.68	0.68	0.00
Atypical sex roles	0.76	0.76	0.00
Partner seeking	1.04	1.04	0.00

Source: Susan Franzblau, Joyce N. Sprafkin, and Eli Rubinstein, "Sex on TV: A Content Analysis," *Journal of Communication* (Spring 1977), 164–170.

Sex on Television

To assess the quantity and quality of sex portrayed on television, Susan Franzblau and her associates systematically analyzed the content of sixty-one programs from all three networks shown between 8 P.M. and 11 P.M. during early October in 1975 [9] They used careful and precise procedures to isolate, describe, and classify every kind of sexual or intimate action on the program. Table 11.2 summarizes their findings.

Franzblau and her colleagues found a great deal of kissing, embracing, and touching, but — not surprisingly — no overt portrayals of sexual intercourse. Such controversial acts as rape and homosexual conduct were only referred to, not shown. Another finding was more surprising. The amount of nonaggressive touching, innuendo, and physically intimate behavior was greater during the two-hour family viewing time — from 8 to 10 P.M. — than later in the evening. By Franzblau's measures, situation comedies and variety shows were the sexiest programs. In comparison, crime-adventure shows, which are usually shown later in the evening, had little sexual content. Thus the times when children are most likely to be watching and the kinds of programs that are most popular among families had more sexual content than programs later in the evening, which are viewed more by adults.

The following year Carlos F. Fernandez-Collado and three associates studied seventy-seven programs broadcast during the 1976–1977 season, including Saturday morning as well as prime-time programs.[10] In addition these researchers polled fourth-, sixth-, and eighth-graders to see which programs they viewed regularly. These researchers counted as "intimate sexual behavior" any "explicit, insinuated or endorsed act of sexual intercourse."[11] As a result, they came up with different findings. They found that the amount of sex portrayed on television was much higher than in the Franzblau study. But like Franzblau they found that sexual content was most frequent during family viewing time. Interestingly (and presumably because of the legacy of fear), these researchers also searched for portrayals of the use of tobacco, alcohol, and illegal drugs. They found that these were also most frequent during the early evening. Saturday morning shows, in contrast, showed little sex, alcohol, tobacco, or dope.

The differences in the findings of the Franzblau and the Fernandez-Collado studies prompted yet a third investigation. A research team led by L. Theresa Silverman analyzed a sample of sixty-four programs appearing between 8 P.M. and 11 P.M. during October 1977.[12] These researchers had carefully reviewed the previous two studies and noted:

> Contrasting sharply with the [earlier study by Franzblau et al.] the 1976 sample contained at least 100 portrayals of or references to controversial sexual topics, specifically "sexual intercourse, any type of illegal sexual behavior, or homosexuality. . . ." Unfortunately, the authors failed to differentiate physical, verbal, and contextually implied presentations, leaving in question the level of explicitness of the references included in their tabulation.[13]

Noting this deficiency, Silverman's research team set out to gain a more comprehensive picture of how physical intimacy and sexuality were portrayed during one season. Their findings were complex, but they did not parallel the Fernandez-Collado study. There was not as much sex portrayed in the programs they analyzed. Mainly the investigators found that flirtatious behavior, sexual innuendo, and implied intercourse had increased substantially since the Franzblau study. They concluded: "There is still no explicit sex shown on prime-time TV. However, there does ap-

Sex on television, a subject of concern to media researchers, has changed radically in television's short history. The somewhat sanitary relationship of Rob and Laura (Dick Van Dyke and Mary Tyler Moore) on The Dick Van Dyke Show *in the 1950s and 1960s seems tame indeed when programs in the 1980s take up such subjects as premarital sex and homosexuality.*

pear to be an increasing tendency to "tease" the audience behaviorally (through flirting), verbally (through innuendo), and visually (through contextually implied intercourse)."[14] Thus in this study the researchers probed more deeply and corrected what the researchers thought to be an error in the second study. An important point to note is how these three studies illustrate very well the innovative, self-policing, and accumulative nature of science.

But notice that these studies, in themselves, do not answer our initial question; that is, they do not tell us whether social pressures on communicators controlling the media led to an increase in sexual content. Neither can these studies tell us what influence, if any, the content had on individuals or society. One limitation of many content analyses is that their purposes and implications are not clear. Do these studies assume that this content has influence through modeling? Or that it influences meanings in the social construction of reality? As we made clear earlier, by itself, content analyses tells us nothing about the effects of that content on audience members.

Violence on
Television

The presence of violence — in reality and in the media — has long been a source of concern and controversy. Especially in the 1960s, there was widespread anxiety about political assassinations, unrest among youth, destructive urban riots, and sharply rising crime rates. In response President Lyndon Johnson appointed the National Commission on the Causes and Prevention of Violence.

The influence of the mass media on violence was one concern of the commission. Several researchers were approached and asked to conduct studies or provide other analyses on the broad topic of violence and the media. Their report was a document of over 600 pages of findings on almost every aspect of the topic.[15] One chapter provided an important overview of how much violence was shown on network television.

Using content analyses completed by George Gerbner and his associates, this research report focused on all prime-time television programs plus Saturday morning cartoons shown during a typical week in 1967 and a comparable week in 1968. Gerbner and his investigators carefully defined what they meant by violence and made detailed tallies of the frequencies with which many kinds of acts were portrayed. They kept track of what kinds of people were shown as violent and toward whom. They recorded numerous details concerning the victims, consequences, means, times, places, and public responses to violence depicted on television. They concluded that the portrayal of violence on television was very pervasive and that the public believed it to be excessive.

Out of this project grew an ongoing effort to monitor television's portrayal of violence. Each year since 1969 the Violence Profile has provided several measures of the prevalence, rate, and role of violence in prime-time television dramas. From these observations a quantitative *violence index* is prepared, mainly to show trends in the portrayal of violence. For any year comparisons can be made between different hours of viewing, between different networks, between children's and adults' programs, and so on.[16]

The profile and the index provide data that reveal how the networks are depicting violence. These content analyses have been of considerable interest to those who fear that television stimulates aggressive or violent behavior, especially among children.

The Violence Profile provided the stimulus for an even larger ongoing research program called the Cultural Indicators Project, of which it is now a part. Headed by George Gerbner, this project analyzes other kinds of content besides violence. It monitors the "geography, demography, thematic and action structure, time and space dimensions, personality profiles, occupations and fates" that are portrayed in "large and representative aggregates of television outputs."[17] Gerbner and his associates call this broad study of television content *message system analysis*. It focuses on the manner in which the content of television depicts almost every conceivable kind of social relationship. Thus it contrasts with other content analyses, which focus on much narrower issues, such as the use of alcohol, how boys and girls are shown, and sex behavior. The project also attempts to probe the influence of television programs on people's behavior, as we shall see later in this chapter.

Comparing Channels of Communication

Whatever the content of a message, is one medium more effective than others in communicating it and influencing the audience? Is one medium more effective than others in communicating particular kinds of content or exerting certain influences? These questions are especially important to educators, propagandists, and advertisers. For example, if the goal is to impart the greatest possible amount of factual information, is it more effective to present the message through a lecture, print, film, or a tape? If one wishes to change attitudes, is it better to use television, posters, radio, or some other medium? Is one medium more effective than others for a certain type of audience?

Concern with these issues predates the emergence of some of our mass media. During World War I, for example, various kinds of filmstrips, graphics, and even silent films were studied as aids for teaching recruits such things as how to avoid venereal disease, how to care for a rifle, and what to do to ensure proper foot hygiene.[18] As new media became available, various kinds of presentations with different media were explored in campaigns to promote better nutrition, stop forest fires, encourage chest x rays, reduce prejudice, improve dental hygiene, and raise funds. In developing countries, studies comparing the effectiveness of different media in persuading people to adopt new ways have been popular. Advertisers have studied the effectiveness of various media in promoting sales. In other words, many kinds of people with numerous goals have tried many ways to determine the effectiveness of different media.[19]

Effectiveness in Teaching Facts

Two recent studies illustrate the tradition of comparing media to see which is most effective for achieving a specific goal. Neither is particularly dramatic or likely to provide final answers to the questions they probe. They represent instead the kind of patient accumulation of evidence on which science depends. Only after a sufficient number of such studies have given similar results will science permit the conclusion that a reliable generalization has been found.

David L. Nasser and William J. McEwen were interested in comparing how well a set of subjects could recall ideas presented through three media: television videotape, a presentation with sound only, and a printed version of the material.[20] They prepared the content carefully so that each version contained the same set of ideas on trade with China. The design was simple. A different group of university students was assigned to each medium. After viewing, hearing, or reading the message, the subjects were tested for factual recall. The essential finding was that there were no statistically significant differences in the effectiveness of the three media.

Although this finding did not set the scientific world aflame, it did raise some nagging questions. It challenged the proposition that television is by nature somehow more powerful than other media. That did not seem to be the case for factual recall when care was taken to control the content of the message and the type of audience.

Another study along the same lines was done by Karen Browne.[21] Documentary material concerning the Oklahoma legislative process was shown on film to one group of people and was presented in print to a second group. Care was taken to equate the groups and to keep the reading level of the print version low (at a seventh-grade level). The results showed that the subjects who received the information via print remembered more facts than those who saw the same information on film. In this case, the difference was statistically significant.

Again, this modest study sent no great stir through the scientific community. However, a substantial body of research has already indicated that material presented via print is recalled better. (Other research shows that with children the reverse seems to be the case.) Thus, the Browne study adds a bit of confirming evidence to an emerging principle.

Generally, studies of the effectiveness of different media in achieving specific goals are an important, no-nonsense trend in contemporary research. Such studies offer important checks on those who are ready to adopt as eternal verities unproven speculations about how "the medium is the message," the "natural power" of television — or some other untested chiché. In addition, we need to pursue the search for the most effective media to accomplish specific goals under defined conditions with particular categories of audiences.

Ways of Learning

Media can also be compared in a broader way, as the research of Project Zero illustrates. Rather than asking which medium is most effective for teaching facts or some other goal, researchers at Project Zero have compared how and what children learn when different media are used. In one study reported by psychologist Howard Gardner, the Project Zero investigators prepared a story called *The Three Robbers*. It was about three violent bandits who reformed after getting to know a charming young orphan girl.[22] Then the investigators read the story in picture-book form to one group of children, who looked at the accompanying pictures. Another group saw a television version of the story. Great care was taken to make the two versions as similar as possible.

A number of intriguing differences between the two groups were found. The "book children" were able to recall more of the story on their own and in response to cues. They were able to quote many of the phrases from the story quite accurately. When they were asked to draw inferences from the story, the book children tended to draw on their own experiences. In contrast, the children who saw the story on television were more likely to paraphrase the story rather than quote it accurately. They were less able to go beyond the content and relate it to their own experiences in making inferences.

Gardner related these results to basic differences between books and television. Television provides the visual experience of moving pictures, but watching and listening to television is a passive experience compared with reading, which demands that the reader exercise his or her imagination. Although it is too early to tell the significance of this line of research, it suggests that television and books have quite different effects on children's thinking. This does not mean that one or the other is "better"; they simply stimulate different experiences. Ultimately, this type of research may reveal ways in which children who watch a great deal of television but read few books develop characteristic patterns of imagination and reasoning.

Studying Audiences

Numerous studies continue to assess the exposure of various categories of people to the media, examining their habits and motives. This kind of research falls into two subtypes. The first is rather simple in that it merely analyzes audience composition. Its goal is to determine what kind of people attend to what medium to what extent. In other words, it assesses patterns of attention. This research can reveal trends, shifts from one medium to another, the kinds of people who attend to a medium at different times, and the type of content most suitable for a given television hour. To advertisers and television programmers, this research is an essential

Two target audiences that have captured the attention of researchers who study media effects are the young and the elderly. Both audiences, for example, watch television more regularly than do people of middle age — but their responses to what they see differ, often considerably.

tool. The second type of research on audiences is more complex and is called *uses and gratifications research.* Here, the goal is to discover the reasons behind patterns of attention. Why do people turn to particular media or particular kinds of content? In this type of study researchers use numerous behavioral theories to try to explain what satisfactions people obtain from their viewing. Both audience analysis and gratification research are very popular today.

Patterns of Attention

Currently, the structure of television audiences attracts more research attention than other media. Interest in the audience for print remains relatively high, but movie and radio audiences are being neglected by comparison. Usually the audience is described in terms of its age, sex, education, and income.

Robert Leibert and Neala Schwartzberg have provided an excellent review of recent findings on audience composition.[23] In general, they found that during the last two decades adults have steadily increased their television viewing. On the average an adult now spends more than 3 hours a day watching television. In 1961 the figure was about 2½ hours, on the average. Research has not clarified the reasons for this increase, but the spread of color television, the rise of popular programs such as sports broadcasts, the increasing availability of cable television, and similar developments probably account for it. (Note that even though the public remains convinced that television may be harmful, audiences are larger than ever and people devote more and more time to viewing.)

People in their forties watch television the least, whereas those over sixty-five tend to be very heavy viewers. Television remains popular with young children as well. First-graders now spend from 2 to 3 hours daily with their sets, depending on the social level of the family; the lower the level, the more television the child watches. A third of preschool children under six spend 4 or more hours daily watching television. Some 25 percent of sixth- and tenth-graders view as much as 5½ hours on school days. In fact, about one-fourth of sixth-graders are still watching at 11:30 P.M. on school nights.

The use of print follows a rather predictable pattern. Newspaper reading and attention to public affairs and political topics in other print media are low among young people. Children read less than adults; young adults read less than older adults. After retirement, reading reaches a peak, but it falls off sharply among the very old.[24]

Generally, research reveals differences in attention to the media between almost every kind of social group — between males and females, blacks and whites, the old and the young, the rich and the poor, the educated and the untutored. Differing patterns of attention are found even among those of different religions, ethnic groups, and regions.

In spite of all these variations, however, one conclusion is obvious: Americans of all circumstances and backgrounds spend many hours a week with television. Surprisingly, even older Native American women in the pueblos of the Rio Grande valley, whose command of English is often very limited and who still follow their traditional culture patterns, avidly watch television soap operas. Neighbors who are versed in the ways of whites provide interpretations and explanations. This observation indicates that social categories are not the only influence on patterns of media attention. Social relationships also affect these patterns. The tastes, social skills, preferences, and habits of peers, parents, and associates all play a part in determining an individual's patterns of attention to mass communication.

But what does all this mean? The figures on media attention are impressive. We can easily show that so many millions of people watched *Roots* or something else. But massive attention does not necessarily mean massive influence. Making this connection

Television entertainment programs are not simply all laughs. In the 1970s All in the Family often touched on controversial and once-taboo practices and beliefs. Mike and Gloria's disagreements with Archie frequently pointed up the differences between contemporary young people and their parents.

is a common logical fallacy, and it continues to be made regularly — even by researchers. The following non sequitur illustrates the point: "With American children averaging between 2 and 3 hours of television viewing daily throughout their entire childhood, the medium is *clearly a powerful agent of socialization that can inculcate undesirable social lessons.*[25] (Italics added) Such conclusions about "power" and "undesirable lessons" (or any other effect) must be based on systematic observations of overt behavior, not just on habits of attention.

Uses and Gratifications

What psychological rewards do people receive from reading, hearing, or viewing specific content? Investigations of this question began many years ago when studies probed the gratification associated with the daily newspapers, western movies, comics, radio quiz programs, serious music broadcasts, and the ubiquitous soap operas.[26] Contemporary research indicates that people seek various forms of media content for many reasons.

One way to categorize audience gratifications is to contrast people's need for *fantasy-escape* with their need for *informational-educational* content. More complex classifications sort out categories such as (1) the need to acquire desired information (for example, Where is a given product on sale?); (2) catering to an established media habit (watching the news every night); (3) using a medium for relaxation or excitement (watching a favorite team battle a rival); (4) escaping boredom (going to a movie to avoid a dull evening at home); and (5) companionship (having a radio or television in the background when one is alone).[27] An excellent review of this research was given in a special issue of *Communications Research* examining the evolution of uses and gratifications research, the theories at stake, problems of measurement, and current controversies.[28]

The study of uses and gratifications is difficult. It seeks to understand not only what people attend to but why. Usually, gratifications research tries to see media content as providing the fulfillment of needs, satisfaction of wants, or realization of wishes, in one form or another. It studies how such factors as content, type of medium, circumstances of exposure, and social context can influence the kinds of satisfactions and rewards obtained. Although such research is promising, it is as yet rather disorganized, and no body of consistent findings or convincing theories has been advanced.[29] Hopefully, these problems may be solved in the future.

Measuring the Media's Influence on People

The question of the effects of mass communication is, as we noted in Chapter 1, the "bottom line." Research on this question interests the public more than any other. It is this concern that has brought so much research attention to the impact of portrayals of sex and violence in the media. Public interest, in fact, led the government in recent years to establish commissions that did much to stimulate research on the media, especially on their relationship to violent and sexual behavior. One example is the Commission on Obscenity and Pornography established by President Johnson in the late 1960s.

Sexual Portrayals and Behavioral Consequences

The Commission on Obscenity and Pornography had the task of reviewing all available research, conducting studies, and hearing reviews from all segments of society on the issue. In particular, the commission wanted to know whether the explicit portrayal of sexual acts in the media leads to antisocial behavior. Many people believe that seeing erotic portrayals excites people sexually and that this in turn leads some people to socially disapproved, overt sexual activity. A first question, therefore, is whether watching erotic portrayals is indeed sexually stimulating.

A study of the reactions of undergraduate students to pornographic films showed that both males and females were sexually aroused by the content. Eighty percent of the males who viewed the films reported partial or full erections, and 85 percent of the females experienced genital sensations.[30] But a *satiation effect* was also found. That is, college-age males who repeatedly viewed pornographic material reported that repeated exposure diminished their sexual excitement.[31] Additional research showed that interpersonal sexual activity often followed exposure to explicit portrayals (for example, the probability of intercourse among married couples increased). The frequency of masturbation (for both males and females) also generally increased.[32]

The most significant finding in this extensive report, however, was that pornographic portrayals play little part in the generation of deviant or antisocial sexual behavior. Pedophiles (people aroused by children) and homosexuals were less likely than sexually conventional people to have seen pornographic materials as adolescents. Rapists in prisons reported seeing pornographic depictions later in life than a comparison group of nonoffenders. When restrictions on pornography were lifted in Denmark, no increase in sexual offenses followed. The report of the commission concluded:

> If a case is to be made against "pornography" . . . it will have to be made on grounds other than demonstrated effects of a damaging personal or social nature. Empirical research designed to clarify the question has found no reliable evidence to date that exposure to explicit sexual materials plays a significant role in the causation of delinquent or criminal sexual behavior among youth or adults.[33]

In spite of this report, the issue remains controversial. It involves a conflict of values, which science cannot resolve. To liberals, the scientific conclusions support their convictions that people should be free to view whatever sexual portrayals they wish. The evidence shows that these portrayals do little harm. To conservatives, however, the data are not important. The explicit portrayal of sex itself seen as a moral transgression, even if it has no effect on other behaviors. It is at this point, where the ultimate resolution is decided by values, that the usefulness of scientific evidence reaches its limits. Scientific findings can show what situation *does* exist, but they cannot show what situation *should* exist.

Influence on Beliefs: The Cultural Indicators Project

President Johnson also appointed a National Commission on the Causes and Prevention of Violence, out of which grew the Cultural Indicators Project. Through its Violence Profile the project has told us much about the violence shown on television, and through message analysis it has expanded the techniques of content analysis. It goes beyond much content analysis research, however, not only in its scope but also in its attempt to measure the actual influence of content on the beliefs of people who have involved themselves deeply in television's fictional world. The researchers term this phase of their work *cultivation analysis* because it "inquires into the assumptions television cultivates about the facts, norms and values of society." [34]

"NOW REMEMBER, DON'T GET UPSET DURING THE FIGHT SCENE, AND DON'T WORRY WHEN THE SHIP STARTS SINKING. YOU MUST REALIZE THESE ARE ALL ACTORS WHO ARE JUST DOING THEIR JOBS, AND THE BAD GUYS ARE REALLY VERY NICE PEOPLE."

Cultivation Analysis. Specifically, the Cultural Indicators Project tries to assess the way television viewing influences perception and interpretation of the real world. They rely on strategies that include two specific techniques.

The first technique is a modernized version of an old method of research into the media's effects: they compare those who have been heavily exposed to television with those who have been lightly exposed. Without an additional precaution, however, findings from this procedure would be untrustworthy; the investigators must control for the influence of other factors that can lead to heavy or light exposure. For example, education, age, sex, and other social characteristics are strong influences on habits of using the media. But these researchers take this fact into account. They compare heavy and light viewers *within* such categories. Thus they contrast heavy and light viewers among college respondents and among no-college respondents, among regular and among occasional watchers of the news, among males and among females, and so on.

Second the investigators pose a series of questions to respondents concerning their interpretations and beliefs about specific aspects of the social environment. For each question, however, the researchers also have a *television answer*. That is, from content analyses of television programs they have formulated the answer that television programs give to the question. For example, many content analyses have shown that television depicts an unrealistically large portion of its fictional labor force employed in law enforcement. Respondents can be asked what portion of the real labor force is employed in law enforcement. The television answer to this question exaggerates the actual percentage substantially. The difference between the television answer and reality is known as the *cultivation differential*.

Figure 11.1 shows the results obtained on this question. Heavy and light viewers within each category are compared. The results seem striking. In all categories the heavy viewers gave answers more consistent with the television answer than with the real facts. Figure 11.1 also shows the results obtained when respondents were asked about their potential involvement in violent incidents. The researchers concluded that heavy viewers believed themselves to be much more likely to be involved than light viewers did — a result that is again consistent with the television answer. Thus this research seems to show that television's content can have a strong influence on the audience's beliefs about reality.

Figure 11.1

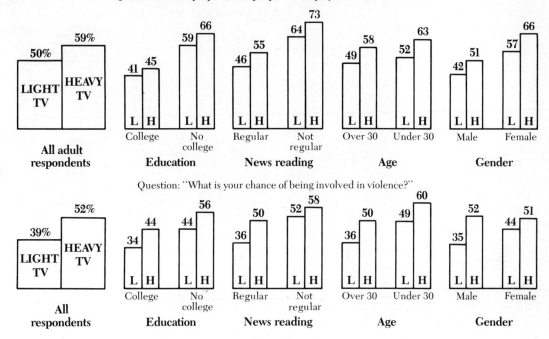

Question: "What proportion of people are employed in law enforcement?"

Question: "What is your chance of being involved in violence?"

Conflicting Findings. The finding that people who view a lot of television are more likely than light viewers to fear their neighborhood stirred much interest. Other researchers tried to replicate the study (that is, reach the same conclusions by repeating the study), but their findings were very different.

In Toronto, Canada, Anthony Doob and Glenn MacDonald tested whether people who watch a lot of television are afraid of being victimized in their neighborhoods.[35] But they added conditions not present in Gerbner's study: they looked at different *types of neighborhoods,* distinguishing high-crime from low-crime areas. They suspected that people in high-crime neighborhoods would, quite reasonably, fear their environment whether they watched a lot of television or not, and that those in low-crime neighborhoods, however much they watched television, would not. In other words, they suspected that the actual amount of crime in the neighborhood — and not patterns of television viewing — is the cause of fear.

The results obtained in the study support this hypothesis. When Doob and MacDonald compared heavy viewers with light

Ongoing Concerns in Mass Communication Research   407

One way that television acts as a socializing agent is by showing behaviors that viewers may deem appropriate to their own lives. Characters in such soap operas as The Young and the Restless *regularly consume alcoholic beverages.*

viewers in low-crime neighborhoods, there was no difference between them in their fear of being victimized. In the high-crime neighborhoods most people tended to watch a lot of television, and most feared crime in their area. But the overall results indicated that there is no relationship between viewing patterns and fear of crime when the realities of the neighborhood are taken into account. People in high-crime neighborhoods feared that they would be victims; those in low-crime areas did not. The amount of television viewing was not a critical factor.

Do these findings discredit Gerbner's research? It's hard to say. Perhaps there's something unique about people in Toronto. What can be said is that additional research is needed to see which conclusions are best. After more studies are completed, with adequate controls for neighborhood crime rates, the weight of evidence will decide the issue. Science does not rest its case on only one or two studies. If incorrect conclusions are reached, further studies allow revision. An important point here is that this controversy illustrates the self-correcting nature of science.

Cultivation Analysis and Meaning Theory. The cultivation analysis of Gerbner and his associates touches on many of the same issues as the meaning theory presented in Chapter 10. Both are concerned with the derivation of conceptions of reality from exposure to mass communication. But the two have important differences. Meaning theory is concerned with the culturally shared conventions people use to interpret symbols and how such interpretations are embedded in a person's trace configurations (as discussed in Chapter 1). Cultivation analysis does not go into such areas. Whereas cultivation analysis is formulated around one medium — television — meaning theory encompasses all the media. Meaning theory begins with an individual's memory, with imprinted traces and their role in communication. From this analysis it moves to portrayals of social reality in mediated communication. Cultivation analysis reverses this direction. It begins with the mediated communications of television and tries to sort out the beliefs of people influenced by them.

There is yet another difference between the two approaches. Because of its origins, cultivation analysis, unlike meaning theory, has been applied mainly to the issue of violence. Generally, the Cultural Indicators Project has provided imaginative if controversial research.

Beyond Scientific Analysis

This review of current trends has shown that communications researchers have come a long way in fifty years but still have far to go. Lasswell's question, "Who says what in what channels to whom with what effect," continues to challenge social scientists. But the question does not exhaust the issues in mass communication, and scientific research is not the only way to explore the issues. Public leaders, media critics, industry representatives, and others also probe and debate Lasswell's question and other issues.

To get an idea of the full scope of scholarly writing on the mass media, we can look at the overview provided by the *Journalism Quarterly*, which monitors and classifies all the articles on mass communication published in a broad spectrum of popular and industry magazines, as well as academic and research journals. Every year it reviews and classifies more than 700 articles. Table 11.3, which is based on nearly 1,500 listings in the *Journalism Quarterly*, shows the principal topics of articles monitored during 1977 and 1978. Those near the top of the table appeared more often and those near the bottom less often. Notice that topics such as research methods and communications theory are not high on the list.

Still, despite the wide range of writings and topics that fall outside the framework for scientific research, we have chosen to concentrate on the work that falls within it, for several reasons. Our

Table 11.3 Relative Frequency of Topics of Published Articles on Mass Communication as Monitored by the *Journalism Quarterly*, 1977–1978

Rank order	Topic or category	Rank order	Topic or category
1	International issues	11	Audiences
2	Education in journalism	12	Communicators
3	History and biography	13	Public relations
4	Courts and law	14	Advertising
5	Government and media	15	Technology
6	Criticism/defense of media	16	Management
7	Broadcasting	17	Visual communication
8	Magazines	18	Minorities
9	Editorial policy and methods	19	Communication theory
		20	Women and media
10	Research methods	21	Community journalism

space after all is limited, and we believe that scientific research provides the surest guide to understanding the process and effects of mass communications. Nonscientific writing has much to offer, but it is the rules of science that demand systematic efforts to correct past errors plus a careful accumulation of knowledge as well as innovation. Even the brief review of research in this chapter has illustrated the value of these requirements.

Today, comprehensive studies in the field continue to open new understandings of the nature and influences of the media. Communications research sometimes seems preoccupied with studying television's portrayal of violence, sex, minorities, and female role models. These are central concerns of the public. Nevertheless, the tradition of comparing media is still alive and is certainly needed. It is fashionable to probe the content and influence of television programs, but in the long run it may be more important to press on in the search for the most effective ways of mediating messages to achieve clearly defined goals. It is this kind of more basic research that holds the best promise of uncovering important principles regarding the use of mediated communication for specific purposes. Meanwhile, new approaches in comparing the media, illustrated by the research at Project Zero, may lead to a far deeper understanding of the psychological processes at work in mediated communication. The search for methods to detect less direct, longer-term effects of the media (such as those discussed in Chapter 10) offers yet another challenge to researchers.

Summary

The search for understanding more about mass communication is being vigorously pursued through research. The basic framework that continues to guide these efforts is that set forth by Lasswell decades ago, when he identified the five basic topics for the systematic study of communication. There is a vast outpouring of analyses, commentaries, criticisms, and other writings about mass communication that has little to do with research. These go beyond Lasswell's guidelines and many are important in themselves, but his formulation continues to shape research on the media.

A good example of the "who" factor is Altheide's analysis of constraints on the television news industry at both the local and national level. The "news perspective" is shaped only in part by what is actually happening. Commercialism, the ratings, the functioning of media bureaucracies, the lack of genuinely important events to report on, journalists' belief that the audience is not very bright, and competition with other media result in both distortions and limitations on news reports.

The "what" factor in contemporary research is illustrated by content analyses of television programs. The conclusions of three studies on the portrayal of sex on television showed an increasing trend in this content but in different quantitative patterns. These studies also illustrate how science is innovative, self-policing, and cumulative.

Research on "channels" remains an important topic in mass communication studies. Recent investigations on the factual recall of information presented via different media showed that popular conceptions — that one form of mediation (such as television) is "by nature" always more powerful — cannot be supported by evidence. Comparisons of children's learning from picture books and television showed that books stimulated the imagination and led to different kinds of recall.

Studies of audience composition have many practical uses. Different categories of people (male, female, old, young, rich, poor) show varying patterns of attention to various media. A related line of research probes the uses and gratifications that motivate attention to different types of content and different media. This difficult area of research seeks to understand not only what people attend to but why they do so.

Studies of the media's effects continue to dominate mass communication research. In the late 1960s extensive research indicated that the evidence does not support the belief that viewing pornographic material leads to deviant sexual behavior. A good illustration of a contemporary direction in research on effects of the media is the Cultural Indicators Project, which includes studies of many kinds of television content and the influence of that content on viewers' beliefs about the world in which they live. This project has some similarities to the meaning theory of media influence. Comparisons of the beliefs of heavy and light viewers — while controversial — show significant differences. Television may have important measurable effects on the audience, but further research is needed.

Notes and References

1. Harold D. Lasswell, "The Structure and Functions of Communication in Society," in *The Communication of Ideas*, ed. Lyman Bryson (New York: Harper and Brothers, 1948) pp. 37–51.

2. Pioneering studies in this tradition are those of sociologist Robert E. Park, *The Immigrant Press and Its Control* (New York: Harper, 1922), and "The Natural History of the Newspaper," in Robert E. Park and Ernest W. Burgess, *The City* (Chicago; University of Chicago Press, 1925), pp. 8–23. A classic study is Warren Breed, "Social Control in the News Room: A Functional Analysis, *Social Forces*, 33 (1955). More recent efforts include J. C. Jarvie, *Movies and Society* (New York: Basic Books, 1970); and R. J. Glessing, *Underground Press in America* (Bloomington; Indiana University Press, 1970).

3. David L. Altheide, *Creating Reality: How TV News Distorts Events* (Beverly Hills, Calif.: Sage, 1976).

4. Walter Lippmann, *Public Opinion* (New York: Macmillan, 1922).

5. Will Irwin, "The American Newspaper," *Colliers Weekly*, January 21, 1911, p. 18.

6. Altheide, *Creating Reality*, p. 173.

7. Ibid.

8. Paul F. Lazarsfeld and Robert R. Merton, "Mass Communication, Popular Taste, and Organized Social Action," in *The Communication of Ideas*, Lyman Bryson, ed. (New York: Harper, 1948).

9. Susan Franzblau, Joyce N. Sprafkin, and Eli A. Rubinstein, "Sex on TV: A Content Analysis, *Journal of Communication*, 27 (Spring 1977), 164–170.

10. Carlos F. Fernandez-Collado and Bradley S. Greenberg, with Filipe Korzenny and Charles K. Atkin, "Sexual Intimacy and Drug Use in TV Series," *Journal of Communication*, 28 (Summer 1978), 30–37.

11. Ibid, p. 32.

12. L. Theresa Silverman, Joyce N. Sprafkin, and Eli A. Rubinstein, "Physical Contact and Sexual Behavior on Prime-Time TV," *Journal of Communication*, 29 (Winter, 1979), 33–43.

13. Ibid, p. 34.

14. Ibid, pp. 41–42.
15. David L. Lange, Robert K. Baker, and Sandra J. Ball, "The Television World of Violence," *Mass Media and Violence*, (Washington, D.C.: Government Printing Office, 1969) pp. 311–339. A report prepared from research evidence obtained by George Gerbner and his associates.
16. George Gerbner and Larry Gross, "Living With Television: The Violence Profile," *Journal of Communication*, 26 (Spring 1976), 181–182.
17. Ibid., p. 182.
18. Charles F. Hoban Jr. and Edward van Ormer, *Instructional Film Research 1918–1950* (New York: Arno Press and the New York Times, 1970).
19. Examples of such diverse efforts can be found in the following: Goodwin C. Chu and Wilbur Schramm, *Learning from Television; What the Research Says* (Stanford University, Institute for Communication Research, 1967); Raymond Winman and Wesley C. Meyerhenry, eds., *Educational Media* (Columbus, Ohio: Charles Merril, 1973); L. C. Barrow and B. Westley, "Comparative Effectiveness of Radio and Television," *AV Communication Review*, 7 (1959), 14–23; P. Deutschmann, L. Barrow, and A. Macmillan, "The Efficiency of Different Modes of Communication," *AV Communication Review*, 9 (1961), 263–270.
20. David L. Nasser and William J. McEwen, "The Impact of Alternative Media Channels: Recall and Involvement with Messages," *AV Communication Review*, 24 (Fall 1976), 263–272.
21. Karen Browne, "Comparison of Factual Recall From Film and Print Stimuli," *Journalism Quarterly*, 55 (Summer 1978), 350–356.
22. Howard Gardner, "Reprogramming the Media Researchers," *Psychology Today*, 13 (January 1980), 6–14.
23. Robert M. Leibert and Neala S. Schwartzberg, "Effects of Mass Media," *Annual Review of Psychology*, 28, 142–143.
24. S. H. Chaffee and D. Wilson, "Adult Life Cycle Changes in Mass Media Use," Paper presented at the annual meetings of the Association for Education in Journalism, 1975.
25. Rita Wicks Poulos, Susan E. Harley, and Robert M. Leibert, "Saturday Morning Television: A Profile on the 1974–75 Children's Season," *Psychological Reports,* 39 (1976), 1047.
26. Elihu Katz, Jay G. Blumler, and Michael Gurvitch, "Utilization of Mass Communication by the Individual," in *The Uses of Mass Communications*, ed. Jay G. Blumler and Elihu Katz (Beverly Hills, Calif.: Sage, 1974) p. 20.
27. See especially chapters 4, 8, and 12 in Blumler and Katz, *Uses of Mass Communications.*
28. *Communications Research*, 6 (January 1979).
29. Katz, et al., "Utilization of Mass Communication by the Individual," p. 22.
30. D. L. Mosher, "Psychological Reactions to Pornographic Films," as reported in H. Abelson, et al., *Report of the Committee on Obscenity and Pornography* (Washington, D.C.: Government Printing Office, 1970) pp. 255–312.

31. It can be noted that the satiation effect has been well demonstrated by several similar research studies. See: *Report of the Commission on Obscenity and Pornography* (Washington, D.C.: Government Printing Office, 1970) pp. 97–132.

32. Ibid., pp. 133–169, 170–254, 295–312.

33. *Report of the Commission on Obscenity and Pornography,* (Washington, D.C.: Government Printing Office, 1970) p. 139.

34. Gerbner and Gross, "Living with Television," p. 182.

35. Anthony N. Doob and Glenn E. MacDonald "Television Viewing and Fear of Victimization: Is the Relationship Causal?" *Journal of Personality and Social Psychology,* 37, No. 2 (1979) 170–179.

IV The Outgrowth and Outlook of Mass Communication

12 The Media and the News

All I know is what I read in the papers.

WILL ROGERS

It happens every day in every city where there are news organizations. Reporters from newspapers and broadcast stations fan out to gather the day's news. They go on routine calls to police stations and firehouses, and they are ready at a moment's notice to follow an unexpected lead. They talk on the telephone frequently and sift through endless piles of paper. In all these activities they are after the raw material that will be sorted and sifted and processed in the newspaper or newscast. They are carrying out what Lasswell called *surveillance* of the environment, trying to inventory "what is happening." The result, however, is not a mirror of that environment but a creation molded by many factors.

Several times in earlier chapters we have looked at how the news provides surveillance, at the forces that shape it, and at its effects. In this chapter we pull together those ideas and fill them out to present a comprehensive, integrated discussion of the news. Included here is a search for a definition of news, a behind-the-scenes look at how it is shaped, and an examination of recent trends in reporting. Finally, we will review the functions and effects of the news.

What Is News?

News is one of those things most people think they know about until they are asked to define it. Henry David Thoreau offered a striking, and scornful, view of the news:

I am sure that I have never read any memorable news in a newspaper. If we read of one man robbed or murdered, or killed by accident, or one house burned, or one vessel wrecked, or one steamboat blown up, or one cow run over on the Western Railroad, or one mad dog killed, or one lot of grasshoppers in the winter — we never need read of another. If you are acquainted with the principle, what do you care for a myriad instances and applications? To a philosopher all news, as it is called, is gossip, and they who read it or edit it are old women over their tea.[1]

Idealistic journalists might reply to Thoreau that they're looking not for gossip but for truth. To get a clearer view of what the news is — gossip or truth or something in between — we'll look at it from several perspectives, beginning with a rather philosophical attempt to define it.

Gossip, Truth, and the News

Columnist Walter Lippmann once pointed out that news gathering and truth seeking are in fact quite different: "The function of news is to signalize an event; the function of truth is to bring to light the hidden facts, to set them into relation to each other, and to make a picture of reality on which men can act."[2] News gathering often stops at the facts, which "signalize the event"; in Thoreau's terms, it's concerned not with the principle but with the "myriad instances and applications," with the who, what, when, where, and how of a story. But as alternative journalist Raymond Mungo said: "Facts are less important than Truth and the two are far from equivalent, you see; for cold facts are nearly always boring and may even distort the truth; but Truth is the highest achievement of human expression."[3]

The pursuit of truth is the work of a lifetime and more — it's the work of generations. In contrast, news is a view of reality gathered quickly under difficult circumstances. A journalist works under limitations quite different from those facing the philosopher, scientist, or scholar. Journalists, said critic Edward Jay Epstein, are in "a simple but inescapable bind: journalists are rarely, if ever, in a position to establish the truth about an issue for themselves, and they are therefore almost entirely dependent on self-interested 'sources' for the version of reality that they report."[4] Moreover, all the news can give is a very selective fragment of human activity "photographed" in time, a fragment which suggests a larger view of human endeavor. Contrast, for example, the journalist working on deadline to file a story about the Supreme Court's decision to allow new life forms created in laboratories to be patented with the work of generations of scientists that led to the creation of these new life forms. Contrast the journalist's report, too, with the work of generations of philosophers, theologians, and scientists who have tried to find out what life is and how human beings relate, or should relate, to the rest of the universe.

But to say that news gathering is different from truth seeking is not to say that journalists don't ever seek the truth or that we must agree with Thoreau that all news is no more than gossip. As sociologist Robert Park observed, news is a form of knowledge.[5] But we can distinguish at least two kinds of knowing: "acquaintance with" and "knowledge about."[6] If you read an article about the volcanic eruptions at Mount St. Helens in 1980, you might say you "know" about volcanoes, but what you probably mean is that you are now acquainted with the subject. Bernard Roshco therefore reasoned that all news can be defined as *timely acquaintance with*. News, he said, is immediate knowledge of sufficient information that touches people's personal experience enough for them to share the meanings intended by the communicator. News is usually surface information; it rarely has deep significance.[7] To Roshco, "timely acquaintance with" is a superficial point of information that makes the bulb in people's heads light up immediately. "Knowledge about," on the other hand, requires formal or systematic investigation. As Robert Park observed, news "is not systematic knowledge . . . news remains news only until it has reached the person for whom it has 'news interest.' "[8]

Roshco's view of the limited, superficial nature of the news is consistent with Walter Lippmann's eloquent commentary:

> The news is not a mirror of social conditions, but the report of an aspect that has obtruded itself. The news does not tell you how the seed is germinating in the ground, but it may tell you when the first sprout breaks through the surface. . . . It may even tell you what somebody says is happening to the seed underground. It may tell you that the sprout did not come up at the time it was expected. The more points, then, at which any happening can be fixed, objectified, measured, named, the more points there are at which news can occur.[9]

News, as Roshco pointed out, usually concentrates on overt incidents, not ongoing processes. And because it is "acquaintance with," it is usually descriptive, not analytic.[10]

These are definitions of news from a rather abstract, philosophical point of view. Although they do help us distinguish news gathering from truth seeking, they tell only part of the story in distinguishing what is news from what isn't. They point to the limited, superficial nature of news; but, after all, many overt incidents that we might be given "timely acquaintance with" are never reported. A more practical and empirical view, looking more closely at news items themselves, can supplement these definitions.

An Empirical View

From a practical standpoint, you might be tempted just to say that news is the stuff that fills news columns and newscasts. That definition, however, isn't much help to working news people. Each day thousands of journalists must decide just what is news and what, therefore, belongs in their newspapers and newscasts. Moreover, the standards for what is newsworthy change over time.

News, some journalists say, is the fodder from which the content of newspapers and newscasts is fashioned. It is something that steps beyond the commonplace, the usual. As John Bogart of the *New York Sun* said in 1880, "When a dog bites a man, that's not news because it happens so often, but if a man bites a dog, that is news." Turner Catledge of the *New York Times* suggested that "news is anything you didn't know yesterday." To David Brinkley of NBC News, "News is the unusual, the unexpected. Placidity is not news. If an airplane departs on time, it isn't news. If it crashes, regrettably, it is." [11]

These comments tell us more about what news is not than about what it is, and many news reports don't fit these definitions. Lou Cannon suggested that they "flunk an empirical test" because "they are not really definitions at all but descriptions of what might be called 'exceptional news.' It is obvious . . . that insufficient 'man-bites-dog' items exist to fill the ravenous news requirements of a modern metropolitan daily." [12]

Some of the characteristics most frequently offered to describe what makes something news are:

1. Conflict (tension-surprise)
2. Progress (triumph-achievement)
3. Disaster (defeat-destruction)
4. Consequence (effect upon community)
5. Eminence (prominence)
6. Novelty (the unusual and even the extremely unusual)
7. Human interest (emotional background)

8. Timeliness (freshness and newness)
9. Proximity (local appeal)[13]

Any one, several, or all these factors may be found in a news story. Sociologist Tamotsu Shibutani explained the timeliness of news further:

> Since news has immediate relevance to action that is already under way, it is perishable. This suggests that news is not merely something new; it is information that is timely. Even if it is about events long past, the information is necessary for current adjustment; it relieves tension in the immediate situation.[14]

Even with all these characteristics, however, we cannot distinguish all those events that are reported as news from those that are not. A definition of news must take into account something more than the processes or events described.

A Definition

News, said Mitchell V. Charnley, "is not an event or happening; rather it is the report of such."[15] News isn't something that just exists "out there" and is reflected in newspapers and newscasts. To define and distinguish the news, we need to recognize, as Bernard Roshco said, that "published news has a dual origin. As a social product, the press's content reflects the society from which it emerges; as an organizational product, press content is a result of the workings of specialized organizations whose function is to gather and dispense news."[16]

Thus Roshco says that news is two things: (1) a selective assessment of the society, and (2) the product of a particular news organization. Any evaluation of news by a reader or viewer will constitute a judgment of how well they think the news reflects the world as they know it, how accurately it assesses the society. Almost everyone can agree with the Commission on Freedom of the Press, which proposed that the news media should present a "representative picture" of the constituent groups of society, and thus the world. But how that should be defined isn't so clear, and the definition has changed as society itself changes. Understanding the news, however, also means understanding the organization in which the news is processed — the newspaper, news magazine, or broadcast news department. What news is, is determined by how this organization works, the decisions it makes, and how its members view the world. Understanding the news therefore means understanding how the news is manufactured.

Thus news can be something that journalists know when they

see, something that scholars ruminate about, something that public officials try to influence. Essentially, though, news must be defined as a *report that presents a contemporary view of reality with regard to a specific issue, event, or process.* It usually monitors change that is important to individuals or society and puts that change in the context of what is common or characteristic. It is shaped by a consensus about what will interest the audience and by constraints from outside and inside the organization. It is the result of a daily bargaining game within the news organization that sorts out the observed human activities of a particular time period to create a very perishable product. News is the imperfect result of hurried decisions made under pressure.

Manufacturing the News

The news is a report designed to be consumed by readers and viewers. It is shaped by many forces both outside and inside the newsroom. Among the outside forces are:

- the audience. Who are they, and what are their tastes and interests?
- the community and society itself. What are their traditions, taboos, and patterns of life?
- events. What, in fact, is happening?
- news sources. Who are they? Are they cooperative? To what extent are they self-serving?
- interest groups. Who is trying to get their cause publicized or who is objecting to the media's coverage of events?
- government. What information is the government letting out, and what is it trying to keep secret? How are guarantees of free speech and regulations about libel, equal time, and so on being interpreted?
- economic forces. Is the country's economy dominating people's attention, or increasing or decreasing the media's audience? Is the economy in such a state that the survival of news organizations is in jeopardy? Are costs going up faster than revenues?

Forces inside the newsroom also shape the product we call news, including

- journalistic forms and styles. Reporters sent to cover a fire are expected to return with a short, terse report that assembles the facts about the fire. They cannot return with a poem, a reflective essay, or a lament — not if they want to keep their jobs.
- craft attitudes. What standards and views about how things should be done do reporters and editors hold?

Editors are on the receiving end of a continuous flow of information. In selecting the news to be published or broadcast, they must consider such factors as the policies of their newspaper or station, the amount of space or time available, and the extent to which the public needs the information.

- the medium and technology. Is the report being prepared for a newspaper, radio, or television?
- the organization. Are reporters encouraged to be innovative? To take a particular point of view? How much influence are economic considerations allowed to have on the news?
- time, space, and economic constraints.

In the pages that follow we will look at a few of these factors in more detail.

The Medium and the Message

News is, of course, a message carried by a medium, and that medium — print, radio, or television — can affect both the form and the content of the message. Take radio news, for example, which is known for its short, snappy delivery. The news comes in short summaries, almost like headlines. It is crisp and to the point. If you listen carefully, you realize that it is written for the ear. The order of the words is different from their ordering in newspaper stories. On radio, the action elements are given first, with considerable repetition, to catch the attention of the listener who may not be paying close attention. In newspaper stories the ordering of words is much more complex than in radio broadcasts; it requires the reader to do more thinking.

Television news is still different because images are integrated with the verbal account and it engages both eyes and ears. Thus television news has more tools at its disposal and more creative potential. Television, for example, sometimes uses music in the background plus a montage of images to give an impressionistic portrait of an event or series of events.

The differences between television and newspapers are not simply a matter of spoken versus written words or the addition of images. Television not only *can* use images, but often relies on images. "Talking heads" — a discussion between people — is usually not considered "good television." Television relies mostly on vivid, visual events and has a difficult time covering concepts or issues that don't result in some event that can be shown.

Moreover, according to critic Paul Weaver, the differences between the two media have led to radical differences in the way they tend to present a news report. Newspapers, said Weaver, have a detached or impersonal tone, whereas television takes on the characteristics of storytelling. The sequence of a story in a newspaper emphasizes the key item of the news story immediately, then backgrounds and amplifies it. Television stories are more often chronological, piquing viewer interest and then building to a climax. But a television news story, unless it is just reported by the anchorperson in headline form, is usually given as a narrative. The event is plucked out of its natural context to be reported as news, but then it is given a new context — a beginning, middle, and end. As Weaver said:

> Unlike the newspaper news story, which is designed *not* to be read in its entirety, while still achieving intelligibility, the television news story is a whole that is designed to be fully intelligible only when viewed in its entirety. Its focus is therefore upon a theme which runs throughout the story and which develops as the story moves from its beginning to its middle and then to its end. Information, narrative, sound, and pictures are selected and organized to illustrate the theme and to provide the necessary development.[17]

Given these differences, it is not surprising that television and newspapers select different items and present them differently.

Inherent differences between the media, however, do not by themselves account for the differences in the way news is presented. Generally, the news offered by each medium is the product of the complex relationship between the technical features of the medium itself and the styles of communication required to capture the attention of its audiences.

The Audience and the News

From the consumer's point of view, said communication researcher Wilbur Schramm, the news is read or watched or listened to because of the rewards it offers, which can be either immediate or delayed. *Immediate-reward news* is usually fast-breaking spot news, such as crime, corruption, accidents, disasters, sports, social events, and human interest stories. News of this kind pays its reward to the viewer or reader immediately, said Schramm. "A reader [or viewer or listener] can enjoy a vicarious experience without any of the dangers or stresses involved."[18] *Delayed-reward news* usually involves public affairs, economic matters, social problems, science, education, or health. As the term suggests, delayed-reward news has deferred gratification. "It sometimes requires the reader to endure unpleasantness or annoyance — as, for example, when he reads of the ominous foreign situation, the mounting national debt, rising taxes, falling market, scarce housing, cancer."[19]

Will the audience be interested in delayed-reward news? Many news shows seem to assume that the audience will take only so much of that diet. Local news shows fill many minutes with reports of sports, crimes, and accidents and with happy chatter, and even the network shows usually end with an upbeat, human interest, immediate-reward story.

Expectations about what the audience wants or can assimilate shape the news in many other ways. The news is, after all, communication, and news people often try to take the role of their audience. Interviewers often try to ask the questions that they think their audience would want to ask. Is the audience the elementary-school readers of *My Weekly Reader* or the sophisticated readers of the *Wall Street Journal*, or is it the mass audience of "20/20" or the highly educated viewers of the "MacNeil/Lehrer Report"? Obviously the news is likely to be presented differently to each of these audiences. In a magazine such as *Time* or *Newsweek*, the news is put in a form different from the form in a daily newspaper or newscast. Because they reach a somewhat more educated audience than television or radio news, magazines use a somewhat more sophisticated vocabulary and syntax. The pace is more leisurely and the articles are usually longer and more interpretive in magazines than in newspapers. Newspapers are designed for a busy and hurried reader. Their stories are organized more compactly than magazine stories and have frequent sub-heads.

Not only expectations about the audience but also feedback from them shape the presentation of news. We have said many times that most of the American media are businesses and that newspapers, radio, and television are in the business of selling the attention of their audiences to advertisers; the larger their audience, the higher the advertising revenues are likely to be, and, at least by one standard, the more successful the operation. The audience provides indirect feedback through letters and phone calls, which keep the news people in touch with the audience's interests and sense of what is in good taste and what is fair coverage. Cruder but perhaps more influential feedback comes from circulation figures and ratings. News consultants and market researchers, as we saw in Chapter 7, are sometimes hired to interpret these figures and tell newspapers or stations how to change their news to increase the audience. In the end, the influence of commercialism and of the audience depends on the news organization.

Inside the Newsroom	The news we read, watch, or hear is the result of several levels of decision making. As editor Ronald Buel put it, news is essentially data and data must be fashioned into a product. This fashioning is done through a series of decisions, which can be summarized as follows:

1. Data assignment: What is worth covering and why?
2. Data collection: When has enough information been gathered?
3. Data evaluation: What is important enough to be put into a story?
4. Data writing: What words or images will be used?
5. Data editing: Which story should get a big headline and go on the front page or begin a broadcast, which stories should be buried, which should be changed, and which should be cut?[20]

Who makes these decisions, what standards are they based on, and what limitations influence them? The answers depend on the people in the organization, its structure and the technology available.

The News and Individuals. At some point, individuals must make each of the decisions we listed. Obviously their talent will influence the result and may influence the type of news that is covered. For example, from the standpoint of the way news is managed and organized in the newsroom, journalism educator Todd

Hunt found two kinds of news: event-centered and process-centered. *Event-centered news* is current; it concerns immediate happenings and events. It is collected by journalists "whose primary skills are maximally efficient observation and minimally biased description."[21] Whereas event-centered news provides fragmented accounts of the events and issues of a particular day, *process-centered news* probes the longer-term patterns. It is written when editors find a writer who can integrate and interpret information in a context that results in an understandable and worthwhile report.

Individual ethics, standards, and attitudes also mold the decisions by which the news is manufactured. As Stanley Cohen and Jock Young explained, the news media operate

> with certain definitions of what is newsworthy. It is not that instruction manuals exist telling newsmen that certain subjects (drugs, sex, violence) will always appeal to the public or that certain groups (youths, celebrities, immigrants) should be continually exposed to scrutiny. Rather, there are built-in factors, ranging from the individual newsman's intuitive hunch about what constitutes a "good story," through precepts such as "give the public what it wants" to structured ideological biases, which predispose the media to make a certain event into news.[22]

The ethics of an individual journalist may lead him or her to delete from a story details that would discredit an individual. A news director or editor may support or resist efforts to mold the content of a paper or newscast to the demands of the advertising department or news consultants. A particular editor or news director may have strong views on particular subjects or issues, and his or her policies may reflect these biases. Reporters may then deliberately or unwittingly slant their stories to fit those policies. Failure to do so, after all, might slow promotion, limit raises, or even put a journalist on the unemployment line. Even without these penalties, subtler forces might encourage conformity. Most people, after all, value friendships and like a smooth-running organization. Conflict over a particular news story might not seem worth the unpleasantness. While all these things are possible, of course, there are also strong professional values that push journalists toward ethical decisions.

The Organization. The extent to which such formal and informal controls can influence the individual's work will vary with the structure of the organization. How tightly is it controlled? How much nonconformity or participation in decision making does it allow?

Moreover, to some extent at least, news people learn their attitudes and standards on the job, in the organization. They learn what is important and unimportant by interacting with their fellow journalists. This interaction plus the more explicit rewards offered by the organization in the form of raises and prestige can shape their attitudes, standards, and styles. For example, one newsroom may place the highest value on objectivity; another may be willing or even eager to use stories expressing a point of view. Standards of completeness and fairness may be more or less strictly enforced by management, editors, or colleagues.

More directly, the organization shapes the manufacture of news by deciding who makes the decisions. Usually, reporters descend on news sources first and ferret out information. They then make decisions about how stories are to be crafted, sometimes in consultation with editors, but always under their supervision. Editors make decisions about what to include in the paper and what to discard; they also (sometimes in consultation with others) decide on the emphasis and placement of stories. Top management may make policies that shape and guide all the other decisions.

But within this general framework there are myriad variations in the balance of power. How free is a reporter to find his or her own stories and follow them up, and how much is he or she under the editor's control? How free are reporters and editors to pursue stories that might offend advertisers or audience? If a major story suddenly develops, how much advertising space will be given up for it? In 1966 Fred Friendly resigned as president of CBS News because the network refused to continue preempting regular (and profitable) programs to give live coverage of congressional hearings on Vietnam. Do the owners or top managers impose a "company line"? An editor of the conservative McGoff newspaper chain quit his job after being ordered to run what he felt was a biased personal attack on Senator Edward Kennedy in the late 1970s. And even organs of media criticism aren't immune. In 1980, the editor of *Columbia Journalism Review* was allegedly fired for running too many stories that were strongly critical of newspapers, including the *Wall Street Journal*. These instances, though, seem to be more exceptions than the rule.

The organization also affects the news in more practical ways. How much time does the reporter have to prepare the story? Will it appear on the same day or in a magazine six months from now? How long is it supposed to "last" — just until tomorrow's paper or

News reporters cover everything from what has been called "immediate reward news" (news of fast-breaking events) to established beats (such as Capitol Hill in Washington) from which they offer periodic commentary in newspapers or in news broadcasts.

newscast? Stories must be ready on time, even if a delay would allow reporters to obtain more details or viewpoints. Time and space are limited, and a story must be cut to fit its allotment — or puffed up to fill it. How much money is available? Is there enough for traveling to interview a source in person, or even to make sufficient long-distance calls for information? All this will affect the final product, the news. Related to the constraints of time and budget are the technological resources at hand.

Technology. In earlier times the telegraph, the steamboat, and the railroad affected the manufacture of news. As we saw in Chapter 7, the telegraph changed not only the content of news by expanding the sources and audiences but also the style. Because news stories sent over the wire cost a certain amount per word, the very descriptive language of the nineteenth-century newspaper gave way to simpler, more direct (and cheaper) language.

Technology continues to shape the news product. During the 1970s the use of small, lightweight cameras with portable transmitters and of videotape instead of film (which takes longer to process) ushered in an era of short live reports on television. Some news staffs were so enamored with the equipment that they let an emphasis on immediacy interfere with their news judgment. Viewers were treated to live reports from the scene even if the report came at a moment when nothing was happening. As the anchorperson said, "Now we take you live to the scene of the fire for an action mini-cam report," an embarrassed reporter appeared on the screen and said, "This is the scene where the fire was raging just minutes ago. Now it is over with and the firefighters and trucks have departed." In time newscasters stopped playing with the equipment and used it to provide more and better reports from the scenes of events.

On newspapers electronic editing machines and computers now allow reporters to retrieve material from various sources more easily and edit their stories more efficiently. Of course, the real benefit of this technology will be in its information storage and retrieval capabilities. Reporters will be able to do detailed information searches from their desks and to retrieve facts in a manner that would have been costly and unlikely in the past.

Thus the news media give us a picture of the world that is in large measure something they have created and tempered by the constraints imposed by their medium, their audience, their organization, time, money, and technology. The definition and presentation of the news change as all these factors and society as a whole change.

**News
Reporting:
Changing Styles
and Standards**

In 1950 Alan Barth of the *Washington Post* wrote with great pride, "The tradition of objectivity is one of the principal glories of American journalism."[23] Nineteen years later, Herbert Brucker of the *Hartford Courant* agreed. He concluded, "We can do a good job . . . as long as we keep the flag of objectivity flying high. That will give a more honest and more accurate view of this imperfect world than trusting a latter day Trotsky, or any other partisan on any side, to tell us what's what."[24] Meanwhile, however, the ideal of objectivity had become an object of scorn and derision. "There's no objectivity," said many critics in the late 1960s. "No human being is capable of complete objectivity. Everyone is subjective, and journalists are no different." NBC's David Brinkley even said that objectivity is an impossible goal and urged reporters to adopt fairness as their standard instead.

Objectivity, as we saw in Chapter 7, is a style that is characterized by:

- separating fact from opinion.
- presenting an emotionally detached view of the news.
- striving for fairness and balance, giving both sides an opportunity to reply in a way that provides full information to the audience.

By world standards, American reporters are quite objective. In France, for example, the press is very partisan, mixing fact and opinion throughout news reports. In contrast, American print and broadcast journalists for decades tried hard to separate fact and opinion, keeping factual accounts in the news columns and opinions on the editorial page.

Still, it is true that objectivity had been under fire for generations, as an examination of the trade journals of the 1940s and 1950s quickly shows. But for a few decades there was a consensus among the majority of journalists and consumers that objectivity was a worthwhile goal and a vast improvement over the turbulent and sensational journalism that characterized the American press of the 1920s and earlier, when blatantly biased reporting was common.

Why, then, did objectivity come under such strong attack in the 1960s? In part, its critics came to feel that American journalism was lifeless, unemotional, and incapable of dealing with great social problems. There is much to be said for this view. The press had virtually ignored the predicament of blacks, other minorities, and the poor and the rising tide of their frustration in the 1960s. In addition, the press in the 1960s trumpeted its success vigorously enough to help reopen old debates. Many American journalists acted as if objectivity were an established characteristic, rather than a yet-to-be-achieved ideal. The typical response to those who said coverage was unfair or inadequate was, "We're objective. We just report the news." This rather arrogant refusal to face complaints often enraged critics.

For a while, the press was criticized with a vigor it had not encountered before. In this fate it had much company: during the 1960s most American institutions were challenged by widespread distrust and a search for alternatives. The status quo of the press was said to be a lifeless, bloodless, uncaring journalism. As we saw in Chapter 4, several alternatives emerged, and although they did not revolutionize mainstream journalism, they did have some influence. Here we examine a few of these alternatives more closely: new journalism; adversarial, investigative, and advocacy journalism; precision journalism; and the marketing approach. These approaches can be found in both the print and broadcasting media, although because of government regulation most of them are more difficult to implement in broadcasting.

The New Journalism

The new journalism was never an issue of great concern to the public. It was a movement that concerned mostly journalists and literary people, but it did alter the reigning definitions of news and writing styles.

The first stirrings of the new journalism came from three sources: (1) journalists on newspapers and magazines who felt restricted by the traditional journalistic styles such as the inverted pyramid; (2) literary figures, especially novelists, who wanted to say something in a direct way about the nation's discontents; and (3) broadcast journalists eager to explore less conventional sources and language. The journalists looking for change felt that traditional procedures were not effectively capturing the essence of the great social movements of the day or the changes in lifestyle. They felt that both the traditional reliance on official sources (mainly public officials) and the conventional avoidance of rich description prevented them from capturing the tone of the 1960s. As a result, they maintained, it was impossible to give the public the full story of what was happening. For example, the counter-culture — which influenced millions of young people — for a while was not presented fully in newspapers and newscasts because it was not tied to "authoritative" sources.

Of course, not everyone agreed with this assessment. In fact, most journalists disagreed; and they continued to defend objectivity and traditional standards. But several young writers began experimenting, mainly in magazines but later in newspapers as well. They began to use new techniques in their writing, including:

Scene setting   The new journalists made frequent use of descriptive adjectives to give the reader a sense of being on the scene.

Extended dialogue   Instead of a few well-honed quotations, the new journalists used long stretches of dialogue to capture the essence of a person's language.

Point of view   Rather than trying to be detached and objective, the new journalists sometimes allowed the attitudes or values of their sources to dominate their stories.

Interior monologue   The thoughts of the people who were the news sources, as they reported them to the journalist, might be included.

Composite characters   Instead of quoting all sources by name, the new journalists sometimes created a composite character who brought together the characteristics of several persons and stood for, say, the average prostitute or policeman.

Notice that these devices are old tools of writers of fiction. The new journalists claimed that these methods allowed them to offer a richer and truer, more objective, portrait than the traditional news style permitted. Most of these new journalists were not political activists; they wanted to observe and report on America's manners and morals in an exciting way instead of merely quoting official sources. The methods of fiction writers helped them do this.

For their subjects, the new journalists turned mainly to "(1) celebrities and personalities; (2) the youth subculture and the still evolving 'new' cultural patterns; (3) the 'big' event, often violent ones such as criminal cases and antiwar protests; and (4) general social and political reporting."[25]   Their stories appeared first in *Esquire, New York,* and *Playboy* and then spread to *Harper's* and many other magazines. (Some critics said that magazines with a strong literary tradition like the *New Yorker* had been using the new journalists' techniques for years.) *Rolling Stone* became well known for its receptivity to the style. Before long, new journalism swept into the mainstream of the magazine world, until it became the dominant style in the mid-1970s. By then conventions in

The Media and the News   433

newspapers had loosened, and the new journalism appeared there, too, especially in feature stories and background pieces. Novelists began to apply their skills to actual rather than fictional events.

The new journalism also touched broadcasting. National Public Radio's "All Things Considered" uses creative news-gathering techniques and a literary flair; sometimes the testimony of news sources is re-created, and sometimes their roles are acted out. Television documentaries, too, sometimes use new journalism techniques. The style is also evident in Charles Kuralt's poetic or whimsical "On the Road" interviews with little-known people in out-of-the-way places, although Kuralt's reports predate the new journalism. Heywood Hale Broun's colorful description of Saturday afternoon sports also are kin to the style of the new journalists.

The best of the new journalism reads with the grace and color of short stories and novels. Among its masterpieces or milestones are Gay Talese's portrait of fighter Joe Louis at fifty; Tom Wolfe's *Radical Chic and Mau-Mauing the Flak Catchers*, depicting a party that composer Leonard Bernstein held for the Black Panthers; Truman Capote's *In Cold Blood*, an account of a gruesome murder; and Norman Mailer's *Armies of the Night*, a portrait of the 1967 march on the Pentagon, and *The Executioner's Song*, a gripping account of murderer Gary Gilmore's last days. More radical and less literary were Hunter S. Thompson's books, written in a style he called "gonzo journalism."

It is hard to draw a balance sheet of the quality or impact of the new journalism. Abuses by some writers who were not much concerned with accuracy led to justified criticism. A good deal of the criticism, however, came from people threatened by the new style — from news people who practiced the traditional style and from literary people who felt the nonfiction novels (as Capote's and Mailer's books were called) poached on their territory. Despite the criticism, the new style had some influence on the conventions of journalism. By the 1980s the new journalism's techniques were commonplace in magazines; nonfiction novels were popular; and news writing — for newspapers and broadcasting — was less rigid. For the most part, however, the influence of the new journalism was not overwhelming or revolutionary but subtle and indirect.

Changes in Substance

Whereas the new journalism is concerned mostly with style, adversarial, investigative, and advocacy journalism are more caught up with substance. The new journalism was somewhat obscured from the public; after all, most Americans don't sit around and talk

Reporters Bob Woodward and Carl Bernstein of The Washington Post *became national folk heroes in the early 1970s with their investigative coverage of the Watergate crisis. The pair helped give investigative reporting a new momentum.*

about the usefulness of literary devices. But other innovations were more visible. Most dramatic was the spectacular success of the investigative journalism of Bob Woodward and Carl Bernstein of the *Washington Post,* whose Watergate reporting became famous. By the time their book, *All the President's Men,* was dramatized in a film, investigative reporters had become folk heroes.

Investigative and Adversarial Journalism. Investigative reporting is not particularly distinguished for its writing; it focuses on news-gathering techniques, on strategies for ascertaining information, not on style. It is a method of reporting whereby the journalist essentially investigates a story deeply. At its best, it is an exhaustive process involving numerous sources, including personal interviews, documents, records, and long periods of painstaking observation. Some say that this should be standard operating procedure in all reporting, that all journalism should be investigative. True enough, but those who call themselves investigative reporters often work with an intensity and give investigation an emphasis that are lacking in more routine, general reporting.

Presumably, an investigative reporter could do a probe that would result in a clean bill of health for an individual or agency under fire. More often it exposes something illegal or immoral. In fact, a "whistle-blowing" government aide who makes charges against an agency or individual often starts the reporter on the trail of an investigation. (There is much less investigative reporting of the private sector than of government, probably because reporters have less access to records and other information in business and industry.) Unlike traditional news reports, investigative journalism does not pretend to be disinterested. Instead, it aims at a target, attempting to expose corruption or other abuses through evidence. Persons whom the journalist portrays as guilty of questionable practices are given a chance to reply in the stories, although the material may be heavily weighted against them. In fact, investigative journalism is an outgrowth of the long-standing belief that the press should be an adversary of government. Central to this belief is the idea that the press can and should act as a fourth branch of government, checking and balancing the other three.

Nowhere does the power of investigative reporting glow brighter than on CBS News's television program "Sixty Minutes." The show takes on targets from faith healers to public officials. As it came down hard on consumer fraud and corruption and vividly presented the conflicting statements of its sources, "Sixty Minutes" soared in the ratings. By 1979 it was number one in the ratings of network television. Even on local television there is investigative reporting, although it is still somewhat infrequent.

Some critics worry that the adversarial approach of investigative reporting results in too much emphasis on what is bad and too little on solid analysis and building public understanding of issues and problems. Indeed, investigative journalism lost some of its glow as early as 1976. A team of reporters calling themselves Investigative Reporters and Editors (IRE) went to Arizona to investigate the killings of reporter Don Bolles while he was on assignment — perhaps the first use of a team approach to investigative journalism. The result was a series that ran in newspapers in several cities. It was sharply criticized for its lack of documentation and faulty conclusion, although the IRE stoutly defended its work.

In 1980 another product of investigative journalism was the object of both intense interest and scathing criticism. *Washington Post* reporters Bob Woodward (of Watergate fame) and Scott Armstrong wrote *The Brethren*, which claimed to be the inside story of the U.S. Supreme Court. It was based on hundreds of unnamed sources, many of whom were not witnesses to the events they were discussing. Woodward and Armstrong's use of confidential sources and their generally poor documentation brought them scores of critical reviews. As one reviewer put it, "If this book had been a school term paper, it would have been given an F." The book was not without supporters who praised the effort to penetrate the secrecy of the Supreme Court, but its shortcomings may have set investigative journalism back considerably in public opinion.

Advocacy Journalism. Another alternative reporting style is advocacy journalism, which was much discussed in the 1960s and 1970s. In advocacy journalism the reporter takes a point of view and identifies with a cause or position, perhaps advocating a populist, New Left, or feminist perspective. Advocacy journalism is different from editorial writing. It appears within the form of the news story and in news columns. Although it may express strong value judgments, it is not a simple statement of opinion. In a sense, it is a kind of hybrid news story with a point of view. Thus it departs from traditional journalism and from investigative reporting.

Advocacy journalism appears mostly in magazines, although a few well-known broadcast journalists, such as Geraldo Rivera of ABC, are unabashed advocates, making no pretense of balance or fairness in their stories. Rivera is famous for his exposés of mental hospital conditions, inner city problems, and issues affecting the poor and minorities. Advocacy journalists see themselves as torchbearers for a viewpoint and pursue their mission knowing that there are plenty of people promoting an opposite point of view. For example, several feminist journalists feel that society is so sexist that their work represents only a small step toward redressing the balance. Advocacy reporting is not widely practiced, and most studies of journalists show that it is not particularly admired.

Precision Journalism

Probably the least known of the new methods of news gathering and reporting is precision journalism. Essentially, *precision journalism* is the use of social science methods and information by journalists, and it takes two forms. In *active* precision journalism, reporters conduct survey research or other studies. In *reactive* precision journalism, they use reports already assembled by government agencies, universities, and private firms.

Precision journalists attempt to make journalism more scientific. They assess the views of citizens through systematic sampling rather than through random interviews. Precision journalism differs from the standard use of polls mainly in that it presents statistical information within the context of traditional news stories. Tables, graphs, and statistics are used along with individual interviews serving as examples. Thus precision journalism can provide a fuller and more exact view of the community as a whole. To use this technique, reporters must be trained in social science methods such as survey research, experimental design, and content analysis. They need to understand how to apply statistical tests and how to use a computer or direct someone else to use one.

Since the 1960s, when precision journalism was first introduced and later championed by Philip Meyer of the Knight-Ridder Newspapers, precision journalists have examined such diverse subjects as race relations in Detroit and Miami, criminal justice in Philadelphia, parking problems in Dubuque, and politics and elections almost everywhere. Meyer has said that journalism may someday be known as "social science in a hurry" if precision journalism catches on. The approach is being promoted by a national organization with a small but dedicated membership, a newsletter, occasional summer seminars, and several books and articles. The number of precision journalists is small but growing. The approach is found mainly in newspapers, but newsmagazines, network television, and, to a lesser degree, local stations also use precision journalism. As one writer put it:

> This radical new direction in American journalism has produced an avalanche of research of a type that was once the exclusive province of the social scientist. Since the . . . late 1960s, precision journalists have turned out literally hundreds of political preference polls and dozens of more substantial studies. These have ranged from sophisticated content analyses of court records to criminal victimization studies, to descriptive surveys of special population groups. In many of these studies, reporters have worked hand-in-hand with social scientists, who provide the refined judgment and technical knowledge that minimally-trained journalists do not yet possess. There is every indication that this pairing of academic and practitioner will become more common.[26]

Precision journalism pushes the whole field of reporting toward science while the new journalism pushes it toward literature. Both are helping to refine the definition of news.

The Marketing Approach

Yet another alternative to traditional journalism begins with statistical data — data on the audience. These data are then used as one factor in determining what material will be offered in what manner. In this *marketing approach* to journalism, the content of the news is matched to the interests and potential interests of the audience. Regular reviews of research on the audience determine what stays in and what goes out.

Of course, newspaper editors and publishers for decades have been concerned with what will and won't sell papers. The marketing approach, however, takes this concern a giant step further. Now news organizations invest time and money to answer that question systematically and to apply the answers methodically to shape their products. The marketing approach institutionalizes concern with the audience and revenues and gives this concern new stature in the process of manufacturing the news.

For years the marketing approach has been applied to television news. Changes in format and style were made in order to attract a larger audience — a practice which print journalists often treated with contempt. But soon print journalists had their own consulting news doctors. In the early 1970s managers and owners of metropolitan daily newspapers were appalled by their declining circulations (although total nationwide circulation continued to mount). Television, the growth of the suburbs, new lifestyles, and a lack of relevance in the papers were all blamed. The newspapers responded with market research designed to diagnose the ills causing the decline. The prescription: add new sections on topics such as lifestyles, entertainment, gardening, and housing — sections that help readers use their communities, their environment.

These new sections were edited and written for audience approval. In part they represented just extended and repackaged coverage. For example, many newspapers had covered real estate for years, but, as a result of the marketing approach, some renamed the section Shelter and began to treat the topic from the consumer's point of view — adding, for example, very personal stories about how to find an apartment or remodel a home. Similarly, in their lifestyle sections, through interviews with experts, the newspapers try to tell people how to solve their everyday problems — from how to get rid of those stubborn stains to how to deal with a sulky child or your spouse's affair.

For the most part the new material, sometimes called the *new news*, supplements standard news coverage. It has not replaced the traditional content of the press, but it is taking a larger and larger share of the space or time available for news. In a sense it

These special sections from Dallas, Los Angeles, and Boston newspapers reflect a trend toward a marketing approach to news, in which newspapers carry more feature material and more stories of immediate practical interest to readers.

reflects the goals of the new journalism, which tried to make reporting more appealing through literary devices, and is related to precision journalism, since both emphasize the use of statistical data.

Critics ask whether newspapers and broadcasters, by relying on the advice of news consultants to shape their product, have become followers rather than leaders of taste. As Dennis and Ismach have pointed out, the marketing approach revives

> the old debate of giving readers what they want vs. providing editorial leadership and giving citizens what they need. We believe that the two goals are not incompatible, that newspapers need not go the way of the *National Enquirer* pandering to morbid curiosity, but can and do provide a mix of public affairs news and guides to leisure time and culture.[27]

Does the marketing approach serve readers better or does it pander to the lowest tastes? Philip Meyer, a leader in the precision journalism movement, suggested that it helps newspapers obtain and respond to feedback from their audiences and thus communicate with them more effectively.[28] On the other hand, perhaps it is too early to predict much about the marketing approach, which is a product of the late 1970s. If it becomes commonplace, however, the definition of news is likely to shift further away from an emphasis on public affairs and specific events.

Surveillance and Its Implications

All the journalistic trends we've mentioned — the new journalism, adversarial and investigative journalism, advocacy journalism, precision journalism, and the marketing approach — have something to offer. It is likely that in the 1980s we will see a conception of news based on a blending of these approaches. The new journalism piques reader interest; investigative journalism helps keep people honest; advocacy journalism points to potential problems; precision journalism helps us understand what the whole community — or a segment of it — is thinking; the marketing approach helps to tune the news to the interests, demands, and expectations of consumers.

These techniques sometimes seem to take journalists away from the most basic function of the news: surveillance of the environment. But to "work" and "succeed" news must provide information that people will bother to read or listen to in large enough numbers to make it worthwhile for publishers or broadcast organizations to produce it. Thus the new techniques may help journalism perform its functions better.

*Newsstands carry a variety of newspapers
and magazines to appeal to all interests.*

Sociologist Charles Wright has said that the news, and specifically its surveillance of the environment, has several implications
for society and for individuals. It provides warnings about imminent dangers such as an impending hurricane or military attack,
and it provides a flow of information about everyday life such as
the state of the stock market or traffic. The news can help individuals cope with daily life, bestow prestige on individuals by making them better informed than their neighbors, and build up the
prestige of the person who is the subject of a news report.[29] It
might also be said that the news reduces uncertainty and helps to
hold the society together. It can also have negative effects: it can
stir things up, threaten stability, foster panic, cause anxiety or
apathy, or ruin someone's reputation as rapidly as it can build it.

But assessing the extent to which the news has these and other
effects is difficult. As we saw in Chapters 8–11, research on the
influence of the media in general has not supported the belief that
the media have powerful, direct effects on individuals or society.
The effect of the news is likely to depend on individual differences and social categories and to be long-term and indirect.
Its effect is likely to depend, too, on the interpersonal channels of
communication that spread and interpret information presented in
the news.

One news report is thus unlikely to change opinions and behavior. However, as we saw in Chapter 9, the news media can be agents of change by spreading information about innovations. Moreover, it is most likely that the news, like other content presented by the media, affects the social construction of reality. It probably has its most direct effect, as we saw in Chapter 9, in "creating" social problems by raising public awareness of troublesome conditions. Less directly, the agenda of issues set by the news media probably influences the public's agenda — the issues that the public thinks about, talks about, and considers important.

Some people argue that the press more often follows public opinion than leads it, and the press itself often claims that it merely reflects "what's happening." These claims, as well as our examination of how the news is made and how recent trends have modified the definition and presentation of news, point to an important if not very satisfying conclusion. It is usually a mistake to try to see the press as just a cause or just an effect; it is often both, affecting and being affected by society. To understand the world we can turn to the news media for much helpful information. But we will understand the news and our environment much better if we understand that the media in part create the news and that the news does not have a magical, controlling influence on us — or our neighbors.

Summary

News gathering is not the same as truth seeking. Journalists operate under many limitations, and what they give us is usually not "truth" but something more limited and more superficial: a timely acquaintance with selected facts. They survey the environment to give us the news, but the news is not just a reflection of what is happening. It is a manufactured report of selected events or processes. That report reflects both an assessment of society and the organization within which it is produced. Among the most important forces shaping the news report are the medium, the audience, and the news organization. The organization determines who makes the decisions that produce the news, and it influences the psychological and philosophical constraints as well as the practical ones (such as time and money) that mold the report.

Several trends in the last ten or fifteen years have modified the definition of news and the way it is presented, including the new journalism, investigative and adversarial journalism, advocacy journalism, precision journalism, and the marketing approach. These innovations illustrate that news is the result of social currents as well as of the internal dynamics of an organization. News is always served up to meet the interests, needs, and demands of a particular audience. When it fails to do so, the vehicle that carries it usually dies.

Notes and References

1. Henry David Thoreau, *Walden, Or, Life in the Woods* (Boston: Houghton Mifflin, 1854), II, 148–49.
2. Walter Lippmann, *Public Opinion* (New York: Free Press, 1967), p. 226, originally published in 1922.
3. Raymond Mungo, *Famous Long Ago: My Life and Hard Times with Liberation News Service* (Boston: Beacon Press, 1970).
4. See Edward Jay Epstein, *Between Fact and Fiction: The Problem of Journalism* (New York: Vintage Books, 1975), p. 3.
5. Robert E. Park, "News as a Form of Knowledge," *American Journal of Sociology,* March 1940, pp. 669–686.
6. Ibid., p. 669.
7. Bernard Roshco, *Newsmaking* (Chicago: University of Chicago Press, 1975), p. 5.
8. Park, "News as a Form of Knowledge."
9. Lippmann, *Public Opinion*, p. 25.
10. Roshco, *Newsmaking*, p. 14.
11. Quoted in Ivan and Carol Doig, *News: A Consumer's Guide* (Englewood Cliffs, N.J.: Prentice-Hall, 1972), p. 8.
12. Lou Cannon, *Reporting: An Inside View* (Sacramento: California Journal Press, 1977), p. 23.
13. Taken from Julian Hariss and Stanley Johnson, *The Complete Reporter* (New York: Macmillan, 1965), pp. 32–33.
14. Tamotsu Shibutani, *Improvised News: A Sociological Study of Rumor* (Indianapolis, Ind.: Bobbs-Merrill, 1965), p. 41.
15. Mitchell V. Charnley, *Reporting*, 2nd ed. (New York: Holt, Rinehart & Winston, 1975). p. 44.
16. Roshco, *Newsmaking*, p. 5.
17. Paul Weaver, "Newspaper News and Television News," in *Television as a Social Force*, ed. Douglass Cater (New York: Praeger, 1975), p. 86.
18. Wilbur Schramm, "The Nature of News," *Journalism Quarterly*, Sept. 1949, p. 260.
19. Ibid.
20. Ronald A. Buel, *Dead End: The Automobile in Mass Transportation* (Baltimore: Penguin, 1973), p. 220.
21. Todd Hunt, "Beyond the Journalistic Event: The Changing Concept of News," *Mass Communication Review*, April 1974, p. 26.
22. Stanley Cohen and Jock Young, eds., *The Manufacture of News, A Reader* (Beverly Hills, Ca.: Sage, 1973), p. 7.
23. Herbert Brucker, "What's Wrong With Objectivity," *Saturday Review*, Oct. 11, 1969, p. 77.
24. Ibid.
25. John Hollowell, *Fact & Fiction, The New Journalism and The Nonfiction Novel* (Chapel Hill: University of North Carolina Press, 1977), p. 40.
26. Arnold H. Ismach, "Precision Journalism: Implications for

Sociologists." Paper read at Pacific Sociological Association, Sacramento, Ca., April 20–23, 1977, pp. 2–3.

27. Everette E. Dennis and Arnold H. Ismach, "The 'New' News: Hype or Real Hope?," *Saturday* (weekend magazine of the *Minneapolis Star and Tribune*), April 15, 1978, p. 4.

28. Philip Meyer, "In Defense of the Marketing Approach," *Columbia Journalism Review*, January–February 1978, pp. 60–62.

29. The concept of status conferral was first introduced in Paul F. Lazarsfeld and Robert K. Merton, "Mass Communication, Popular Taste and Organized Social Action," *Mass Communication*, ed. Wilbur Schramm, 2nd ed. (Urbana: University of Illinois Press, 1960), p. 497.

13 Advertising and Public Relations

Promise, large promise, is the soul of an advertisement.

SAMUEL JOHNSON

As the English historian and essayist Thomas Macaulay wrote, "Advertising is to business what steam is to industry — the sole propelling power. Nothing except the Mint can make money without advertising." Almost without exception, Macaulay's principle holds true for businesses today, and it is especially true for the mass media. Their solvency as businesses depends to a great extent on advertising, and advertising depends heavily on the mass media as its vehicle. It is impossible to imagine the American mass media without advertising, for they have grown up together and each depends on the other.

Advertising is basically a form of mass communication. We will examine how it is distinguished from other types of communication, what its functions and content are, and how it has developed. We will look, too, at how the advertising message is manufactured: How large is the industry? Who produces the messages? How are they organized? Advertising messages, we will see, are very closely tuned to public taste, but still they are the object of much criticism. Finally, we examine a field that is related to advertising: public relations.

Advertising as Communication

Advertising is not a mere appendage to the mass media. It has a structure and existence of its own, and it is an important part of the American economy. Moreover, as economic historian David Potter wrote, "Advertising now compares with such long-standing institutions as the school and the church in the magnitude of its social influence. It dominates the media, it has vast power in shaping popular standards, and it is really one of the very limited group of institutions which exercise social control."[1]

But we should look at advertising not only as an economic and social force but also as a form of communication. A television commercial, a catchy slogan, a full-page spread in a magazine, a pencil with the name of a firm embossed on its side, a card above your seat on a bus or subway — all these are forms of advertising. What do they have in common? We begin our examination of advertising with a look at its definition, functions, content, and history.

What Is Advertising?

One definition suggests that advertising is simply "the action of attracting public attention to a product or business [as well as] the business of preparing and distributing advertisements."[2] According to the American Marketing Association, advertising is "any paid form of nonpersonal presentation and promotion of ideas, goods, and services by an identified sponsor."[3] But neither of these definitions notes the role of the mass media in advertising. To correct this deficiency, a leading advertising textbook has defined advertising as "controlled, identifiable information and persuasion by means of mass communications media."[4]

In terms of the meaning theory of mass communication's effects that we presented in Chapter 10, advertising can be defined as an attempt to establish, extend, substitute, or stabilize people's meanings for symbols that label the advertiser's products or services. Advertisers seek to influence language conventions, individual interpretations, and the shared meanings of such symbols so that people will make choices in their personal behavior that are favorable to the advertiser's purposes. In other words, they hope that through communication they can get people to like and purchase their wares.

Advertising is *controlled* in that it is prepared in accordance with the desires of the firm or other group it represents. Unlike a person who grants an interview to the press not knowing how his or her words will appear, the advertiser knows exactly what the message will say. Furthermore, advertising is *identifiable* communication. The message may be subtle or direct, but you know it *is* advertising and not, for example, news. Advertising can be entertaining, but few would claim that this is its primary goal. If advertising entertains, that is only a means to an end. The end is to increase sales. Advertising tries to *inform* consumers about a particular product and to *persuade* them to make a particular decision — usually, the decision to buy a product. Its avowed goal is to guide and control buying behavior, to move the consumer toward one product instead of another. It is thus a form of social control, urging the consumer to conform within a range of product choices, "providing norms of behavior appropriate to current economic conditions."[5]

The Content of Advertising

To accomplish its ends, advertising must make a persuasive appeal. Sometimes that appeal is simple and descriptive; sometimes it is subtle and sophisticated. Communication critic James Carey says advertising is persuasive — and thus acts as a form of social control — mainly by providing information.[6] Indeed, some advertising content is direct and makes rational appeals, mentioning characteristics of the product, relative advantages, and price. A Firestone tire commercial, for example, talks about the durability of the tire and its worth compared to competitors' tires.

Much advertising, however, has little to do with direct information or rational appeals. Instead it attempts to manipulate the consumer by indirect appeals. As David Potter has written, "Advertising appeals primarily to the desires, the wants — cultivated or natural — of the individual, and it sometimes offers as its goal a power to command the envy of others by outstripping them in the consumption of goods and services."[7] Thus advertising may try to get you to buy a product, not because of its advantages and not because of your existing needs, but because of a need or desire that the advertisement itself tries to create.

Almost every appeal imaginable has been used in advertising. Some ads have traded on prestige; others have used fear. Some have promised glamour and the good life. Some have embraced fantasy and others have been firmly fixed in reality.

To make these appeals advertisers associate their product, verbally and visually, with other images, symbols, and values that are likely to attract consumers. An appeal to love of the underdog, for example, was seen vividly in advertising for the auto rental firm Avis that promised, "We try harder." Another kind of dog — the trustworthy family dog — was used by the manufacturer of the first record player. RCA advertised its Victrola with the slogan "his master's voice" and showed a dog listening to recorded music. The starched but debonair look of "the man in the Arrow shirt" provides a model for the well-dressed man. Elegant, tastefully designed advertisements for Cadillacs convey an image of quality and excellence. Coca-Cola's successful "it's the real thing" advertisements show happy, fun-loving, youthful people

drinking Coke against the backdrop of melodious music —
without saying anything about taste, nutritional value, or price.

Institutional advertising is even less direct. For example, a
firm that makes paper and other forest products presents a commercial about the virtues of a beautiful, well-managed forest —
showing cute animals but saying nothing about its specific product. The company hopes, of course, that the public will associate
it with the "selfless" ad and lovely images.

The visual and verbal content of advertising has changed considerably over time — from the ornate and highly decorative soap
and cosmetic ads of the 1890s to the cleaner lines of the Art Deco
designs of the 1920s and 1930s and the bizarre psychedelic
posters of the 1960s and 1970s. These changes reflect the efforts
of entrepreneurs to fashion effective messages. Obviously, in
order to be effective an advertisement must have an appeal to its
audience; it must reflect shared values. Advertising that works is
therefore an index to popular culture. As Norman Douglas wrote,
"You can tell the ideals of a nation by its advertisements."[8] Thus
changes in advertising over the years have been closely tied to
changes in America.

Advertising in America: A Brief History

Until recently, social histories all but ignored advertising. Even
histories of journalism failed to deal with advertising's role in
creating the modern mass media. But since our country's beginnings, advertising has had an important place in the life of the nation. According to Daniel J. Boorstin,

> Advertising has remained in the mainstream of Ameri-
> can civilization — in the settling of the continent, in the
> expansion of the economy, and in the building of an
> American standard of living. Advertising has expressed
> the optimism, the hyperbole and the sense of commu-
> nity, the sense of reaching which has been so important
> a feature in our civilization.[9]

American society provided one important precondition for advertising: abundance. According to David Potter, advertising can
thrive only in a society where there is abundance. When resources are scarce, there is little or no need for manufacturers or
producers to promote their wares. As Potter wrote:

> It is when potential supply outstrips demand — that is
> when abundance prevails — that advertising begins to
> fulfill a really essential function. In this situation the
> producer knows that the limitations upon his operations

and upon his growth no longer lies, as it lay historically, in his productive capacity, for he can always produce as much as the market will absorb; the limitation has shifted to the market, and it is selling capacity which controls his growth.[10]

America has usually provided the relative abundance necessary for advertising to be useful. And American businesses, with the help of advertising, have been very successful at increasing selling capacity. The result is today's so-called consumer society.

Of course, advertising is older than America. The earliest advertising messages were probably those of criers or simple signs above shops. Modern advertising had its origins in the trademarks used by craftsworkers and early merchants to distinguish their wares from those of others. With the advent of printing and an expanding world trade, there was even more advertising. The watermarks of printers were distinctive forms of advertising. Coffee, chocolate, and tea, to name a few, were hawked in messages on broadsides and in newspapers and other periodicals. Proving that advertising could be compelling and useful, the London *Gazette* in 1666 published an advertising supplement to help lost and homeless fire victims get in touch with each other.

In Colonial America advertising had many vehicles — newspapers, pamphlets, broadsides, and almanacs. Early communications media thus became factors in the marketplace for goods and services. But advertising was not a very important source of revenues for early newspapers. They depended more on government printing contracts and the price paid by the reader. This early advertising was somewhat subdued by our standards, and it rarely overshadowed the editorial content of the papers. Still, it often got front-page billing, probably because the news was often less than fresh reports from distant Europe whereas the advertising was current and local.

From the early days of the Industrial Revolution onward, advertising grew naturally as markets expanded and factories tried to sell their goods. In the nineteenth century advertising came to account for more of the content of newspapers and magazines — and for more of their revenue. Like the press itself during this time, advertising was fiercely local and was paid for by local merchants.

Then, around the middle of the nineteenth century, national advertising developed. In America the first advertising aimed at a national audience appeared in magazines, which were really the first medium of nationwide communication. Many of the new national magazines appealed to women, and soaps, cosmetics, and

The forerunner of modern product advertis-
ing was found even in the colonial press in
America. This 1767 advertisement from the
New York Gazette *quaintly calls attention to*
"Sarah's muffins."

patent medicines were among the products frequently advertised
in their pages. These ads created a market for new products; that
is, advertising proved that it could accelerate acceptance of new
products and get people to change their buying habits. For example, in 1851 people still bought soap by the pound. Then a
soap manufacturer named B. T. Babbitt introduced the bar of soap.
When the public was unresponsive to the product, Babbitt introduced a premium. That is, for every 25 empty soap wrappers,
Babbitt promised the buyer a handsome color picture. The lure
attracted buyers, and the idea of premiums took hold. Premiums
are still with us today on cigarette wrappers, cereal boxes, and
other products.

The nineteenth century saw the use of yet another advertising
gimmick: the testimonial. Some firms used photos of beautiful
women and even prominent women such as the First Lady (without her permission) to promote their products. Later, movie stars,
athletes, and television stars would be used.

In the late nineteenth century the happy combination of new
postal rates favorable to regularly issued publications, improved
transportation, and the desire of business for national markets
stimulated the growth of the national magazines and advertising.
Magazine publishers, like newspapers publishers, adopted the
revolutionary idea that the reader should be able to buy a magazine for a fraction of its actual cost (that is, the cost of production);

Truth in advertising has long been an issue. Nineteenth-century advertising frequently resorted to false or misleading claims, as is only too obvious in this promotion for a "bust developer" from a Sears & Roebuck catalogue.

advertising revenue would pay most of the cost. By the 1890s nickel and dime magazines flourished even though the cost of production was much more.

The importance of advertising in delivering information and entertainment products accelerated as radio and television entered the marketplace. It could be said that "Marconi may have invented the wireless and Henry Luce may have invented the news magazine, but it is advertising that has made both wireless and newsmagazine what they are in America today."[11]

The go-getters of American business fought vigorous battles for larger sales in an expanding economy. One of their weapons in this war was advertising. At first essential goods and services had been advertised, then luxury items, and then new products and services. Advertising became the expression of America's commercial self.

As the advertising industry grew, newspapers and magazines developed advertising departments catering to the commercial interests that wanted to buy advertising space. Publications began to compete aggressively for the advertiser's business, especially in towns where there were competing media. Large retail organizations placed large amounts of advertising, and eventually they too established advertising departments to plan their advertising and place ads. By the 1930s there were middlemen who facilitated the relationship between the commercial enterprise and the media organization. At first these middlemen were space brokers — just arranging for the placement of ads — but later they expanded their operations and became the world's first advertising agencies, organizations that eventually provided creative and research assistance and advertising strategies.

Thus the main features of the modern advertising industry were established. Its development both depended on and stimulated the growth of the mass media, of businesses eager to expand, and of consumers who might be persuaded to buy. It has become a mass communication content important to the survival of the mass media and most other businesses as well as a rather large industry in itself.

The Advertising Industry

The advertising industry exists for the purpose of putting businesses who want to market and distribute goods and services in touch with consumers who want to buy and use them. Viewed in this way, the advertising industry itself is a kind of middleman. Components of the industry include:

- advertising agencies
- media services organizations
- suppliers of supporting services ranging from public opinion research to commercial art
- advertising departments of retail businesses
- advertising media: print and electronic media, outdoor advertising, specialty advertising, direct-mail advertising, and business advertising (and the various departments of these organizations that deal with advertising)

These are only the bare bones of the industry. Everything on the list comes in several sizes. Take advertising agencies, for example. There are massive national advertising agencies with offices in scores of cities in the United States and abroad, and there are small, local agencies with only a few accounts.

Although the advertising industry is made up of independent business interests and is by no means a tightly controlled national entity, it is held together by various voluntary organizations and associations. There are, for example, associations of advertisers and advertising agencies. These include the important American Association of Advertising Agencies (or 4As, as it is called) and the Association of National Advertisers (which are the agencies' accounts), as well as regional and state groups. There are also media associations concerned with advertising, including the Newspaper Advertising Bureau, the Outdoor Advertising Institute, and the Television Bureau of Advertising, to name only a few.

These organizations and others produce regular publications that carry news of the advertising industry. Some are general interest publications for advertising (like *Advertising Age*) whereas others are very specific (like *Art Direction*, which deals with graphics). Each category of advertising (direct mail, outdoor signs, packaging, and so on) has its own publications. Information and research services as well as publishing houses and organizations produce much on the subject of advertising.

All this adds up to an industry with a substantial economic impact. In 1977, for example, American businesses spent more than $36 billion on advertising, with advertising agencies taking in about $9 billion of this amount. It has been estimated that more than 105,000 people are employed in advertising, approximately 75,000 of them in advertising agencies. The U.S. Bureau of the Census has estimated that there are nearly 9,600 establishments engaged in the advertising business, including 6,719 advertising agencies.

The trend toward concentration into large firms that we have seen elsewhere in the communications industry is present in advertising as well. A breakdown of agency billings, as shown in Table 13.1, reveals that 200 agencies (or 4 percent) do almost 70 percent of the total business! J. Walter Thompson, the world's largest agency, has billings of $750 million annually and offices in many foreign countries.

The various elements of the advertising industry are interrelated parts of a dynamic system that is very competitive. The image of the harried advertising account executive often presented in movies and television may be an overstatement, but advertising is a field marked by much stress and competition as the various agencies and other firms do battle for accounts. We look next at each of the major components of the industry.

| Advertising Agencies | Advertising agencies have come a long way since the nineteenth century, when they were essentially space brokers. Today, the full-service agency employs writers, artists, media experts, researchers, television producers, account executives, and others as |

Table 13.1　The Advertising Agency Business in Review

Group	Number of agencies	Billings (billions of dollars)	Number of employees
A	200 (4%)	5.2　(70%)	40,000
B	1,300 (23%)	1.7　(22%)	22,000
C	4,200 (73%)	0.56　(8%)	13,000

Source: Otto Kleppner, *Advertising Procedures,* 6th ed. (Englewood Cliffs, N.J.: Prentice-Hall, 1973).

part of the organization. (There are also smaller *boutique agencies* with limited functions and services.) John S. Wright and his colleagues have identified three main functions for the advertising agency:

1. *Planning*　The agency must know the firm, its product, the competition, and the market well enough to recommend plans for advertising.
2. *Creation and execution*　The agency creates the advertisements and contacts the media that will present them to the intended audience.
3. *Coordination*　The agency works with salespersons, distributors, and retailers to see that the advertising works.[12]

Within the agency there are several major functions and groups:

1. *Account management*　The account executive and his or her staff provide services to a firm or product. An account management director is responsible for relations between the agency and the client.
2. *The creative department*　The creative director supervises writers, directors, artists, and producers, who write and design ads.
3. *Media selection*　A media director heads a department in which the specific media to be used for particular ads are chosen.
4. *The research department*　Advertising messages are pretested and data are gathered to help the creative staff fashion a specific design and message. The research director supervises in-house research and hires public opinion firms for more extensive national and regional studies.

5. *Internal control* The administrative operations of the agency, including public relations, are concentrated in one department.

An administrative director runs the agency. Of course, large agencies have a board of directors and the usual trappings of a big business.

Unlike the full-service agency, a *boutique* has more limited goals and services. It is essentially a creative department and may hire other agencies and independent services to provide advertising services for particular clients and products. Often boutiques work closely with in-house agencies — that is, a small ad agency formed by a business to handle its own products. Most boutiques are small agencies established by persons who once worked for full-service agencies.

Inside the Agency

What an advertising agency offers is service, and it is confidence in that service that brings clients to pay 15 percent of their total billings to the ad agency. Just what happens from the initial contact between an agency and a client to the finished advertising campaign varies considerably, depending on the size of the agency and the nature of the account. But, essentially, this is how it works:

The account management director either calls on a business — say, a local company that manufactures solar heating devices — or someone from the business contacts the advertising agency. Indeed, the solar heating company may contact several agencies and ask all of them for proposals, with the understanding that only one will receive the account. The account management director selects an account executive from within the agency, who arranges a meeting of executives from the solar heating company, his or her boss, the account management director, and other appropriate people from the agency. They discuss potential advertising objectives with the client. For example, who are likely consumers for the device? How can they best be reached? Through what medium? With what appeals?

Then the account executive goes to work inside the agency. Research is done to answer some of the questions about potential consumers. The agency's creative department has brainstorming sessions, discussing ideas for potential ads and a potential campaign. Artists and writers draw up sample ads. These may be rough sketches of newspaper and magazine advertisements as well as broadcast *story boards*, which are a series of drawings on a panel indicating each step of the commercial. Depending on how complex and detailed the campaign is to be, a variety of other spe-

"NIPPER" WITH "HIS MASTER'S VOICE"

"HIS MASTER'S VOICE"

Some of the earliest ads were simple signs and symbols. Trademarks, symbols, and logos are still an important force in modern advertising. The dog "Nipper," listening for "his master's voice," remains the symbol for RCA.

cialists may be involved, such as sound engineers, graphic artists, lighting experts, and actors.

What results from all this are sample ads, which are then pretested on potential consumers. The agency's research department goes over this pretesting and suggests which of several alternative advertising approaches would be best for the client. This research also guides the agency and client in deciding what media to use — print or broadcast, outdoor advertising, or matchbook covers.

The account executive then pulls this information together and, along with other agency personnel, conducts a presentation for the company. But first, potential costs are clearly laid out so that the solar heating company can evaluate the proposal. The presentation is often elaborate, with slide and tape presentations and sample ads. Research and creative personnel are called on to discuss the ads, and people from the media department discuss the advantages and disadvantages of using particular media for the campaign. Now the ball is in the company's court. They either accept or reject the agency's proposal. Their acceptance may, of course, be conditional on various modifications.

Once the green light is given, the account executive coordinates activity within the agency to produce the actual ads and then works with the media department to contact the media and arrange that the advertising campaign actually reaches the public. The research department usually prepares to evaluate the campaign so that the agency can present evidence about whom the campaign reached and with what effect — and thus ensure that the account will be renewed in the future. Eventually, the advertisement for solar heating devices reaches the consumer. The success or failure of the campaign depends on whether an ample number of consumers head toward a local store to buy the device.

Media Service Organizations

There are also specialized organizations that spend their time on particular advertising functions, such as buying space in the media and negotiating with advertising agencies for it. Many people in these *media service organizations* once worked for advertising agencies. One type of media service organization is the *national advertising representative,* which has special expertise about network television rates and knows the ideal times to display particular kinds of products. Often, national advertising representatives buy blocks of television time in advance and then sell the time to various advertising agencies for particular accounts. They get involved with an account late in the game, usually after much planning has been done. Other kinds of media service organizations include independent design firms and television production companies. Generally they work with the advertising agency, not directly with the advertiser.

Advertising Departments

Whole industries as well as large department stores sometimes have advertising departments. Unlike advertising agencies, which are independent middlemen serving several accounts or businesses, the advertising department of a business works with that firm's products and is part of its staff. This department has an intimate knowledge of the business or industry and makes proposals for advertising plans and strategies. Its main concern is the final outcome: increasing sales or heightening the awareness of a particular product or service. Advertising departments work closely with advertising agencies, which compete for their business and present alternative proposals for the advertising campaign. Some retail advertising departments resemble small advertising agencies and place advertising directly with local media. For more complicated transactions that involve research and other specialties they look to the agency for assistance.

Advertising Media

The standard mass media are, of course, advertising vehicles. Newspapers, magazines, television stations, radio stations, cable companies, and other media outlets have advertising departments.

Billboards or outdoor advertising are one form that advertising agencies can use as an outlet for messages. Many "strips" — highly commericalized areas along national highways — reflect the abuses, as well as the uses, of this practice.

At both the national and the local level, the media compete vigorously for advertising dollars. Each of the major media has some kind of national advertising association that gathers data and tries to show that that medium is the "best buy" for reaching a particular audience. At the local level advertising salespersons who work for media organizations sell space, either directly to a business or to a business through an advertising agency or media service organization.

In selecting a medium, the business or advertising agency considers the target audience to be reached, cost of advertising, and effectiveness of a medium in doing the job that the advertiser wants done. Newspapers get the largest share of the advertising dollar among the traditional mass media (30 percent), followed by television (19.7 percent), radio (6.7 percent), and magazines (5.3 percent). Other types of advertising account for 38.3 percent.

These "other types" of advertising include retail advertising (signs and displays in stores), specialty advertising (pencils, calendars, and similar items), direct-mail advertising (which takes advantage of special mailing rates to send fliers and brochures to

Advertising and Public Relations   459

people's homes), outdoor advertising (billboards and various signs), and transit advertising (cards on buses, and so on), as well as business advertising (special advertising directed to an industry or business as in trade magazines and displays at trade shows). But even this listing gives only a hint of the diverse media for advertising. There are firms that specialize in exhibits for trade shows and fairs, firms that do skywriting, and many, many other outlets.

Research on Advertising

The advertising industry is a great generator of research. Each of the advertising media hires research firms, rating services, and other groups to gather data that show the pulling power of that medium; agencies conduct research on the effectiveness of their ads, awareness of their clients' products, and the public's response to them. And, of course, academics — including sociologists, psychologists, and anthropologists — conduct research on the industry and its effects, studying topics such as marketing, product appeals, the psychology of advertising, and consumer behavior. Marketing researchers probe the effects of different appeals on various audiences, and mass communication researchers examine the role of particular media in communicating advertisements, among other things.

All this research can be found in many sources. Trade publications and trade journals as well as the *Journal of Advertising* and *Journal of Advertising Research* publish some of it. Some associations and groups will provide a copy of research (for example, on the ability of magazines to sell a particular product such as whiskey) to anyone who asks for it.

Much of the research on the effectiveness of advertising, however, is hidden from the public. Some of it is gathered by research firms and then sold to the highest bidder; some of it is conducted by a specific company for its own use; and some of it is conducted by agencies for particular clients. Moreover, much of this research is self-serving, designed to demonstrate that a consumer or advertising agency or business should take a certain action. As a result, businesses sometimes hire consultants to help them sort out the various claims of researchers.

Studying the Effectiveness of Advertising. Advertising researchers may use surveys, panel studies, or experiments. In panel studies they take a group of subjects and analyze their attitudes or behavior over time. In experiments they might set up experimental and control groups in order to determine the effect of advertising messages. But whatever the method, Russell Colley has claimed that good research on advertising effectiveness must make "a systematic evaluation of the degree to which the advertising succeeded in accomplishing predetermined goals."[13]

What are these goals? If advertising is successful, said Colley, it results in a sale, and to do that it must carry consumers through four levels of understanding: (1) awareness of a brand or company, (2) comprehension of the product and what it will do for them, (3) a conviction that they should buy the product, and (4) action — that is, buying the product.[14] Colley urged advertisers to use precise research to evaluate whether an advertisement has succeeded, including the following types of research:

Audience research Basic data are gathered on the audience to be reached, including the number of people in various groups (based on age, sex, region, and so on) who see and respond to advertising.
Media research The particular characteristics of each medium and what it can do, including comparisons of the pulling power and persuasiveness of various media, are studied.
Copy research Comparisons are made of audience reactions to particular advertisements. For example, researchers might compare the effectiveness of ads using an underdog appeal and others that arouse fear, instill pride, or reinforce old values.

Consumer and Lifestyle Research. More accessible than research on advertising effectiveness is research on consumer behavior, though some of it, too, is privately funded and hidden from public view. From their studies of consumers, researchers help businesses and ad agencies learn who their most likely consumers are and what kind of advertising is most likely to reach them. They might study how needs, drives, and motives affect consumers' buying; how perception of an advertisement might vary among consumers; what opinions, attitudes, beliefs, and prejudices should be taken into account in fashioning a message.[15] Some researchers focus on one group, such as children. These specialists might examine children at different stages of their development and then predict what kinds of things children like at certain ages and what influence they can have on their parents' purchases of toys, food, and so on. Advertising agencies then use this information to prepare commercials for Saturday morning cartoon shows.

Another area of study is lifestyle research, which grew out of research surveying trends in American living patterns and buying

"Hard-sell" advertising makes a direct pitch
for a product, often in superlatives.

behavior. These studies tell advertisers about the changing attitudes and lifestyles that characterize potential consumers at different ages and stages — information that can be immensely helpful in fashioning an advertising campaign. For example, if older people tend today to be moving out of large old houses into small new apartments where they live alone, and if they are interested in simplifying the tasks of managing their new homes and having more free time, then they are new potential consumers for several types of goods — such as frozen foods packaged for just one or two servings, toaster ovens, and airline tickets.[16] It might be worthwhile, then, for companies providing these items to use ads that might have special appeal to older people. Or if college women

The Tree Growing Company.

"Soft-sell" advertising can appeal subtly to the instincts or preferences of a certain audience. At times, too, it is used to convey a public service message not necessarily related to the firm paying for the advertising.

tend not to be attracted these days by "back to nature" lifestyles, then the cosmetics and clothing industries might recapture a large source of revenue, and they should use fashion ads to "hook" these potential buyers.

Generally, advertising research is mostly applied research; its purpose is to help stimulate sales. This use of research to manipulate people has, not surprisingly, aroused considerable criticism, as has advertising itself.

Criticism and Control of Advertising

Few people doubt that advertising has a significant impact or that it plays an important role in America. Most would agree that it reflects the culture and ideals of America — although many people also find that idea appalling. Noting its importance, however, is far different from granting approval, and advertising has been criticized on many grounds. Some critics take on advertising in general, analyzing its economic and social effects; others criticize the content of some advertisements or the effect of advertisements on some groups. These criticisms, as we shall see, have led to attempts to regulate advertising.

The Nature of Advertising: Economic and Social Criticisms

A favorable view of advertising claims that it stimulates competition, which is good for the economy, and stimulates the development of new products, which can be good for the consumer. Proof of the pudding, defenders say, is that people choose to buy the new products. And consumers are happier because they can choose from a great diversity of goods — a diversity stimulated by advertising. By encouraging people to buy more, advertising helps keep the economy, and the number of jobs, growing. By giving consumers information, advertising helps them buy wisely. Advertising, then, is a key cog in the economic machine that can give us the good life, the fruits of capitalism, the American dream.

Critics have many answers to these comments. First, much advertising has nothing at all to do with objective information; it does not help consumers make wise choices. Still, they must pay for advertising, since its cost raises the price of the goods they buy. Thus, say its critics, advertising is wasteful. It makes consumers pay higher prices, and it directs money away from channels that would be far more useful than advertising.

What's more, say its critics, far from helping competition, advertising contributes to monopoly. Large firms can afford to invest in expensive national advertising, whereas smaller firms perhaps cannot. So larger firms can perpetuate and even expand their hold on the market; in other words, those that have, get. Even in the absence of an actual monopoly, some economists see advertising as hindering the development of perfect competition and leading to the condition called *imperfect competition*. Several consequences follow, including, according to Neil Borden, "improper allocation of capital investment," "under-utilization of productive capacity and underemployment," "relatively rigid prices," and increasingly severe cyclical fluctuations — from inflation to recession and back again — in business.[17]

According to Borden, even the diversity of goods stimulated by advertising is not beneficial. Consumers, said Borden, "are confused by the large number of meaningless product differentiations and consequently do not make wise choices."[18] Other critics point to more general supposed effects of advertising on individuals and society: Advertising is said to be often manipulative and deceptive, indirectly teaching people that other people are objects to be manipulated and deceived. By creating new wants and desires, advertising is said to distract people from their "true" selves, to contribute to their alienation and dissatisfaction. It makes of life an unending, hopeless quest for trivial goods or the perfect image.

We certainly cannot evaluate point by point either the economic or the social analysis of advertising's critics here, and we have stated their complaints rather succinctly. But note that advertising is a form of mass communication, and the principles we have reviewed in earlier chapters regarding the media's influence on the individuals and society apply in general to advertising as well. That is, we should not think of advertising as a magic bullet, or the people seeing or hearing them as passive dolts receiving the message in identical ways. Nor should we think of advertising as a single, isolated cause; it not only affects society and culture but is affected by them. Perhaps in the future economics and other social sciences will progress enough to allow us to know and weigh more precisely the benefits and the harms coming from advertising.

Children and Advertising	Few aspects of advertising have generated more concern or more research than advertising directed at children, specifically television commercials. Critics fear that this advertising creates in children wants that cannot be fulfilled; that by prompting them to ask their parents for innumerable things, it generates tension and conflict in the family; and that it "teaches" many lessons that are simply wrong because the children mistake the advertisement for realistic portrayals of the world. In defense of advertising, other observers note that it helps children learn to be consumers.

Any good evaluation of advertising's effect on children, however, requires answers to several questions, including:

- To what extent do children pay attention to commercials?
- What if any effect do commercials have on children's thinking processes? Can they, for example, distinguish between fact and fantasy in a commercial? Do they know that the "Man from Glad" isn't real?
- What if any influence do children exert on their parents' buying as a result of commercials?

Government, foundations, ad agencies, and businesses have spent much money to answer these similar questions. Research by the advertisers and ad agencies, however, is devoted, understandably, to one purpose — finding out how to make better and more persuasive commercials — and their findings are usually kept secret. From other researchers, however, we are beginning to get some answers to these questions.

To date, research suggests that the younger the child, the fuller the attention he or she pays to commercials.[19] Very young children don't know the difference between commercials and programs. Young children pay a good deal of attention even to commercials that would seem to be irrelevant to them, such as ads for cleaning products and commercials; perhaps they are simply using the commercial to learn about what is unfamiliar to them. As they get older, children pay less attention to commercials, and many adolescents scorn them. The available evidence so far indicates that children are influenced by commercials and that they pressure their parents to buy the products they've seen advertised.[20]

In fact, we don't know a great deal yet about advertising's effect on children. Many of the research findings are still tentative; many questions have yet to be explored in depth. Meanwhile, critics such as Action for Children's Television are taking their concerns to the government, seeking controls on advertising.

Controls on Advertising

From its earliest times advertising has been criticized on more specific grounds than the complaints we've reviewed. Whatever the general effects of advertising, the specific content of many advertisements has often been attacked for poor taste, exaggerated claims, and annoying hucksterism. As a result of these specific sins, some controls on American advertising have developed. Shabby practices led to a gradual erosion of the ancient principle of *caveat emptor* ("let the buyer beware") toward one of *caveat venditor* ("let the seller beware"), that is, toward regulation. Advertisers today live with certain constraints — some imposed by the government, some by the industry itself.

As early as 1911, *Printer's Ink* magazine called for greater attention to ethics in advertising and proposed a model statute that made fraudulent and misleading advertising a misdemeanor. Before long, with a strong push from the Better Business Bureau, most states enacted the model statute. Although there is much doubt about its effectiveness, the law was a statement on advertising ethics as well as a standard setter.

A few years later, in 1914, the Federal Trade Commission (FTC) also set up some ground rules for advertising. In administrative rulings over the years, the FTC has written rules related to puffery, taste, and guarantees, and in general it has taken a considerable interest in the substantiation of advertising claims (for examples, see pages 103–104). At times the FTC has demanded "effective relief" for those wronged by misleading advertising, and it has levied fines against companies engaging in unfair, misleading, and otherwise deceptive advertising.

As we saw in Chapter 3, the Federal Communications Commission (FCC) also scrutinizes advertising. It regulates abuses regarding the total amount of time that a radio or television station devotes to advertising and examines the number and frequency of commercial interruptions. In addition, several other federal agencies also influence advertising — including the Food and Drug Administration, the Post Office Department, the Securities and Exchange Commission, and the Alcohol and Tobacco Tax Division of the Internal Revenue Service. State and local governments have passed laws on lotteries, obscenity, occupational advertising, and other matters.

In the private sector, various advertising organizations and individual industries have developed codes of ethics to govern advertising. The broadcasting industry, for example, has codes that set standards for the total amount of nonprogram material (which usually means advertising) per hour and the total number of interruptions permitted per hour. The standards differ for broadcasts during prime time and other times and for broadcasts directed mainly to children. In many states local industry organizations such as advertising review committees and fair advertising groups promote truth in advertising. The National Advertising Review Council promotes ethical advertising and fights deception, and Better Business Bureaus prepare reports on particular firms and their advertising.

In recent years both the public and the private sectors have followed closely various court decisions regarding whether or to what degree the First Amendment's guarantee of freedom of speech and of the press can be extended to advertising. To date, the courts have drawn a line between advertising that promotes one's views — which is protected by the First Amendment — and advertising that is designed for commercial gain — which is not — although at times it is difficult to separate the two.

In addition, many consumer groups monitor advertising and protest when they object to particular content. These groups range from Action for Children's Television, which opposes much of television advertising aimed at children, to religious groups that object to newspaper ads for sex. Advertisers have in the past responded to public criticism and pressure, and advertising has undergone constant change. For example, for many years radio and television commercials included very few blacks or other minorities; and when, occasionally, they did appear, these people were often shown in trivial and demeaning roles. But by the late 1960s advertisements began to include blacks and other minorities more frequently and more realistically. Similar changes have begun to take place in the portrayal of women — who were shown most often either behaving rather idiotically in domestic situations or as passive sexual objects — and of elderly people — who were often made to look like doddering simpletons.

If a large part of the public becomes unwilling to accept demeaning stereotypes, soon advertising will probably follow the public's lead. Advertisers, after all, are not trying to mold society or public opinion — though they may in fact affect both. They are trying to sell goods, and they will change their messages if need be to appeal to the public. If critics can arouse the public to complain enough or can convince advertisers that the public is annoyed, they have a good chance of changing specific aspects of advertising messages.

Critics who object not to specific aspects of some advertisements but to advertising's broader effects on individuals or the society or the economy will have longer to wait for the changes they desire. Government is unlikely to impose stringent controls. Advertisers are likely to continue to appeal to our desire to be attractive or liked or somehow better than our neighbor, to have more or better of just about anything, whatever the psychological or cultural or economic effects of these appeals, as long as they think the messages work. And advertisements are likely to remain nearly ubiquitous unless there are monumental changes in the economy and society. The media, the economy, and advertising are too interwoven today for a workable alternative to the status quo to be evident or for significant change in the near future to be likely.

Public Relations

Public relations is probably the inevitable result of the growing complexity of society generally and of the communication system that holds it together. If an individual or a unit of society wants to be known and understood by the public at large, it must master and use mass communication. This is true whether we are talking about a little-known politician who wants to run for president, a giant oil company that wants the public to think well of it, or a mental hospital that wants its patients to be treated with dignity and respect. In all three instances, it is difficult to think that these goals can be accomplished without some access to and receptive treatment by at least part of the media.

Individuals or social units wanting to achieve a positive public image through the mass media face at least two barriers. First, the media and the organizations that service them, such as advertising agencies, are independent entities with their own goals, which might be far different from those of the publicity seekers. For example, the politician who wants to be seen in a positive light on

Drawing by Stevenson; © 1974 The New Yorker Magazine, Inc.

"Well, Senator, we've sharpened your image, and your recognition factor is way up. Unfortunately, they're all against you."

the 6 P.M. news might not merit any coverage at all in the view of the local television news staff. Or, worse yet for the politician, reporters might be preparing an exposé of his or her alleged wrongdoing. Second, there is great competition for space and time in the news media, and many worthy individuals and causes simply won't get media attention and public exposure. Thus, people and institutions who want public understanding need help. Enter public relations.

A Definition

Because the term *public relations* is used in several ways, it is difficult to define it to everyone's satisfaction. There is agreement, however, that public relations is a planned and organized communications process that links particular elements of society together for particular purposes. A leading public relations text says:

> The term public relations is used in at least three senses: the *relationships* with those who constitute an organization's publics or constituents, the *ways and means used* to achieve favorable relationships, and the *quality or status* of the relationships. Thus the one term is used to label both *means and ends,* to name a *condition,* and to express *the conduct or actions related to that condition.*[21]

The term is also used to describe a group of professional communicators who call themselves public relations people and who have a code of ethics and a professional accrediting process. Sometimes the term is used to describe an attempt to mislead the public. For example, during the Watergate scandal President Richard Nixon used to speak of finding a "public relations solution," meaning a seemingly plausible explanation for the potentially scandalous activity that would get the public and the press off his back.

   Scott Cutlip and Allen Center, authors of a leading public relations text, settled on a rather upbeat definition: "Public relations is the planned effort to influence public opinion through good character and responsible performance, based upon mutually satisfactory two-way communications."[22] This flag-waving definition, however, may be more wishful thinking than reality. It may describe a desirable goal but it hardly offers a neutral description. More accurate is Edward L. Bernays's definition of public relations as a "profession that deals with the relations of a unit and the public or publics on which its viability depends."[23] Bernays added that public relations should serve the public interest, but people have been squabbling for years about just what that is.

Notice that these definitions of public relations sound remarkably like advertising. Like advertising, public relations is a communications process. It is planned and organized and depends, at least in part, on the mass media to carry its messages. But unlike advertising it is really not controlled. Advertising is controlled because it consists of purchased space and time. Public relations personnel, on the other hand, use persuasive means to build a favorable climate of opinion but rarely pay for it directly. Nor is public relations always identifiable. You know an ad when you see it in a magazine, but you don't always know that the sources for a news article were public relations personnel or that a public event, be it a demonstration or a neighborhood block party, was planned as part of a public relations campaign. Rarely do public relations people announce exactly what they are doing. In fact, public relations personnel may use advertising as part of their overall activities, but they are much more involved than advertising personnel in the total process of communication — from initiating the message to getting feedback from the public.

What, then, is public relations? Basically, it is a communications process whereby an individual or unit of society attempts to relate in an organized fashion to its various constituent groups or publics for particular purposes. The purposes usually center on a positive public image. But some institutions — for example, foundations with limited purposes — may want to have a low profile or be regarded as crusty and arrogant in order to avoid public contact and public curiosity. Clearly, public relations is a type of manipulation of meanings, although that manipulation need not be deceptive.

| How It All Began: Origins of Public Relations | Public relations is a rather new field. It began just a few decades ago with publicity campaigns designed to persuade the public to a particular point of view. Its roots are found in the efforts of both private press agents and government propaganda machines. |

In part the field of public relations grew out of reactions to the "public be damned" era when big business did as it pleased regardless of public opinion. Early in this century Ivy Lee, a former newspaperman, recognized the value to business of a positive public image and the possibilities of creating such an image through favorable publicity. He set up an agency to help businesses communicate with the public, and his clients eventually included the Pennsylvania Railroad and John D. Rockefeller, Jr.

Governments also saw the need for persuasive communication with the public. Around the time of World War I, government propaganda machines were competing for the minds and hearts of Americans. The U.S. government set up the Committee on Public Information under George Creel to create public confidence in the war effort and in war bonds.

After World War I, men like Carl Byoir and Edward L. Bernays who had been impressed with Creel's success set up their own firms and began using the term *public relations* to describe their activity. Bernays, who is sometimes called the father of public relations, described his efforts as the "engineering of consent." He developed an eight-stage process from planning to feedback and reevaluation, wrote the first book on public relations, and organized the first university course on the subject.

The Great Depression of 1929 gave business a black eye, and, not surprisingly, public relations practitioners went to work to create a positive image for commerce and industry. During the 1930s and 1940s, business, labor, and government began to employ public relations practitioners in greater numbers, both to generate greater public confidence and support and to help the public understand the growing complexity of society. During the 1950s and 1960s, political and social movements also began to use public relations to achieve their aims and purposes. In the 1970s the consumer movement spurred much public relations activity, in both the private and the public sector. Business responded to the movement's criticisms both defensively and with reforms; consumer groups tried to reach target audiences to warn them of dangers and to seek their support; and the government set up special consumer protection and environmental safety offices. All this activity was closely linked to public relations.

From World War I to the 1980s, public relations practitioners have become more sophisticated, in the research techniques they use as well as the means they choose to reach the public. Even on the international scene, the means and methods of public relations have been evident. For example, some commentators wondered how the Ayatollah Khomeini had managed to come to power in Iran in 1979, given the fact that the Shah of Iran had controlled the mass media in that country while Khomeini was in exile in Paris. Khomeini's supporters revealed that they had made telephone calls to Khomeini that were recorded on cassettes and passed from person to person. In addition, copies of other messages were reproduced on photocopy machines and distributed widely. Clearly, this was a public relations program that worked even without the mass media.

Public Relations in Practice

An industrial polluter wants to convince us that it is doing something to benefit the environment; a health organization wants to break down the stigma attached to mental illness; a government agency wants citizens to make better use of its services. How do they achieve these goals? Public relations.

According to Cutlip and Center, any public relations program must include four basic steps:[24]

1. *Fact-finding and feedback* This stage includes background research on the audience to be reached by the program, including impressionistic observations by knowledgeable observers as well as scientific studies of public opinion. The public relations practitioner uses this information to define the problem and identify the publics to be reached.

2. *Planning and programming* The public relations practitioner takes the information from the fact-finding stage and puts it to work by plotting a broad strategy for the public relations program. This strategy includes a timetable, budgets, and probable targets for the message.

3. *Action and communication* In this stage the public relations program is initiated, using whatever tools and media are appropriate. This is the actual communication in which pamphlets are distributed, speeches are given, or news releases are sent to media organizations.

4. *Evaluation* After the program is initiated and carried out, it is assessed in several ways — by measuring attitude and opinion change among particular publics, by considering the success of contacts with the news media by counting news clippings or reports on radio and television, or by interviewing key opinion leaders. If carried to its logical conclusion, evaluation should affect future public relations activity, depending on what worked and what didn't.

In actual practice, a public relations campaign begins with the recognition of a problem or a perceived need for an image change of some sort. Let's say, for example, the tourism board of the State of New York is unhappy with the state's tourism revenues and thinks this might be caused by a poor public image. The group decides to investigate further and hires a public relations firm. The firm conducts research, including making surveys of selected publics that include Americans who regularly take vacations, travel agents, and perhaps newspaper and magazine travel writers. The survey assesses what these people know about vacation possibilities in New York State; also points up ignorance and misconceptions. And, further, it reveals some genuine worries that keep people from vacationing in New York City.

Advertising and Public Relations   473

The public relations firm then prepares a campaign proposal. It suggests a variety of means to reach the publics most likely to increase tourism in the state. Because all Americans cannot be reached through a limited campaign, the firm decides to aim its efforts at travel writers, in the hope that they will write something about the state as a good place to vacation. This is done by means of news releases, press briefings, and a series of arranged tours for the travel writers. In addition, special mailings go to travel agents who could direct their clients to select New York State for their vacations.

To reach the general public, a series of advertisements are purchased on national television and in the news magazines. Decisions as to specific media are made on the basis of advice from advertising agencies and research on the demonstrated effectiveness of particular media. The proposed campaign is presented to the leaders of the tourism board. They accept it with a few minor modifications and the public relations firm is commissioned to carry out the campaign, which they do over several months. At the end of the campaign they conduct an evaluation that includes making another survey of the same groups who offered the initial evaluation of attitudes and opinions. In addition, the members of the firm look at tourism figures and attempt to ascertain whether the campaign had anything to do with the increases, decreases, or status quo situation that exists.

This is one of the real problems with public relations: the people who carry out information campaigns are not disinterested social scientists, but profit-making enterpreneurs (or government employees eager to keep their jobs and get advanced), and thus they look for "proof" that their information campaign has worked. If it clearly has not, they may try to convince those who hired them that other factors — the economy, overwhelming negative public events, like violent murders — caused the public relations program to fail. Naturally, those who do the hiring are free to make their own judgments about what works and what doesn't. Scholarly evidence about information campaigns — and there is little of it — suggests that many public relations efforts are not successful, but practitioners would dispute this with practical and often compelling examples.

Leaders in public relations are quick to point out that their work includes a great deal more than mass communication. Sometimes they distinguish between internal and external communication. *Internal communication* is communication within the organization itself — to its internal publics. For example, a labor union communicates to its members through newsletters, meetings, bulletin boards, and other media. Internal messages are aimed at a discrete group of people. This is not communication with the general public through public media. *External communication,* on the other hand, is communication to large, diverse publics, or to particular segments of the population outside the organization, usually through the mass media.

The Public Relations Industry

Public relations practitioners today go by many names: public relations counselors, account executives, information officers, publicity directors, house organ editors, and many more. They are nearly everywhere — in the private sector in business, industry, social welfare organizations, churches, labor unions, and so on; and in the public sector in government at all levels from the White House to the local school or fire station. The number of people employed in public relations is almost staggering. The U.S. Department of Labor estimated that there were about 19,000 persons engaged in public relations and publicity work in 1950; 76,000 by 1970; and nearly 125,000 by the early 1980s.

Public relations organizations take many forms, including the following:

1. *The independent public relations counselor or agency* This person or firm operates much like an advertising agency or law firm. It takes on clients and represents them by conducting public relations activities on their behalf. The client may be an individual who wants to be better understood by the public or a large company that wants an experienced firm with such special services as the ability to conduct research or to design publications in order to help the company's own in-house public relations staff.

2. *Public relations departments of businesses or industries* These departments act as part of the overall management team and attempt to interpret the firm to the public and internal constituents and to provide channels for feedback from the public to management. These departments are expected to contribute to the firm's profits by helping it to achieve its overall business goals. The public relations department of General Motors, for example, will set communication goals to support and enhance the corporation's general goals.

3. *Public relations departments of nonprofit or educational institutions* Public relations for organizations such as colleges and labor unions usually involves a range of internal and external activities from publications to fund drives.

4. *Governmental or public-sector public relations* In government the terms *public information* or *public affairs* are most often used to describe activity that communicates the purposes and work of the agency to the public generally or to particular users of the agency's services. For example, welfare recipients may need to know about the policies of the state welfare department and taxpayers need to know how their money is being spent.

5. *Political consultants and other public relations specialists* There are many, many types of public relations practitioners ranging from political consultants who work exclusively on election campaigns to information specialists who are experts in both communications and a field such as health, transportation, or insurance.

6. *Communication policy consultants* A new type of practitioner is the consultant who formulates plans and suggests courses of action to public and private institutions that want to develop a policy on the use of information resources. They may want to affect the policies of Congress or the Federal Communications Commission or to develop an early-warning system for a corporation to assess and trace the impact of a particular issue or program. This new area of public relations is expected to expand considerably in the 1980s.

Criticizing Public Relations

Almost from its beginning, public relations has had its critics. Early efforts were often called propaganda, which took on a negative connotation even though the term originally had a neutral meaning. Public relations, in one view, is manipulative, self-serving, and unethical. It distorts and blurs issues in its attempts to persuade the public, say its critics, and practitioners use just about any means to assure a favorable image for their clients.

Certainly there are some unscrupulous people in public relations, as there are in any profession. Public-spirited groups and the news media, however, try to ferret out deceptive activities. As a result, public relations practitioners are in the public eye much more often than they once were, and therefore unethical practices can backfire, harming the image that public relations is meant to polish. Abuses are discouraged, too, by the growing professionalism of the field. To be accredited by the Public Relations Society of America, public relations personnel must pass tests of their skill in communications and ascribe to a code of good practice. In addition, colleges and universities now have training programs in public relations.

These changes seem likely to decrease the frequency of flagrant deceptions of the public, but they are not relevant to those who criticize the basic task of public relations. The question of whether there is something a bit less than honorable in working just to polish the image of a corporation or individual remains. Defenders say that a corporation or individual has every right to try to put the best face possible before the public. Moreover, public relations does provide useful information to a public sometimes confused by an increasingly bureaucratic world — although that information should be balanced, when possible, with information from more reliable, more objective sources.

Summary

Both advertising and public relations are activities of professional communicators who attempt to influence audiences through the manipulation of meanings. They try to establish, extend, substitute, or stabilize the interpretations those audiences place on products, services, groups, or individuals through the deliberate use of mass communications.

Advertising is a form of mass communication that puts businesses in touch with consumers through paid, controlled, identifiable messages that try to persuade the receiver to make a specific decision — usually, the decision to buy a product. Advertising may also provide information to consumers, but it often appeals not to a rational consideration of the product's costs and benefits but to the consumers' needs and desires; it may in fact try to create new needs and desires in order to sell a product. To be effective, advertising must appeal to its audience. It has therefore been closely tied to public taste and popular culture and has changed as America has changed.

The history of advertising is very closely tied not only to public taste but also to the growth of the American economy and the mass media. Unless there is relative abundance in a society, businesses are not likely to find advertising worthwhile. The nineteenth century in America saw the growth of national media, national markets, and national advertising. Advertisers showed that they could create markets for new products, and newspapers, magazines, and broadcasting stations eventually became dependent on advertising for most of their revenues.

As advertising grew, organizations that specialized in the production of advertisements developed. Today advertising agencies include managers, writers, artists, researchers, and other specialists. Boutique agencies and various media service organizations offer more limited, specialized services, and many businesses and media organizations have departments that deal exclusively with advertising. Advertising today employs more than 100,000 people in America. Concentration into large firms seems to be a trend here, as in other industries.

The advertising industry has many critics. Some economists claim that advertising is economically wasteful, decreasing competition, adding to consumers' costs, and channeling investment away from more productive uses; other economists claim that it promotes competition, diversity, and wise buying decisions. Some critics are most concerned that advertising somehow debases individuals and the culture. Yet other criticism is directed more specifically at advertising that makes exaggerated claims, is in poor taste, is directed at children, or presents negative stereotypes of particular groups. In response to such complaints, both government and the advertising industry have set up guidelines to prevent misleading, offensive, and excessive advertising. And advertising has changed frequently to suit public taste.

Unlike advertising, public relations communications are not always controlled and identifiable, but the two fields have some similarities. Public relations is a process of communication in which an individual or group attempts to relate in an organized way to various groups or publics for particular purposes — generally, to promote a good public image. The field developed after World War I, growing out of the efforts of press agents and government propaganda machines. Today it includes both internal and external communications and both the public and the private sectors. It takes a number of forms, including independent public relations counselors or agencies, the public relations departments of business, industry, or nonprofit organizations, governmental public relations, political consultants and specialists, and communication policy consultants.

Notes and References

1. David M. Potter, *People of Plenty*, 2nd ed. (Chicago: University of Chicago Press, 1969) p. 167.
2. *The American Heritage Dictionary of the English Language*, ed. (Boston: Houghton Mifflin, 1970) p. 19.
3. John S. Wright et al., *Advertising*, 4th ed. (New York: McGraw-Hill, 1977) p. 6.
4. Ibid., p. 9.
5. James W. Carey, "Advertising; An Institutional Approach," in *The Role of Advertising*, ed. C. H. Sandage and V. Fryburger (Homewood, Ill.: Richard D. Irwin, 1960) p. 16.
6. Ibid.
7. Potter, *People of Plenty*, p. 172.
8. Norman Douglas, in *South Wind* (1917, See *Bartlett's Familiar Quotations*, 13th ed., p. 840.

9. Daniel J. Boorstin, "Advertising and American Civilization," in *Advertising and Society*, ed. Yale Brozen (New York: New York University Press, 1972) p. 12.

10. Potter, *People of Plenty*, p. 172.

11. Ibid., p. 168.

12. Wright et al., *Advertising*, pp. 161–62.

13. Russell H. Colley, *Defining Advertising Goals for Measured Advertising Results* (New York: Association of National Manufacturers, 1961) p. 35.

14. Ibid., p. 38.

15. Wright et al., *Advertising*, p. 392.

16. Otto Kleppner, *Advertising Procedure*, 6th ed. (Englewood Cliffs, N.J.: Prentice-Hall, 1973) pp. 301–302.

17. John S. Wright and John E. Mertes, *Advertising's Role in Society* (St. Paul, Minn.: West, 1974) pp. vii–viii.

18. Ibid.

19. George Comstock, *Television and Human Behavior* (New York: Columbia University Press, 1979).

20. Ibid.

21. Scott M. Cutlip and Allen H. Center, *Effective Public Relations*, 5th ed. (Englewood Cliffs, N.J.: Prentice-Hall, 1978) p. 4.

22. Ibid., p. 16.

23. Edward L. Bernays, "Public Relations," Lecture at School of Journalism and Mass Communication, University of Minnesota, October 19, 1979, also mentioned in his several books on the subject. Other information about Bernays in this chapter comes from several personal interviews conducted by one of the authors (Dennis) of this text while on sabbatical in Cambridge, Massachusetts in 1978–1979.

24. Cutlip and Center, *Effective Public Relations*, pp. 138–230.

14 Careers in Communication

If you wish to be a writer, write.

EPICTETUS

To speak of careers in mass communication is to speak of diversity. Each of the industries involved in mass communication is made up of organizations of differing sizes, from multinational conglomerates and large chains to one-person syndicates. Naturally, these very different entities employ persons with a diverse range of training and skills. Some jobs, such as writing, require solitary work and minimal contact with others; some are managerial jobs orchestrating the talents of thousands of other persons. Some roles require graduate degrees; others require no formal training at all. Some people in mass communication are highly paid; others eke out only modest livings. In such a field it is little wonder that there is controversy about the nature of the job market, the best kind of training, and the best pathways to a satisfying career. In this chapter we survey the pathways and possibilities for careers, as well as some of the rewards and frustrations of working in mass communication.

Pathways to a Career

Mass communication includes a great diversity of jobs, but most people would agree on several characteristics of careers in this field. First, they are flexible; they allow talented persons to move in and out of different roles, even in and out of the different industries. A person may at various times be a newspaper reporter, an editor, and perhaps a public relations executive. In fields like public relations a person may go from the public to the private sector. Without a major change in career, a person may have a job that requires much creativity and then shift to a managerial position. The rate of movement in, around, and among the various industries is high indeed.

There is also general agreement that at least some careers in mass communication are glamorous. The images of the investigative reporter, the foreign correspondent, the advertising executive, the film maker, and others have been heralded and celebrated in popular literature and film. Indeed, when the movie *All the President's Men* was cast in 1976, it seemed natural that the investigative reporters were played by two of America's most popular male actors, Robert Redford and Dustin Hoffman. Although mass communicators do not always rank very high in polls of how well the public regards various occupations, the relative status of the communicator seems to be on the rise. For example, the bawdy image of the journalist from movies like *Front Page* is on the decline. "Journalism," wrote Jeremy Main, "*is* fun and it's in the prime of its life. Once an ill-paid and rather raffish trade for disillusioned idealists, journalism is now respectable and reasonably remunerative."[1]

Another point of agreement: jobs in mass communication have changed greatly in recent years, and among those changes are better working conditions, better salaries, and greater social recognition.

There is great social utility in mass communication. American society is founded on the premise that the free flow of ideas is essential to democratic government, and the communications industries are the custodians of that flow. Many people find that it is more satisfying to provide the public with information, entertainment, opinion, and advertising than to produce goods like cars or pencils, useful and necessary though they may be. The people working in mass communication provide the public with obvious social benefits. They may help set the agenda of public discussion, teach children how to be consumers, or entertain millions. The steady flow of criticism of mass communication and public concern about its effects add to the image of mass communication as significant work. Communication has achieved a status and glamour unequalled by many other fields.

Unlike law or medicine, the path to a career in communications is not clearly and tidily laid out with precise requirements, examinations, and licenses. As Jeremy Main said of journalism, it "is a profession only in the loose sense of the word. Its standards range from the eye-popping sensationalism of the *National Enquirer* to the meticulous scholarship of the *Scientific American,* from the

flat objectivity of the Associated Press to the highly personal journalism of *Rolling Stone*."[2]

The path to a career, and connections between education and
the professional world, are determined by a coalition of interests:
those doing the hiring, those doing the training, and the available
pool of trained personnel. Various other forces also influence the
market, such as organized efforts by women and various minority
groups to increase their access to the work force. Basically,
though, pathways to a career in communications break down along
two lines — *general* education and *professional* education. There
are, of course, some combinations of the two.

Traditionally, a prospective journalist, broadcasting executive,
or advertising professional earned a bachelor's degree in liberal
arts and then learned the demands of a particular medium or organization on the job. This pattern changed somewhat as schools of
communication and departments of journalism and related media
developed, especially in this century. Today, the distinction between general and professional preparation has become a bit
blurred. Professional schools and departments that train people
for the communications industries are integrated with general education. Professional programs at the undergraduate level in journalism, for example, typically demand that students take three-
fourths of their work in other arts and sciences and one-fourth in
journalism or related areas. Thus, journalism educators argue that
their students are liberal arts graduates with special capabilities as
writers.

Professional training programs are wide ranging. They include
specialization in such areas as news-editorial journalism (newspapers and magazines), broadcasting, advertising, public relations,
photo-journalism, and technical journalism. In addition, there are
general programs in departments of communication, radio-
television, speech-communication, and media studies. Some
business schools offer work in advertising and public relations;
and departments of film studies help prepare people for that
industry.

At the graduate level there are master's programs that provide
more advanced professional training (and credentials) for persons
entering the communications field. Some people come to professional schools with undergraduate degrees in such fields as political science, sociology, and English; others have degrees in journalism and advertising and want to increase their knowledge and
skill.

At both the graduate and undergraduate level most professional schools have a difficult, dual identity. They must maintain contact with (and the confidence of) the media industries, and they must survive within the academic community. Thus, they speak to at least two constituencies and yet have their own distinct functions. As educator John Hulteng said, "Schools of mass communication must not be mere hiring halls operated at the whim of the industry."[3] Instead, he said, they must be centers for learning and for the advancement of knowledge about mass communication. Sometimes this stance angers media professionals who scorn the broader social and theoretical concerns of the academics. Still, the academic and business worlds manage to work together, and a steady flow of trained people enters the professional world of mass communication.

In the final analysis, employers want competent people with a sense of professionalism who can perform the work desired; good writing skills are essential to many jobs in communications. Some employers prefer persons who have developed professional skills in colleges and universities. Others prefer to provide professional training themselves, either on the job or in special programs. But we can distinguish two broad categories of training most frequently offered by American schools today: journalism and speech-communication.

A Journalism Perspective

Although schools have particular characteristics, their professional programs are similar. Accredited schools and departments of journalism, for example, are monitored by the American Council on Education in Journalism, which is made up of leading media professionals and educators. The council sets standards for class size, student-teacher ratios, faculty qualifications, physical space and equipment, and other matters. Accreditation is granted only to those schools that conform to certain norms and meet certain standards.

Most graduate-school educators in fields concerned with mass communication go to the same academic and scholarly meetings, share similar values, and generally agree on the nature and characteristics of professional education. Still, there are differences. Some institutions, such as Columbia University, Northwestern University, and the University of Missouri, have strong industry-oriented programs in journalism that give much practical, hands-on experience during graduate school. Others, such as the University of Pennsylvania's Annenberg School of Communication, are very academic, believing that the student is best served by a rigorous study of research and theory. Still others, like the journalism schools of Minnesota, Wisconsin, and Ohio State, look for more of a balance between theory and practice.

In a recent nationwide study of American journalists, John Johnstone and his colleagues concluded that "formal training in journalism is by no means typical"[4] among practicing journalists. But this statement is somewhat misleading. Among those studied, 27 percent had majored in journalism either at the undergraduate or graduate level. Journalism majors were outnumbered about two to one by persons with other types of college training. But the schools of journalism were the largest *single* source of trained personnel, although they were by no means the only source.

In the late 1970s, in the wake of the popularity of journalism generated by reporting on Watergate, respected press critic Ben Bagdikian delivered a scathing attack on journalism schools. He charged that they were engaged in the "mass production and questionable education of journalists."[5] Educational programs, he maintained, were out of tune with the realities of the job market. So swollen were the journalism schools with students, he said, that there were more people enrolled in school than there were jobs in the marketplace. He added that there were enough journalism students to replace every professional journalist now employed on an American newspaper.

The Bagdikian report sent shock waves through journalism schools, which were already trying to curb their enrollments. But the "facts" in Bagdikian's report were sharply disputed. Although in 1976 there were about 65,000 students enrolled in journalism schools and only 70,000 news-editorial jobs in the United States, these figures distort the picture somewhat. Actually, only about 14,000 students were graduating each year, and less than half of this number were looking for newspaper jobs. Many journalism schools would more properly be called schools of communication or mass communication, and they provide programs in advertising, public relations, film, broadcasting, and related areas as well as newspaper journalism.

During the 1970s, though, there was a constant debate between professionals and educators about whether the pool of job seekers had grown too large. The numbers of students majoring in mass communication had been accelerating rapidly — faster than the number of available jobs. But by the early 1980s educators reported that they were placing almost all their graduates in jobs. It also appears that enrollments in professional schools are stabilizing.

**A Speech-
Communication
Perspective**

Students in departments of speech-communication in colleges and universities have broad training for several careers. The primary aim of study in these departments is:

> to advance the discovery and application of humanistic, behavioral, and linguistic knowledge of human symbolic interaction. Communication is examined in its various forms, verbal and nonverbal; as it occurs in all media — conference, platform, print, radio, film, television — and institutions; as it is affected by cultural context; and for its influence in the course and quality of public policy and social change.[6]

In addition to studying the liberal arts, speech-communication majors are trained in such areas as rhetoric and public address, communication theory, organizational communication, small-group communication, inter-cultural communication, and radio-TV-film.

Although speech-communication departments do not always attempt to train people for specific careers (as journalism schools prepare students for jobs as reporters), competent graduates have considerable skill in writing, speaking, and organizing meetings and conferences. Thus, they can engage in a wide range of work based on human communication from analysis of nonverbal communication to small-group work and planning public communication programs. Several studies of employers' attitudes toward young job seekers indicate that the ability to communicate is highly valued when compared with other attributes. Employers want people who can write and communicate ideas, who can pull complex or fragmented ideas together into coherent reports. Skills in interpersonal communication and in giving oral reports are also much in demand. By blending education in the liberal arts with the study of communication and its application, speech-communication graduates should be uniquely suited to meet the needs of many employers.

Indeed, the speech-communication graduate should have something that the pioneer public relations counselor Edward L. Bernays has advocated for years: a broad-based education grounded in the social sciences and liberal arts with a sense of a strategy behind communications. Too many people have the tactics (for example, specific job skills and writing), said Bernays, but too few understand social psychology, linguistics, and other fields that provide a strategy — that is, the basis for planning and thinking about communication in its fullest sense.

There is, however, one key problem in this career path: few employers advertise for communicators as such. They want editors, technical writers, conference coordinators, and other personnel. Thus speech-communication graduates must tailor their descriptions of their credentials for a specific position and persuade the employer that they are equipped for the job. Getting a job can be a first test of their skill. There is ample evidence that speech-communication graduates have been successful in doing so. One study found that speech graduates were working in many fields, including public relations, advertising, personnel, communication in business, social services, sales, the ministry, and teaching.

Career Choices and Job Prospects

Even the obvious possibilities for careers in mass communication are tremendously diverse. If you know you want to write, you might look for a career in newspapers, consumer and industrial magazines, public relations, broadcasting, technical journalism, or even screenplays. If you're interested in broadcasting, you might try reporting, camera work, directing, producing, writing, editing, or advertising. Other jobs seem more distant to the beginner — management positions that lead to administrative careers. There are also careers in the auxiliary agencies that serve the media — the wire services, feature syndicates, rating services, and so on — and in research and education. Careers in research require higher degrees. They are usually found in private or public research agencies that probe various aspects, uses, and effects of communication. There are also research jobs in universities and the federal government. And there are jobs for mass communication educators in the secondary schools, community colleges, and universities. A communication educator is usually some combination of professional, researcher, and teacher. Usually these careers require earlier professional experience, but not always.

The qualities needed in communications jobs are as diverse as the jobs themselves. Some demand visual competence; some are entirely verbal. Some require artistic creativity; others, meticulous craftsmanship. But most demand communications skills — whether in writing, public speaking, drawing, or organizational communication. Often, the communications professional is expected to be a synthesizer, a generalist who can organize lucid presentations out of complex and scattered facts. Usually, the communications professional must be able to get along with others and work in a large organization. There are, of course, exceptions to all these statements.

Seeking a Job

Economic trends and hiring patterns are important to anyone planning to enter the communications field. In the affluent 1960s there were more jobs than people to fill them, and employers tried to make their workplaces more attractive. By the early and mid-1970s, as a recession hit the country, even some of the best graduates had difficulty finding satisfying jobs. By the early 1980s there was again a surge in hiring.

But information on the current job market should not be the only factor considered. A career choice is a long-term decision and should not be based mainly on short-term trends. Besides, the so-called job market is a national profile. In a particular city or a particular medium, your chances may have nothing to do with the national market. A national profile says nothing about the chances of a particular individual in a particular situation. As one broadcast personality put it in a meeting with journalism seniors, "There are no openings at our station, but you can get a job there tomorrow if you are the right person." Translated by an optimistic professor: "There are always openings for good people."

In fact, however, the shifting market has meant that persons interested in careers in mass communication have taken their first job in a less than desirable location. Many now-famous journalists and advertising professionals in major cities had to start in smaller cities and with smaller organizations. Some people decide that they like these settings and never move, while the more ambitious strike out for bigger and more glamorous rewards.

What should a student who is interested in a communications career do? A step-by-step approach offered by educators James McBath and David Burhans seems as practical and useful as any. They think that students can enhance their marketability by following these recommendations:

1. Seek career counselling early.
2. Develop key marketable skills.
3. At least learn to speak the language [of the area or field where you plan to seek a job].
4. Get some relevant career experience.[7]

Various professional organizations can help job seekers find and prepare for positions. In advertising there are organizations like the American Advertising Federation/Alpha Delta Sigma and the American Academy of Advertising; in broadcasting, the American Federation of Television and Radio Artists (a union, AFTRA), American Women in Radio and Television, and Broadcast Education Association; in film, the American Film Institute and the

The media employ people in a considerable range of roles. Reporters, writers, editors, broadcasters, advertising agents designers, lighting technicians, camera operators, film makers — these titles only begin to suggest the kinds of career opportunities offered by the communications industries.

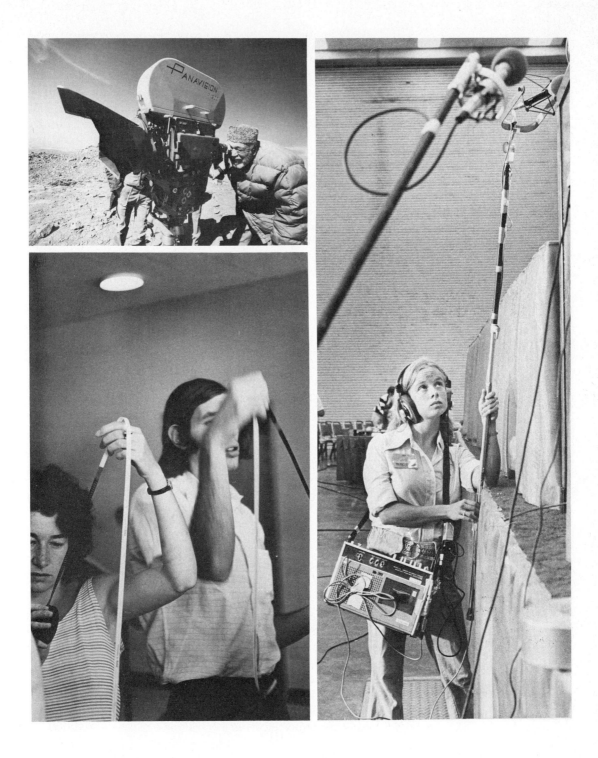

Motion Picture Association of America; in photojournalism, the National Press Photographers Association and the National Free Lance Photographers Association; in public relations, the Public Relations Society of America; in journalism, the American Society of Newspaper Editors, the American Society of Magazine Editors, the National Federation of Press Women, and many, many others. Some of these organizations have placement bureaus. Some are dedicated to advancing professional standards in a particular area; others are trade associations, like the Magazine Publishers Association; still others are specialty groups. Many prepare materials helpful to young people interested in careers.

Rewards and Frustrations

Salaries in mass communication are accelerating. For example, in newspaper reporting, once one of the most underpaid professions, persons who have worked for three to five years on unionized newspapers now earn around $25,000 per year. Journalism school graduates going to newspapers in the early 1980s on the average earned from about $8,000 to $12,000 per year on their first job. More financially rewarding is the field of public relations. The average accredited practitioner was earning $30,000 to $40,000 by the 1980s.

In a 1976 article *New York* magazine demonstrated the variation in incomes, ranging at that time from $12,000 per year for a sportswriter at the *Yonkers Herald-Statesman* to anchorwoman Barbara Walters' legendary $1 million per year. Even though these figures would now need to be updated and adjusted for inflation, they still illustrate the tremendous range of salaries in communications. Some examples from the magazine's report: [8]

Dr. Martin Abend, news commentator	$31,000
Fred Benninger, chairman, Metro-Goldwyn Mayer, Inc.	$194,445
Ralph Blumenfeld, reporter, *New York Post*	$37,000
David Brinkley, newscaster, NBC	$250,000
Steven Clark, sportswriter, *Yonkers Herald-Statesman*	$12,000
Sam Cohn, film agent	$150,000
Richard Curtis, literary agent	$55,000
Hedley Donovan, editor, Time, Inc.	$263,000
Joanne Edgar, Editor, *Ms*	$16,000
Shelton Fisher, chairman, McGraw-Hill Publishers	$195,000
Hugh Hefner, chairman, Playboy Enterprises	$276,300
Judy Klemesrud, reporter, *New York Times*	$34,000

Monica Mayper, editorial assistant, Delacorte Press	$7,400
William S. Paley, chairman, CBS	$731,000
Bob Reiss, student, free-lance writer	$1,000
Eileen Shields, correspondent, *Time*	$21,000
Tom Snyder, newsman, NBC	$500,000
John Stapleton, inquiring photographer, *New York Daily News*	$22,750
Barbara Walters, anchorwoman, ABC News	$1,000,000
Will Weng, puzzle editor, *New York Times*	$33,000

For the most part, salaries in communications are similar to those in other profit-making businesses in America, although it took some branches of the communications industry a long time to get there. There are some unions in the field, namely the American Newspaper Guild and AFTRA, that set salary standards and have an influence even beyond the newspapers and broadcast stations where they are organized.

There are, of course, many rewards beyond money. Prestige is one. It can come from bylines on news stories or credit for a creative approach to an advertising campaign, for example. The opportunity to influence thousands of persons might be another reward. Studies of communicators in both news and advertising report a high degree of job satisfaction, much of it related to the social worth that these people attach to their jobs. They believe their work to be important and beneficial to society. Supporting this belief are all kinds of awards and prizes given for exemplary work, learned treatises on the virtues of the Fourth Estate, and widespread convictions about the "power of the press." All these things add up to ego gratifications for the journalist, in print or broadcasting. Rewards for those working on books and magazines can be similar. For film makers, artistic satisfactions, a glamorous public image, and the pleasures of entertaining other people can provide comparable benefits.

Careers in mass communications can also bring deep frustrations. Some jobs subject their holders to great stress, which can have a debilitating effect on health and can even lead to early death. In a recent ranking of the stressfulness of various jobs, several communications positions were ranked high. Ranked from 1 (the most stressful) to 130, health technicians came first and dyers last. Ranking sixth on the list was public relations; sixteenth was photography; reporters and editors were forty-sixth. Advertising professionals, who are sometimes thought to be under great stress, were not ranked.

Some commentators have said that advertising is among the most stressful of all occupations, and studies show that people in advertising die sooner than the average American. The national average age at death in the United States in the late 1970s was 67.1 for men and 74.8 for women; for advertising agency personnel in 1974, the average age was 64.6. This was up markedly, however, from a 1950 study that reported an average age at death for workers in advertising agencies of 57.5.[9]

There is also a persistent image that communications professionals, especially newspaper reporters and advertising personnel, are heavy drinkers. A few sketchy studies do show that people in these professions drink more alcohol than the national average, but the difference is by no means alarming or worrisome. No doubt, stressful jobs are accompanied by high rates of alcoholism, mental collapse, and other problems. There is little systematic information about the stresses and frustrations of the mass communications professions, but there is no doubt that the more demanding and stressful jobs take their toll.

Career of the Future: Managing Information Resources

The great future challenge in communications will be to manage information resources for a variety of uses in both the public and private sector. This relatively new field, sometimes called *communication policy*, involves the uses and control of communications. It has been accelerated by the computer revolution. As Anthony Oettinger wrote, "Our concern with information policy is inextricably tied to computers and to the communications network."[10] Oettinger coined a new term, *compunications*, to describe the convergence of computers and communications. Oettinger and others recognize that the flow of information is a critical resource for decision makers throughout society. We can't manage any of our basic resources — energy, transportation, health care, or housing — without also managing information. Thus information resources become valuable commodities that must be planned for, directed, and monitored.

What does this mean, exactly? It means knowing, understanding, and using the services and resources of the various information industries and working within these industries. What are they? In a partial list the Program on Information Resources Policy at Harvard University included telephone, telegraph, specialized common carriers, satellite carriers, mobile radio systems, postal service, private information delivery systems, pulp, paper, and board, photographic equipment and supplies, radio, TV, and communication equipment, electronic components and accessories, computer systems and manufacturers, computer software and service suppliers, broadcast television, cable television, broadcast radio, motion pictures, organized sports, theaters, newspapers and wire services, periodicals, business consulting services, advertising, brokerage industries, book publishing and printing, libraries, schooling, research and development, Census Bureau, national intelligence community, Social Security Administration, county agents, banking and credit, insurance, legal services.[11] This broad-based list suggests the dimensions of the new field of information resource management.

Large and small businesses, government agencies, as well as voluntary organizations like hospitals need help in sorting their way through the communications maze. And all the information industries will need trained professionals — people who can write, edit, engage in interpersonal communication, make presentations, and provide technical assistance.

In a world of duplicating machines and tape cassettes, videotape recorders and cable television, opportunities for persons with the interest and motivation to be communicators abound. The first real test of communication skill may be getting a job, but those who succeed will be on the threshold of a new field. Persons with a strong interest in transportation might make themselves highly sought after transportation communications specialists, while others might become experts on the use of federal documents and records vital to understanding and working with the federal government. Indeed, in both areas persons have carved out exciting and lucrative roles for themselves.

Throughout this book we have seen a tendency toward concentration into large corporations, but there is still room for the venturesome entrepreneur who wants to start something new. Many newsletters providing specialized information have become very profitable businesses and are often started on a shoestring. For example, an energetic person, armed only with the federal Freedom of Information Act (which explains how to get documents and records out of the government) and a little capital, can set up a consulting business to help people get federal grants for local communities. Ingenuity can pay off in this field.

Some industries, for example, cable television, are at a primitive stage of development. Cable has ever-increasing capabilities to deliver signals to people's homes, but little has been done to develop creative and imaginative programming. This is only one of hundreds of examples that suggest that communications is one place for a creative career.

The Challenges

The mass communicator enters a career of the mind, but one deeply rooted in the practicalities of everyday life. There is an excitement and challenge to many jobs in the field, as well as glamour. Some positions demand much of the individual's creative and organizational skills; some demand hard ethical choices in areas with few rules and guidelines. And because public communication is just that — public — the person in communications is likely to find his or her work being assessed by many persons. This scrutiny has rewards, but at times it is also painful and requires a resilient personality. Rare is the person who would not find considerable challenge in any one of dozens of mass communications careers.

In the final analysis, the work of the communications professional is reasonably well regarded, socially beneficial, and potentially satisfying. Only a few occupations can be so characterized. In testimony, there are few fields that have more tightly packed bookshelves of memoirs by professionals recounting the excitement and value of their work.

Summary

There are hundreds of possible careers for the person considering mass communication as a field of work. This chapter has surveyed the diversity of opportunities as well as the pathways toward a career in mass communications. Advantages and disadvantages, rewards and frustrations, have been mentioned. Anyone interested in a career in this field should investigate the present job market as well as long-term projections. Some areas presently offer an abundance of opportunities; others offer fewer. Careful planning in conjunction with professional education and various professional societies and groups will assist a person attracted to this field to examine the career possibilities and make a sound choice.

Notes and References

1. Jeremy Main, "The Professionals: Journalists, A Career That's Hit Its Heyday," *Money*, April 1977, p. 46.
2. Ibid., p. 49.
3. Speech to Oregon Press Conference, February 1976.
4. John W. C. Johnstone, Edward J. Slawski, and William W. Bowman, *The News People; A Sociological Portrait of American Journalists and Their Work* (Urbana: University of Illinois Press, 1976) p. 36.
5. Ben Bagdikian, "Woodstein U. — Notes on the Mass Production and Questionable Education of Journalists," *Atlantic*, March 1977, p. 80.
6. James H. McBath and David T. Burhans, Jr., *Communication Education for Careers* (Falls Church, Va.: Speech-Communication Assn., 1975) p. 1.
7. Ibid., pp. 82–90.

8. Bob Reiss, "The Fifth Annual Salary Roundup: Who Gets the Most Money in Town?", *New York*, May 17, 1976, pp. 41–45.

9. *Advertising Age*, June 23, 1975, p. 3.

10. Anthony Oettinger quoted in speech by Senator Ernest F. Hollings to Computer and Communications Industry Association, Washington, D.C., February 28, 1978.

11. Program on Information Resources Policy, *Information Resources: Performance, Profits and Policy* (Cambridge; Harvard University, 1978).

Glossary

Accuracy (in communication) The degree to which the meanings intended by a communicator arouse similar meanings in a receiver.

Activation An effect of a mass media election campaign. Voters who are predisposed to support a particular candidate (because of their social, economic, and political background) are persuaded to go to the polls and actually vote.

Active precision journalism A type of reporting in which reporters use social science methods (for example, polls) themselves, rather than relying on information obtained by others. Contrast with *reactive precision journalism*.

Adoption The act of taking up and using some innovation.

Adversarial journalism A style of reporting similar to *investigative reporting*, especially related to coverage of governmental activity that leads to exposés of wrongdoing.

Advertising Messages designed to inform and persuade consumers to buy a particular product or service. They are often presented via mass media.

Advertising agency An organization that designs and distributes advertising messages on behalf of businesses that pay fees for their services.

Advocacy journalism A reporting style that openly advocates a position or cause, such as feminist reporting, radical reporting from a leftist perspective, and so on.

Agenda theory An explanation of why the public regards some public issues as more important than others. Basically, the theory holds that the news media present some issues more often and with greater emphasis than others and that this sets the rank order of importance that the public gives to issues.

Alternative press Special-interest newspapers that promote ideas counter to conventional norms or beliefs. Such newspapers were especially popular during the late 1960s and early 1970s, when many people were criticizing established social life.

AM See *amplitude modulation*.

Amplitude modulation (AM) A technique of broadcasting sound via radio waves that uses differences in the strengths of waves to transmit variations in sound. A carrier wave is transmitted and an information wave is superimposed on it, altering its height to produce different sounds. Compare with *frequency modulation*.

Associate editor Often, the editor of an editorial page of a newspaper or a person in charge of special sections; the term is used differently in various settings.

Attitude A person's pattern of evaluative beliefs (feelings of acceptance or rejection) toward a topic, category of people, or public issue. Attitudes can be measured by attitude scales that ask people to record their patterns of belief.

Author A very creative and hard-working individual who is regularly hoodwinked and economically exploited by publishers.

Auxiliaries Groups that provide services for media. Examples are wire services, feature syndicates, rating services, and research organizations. Essentially, they provide content, feedback, or data needed in decision making.

Blacklisting A practice of movie producers during the late 1940s and the 1950s. They agreed jointly to bar specific actors from employment in the industry. The practice has been used in other industries as well.

Block booking The practice of requiring a theater owner to agree to take a whole set of films (good and bad) produced by a studio — or get none at all.

Boutique agency A relatively small advertising agency that subcontracts many of its services.

Cable TV A system for sending and receiving television signals by wire from a central facility in a community to homes or other locations. The central facility can pick up signals from satellites or other broadcasting sources, or it can originate its own material. The set owner is charged a monthly fee for the service.

Catharsis In media theory, a process of reducing the urge to engage in violent acts by seeing violence acted out. More generally, the reduction of emotional stress by vicarious activities or soothing experiences.

CATV Community antenna television. A TV-reception system used mainly in rural locations where it is difficult for the home-owner to pick up a signal. A large central antenna is mounted in a favorable location and home sets are served by cable from this central facility.

Censor To delete part of a message in order to prevent receivers from understanding part of its meaning. A person performing the deletions, usually on behalf of a government, is called a *censor* and the practice is called *censorship.*

Chain A number of newspapers that are owned by one company.

Cinema A term used in Europe for film and/or movies. It has a variety of special meanings among different groups.

Cinema verité A style of film making usually associated with documentaries. It became a fashionable term in the 1960s for what used to be called *candid camera,* a style of recording life and people with hand-held cameras and natural sound.

Circulation The number of copies sold to people who subscribe to or otherwise purchase a newspaper or magazine.

City editor An editor of a newspaper who supervises the coverage of news of a local area or city; in contrast with national, foreign, or state editors, he or she is usually in charge of reporters covering news of a city or metropolitan area.

Classified advertising Brief announcements in newspapers concerning items for sale or rent, services, jobs, and other information; usually arranged by categories such as "help wanted," "apartments for rent," and so on.

Coaxial cable A special way of transmitting television signals. The cable has two main parts: one wire is tightly enclosed inside a plastic or rubber tube (like the lead in a pencil); the other is a flexible metal sheath surrounding the plastic and coated with more plastic. This arrangement prevents signal leakage and electrical interference.

Codex An early form of the book. Mayan codices were folded like an accordion with wooden plates at each end. Roman codices were much like modern books, with binding on one side.

Colonial press The newspapers produced in the colonies that eventually formed the United States. Generally, they were small, controlled by the British Crown, and designed for more educated and affluent members of society.

Commercial paper An early form of American newspaper devoted mainly to announcements of interest to the business, commercial, and financial community such as the recording of sales or purchases of stock, ship movements, and news of specific industries.

Communication The achievement of very similar (parallel) meanings in the person initiating a message and those receiving it.

Communication policy Principles and plans in the development of communications technology and other issues related to communications that involve both the public and the private sector.

Communicator Any person who formulates a message composed of one or more symbols that is intended to result in shared meaning and directs the message toward a receiver or receivers.

Compunications The joining of computers and communications. Anthony Oettinger coined the term.

Configuration A pattern in which the whole is more than the sum of its parts. An example in communication is the meaning that emerges from a grammatically correct arrangement of words (parts) in a sentence (the whole).

Conglomerate A corporation or other business group that owns a number of different companies.

Content analysis A research procedure with many variations used for the purpose of understanding and summarizing the major qualitative and/or quantitative features of mass communications content.

Control group A set of persons used in a research study. They are as similar as possible to another set who serve as an *experimental group* and receive some form of treatment. Because the control group does not receive the treatment, the two groups can be compared before and after the treatment of the experimental group to see if it had an effect.

Conversion An effect of a mass-mediated election campaign. Voters attending to political messages are persuaded to change their loyalty from their party or candidate to another.

Cross-media ownership A situation in which a person, company, or corporation owns both newspapers and broadcasting stations. The extent of such ownership is limited by law.

Culture complex Any pattern of interrelated beliefs, attitudes, things, and behaviors that is widely shared by the people of a society and passed on from one generation to another. Examples are basketball, camping, fast foods, higher education, and political elections.

Culture lag A term from the writings of sociologist William Ogburn referring to the fact that a society's ability to produce technology often surges ahead of its ability to devise adequate means for its social control.

Curve of diminishing returns A plot of some event that accumulates over time in which as more and more time goes by, fewer and fewer events are added to those that have already occurred.

Daguerreotype The first form of photographs in wide use. Produced first by Louis Daguerre in 1839, the process imprinted the image on a polished copper plate coated with silver iodide. There was no negative. Daguerreotypes were clear and sharp.

Daily Usually, a newspaper that appears seven days of the week, including a special Sunday edition.

Data Recorded observations obtained in research studies. Data are usually in numerical form, indicating how many subjects did this or that, exhibited this or that characteristic, or acted strongly or weakly in some way.

Delayed-reward news News that provides context and background for the consumer; for example, coverage of economic issues. Contrast with *immediate-reward news*.

Dependence (on mass media) The degree to which modern urban industrial societies would be unable to carry on their economic, political, educational, and other activities without the services provided by mass communications.

Diffusion The spread of an innovation through a society as its members adopt the phenomenon.

Display advertising Newspaper or magazine advertisements that announce the availability of goods or services from merchants or other businesses.

Docudrama A filmed reconstruction of historical events in which actors portray the parts. The original events are often changed to make a more interesting, fictionalized version.

Documentary A film that attempts to portray and explain some real-life situation, usually by filming the actual people in their own setting rather than by using actors and props.

Elite art Art forms and products produced by talented and creative specialists who invent new aesthetic experiences through their forms and concepts.

Elite press Newspapers prepared for and distributed to well-educated and affluent members of society. More emphasis is placed on information and intellectual content than on diversion and entertainment.

Equal time rule A policy of the FCC regarding broadcasts by political candidates. If one side is allowed to make a broadcast, the same opportunity must be extended to the other in an equal manner.

Establishment function The linking of meanings to symbols for individuals in a shared manner among members of a group; for example, teaching individuals new words and their meanings or developing new language conventions in a group.

Ethnic press Newspapers designed to be read by a particular ethnic group, such as Italian-Americans, Cuban-Americans, and so on. Some are published in the group's language. Such newspapers have a long history among immigrants to the United States.

Event-centered news News concerned with specific, finite events, or issues such as meetings and fires. Contrast with *process-centered news*.

Executive editor The chief editorial officer of a newspaper, who usually supervises other editors and reports to the publisher.

Extension function Adding to the meanings a person has for a given word.

Fairness doctrine The policy of the FCC that grants equal broadcasting time to persons representing different sides of a controversial public issue.

FCC See *Federal Communications Commission*.

Feature syndicate See *syndicate*.

Federal Communications Act of 1934 The basic legislation of the U.S. Congress that established the principle that "the airways belong to the people" and the FCC as the regulatory agency to represent the public interest.

Federal Communications Commission (FCC) Federal agency established by Congress in 1934 to regulate broadcast frequencies and licence persons or groups to broadcast. It regulates all forms of broadcasting including marine, aircraft, police, and citizen's band radio.

Feedback A form of reverse communication in which a receiver sends messages back to a sender, unwittingly or deliberately. Feedback can be subtle, but it clarifies how well communication is taking place.

Film Motion pictures as an art form, a medium of mass communication, and a form of entertainment.

First Amendment The first article of the Bill of Rights — a series of amendments to the U.S. Constitution. For mass communication the most significant part of the First Amendment prohibits Congress from making laws that limit free speech and a free press.

FM See *frequency modulation*.

Folk art Art forms and products produced by ordinary people as part of their everyday life.

Form (of a medium) The physical characteristics of a medium and how it is produced. For example, a newspaper with its thin sheets of paper obviously differs in form from a motion picture, which is projected light through transparent film.

"Freebies" Special favors, gifts, or services provided to reporters, magazine writers, or broadcasters in order to influence their reports on the activities of the giver in a favorable direction.

Free press A social and political arrangement of laws and practices that permits newspapers (or other media) to present whatever they wish to the public. In the United States the idea of a free press is valued, but in practice there are numerous constraints on mass media.

Frequency allocation The assignment of specific frequencies (positions on the radio or television broadcasting band). In the United States these assignments are made by the Federal Communications Commission.

Frequency modulation (FM) A technique of broadcasting sound via radio waves that uses differences in frequencies to transmit and receive variations in sound. The frequency of the carrier wave is altered to produce different sounds. Contrast with *amplitude modulation*.

Frequency spectrum The total range of wave frequencies that can be used in broadcasting.

Function (of a medium) That which is accomplished by a medium, for society or for individuals. Among the media's functions are informing, entertaining, or influencing persons and, for the society as a whole, providing surveillance, correlation, or transmission of the social heritage.

Gatekeeper Individuals or divisions in a group (such as news personnel in a television station) who select some items for release in a medium and reject or modify others. The act of such selection and editing is called *gatekeeping*.

Genre Category or type of film distinguished by theme or content. Examples are westerns, musicals, comedies, horror.

Glyph A nonrepresentational symbol that stands for an idea, event, or thing. For example, a circle with three crossbars can mean "power." Unlike *pictographs* and *ideographs*, glyphs are standardized in meaning but are not pictures of what they represent.

Hypodermic needle theory See *magic bullet theory*.

Identification A complex of attitudes and other beliefs shaping the perceptions of an individual regarding another person. The individual approves of, wants to be like, or feels a similarity with the other person.

Ideographic writing A form of writing in which simple drawings or stylized marks stand for particular ideas. For example, a representation of the moon can stand for a month, a bolt of lightning for a storm, and a ship for a journey by sea.

Immediate-reward news News that is extremely perishable and has an immediate payoff for the reader; for example, reports of crimes, fires, natural disasters, and so on. Contrast with *delayed-reward news*.

Impedance Any reduction in accuracy; that is, any dissimilarity between the meanings intended by a communicator and those aroused in the receiver of the message.

Imprinting (of traces) The process of establishing traces in the brain; traces are the biochemical basis of memory.

Incidental learning The acquisition of ideas or behavior patterns when neither the teaching nor the learning is deliberate.

Individual differences theory The view that a person's habits of selecting particular types of media content and responding to them in distinctive ways is due to that person's particular personality structure.

Influence Changing a person's understandings, feelings, beliefs, opinions, attitudes, or overt behaviors in any way, trivial or significant.

Information In communication theory, the physical events that make possible the transmission of auditory or visual phenomena over distance. Examples are variations in sound or light waves and electrical impulses moving along a wire.

Innovations New ideas, technical inventions, or forms of behavior that a population adopts.

Institution A sociological term indicating a complex of social practices, ideas, and expectations deeply established (institutionalized) in the behavior of people. The media in modern society are a social institution in this sense.

Institutional advertising A form of long-range advertising designed to create a particular construction of reality — the image of a company as wholesome, responsible, or concerned about the important things.

Inverted pyramid style A somewhat standardized format for presenting a news story. In this format the reporter explains clearly what happened to whom with what causes and consequences and gives the most important facts first, those next in importance second, and so on to the minor details.

Investigative reporting (or journalism) A style of reporting that emphasizes the careful assembly of facts in order to gain the inside story and expose wrongdoing.

Jazz journalism A form of *yellow journalism* that persisted into the twentieth century. It was characterized by the *tabloid* format and the extensive use of dramatic photographs.

Journalism review A publication, usually but not always produced by professional journalists, that criticizes the practices of the media.

Kitsch Art forms that are of low quality or are poor imitations of more sophisticated products or styles. Many critics claim that most entertainment produced for the mass media is *kitsch*.

Labeling In communication theory, the activity of assigning a particular word or other symbol to a meaning experience associated with a given object, event, or situation. *Reverse labeling* is the opposite: assigning a particular meaning experience to a given word or symbol that has been perceived.

Law of large numbers The relationship among the size of an audience for a medium, the profit that medium can make from advertisers, and the taste level of the medium's content: the greater the number of receivers, the greater the profit. This relationship leads to an emphasis on content with a low intellectual level and aesthetic taste to attract the largest possible audience. The larger the audience, the larger the profit, and the lower the taste level of the content.

Legacy of fear A set of beliefs shared by the public that mass communications are powerful and dangerous; that is, that they can and sometimes do produce socially undesirable effects on their audiences.

Libel The act of publishing material with the intent of damaging a person's reputation.

Longitudinal study Research that follows the behavior of a group of subjects over a long time, such as several years. The study systematically notes changes in the behavior that can be attributed to known influences.

Magic bullet theory An explanation of the effects of exposure to mass media content. The explanation assumes that *all* subjects will receive some critical feature of the message (the magic bullet) that will change them in the same way. Also called *hypodermic needle theory, stimulus-response theory.*

Managing editor A kind of editorial personnel director on a newspaper, especially involved in hiring and some newsroom supervision of personnel. Reports to the executive editor.

Marketing approach (to journalism) The practice of making editorial decisions on the basis of market research on readers and their needs and wants.

Market research Investigations based on applied social science techniques that try to discover what consumers want in a product, why they do or do not buy it, and what might lead them to purchase it more frequently. A frequent topic of such research is the effectiveness of advertising.

Mass Members of a society with a specific set of characteristics: the mass is made up of relatively unorganized people, not members of binding groups or families, who tend to act and react as individuals rather than as members of a group following norms and roles.

Mass communication A multistage process in which professional communicators use media to send out messages rapidly and continuously to stimulate meanings and to achieve change among large and diverse audiences.

Mass media Devices for moving messages across distance or time to accomplish mass communication. The major mass media in modern society are books, magazines, newspapers, motion pictures, radio, and television.

Meaning The internal experiences of a person responding to an object or event that has a name (a word or other symbol) in his or her language. Shared (parallel) meanings between people are the essence of communication.

Meaning theory An explanation of the part played by mass communication in the social construction of reality. The activities and situations acted out, displayed, or described in media portrayals provide meanings for words and other symbols.

Media access movement Efforts, largely by minority groups and other special interests, to get access to the media for the purpose of having their views heard.

Media service organizations A variety of organizations that for a fee provide specialized services for advertising agencies. They buy newspaper space or time on radio or television, and provide talent or other needed services.

Medical model Explanations of deviant behavior that define it as a sickness that has a causal sequence, that can be treated by therapy, and that can be cured. Rightly or wrongly, this framework has been applied to such deviant behaviors as alcoholism, drug abuse, homosexuality, child abuse, criminality, delinquency, and so on.

Medium (plural, *media*) Any object or arrangement of objects, at rest or in motion, that can be used to represent meanings; for example, smoke signals, drum beats, marker stones, trail blazes, dances, markings on pottery, tattoos, ink on paper, or modern mass media.

Message A symbol or configuration of symbols that can arouse similar meanings in both sender and receiver.

Microwave Electromagnetic waves of extremely high frequency but small amplitude used to transmit television signals from tower to tower over long distances. Microwaves have numerous other applications (for example, in ovens).

Modeling theory An explanation of the influence of mass communication that sets forth the conditions under which a person will adopt a form of behavior after seeing it portrayed (modeled) in media content.

Movies The industry that produces, distributes, and exhibits films to make a profit.

Muckraking A term applied by President Theodore Roosevelt to the activities of some magazine writers who exposed graft, corruption, and social problems in American society during the late nineteenth century.

Multistage flow (of information) A process by which a message is passed on from a person who originally received it from a medium. It passes through a number of additional people, often in complex chains.

National development The process of social and cultural change by which traditional societies are modernized.

Network In broadcasting, a group of radio or television stations that operate as part of the same corporation. Some are owned by the corporation; others subscribe to its services and broadcast the content released by that corporation.

New journalism A style of journalism that emerged in the 1960s in which writers expressed their feelings and values and used techniques usually found in fiction (for example, extensive description and interior monologues).

News perspective A set of criteria used by news personnel in deciding whether and how to present a news item. They take into account a story's commercial value (that is, its likely effect on their ratings), their limited resources, the availability of alternatives, the audience, and their competitors' practices.

Nickelodeon One of the first types of motion picture theaters in wide use. The term came from Harry Davis and John Harris of Pittsburgh, who charged a nickel for admission to their theater in 1905.

Objective reporting An impersonal style of news reporting that emphasizes the facts rather than the reporter's interpretations or opinions.

Ombudsman Generally, a person working in a bureaucratic setting whose task is to solve problems quickly that cannot be handled easily by routine processes.

Opinion leaders Those who are directly exposed to media content and deliberately or unwittingly influence others to whom they pass on such content.

Overt behavior Actions that can be easily observed by another person. Such behavior is usually thought of as going beyond thinking or talking to include physical activity, such as is involved in buying, voting, donating, participating in groups, or other complex conduct.

Pay TV See *subscription TV*.

Penetration See *saturation*.

Penny press The first mass newspapers. Originating in the early 1830s in New York, they sold for a penny in the streets, made a profit from advertisers, and were oriented toward less-educated, ordinary citizens.

Perception (perceive, perceiving) For human beings, the mental activity of organizing the input of one's senses (sight, hearing, touch, and smell) into interpretations that make sense in terms of one's culture and past experience. In other words, interpreting stimuli in meaningful ways.

Personal influence Changes in people's beliefs, attitudes, or behavior brought about by messages received by personal, face-to-face communication.

Phonetic writing A system of writing in which each letter or character indicates a specific sound of human speech. The widely used alphabet, familiar to English speakers, is a good example. Many languages today use phonetic writing, but some, including Chinese, do not.

Pictographic writing An early form of writing in which ideas were represented by simple drawings. Arranged in a sequence, the drawings could tell a story (such as the tale of a military victory, a successful hunt, or a journey); but because the meanings of the drawings were not standardized, interpretation was not always precise.

Political paper An early form of American newspaper controlled and often subsidized by a political party or faction. These papers emphasized the point of view of the political groups who supported and controlled them.

Popular culture Music, drama, and other entertainment content of mass communication that is simple, makes few intellectual demands, is not creative, and is largely repetitive in form.

Popular press Newspapers that are prepared for and distributed to people in all levels of society, especially those in the middle and lower levels. They give less emphasis to intellectual content than to entertainment.

Pornography Printed material, pictures, or movies that give explicit portrayals of people in sexual situations. In particular, material of this type that is, according to the standards of the community in which it is available, obscene and without redeeming social value such as might be found in a work of art.

Portrayal The representation of some aspect of social life or physical events or situations to which words or other symbols are associated. Portrayals in this sense show the meanings we share for words.

Precision journalism A form of reporting that makes extensive use of the methods of social science, such as polls, surveys, and statistical analysis.

Press council A voluntary organization of citizens in a community to provide a forum for criticism of the press. Such groups exist in many nations as a result of a spread of the idea since World War I.

Prior restraint A legal procedure by which a government reviews news releases before giving permission for their release. This is not practiced in countries that have freedom of the press.

Process Any series of activities that transforms something through a set of distinctive operations. The term is widely used in science, engineering, and technology to describe successive stages in the production of a product, outcome, or effect.

Process-centered news Complex news that goes beyond a single, fragmented report or issue to convey a comprehensive, systematic understanding, such as reports of the consequences of governmental activity. Contrast with *event-centered news.*

Professional communicators Those who produce or disseminate mass communication content as an occupation; for example, reporters, newscasters, sportswriters, movie directors, scriptwriters, actors, and so on.

Propaganda Mass communication content — whether news stories, advertisements, dramas, and so on — that is deliberately designed to change the beliefs, attitudes, or behavior of an audience.

Protestant ethic A set of beliefs that places value on hard work, frugality, rational planning, self-denial, and postponement of reward to self. These beliefs originated in early Protestant religious groups but eventually became the "work ethic" of modern capitalism. These issues have been thoroughly analyzed by the German sociologist Max Weber.

Pseudoevent Events of minor significance that the news media build up to make them appear important.

Public opinion poll Measures of the public's beliefs or feelings about an issue or topic. These measures are obtained by interviewing various kinds of samples of persons in the population under study, usually with a standardized questionnaire prepared for the purpose.

Public relations A systematic process of communication that involves the identification of discrete publics and the tailoring of specific messages to them.

Publisher The person or group of persons who exercise top management decisions over a print medium.

Rating services Organizations that for a fee provide research on audience sizes, behaviors, and characteristics. Rating services measure newspaper and magazine circulations, as well as radio and television audiences, in terms of patterns of attention to various content and the social categories of the people attending.

Reactive precision journalism Reporters' use of social science data that have been gathered by others; for example, using census data in a report on a community. Contrast with *active precision journalism.*

Receiver A person to whom a message has been sent and who perceives and understands that message.

Reinforcement An effect of a mass media election campaign. Voters attending to the political messages of their favored party or candidate increase their commitment.

Reliability The degree to which a form of measurement will produce consistent results. For example, a tape measure used repeatedly to measure a given board will give very consistent (that is, very reliable) results. An IQ test given to a person on different occasions may give less consistent results.

Reviewers Persons who view films or other communications and tell consumers how good or bad the product is in terms of general appeal.

Role model Definitions of what activities are suitable and expected of a person in a particular social role. For example, the media portray the elderly in specific ways. The same is true of male and female adults, various occupations, the mentally ill, and so on.

Role-taking The use of feedback (from a receiver) by a communicator to judge which symbols will best indicate to a receiver the intended meanings of his or her message.

Royalty Compensation paid to an author by a publisher, representing a share of the proceeds from the sale of the author's book.

Sample A number of persons or families (or household units) selected from some large population (such as a city, county, or country) in such a way that they represent faithfully the major characteristics of that population; that is, the sample has the same percentage of old, young, black, white, rich, poor, and so on as the population from which it was selected.

Saturation (or penetration) The proportion of workable receivers in a given area to the total number of households in the area. This is one index used in studying patterns of audience attention to broadcast media. It is a measure of potential audience; it does not indicate how many people are listening or viewing.

Sedition Committing any act that brings damage to the government; for example, publishing materials that advocate the overthrow of the government. It has on occasion been illegal in the United States to publish anything that scorned, abused, or showed contempt for the federal government, its flag, or even the uniform of the armed forces (Sedition Act of 1918).

Shield law A law that protects reporters from demands by the police or the courts that they reveal their sources. If reporters obtain information regarding a crime and refuse to divulge their sources, they may penalize the chances of a person being tried for the crime. But if reporters reveal their sources, they may never again get confidential information. This issue remains controversial and is under review by the courts.

Slicks A popular term for general interest, large-circulation magazines that are traditionally printed on rather slick shiny paper.

Social categories theory The view that a person's habits of selecting particular types of media content and responding to them in distinctive ways is heavily influenced by norms and other shared influences that characterize the social categories of which he or she is a member (for example, race, education, income, occupation, and so on).

Social construction of reality The ongoing processes of communicative interaction by which we collectively develop culturally shared meanings for objects, events, and situations. Explanations of the origins and consequences of meanings in terms of these processes have been developed in anthropology, psychology, philosophy, and sociology.

Social darwinism A set of beliefs drawn from the nineteenth-century philosophy of Herbert Spencer. The main ideas are that society is analogous to a living organism and that it develops toward a better condition through a process of natural selection and survival of the fittest leaders and citizens.

Social learning theory A general psychological theory that attempts to explain how people acquire behavioral patterns by observing such patterns in social settings. It is a complex theory that involves many assumptions and factors.

Social relationships theory The view that a person's habits of selecting particular types of media content and responding to them in distinctive ways are heavily influenced by the persons with which he or she has binding social ties (for example, family and friends).

Specialization Generally, the division of functions in any system into increasingly distinct operations. In magazine publishing, the increasing trend toward concentrating a magazine's content on some well-defined interest.

Stabilizing function The institutionalization (standardizing) of a convention linking a word and its shared meaning.

Statistical analysis The use of specialized mathematical procedures to study the characteristics of a set of data (numerically recorded observations). Various procedures are used to determine averages or other central tendencies, variation (scatter, dispersion), and correlations.

Stimulus intensity The strength of a given stimulus. Intensity can be increased by making the stimulus physically stronger (as may be done with sound or light) or more frequent.

Stimulus-response theory See *magic bullet theory*.

Subscription TV (pay TV, toll TV) A system for transmitting television signals over the air or by wire in such a way that a special device is needed on the receiver to unscramble the signal. The owner of a set pays fees for the use of the device. Other technologies are also used in some areas.

Subsidies Generally, any payment to support an activity. Political parties often provided money to support early American newspapers. The federal government today provides cheap postal rates to subsidize magazines, books, and newspapers.

Subsidy publishing See *vanity press*.

Substitution function The development of new meanings for symbols to replace those already established.

Supplemental (wire) service A type of wire service that gathers, prepares, and provides special reports and features to newspapers and broadcasters for a fee. Examples are women's news, gardening information, religious news, science coverage, and financial analyses.

Symbol Something that "represents" a more-or-less standardized meaning among a given set of people. Common examples are words (that stand for the objects or events they name), military insignia, flags, a wedding ring, traffic signs, and so on.

Syndicate (feature syndicate) A group that prepares and provides specialized (feature) material to printed news media for a fee; for example, comics, editorial cartoons, political commentaries, gossip columns, crossword puzzles, and serialized books.

Tabloid A newspaper whose pages are usually about five columns wide or about half the size of a standard newspaper page. Tabloids were originally associated with sensationalism; but today the term more commonly applies only to format, not to content.

Taste publics Categories of people who find distinctive levels of art products, entertainment forms, and aesthetic experiences interesting and appealing. In American society these levels include high culture, upper-middle culture, lower-middle culture, low culture, and quasi-folk low culture.

Technology The application of principles of physical, biological, or social science to provide techniques for solving specific practical problems.

Telecommunication Literally, communicating over distance. The term usually refers to such communication via electromagnetic instruments (telegraph, telephone, radio, and television). *Mass telecommunication* refers to the use of broadcast media mainly to reach large and diverse audiences. *Surveillance telecommunication* scans distant places for specific phenomena such as hostile weapons, weather disturbances, pollution, and so on; radar and satellite photos are examples. *Point-to-point telecommunication* refers to the electronic transmission of signals from one point to another; messages sent by telegrams or telephone are examples.

Telegraph editor See *wire editor*.

Toll TV See *subscription TV*.

Traces Experiences stored in the brain that are capable of being recalled. Traces are thought to be biochemical records that potentially enable us to remember every detail of our conscious experience.

Two-step flow of communication A process by which mass-mediated content reaches a population. In this process only some people attend directly to the media; they pass on the information obtained to others, who are thus indirectly exposed. See also *Multistage flow*.

UHF Ultra-high frequencies. The letters generally refer to channels 14–83 on the second television dial. Ultra-high frequencies are also used in many other applications of radio waves; for example, radar.

Unit (in content analysis) Any type of theme, category of person, type of action word, form, or other element that appears in a message. Such units are counted in a content analysis.

Uses and gratifications research The study of psychological variables that provide motivations and rewards for individuals who develop particular patterns of exposure to media content.

Validity An assessment of how well a given form of measurement actually quantifies what it is designed to measure. For example, a common tape measure provides a rather valid measure of length, but an IQ test may be a less valid measure of a person's actual intellectual ability.

Vanity press (or subsidy publishing) The system for publishing an author's work in which he or she pays all the costs of producing the work.

VHF Very high frequencies. The letters generally refer to channels 2–13 on the television set's main dial. Very high frequencies are also used in aircraft radio and other applications of broadcasting.

Violence profile A chart developed annually that shows trends in the depiction of violence by the major television networks.

Weekly A newspaper that publishes only one day a week. Many are produced in small communities or rural areas; others appear in suburban sections of larger cities. There are many different types.

Wire editor (or telegraph editor) An editor in charge of editing copy from press associations and preparing it for publication.

Wire service An organization that gathers news stories, prepares them in a convenient form, and sends them (by wire or other rapid means) to newspapers and broadcasting stations around the country that pay for the service.

Yellow journalism A late nineteenth-century type of newspaper publishing that placed profit above truthfulness and significance, emphasizing sensationalism, human interest, and reader appeal at the expense of public responsibility.

Photo Credits

Chapter 9

Roger Werth/ © 1980 Longview Daily News/Woodfin Camp, p. 317; Jan Lukas/Photo Researchers, p. 318; Ray McCoy/Black Star, p. 322; Courtesy The New York Post, p. 328; Reprinted by permission of The Wall Street Journal. © Dow Jones & Company, Inc. 1980. All Rights Reserved, p. 329; Paolo Koch/Photo Researchers, p. 334; Jim Anderson/Black Star, p. 335; Ken Robert Buck/The Picture Cube, p. 342; James Scherer for WGBH, p. 343; Roy Lichtenstein, "Good Morning Darling," 1964. Coll. David Lichtenstein, Princeton, N.J. Courtesy Leo Castelli Gallery, p. 347.

Chapter 10

United Press International, p. 356; Cary Wolinski/Stock, Boston, p. 360; Jean Claude Lejeune/Stock, Boston, p. 367; CBS Entertainment, p. 371; Culver Pictures, p. 376, p. 377; New York Public Library, p. 378.

Chapter 11

CBS Entertainment, p. 395, p. 402; Frederick D. Bodin/Stock, Boston, p. 400 (left); Thomas Hopker/Woodfin Camp, p. 400 (right); Sidney Harris, p. 405; CBS Entertainment, p. 408.

Chapter 12

Ellis Herwig/Stock, Boston, p. 423; Peter Southwick/Stock, Boston, p. 429 (top); Joel Gordon, p. 429 (bottom); United Press International, p. 435; Courtesy Dallas Morning News, p. 440 (top left); copyright, 1980, Los Angeles Times. Reprinted by permission, p. 440 (top right); Reprinted courtesy of The Boston Globe, p. 440 (bottom); David Powers/Stock, Boston, p. 442.

Chapter 13

Culver Pictures, p. 451; Minnesota Historical Society, p. 452; Courtesy RCA, p. 457; Sam C. Pierson/Photo Researchers, p. 459; Courtesy Nissan Motor Corporation, p. 462; Courtesy Weyerhauser, p. 463; Drawing by Stevenson; © 1974 The New Yorker Magazine, Inc., p. 469.

Chapter 14

Peter Southwick/Stock, Boston, p. 488 (top); Christopher Morrow/Stock, Boston, p. 488 (bottom); Bettye Lane/Photo Researchers, p. 489 (top left); Bobbi Carey/The Picture Cube, p. 489 (bottom left); J. Bryson/Sygma, p. 489 (right).

Index

DEFGHIJ-D-82

To The Student

We need your help. By answering a few questions below, you can have a hand in shaping the next edition of *Understanding Mass Communication*. Please complete this questionnaire, tear it out, and mail it to:

Melvin DeFleur and Everette Dennis
% College Marketing Services
Houghton Mifflin Co. College Division
One Beacon St.
Boston, MA 02107. Thank you.

School name _____

Title of course(s) in which you used this book _____

Is your school on a quarter ____ or semester basis ____?

Instructor's name _____

Other books used in the course(s), if any, _____

_____

1. What is your overall impression of the book? Did you find it

   ____ enlightening ____ interesting ____ useful ____ not so useful

   Comment, if any, _____

2. Did your teacher assign all sections and chapters of the book, or only some? If any were omitted, please indicate which ones.

   _____

3. How did you find the reading level of the book? Was it: _____ highly

   readable _____ generally interesting _____ fair _____ poor

4. Did anything about the book surprise you? That is, did you find new
   material that you hadn't expected in a text of this kind?

   _____ yes _____ no. If yes, be specific:

   _____

5. Is there any material you would like to see added to the book?

   _____ yes _____ no. If yes, be specific:

   _____

6. Did your instructor test you on the book? _____ yes _____ no

   Describe the tests: _____ objective _____ short essay _____ other

7. Did your teacher's lectures: _____ usually cover the same ground as

   the book; _____ introduce entirely different material _____ some-

   thing in between (describe) _____

   Give the book a grade: _____ A _____ B _____ C _____ D _____ F